Corruption Mocking at Justice

A Theological and Ethical Perspective on Public Life in Tanzania and Its Implications for the Anglican Church of Tanzania

Alfred Sebahene

MONOGRAPHS

© 2017 by Alfred Sebahene

Published 2017 by Langham Monographs
An imprint of Langham Creative Projects

Langham Partnership
PO Box 296, Carlisle, Cumbria CA3 9WZ, UK
www.langham.org

ISBNs:
978-1-78368-334-5 Print
978-1-78368-336-9 Mobi
978-1-78368-335-2 ePub
978-1-78368-337-6 PDF

Alfred Sebahene has asserted his right under the Copyright, Designs and Patents Act, 1988 to be identified as the Author of this work.

All rights reserved. No part of this publication may be reproduced, stored in a retrieval system or transmitted, in any form or by any means, electronic, mechanical, photocopying, recording or otherwise, without the prior written permission of the publisher or the Copyright Licensing Agency.

All Scripture quotations, unless otherwise indicated, are taken from the Holy Bible, New International Version®, NIV®. Copyright ©1973, 1978, 1984, 2011 by Biblica, Inc.™ Used by permission of Zondervan.

British Library Cataloguing in Publication Data
A catalogue record for this book is available from the British Library

ISBN: 978-1-78368-334-5

Cover & Book Design: projectluz.com

Langham Partnership actively supports theological dialogue and an author's right to publish but does not necessarily endorse the views and opinions set forth here or in works referenced within this publication, nor can we guarantee technical and grammatical correctness. Langham Partnership does not accept any responsibility or liability to persons or property as a consequence of the reading, use or interpretation of its published content.

Dedication

I dedicate this work to:
- My beloved wife, Ruth Niyonzima Rubagora Sebahene, known as "Mama Niyo," our children Joanna Niyonkuru and Samuel Niyitegeka, and my nephew Kelvin Tumsifu. You all faced and endured endless challenges in the process of my academic advancement. I thank you for your love and incomparable support.
- To my parents, the late Mr Thobias Baldwin Masumbuko and Mrs Joanna Hakizimana Ntakabozinda Bgoya Sebahene. Since my childhood, you have worked hard to instill ethical values in me. This study has a very strong connection to your ongoing teachings. Thank you.
- To Mr Munyaruko Sebahene, whom I honor posthumously. It is a great privilege to have inherited your name. I have always been, and still am, challenged to live life as you lived, a life of integrity, accountability, transparency and service to humanity. I shall endeavor to do so as long as I live.

Contents

Abstract xi

Opsomming xiii

Acknowledgements xv

Chapter 1 1
Introduction
    1.1 Background to and Motivation for the Study 1
    1.2 Primary and Secondary Research Questions 6
    1.3 Research Design, Methodology and Overview of Primary
        (Literary) Sources 7
    1.4 Possible Contribution of the Research 12
    1.5 Structure of the Study 13

Chapter 2 15
Corruption, Injustice and Contemporary Public Life in Tanzania
    2.1 Introduction 15
    2.2 Corruption and Justice/Injustice – A Conceptual Analysis 16
        2.2.1 Corruption: Secular Perspectives 16
    2.3 Corruption in Tanzania – A Historical and Contextual Analysis . 28
        2.3.1 Tanzania: An Overview of the Country 28
        2.3.2 Historical Overview of Corruption and Ethics in Public Life
            in Tanzania 30
        2.3.4 Tanzanian Perceptions and Forms of Corruption 48
        2.3.5 The Extent of Corruption in Contemporary Tanzania:
            Comparative Statistics 52
    2.4 Corruption: Causes and Consequences 56
        2.4.1 Possible Causes of Corruption: General Observations 56
        2.4.2 The Consequences of Corruption (in Tanzania): Secular
            Perspectives 64
    2.5 Conclusion: Corruption and Corruption as Injustice in
        Contemporary Tanzania 78

Chapter 3 85
Why Corruption? Biblical and Theological-Ethical Considerations of the Nature of Corruption and In/Justice and Corruption as Justice
    3.1 Introduction 85

  3.2 Point of Departure: The Unique Nature of Biblical-Ethical
    Principles on Corruption and In/Justice 87
  3.3 Forms of Corruption and Injustice in the Bible:
    A Short Overview..89
  3.4 On the Character of God: A Methodological Route towards
    Theological-Ethical Principles...92
    3.4.1 God the Creator vs. Corruption and Injustice....................95
    3.4.2 God as Righteous vs. Corruption and Injustice 96
    3.4.3 God as Sovereign vs. Corruption and Injustice 99
    3.4.4 God as Faithful Governor and Sustainer vs.
      Corruption and Injustice..101
  3.5 Preliminary Conclusion: God, In/Justice and Corruption
    from a Biblical-Theological Perspective 103
  3.6 On the Nature of Humankind: Christian Anthropological
    Perspectives in the Context of Corruption and Injustice.............105
    3.6.1 Sin, Corruption as Sin, and the Fallen State
      of Humankind 105
    3.6.2 Corruption and Power and Corruption as Abuse
      of Power 114
    3.6.3 God, Human Dignity and Human Flourishing...............120
    3.6.4 Relationality, Relational Justice and God's Vision
      of a Peaceful and Just Society 128
  3.7 Conclusion 135

Chapter 4 139
*Why the Church . . . and How? The Public Role of the Church in the
Context of Corruption*
  4.1 Introduction 139
  4.2 Point of Departure: What Is "The Church"?.............................141
    4.2.1 The Church: Basic Biblical and Theological
      Considerations...141
    4.2.2 The Many Faces of the Church: Dirk Smit on
      the Social Forms of the Church...145
  4.3 The Fight against Corruption: Why the Church? 148
    4.3.1 The Church in the Public Square – A Centuries-Old
      Question 148
    4.3.2 The Church's Role in the Public Sphere: From History
      to Contemporary (Public-Theological) Perspectives 160
    4.3.3 Corruption and the Church: Baseline
      Biblical-Ecclesiological Considerations 181
  4.4 The Church in the Fight against Corruption – How?................190

    4.4.1 The "How" of the Church's Engagement in
          the Fight against Corruption: Nature, Contours
          and Modes of Engagement 190
  4.5 Conclusion 223

Chapter 5 227
The Anglican Church of Tanzania and Its Response to Corruption
  5.1 Introduction 227
  5.2 The Anglican Communion and the Origins of Anglican
      Church of Tanzania 229
  5.3 The Church's Engagement in Public Life: The UMCA
      and CMS Missionary Methods 232
  5.4 Reflections on Anglican Theology, Identity and Spirituality 234
  5.5 The Anglican Church of Tanzania's Public Witness
      in the Context of Church-State Relations 239
    5.5.1 Strategic Planning: A Popular Contemporary
          Approach in the Church's Public Engagement 243
    5.5.2 ACT's Strategic Plan: Theological Principles Allowing
          for a Public Engagement with Corruption 245
    5.5.3 ACT's Public Engagement as Part of Global Anglican
          Communion 247
    5.5.4 ACT and the Public Discourse on In/Justice 252
  5.6 ACT's Anti-Corruption Efforts 256
    5.6.1 ACT and the Government of Tanzania 258
    5.6.2 ACT's Christian Ecumenical and
          Interfaith Collaboration 262
    5.6.3 Anti-Corruption Clubs in Schools and at Universities:
          An Opportunity for the Teaching of Virtues 266
  5.7 ACT's Anti-Corruption and the Discourse on Justice:
      A Failure or Success? 268
    5.7.1 Corruption within the Church 269
    5.7.2 Fighting Corruption from the Pulpit: A Theological
          Disagreement 273
    5.7.3 A Divided and Fragmented Church
          Fighting Corruption? 275
    5.7.4 ACT, Theological Education and the Challenge
          of Effective and Competent Leadership 277
  5.8 A Final Word: Appreciating a Societal and Political Context
      Conducive to an Anti-Corruption Public Role 280
  5.9 Conclusion 285

Chapter 6 287
    Summary, Conclusion and Recommendations
        6.1 Introduction 287
        6.2 Summary of Arguments and Research Findings 288
        6.3 Recommendations 291
            6.3.1 Theoretical Recommendations 291
            6.3.2 Practical Recommendations 291
        6.4 Concluding Words 295

Bibliography 297

Abstract

In recent years, the world has witnessed an increased global consciousness and attention to the challenges of corruption and injustice and the threats they pose to humanity. In the United Republic of Tanzania, too, such consciousness and attention have intensified as, in terms of corruption, the country currently faces a crisis as never before. This has not only prompted increased efforts by a variety of societal role players seeking solutions to this scourge, but it has also opened up new avenues of inquiry into the harsh realities of corruption and injustice. It is proposed that this also calls for urgent attention to these challenges by churches in general, and the Anglican Church of Tanzania in particular.

In light of the above, this study examines the problem of corruption in Tanzania from a theological-ethical perspective. It proceeds from the view that there is a dynamic and "indissoluble" link[1] between corruption and injustice in that it is proposed that curbing corruption correlates with an appropriately robust understanding of what constitutes justice in the Christian sense of the word and the ways in which corruption constitutes injustice and undermines justice. This study builds on the recognition that, while the Anglican Church of Tanzania has grown considerably in terms of its membership, its role in engaging corruption – as an element of public and personal morality – has in some senses been lagging behind. For this reason, the study identifies theological-ethical guidelines to inform and add theological content to the discourse on the role of the Anglican Church of Tanzania in the public sphere in general and in the fight against corruption in particular.

---

1. Kirkpatrick, "Incarnational Ecology," 41.

This study falls primarily within the field of Christian ethics, but on an intradisciplinary level also finds itself within the relatively new field called "public theology." The study also draws insights from the biblical sciences and, on an *inter*disciplinary level, on input from secular anthropology, philosophy, political science, sociology, economics, and historical studies. The interdisciplinary engagement in this study already acknowledges that a theological-ethical perspective is not the only perspective on the challenges facing anti-corruption and injustice strategies. However, the study shows that the Anglican Church of Tanzania should contribute to the fight against corruption and injustice. And, being a *Christian* church, this can be done only in accordance with the gospel of Jesus Christ. To come to the latter conclusion and to give content to it, the study asks and answers the following interrelated questions: What is corruption, justice and injustice and how does it feature in Tanzanian society? For this a secular conceptual analysis is done as well as a contextual analysis of Tanzanian society in the past and today with regard to corruption. To find an answer to the question of why, from a theological-ethical perspective, corruption is wrong, the focus falls mainly on two elements: first the Christian doctrine of God, and second, the Christian understandings of humanity, or Christian anthropology. When looking at why the church should be involved in the public sphere in general, and especially with regard to the fight against corruption as injustice, different understandings of the nature of the Christian church is investigated and special attention is given to the views on the nature, role and modes of engagement of the church in the public domain in the view of public theologians past and present. Finally, this study asks to what extent these views of the role of the church in the public domain represent the reality of the life and witness of the Anglican Church of Tanzania. The study ends by exploring possible reasons for the current state of the church's involvement in these issues and suggestions as to how this may be stimulated, increased or improved.

Opsomming

In die onlangse verlede is daar 'n wêreldwye toename in die bewussyn van en aandag aan die uitdagings van korrupsie en ongeregtigheid as bedreigns vir die mensdom. Hierdie bewussyn en aandag het ook toegeneem in die Verenigde Republiek van Tanzanië, 'n land wat, in terme van korrupsie, vandag 'n krisis in die gesig staar soos nooit tevore. Hierdie toestand van sake het nie net gelei tot 'n toename in pogings deur 'n verskeidenheid rolspelers in die samelewing om oplossings te vind vir hierdie golf van korrusie nie, maar het ook nuwe weë van ondersoek na die harde realiteit van korrupsie en ongeregtigheid daargestel. Dit word aan die hand gedoen dat hierdie uitdagings ook dringend aandag vra van kerke oor die algemeen en ook in besonder van die Anglikaanse Kerk van Tanzanë.

In die lig van bogenoemde, word 'n ondersoek gedoen na die problem van korrupsie vanuit theologies-etiese perspektief. Die ondersoek gaan van die veronderstelling uit dat daar 'n dinamiese verband bestaan tussen korrupsie en ongeregtigheid in die sin dat om korrupsie hok te slaan, 'n ewe robuuste verstaan vereis word van wat geregtigheid in die Christelike sin van die woord is, hoe korrupsie ongeregtigheid daarstel en dit ondermyn. Hierdie studie is van mening dat, terwyl die Anglikaanse Kerk van Tanzanië aansienlik gegroei in terme van ledegetalle, die Kerk se rol in die aanspreek van korrupsie – as element van openbare en persoonlike moraliteit – in sekere opsigte agterweë gebly het. Daarom identifiseer die studie teologiese-etiese riglyne ten einde die theologies inhoud van die diskoers oor die rol van die Anglikaanse Kerk van Tanzanië, spesifiek mbt die stryd teen korrupsie, te informer en aan te vul.

Hierdie studie resorteer binne die veld van Christelike etiek, maar op *intra*dissiplinêre vlak bevind dit ditself binne die relatief nuwe veld van "publieke teologie." Die studie steun ook op insigte van die Bybelwetenskappe en, op 'n *inter*dissiplinêre vlak ook of sekulêre antropologie, filosofie, politieke wetenskap, sosiologie, ekonomie en geskiedenis. Die *inter*dissiplinêre betrokkenheid van hierdie studie erken alreeds at 'n theologies-etiese perspektief nie die enigste is op die uitdagings wat anti-korrupsie en anti-ongeregtigheidsstrategieë in die gesig staar nie. Tog toon dit dat die Anglikaanse Kerk van Tanzanië moet bydra tot die stryd teen korrupsie en ongeregtigheid. En, as *Christelike* kerk, moet dit gedoen word aan die hand van die evangelie van Jesus Christus. Om te kom tot laasgenoemde gevolgtrekking en om inhoud daaraan te gee, vra en beantwoord die studie die volgende vrae: Wat is korrupsie en on/geregtigheid en wat is die voorkoms daarvan in die Tanzaniese samelewing? Hiervoor word 'n sekulêre konsepsuele analise gedoen asook 'n kontekstuele analise van die Tanzaniese samelewing mbt korrupsie tans en in die verlede. Vir die vraag waarom korrupsie vanuit theologies-etiese perspektief verkeerd is, word gefokus op twee elemente, naamlik die die Christelike Godsleer en die Christelike verstaan van menswees, of Christelike antropologie. Wanneer gekyk word na waarom die kerk betrokke moet wees in die openbare sfeer in die algemeen en mbt die kwessies van korrupsie en ongeregtigheid in besonder, word gelet op verskillende interpretasies van die aard van die kerk met spesiale aandag aan die aard, rol en modus van betrokkenheid daarvan in die openbare domein aan die hand van publieke teoloë, hedendaags en in die verlede. Ten slotte vra die studie tot watter mate hierdie sienings van die rol van die kerk in die openbare sfeer 'n weerspieëling is van die realiteit van die lewe en getuienis van die Anglikaanse Kerk van Tanzanië. Die studie eindig deur te let op moontlike redes vir die huidige stand van sake mbt die Anglikaanse Kerk van Tanzanië se betrokkenheid in hierdie aangeleenthede en met voorstelle vir hoe aangemoedig, vermeerder of verbeter kan word.

Acknowledgements

This study was made possible through the contributions of many individuals and organizations, who believed in me and blessed me with their support, energy, love and time. I would like to extend my gratitude to them all. My academic and spiritual life has been blessed because of the sacrifices they have made on my behalf. It is impossible to mention all of them by name, but I wish to specifically thank:

The Chancellor of St John's University of Tanzania, Archbishop Emeritus of the Anglican Church of Tanzania, the Rt Rev Donald Leo Mtetemela and the first Vice-chancellor Professor Manoris Meshack. Thank you for granting me the opportunity to study towards a PhD.

The community of George Whitefield College, especially the Evangelical Research Fellowship Team under the leadership of Rev Dr Benjamin Dean, for hosting and supporting me in a variety of ways.

To all donors: St John's University of Tanzania, Oversees Council Australia, Langham UK, Langham USA, the Faculty of Theology at Stellenbosch University, Church Missionary Society of Australia, New Zealand Church Missionary Society, George Whitefield College Trust Fund, Culham St Gabriel's Trust, St Barnabas Bible Church in Claremont and all anonymous donors. Thank you for your financial support and your prayers.

The congregation of St Barnabas Bible Church in Cape Town and especially pastor Simon and mama Gillian Clegg, thank you so much for your encouragement and prayers.

My original doctoral supervisor, Dr Clint Le Bruyns, who has since moved to the University of KwaZulu-Natal after guiding me through the proposal stage of my PhD journey. My second supervisor, Dr Gerrit W. Brand, for his brief support and guidance before he was called home to be with the Lord. I appreciate your contribution. May your soul rest in peace! My third and final supervisor, Dr Len Hansen, who has been a colleague, friend, teacher, and advisor to me. In the process of writing this thesis you have been all of these and more. I am immensely grateful for your generosity with time, advice and patience that enabled this project to come to conclusion. Your efforts have helped me to develop into a better student and scholar of systematic theology, public theology and Christian ethics.

To my beautiful wife, Ruth Niyonzima, thank you for being a constant source of support, encouragement and help over the years of study and writing of this dissertation. You managed our home while I was away for long periods of time in pursuit of this goal. The debt I owe to you for the opportunity to work on this project is incalculable. You are my mentor *par excellence* and you remain my best friend.

Finally, I wish to thank the Lord for granting me the peace and strength to face the many challenges of a PhD journey. All blessings and honor, glory and power belong to you, Lord.

CHAPTER 1

Introduction

A corrupt witness mocks at justice, and the mouth of the wicked gulps down evil.

Proverbs 19:28

[Christian] ideas, leaders, institutions and communities are missing links in much of the public conversation about public integrity. That is not as it should be.[1]

1.1 Background to and Motivation for the Study

This chapter serves as an introduction and background to the study and as an overview of the general structure of the study entitled '*Corruption Mocking at Justice': A Theological-Ethical Perspective on Public Life in Tanzania and its Implications for the Anglican Church of Tanzania*.[2] In addition to preliminary remarks on and background to the research problem, the chapter will also

---

1. Quoted in Marshall, "Sin, Corruption."

2. The phrase "mocking at justice" is taken from Prov 19:28 which is a basic theme of this study, namely that there exists a dynamic theological link between corruption and injustice. Corruption in the title of this work is used here also in a wider sense than a mere "corrupt witness" as in Proverbs, as it will refer to corruption in general and not only in the form of perjury. In fact, some exegetical studies, such as those of Kidner (*Proverbs*) and Fox (*Proverbs 1–9*) suggest that such a broad meaning is exactly what is referred to in this verse. It may thus, for example, mean that a "corrupt witness" has the potential to facilitate the false judgment of a judge and in this way open the door to injustice. This type of corruption can be termed judicial corruption. However, it can it can also be a form of injustice that involves the misuse of the law, even though it may not be in a judiciary context. According to Nthamburi ("Morality in Public Life," 110), such injustice, "[is] perpetrated on other humans through neglect [or] indifference . . . [and] [w]hen people do not want to become their neighbor's keeper in violation of God's command that they should love and serve one

1

state the primary and secondary research questions, explain the nature of the research, methodological issues, the possible contribution(s) the research may make, and will offer a chapter outline of the study as a whole.

According to the Implementation Report of the Tanzanian National Anti-Corruption Strategy and Action Plan II (NACSAP II),[3] which will be referred to in detail in this study, corruption is by nature a falsehood; it denies justice. Corruption in this document means gaining an unfair advantage by unfair means. Furthermore, according to the document, corruption is also an obstacle to the principles of democracy, good governance, and human rights and it poses a threat to peace, tranquility and security in society. If this is true, then this research seeks to offer an account of ways in which the church can and why it should appropriate the discourse on justice by becoming actively engaged in the struggle to eradicate the blight of corruption.

This study, then, is in essence one on corruption as it relates to injustice from the perspective of Christian theology. This means that this research wishes to bring to bear biblical and theological perspectives on the challenges of corruption, but in a specific context, that of the United Republic of Tanzania. Furthermore, the study is conducted with a view to explore whether and how theology and Christian ethics may help to equip *the church*, in this case more specifically the Anglican Church of Tanzania, to embark on and sustain responses to corruption, if such responses indeed exist. It is, therefore, also a study that attempts to understand the role of the church in fighting corruption, whether the church has potential for combating corruption and whether this may be still underutilized, and to investigate and offer theological-ethical guidelines that may underpin such a task of and efforts by the church.

With regard to the personal motivation behind this study, three experiences have prompted it:

1) *The effects of the Rwandan and Burundian refugee crisis of the 1990s.*

    I am Tanzanian, born in Ngara, in the Kagera region in northwestern Tanzania. Due to its geographical location, this

---

another and they instead make others poor and destitute by promoting unloving and unjust social relationships, then this is a moral question of the highest order."

3. NACSAP II Implementation Report, 94.

area has been forced to play host to refugees from Burundi and Rwanda since the 1950s. This process reached a climax in April 1994, following the assassination of the heads of state of both Burundi and Rwanda and the genocide that resulted in Rwanda. At the time there was an unprecedented influx of refugees into the Kagera region – over 800,000 Rwandans and Burundians flocked to refugee camps in the area. One started to hear rumors of corruption and bad governance as contributing causes to the situation in Rwanda and Burundi. Refugees pointed toward corruption as a generator and facilitator of civil conflict in their countries, as an inhibitor of peace and as a source of recurring ethnic violence in the two small nations. To many it became obvious that there will be no true peace and security and no real freedom as long as the machinery of law and governance remain compromised, among others, by corruption in countries such as Burundi and Rwanda. For me, however, the rumors also prompted questions about the possible consequences of corruption in Tanzania itself.

2) *Corruption in Tanzania and the current political and moral state of the nation.*

The second motivation for this study concerns the apparent levels of corruption in my country itself. As will be shown, corruption is a major problem and a major public issue in Tanzania.[4] Today corruption scandals often dominate the socio-political scene

---

4. The Presidential Commission on Corruption (The Warioba Commission) will be referred to frequently in this study. In 1996 the president appointed a commission led by the former Prime Minister Joseph Warioba. This Commission catalogued a large number of public grievances on corruption and revealed that the public had lost confidence in both the government's ability and political will to control the problem. The Warioba Report was remarkable in its detailed analysis and the large number of documented cases it referred to. According to a Report of the World Bank Mission to Support the Government of the United Republic of Tanzania's Anti-Corruption Program, the Warioba Report presents a frank, comprehensive, and detailed survey of corruption – sector by sector and ministry by ministry. The report also suggests that it is doubtful that any country has documented its corruption problems as openly as Tanzania. In short, the Warioba Report found that corruption had penetrated to the core of Tanzanian society and had become endemic to it. The Report made it clear that corruption was the result of a fundamental failure of the administrative and political system to impose controls and enforce discipline (see Government of Tanzania, "Commission Report").

in the country and as a result, many Tanzanians speak of a catastrophic loss of moral footing in the world.[5] Not long ago, the Tanzanian CAG (Controller and Auditor General)[6] estimated that over twenty percent of the government's annual budget is lost due to corruption, theft and fraud.[7] Generally speaking, events on Tanzania's political scene, such as pressure on leaders to resign due to corruption scandals, and peaceful demonstrations against corruption, are occurring much more frequently today than in any period since the country's independence in 1961. Despite this, Tanzania has played, and continues to play, a constructive role among its neighbors, for example, by hosting refugees and leading efforts to resolve regional conflicts. However, the country's repute and prominence is on the decline due to the growing scourge of corruption.[8] Commentators have argued that all these are still political disturbances rather than a full blown political crisis, but for how long?

In general, churches in Tanzania[9] have joined the discourse, especially with regard to the need for ethical reflection in conversation with people from all walks of life. The "international community," too, talks about the fact that restoring ethics to public life in Tanzania is no longer a matter of choice, but of urgency.[10] Against this background, Njunwa

---

5. For example, speaking at an anti-corruption public dialogue organized by Agenda Participation 2000 at the Blue Pearl Hotel, Ubungo Plaza in Dar es Salaam on 21 September 2010, well-known Tanzanian journalist Jenerali Ulimwengu stated: "[w]hat worries me most is the level of moral decay one sees today in Tanzania and among Tanzanians. It is catastrophic. We will sooner than later head for a down fall" (quoted by GEPC, "Is Corruption the Result of Moral Decay").

6. The CAG is the statutory auditor of all ministries, independent departments, executive agencies, local government authorities, donor-funded projects and all public bodies and entities whose operations create a liability to the government of Tanzania or who receive public monies for public purposes.

7. cf. Chêne, "Overview of the Corruption"; Kagashe,"Tanzania."

8. cf. World Bank, "Six Questions"; United Nations Development Programme, "Human Development Report," 2011, http://hdr.undp.org/.

9. An overview of the country's population, its political and economic history is given in chapter 2 of this study, with responses of the churches in chapter 5.

10. cf. United Nations Development Programme (UNDP), 2000.

proposes that citizens, political decision makers, civil society, private sectors as well as public service employees need to be reminded of the current concerns about declining confidence in public and private institutions.[11]

What has gone wrong in this country which has normally been regarded as politically stable? Why is the country being shaken by a seeming succession of corruption scandals? These are questions that also motivate this research.

3) *Lecturing and leadership at St John's University of Tanzania.*
Before embarking on my doctoral studies, I served as a lecturer in theology and Christian ethics at St John's University of Tanzania. With it came the opportunity to teach a course called Professional and Business Ethics to business studies students. Among other things, I was tasked with fostering in students an awareness of ethical concerns across a wide range of professions. The focus of this course was on the need for students to understand the strengths and weaknesses of various ethical assumptions and arguments, and also to encourage them to reinforce their personal sense of compassion and fairness with a view to their future roles as Christian businesspeople. In my interaction with students I found that, for them, corruption raised complex questions and that it was indeed one of the most debated topics among themselves. The students were very keen to expose the extent of the challenge of corruption and the ways in which it continues to be a key agent in depriving people from access to basic services, how it manifests itself in a lack of basic fairness in decision making, the embezzlement of investments, misuse of incentives and the general breakdown of trust in public services and institutions. The concerns of these students at St John's also motivated me to start this work.

---

11. Njunwa, "Combating Corruption," 39.

1.2 Primary and Secondary Research Questions

Corruption has reached crisis proportions in Tanzania.[12] For a long time it has mainly been regarded as a political, developmental and judicial challenge.[13] However, this study takes as point of departure that it is also a theological challenge, one which the churches in Tanzania can and should respond to. For a long time, religion and faith have been resources that have inspired and motivated non-governmental organizations (NGOs) and especially faith-based organizations (FBOs) to engage in humanitarian and welfare issues. In its report on the role of churches in the dismantling of apartheid in South Africa, the World Council of Churches recognizes, together with UNESCO, that the church has been and remains among the most influential social forces, not only in that country, but indeed across the African continent.[14] And, referring specifically to Tanzania, Hyden states that "due to its work at grassroots level the church has gained a large measure of influence."[15] But, one may ask, in what way is corruption a *theological* challenge and why should and how may the church in Tanzania, on theological grounds, use this influence that Hyden speaks of to contribute in addressing it [corruption]?

In light of the above the primary research question of this study may be formulated as follows: On theological-ethical grounds and in light of the link that exists between corruption and injustice, what has the Anglican Church of Tanzania done, what is it doing, and what may be expected of it with regard to the challenge of corruption in Tanzanian society?

---

12. A detailed discussion on the magnitude of the problem of corruption in Tanzania will be given in chapter 2.

13. This has not only been the case in practice in Tanzania, but also internationally. For example, while the Bangkok Declaration: Restoring Trust (issued at the 14th International Anti-Corruption Conference in Bangkok, Thailand) strongly emphasizes that corruption is an ethical/moral issue, it stops short of acknowledging any role in addressing it from a faith or religious perspective. The Declaration expressly identifies civil society and the media as catalysts for and driving forces behind raising public awareness of corruption. It also emphasizes the importance of determined leadership and strong political will as critical factors in anti-corruption initiatives, but, the fact remains that more often than not these initiatives include very little involvement from the world of faith (for the text of the Declaration see online at: http://14iacc.org/about/declaration/. Accessed 19 July 2014).

14. WCC & UNESCO, "Final Report"; cf. Kofi Annan referred to in 1.4 below.

15. Hyden, *No Shortcuts in Progress*, 2.

In answering this primary research question, the following secondary questions will be addressed:

- In non-theological terms, what is understood as "corruption" in general and in the Tanzanian context in particular?
- In non-theological terms, what is injustice and what is the relationship between it and corruption?
- What is the extent of corruption in contemporary Tanzania?
- In theological terms, what is corruption and in/justice?
- On theological grounds, should the Christian church be involved in the public (socio-political and economic) sphere – also in the fight against corruption – and how may such involvement occur?
- To what extent is the Anglican Church in Tanzania involved in the fight against corruption in the country and, if this involvement exists, is it effective and what theological-ethical guidelines inform or may inform its involvement?

1.3 Research Design, Methodology and Overview of Primary (Literary) Sources

This study takes the form of a literature study. As such it refers to a variety of forms of literature on corruption and justice – monographs and edited books, journal articles, government reports, reports by NGOs, statistics (which will serve as secondary data on the extent of corruption) and newspaper articles. The focus primarily falls on *theological* literature (especially within the theological disciplines of systematic theology, Christian ethics, public theology and, to a lesser extent, biblical science), but sources from the disciplines of philosophy, anthropology, history, economics and business studies, political science and sociology are also referred to. The following are the most important specific sources that are consulted:

As the *leitmotif* of this study is corruption in Tanzania as a form of injustice as viewed from a theological-ethical perspective, the meaning of corruption, its forms, causes and consequences and the state of ethics in public life in Tanzania are crucial. Regarding the meaning, extent and forms of corruption, a variety of sources are consulted, not only theological sources but also non-theological ones and the United Nations Convention against Corruption

(UNCAC) is a primary example of this. UNCAC is a legally-binding international anti-corruption instrument adopted by the United Nations in 2003; it came into effect on 14 December 2005. Another regional instrument is the South African Development Commission Protocol Against Corruption (SADCPAC). Other sources which pertain particularly to Tanzania and the understandings of corruption in that country are reports by Transparency International (TI), which includes reports on corruption in Tanzania. The latter reports are valuable not only as they provide comparative statistics on corruption globally and on the African continent, but also as they report on key government initiatives and policies that deal directly or indirectly with corruption in the countries under investigation. The texts, implications and commentaries on these government initiatives and policies themselves are of course also crucial. In the Tanzanian context the most important of these initiatives include the seminal National Anti-Corruption Strategy and Action Plan (NACSAP I and II), but also the Development Vision 2025 for Tanzania; the Five Year Development Plan 2011/12 – 2015/16; the National Strategy for Growth and Reduction of Poverty (NSGRP – commonly known as MKUKUTA); and the Zanzibar Strategy for Growth and Reduction of Poverty (ZSGRP – commonly known as MKUZA). Other sources include the Tanzanian Poverty Monitoring Master Plan; the mandate of the Commission of Human Rights and Good Governance (2001); the work of the Prevention of Corruption Bureau (PCB); reports by the Tanzanian Controller and Auditor General (CAG); statements by and activities of the Public Leaders' Ethics Secretariat, the President's Office and, of course, the key document, namely 1996 Presidential Commission of Enquiry on Corruption (the so-called Warioba Commission).

With regard to the theme of justice, much has been written on this subject by scholars of theology as well as those of other disciplines. No reflection on justice can ignore the philosophical discourse on the concept and, with it, of the seminal work in this area, that of *A Theory of Justice* by John Rawls (1971). Even though almost half a century old and not above critique, Rawls's book remains most influential. Rawls's view and theory on the fundamental principles of social justice – for example that each person has equal rights – and Rawls's "principles of redress" of social and economic inequality, have contributed much to this study. Besides, for Rawls, important contributions from a philosophical perspective that are referred to are, for example, those by Amartya Sen and Martha Nussbaum, both known for their work on the so-called "capabilities approach" to human development or their "capabilities ethics,"[16] which will throw additional light on the sections on Christian anthropology from a secular philosophical perspective in the study. However, even more important for the purposes of this study are the works on justice by theologians such as Nicholas Wolterstorff (e.g. his *Until Justice and Peace Embrace* [1983] and *Justice: Rights and Wrongs* [2008]) and North American Christian ethicist Karin Lebacqz's *Six Theories of Justice: Perspectives from Philosophical and Theological Ethics* (1986) and *Justice in an Unjust World: Foundations for a Christian Approach to Justice* (1987).

As mentioned above, as a methodological way toward identifying theological guidelines pertaining to the moral reprehensibility of corruption and/ as injustice, the focus falls on the Christian doctrine of God and Christian anthropology. With regard to the former, a variety of scholars are referred to and all made valuable contributions with regard to this theme in this study, such as proponents of so-called Trinitarian Theology, Thomas F. Torrance in his *The Christian Doctrine of God, One Being Three Persons*, (1996), Colin Gunton's *The Promise of Trinitarian Theology* (1997), and Christian ethicist David Cunningham's *These Three Are One. The Practice of Trinitarian Theology* (1997).

Regarding the Christian understanding of humanity or of being human, David Kelsey's Christian anthropology in his *Eccentric Existence: A Theological Anthropology* (2009), for example, contributes greatly to this study. Alvin Plantinga's reflections on sin and God's vision for humanity in *Not the Way It's Supposed to Be: A Breviary of Sin* (1997) and *Engaging God's World: A Christian Vision of Faith, Learning and Living* (2002) are also among the prominent theological voices on this issue in the study. Especially Plantinga's *Not the Way It's Supposed to Be* presents a powerful picture of the "Vandalism of Shalom" as well as the book Christopher Wright's *Knowing Jesus through the Old Testament* (1992) on the concept of *shalom* in the Bible, which refers to the complete well-being of a society and which is brought in conversation with the issue of corruption in this study.

---

16. cf., e.g. Nussbaum, *Fragility of Goodness*; Sen, *Commodities and Capabilities*; "Capability and Well-Being."

As a key to understanding what may be understood by referring to "the church," Dirk Smit's explanation of the so-called social manifestations of the church is foundational for this study and is referred to often. Furthermore, few theological studies on the nature of the church can ignore the work of prominent contemporary theologian Jürgen Moltmann. This study engages, for example, Moltmann's *The Way of Jesus Christ: Christology in Messianic Dimensions* (1993) and his *The Church in the Power of the Spirit: A Contribution to Messianic Ecclesiology* (1992). Regarding the role or not of the church in the public sphere, works from the theological discipline of public theology are central to this study. Oliver O'Donovan's works are consulted at crucial points in it, especially his *The Desire of the Nations: Rediscovering the Roots of Political Theology* (1999), which offers an in-depth discussion of a Christian worldview and a Christian theological-ethical way of looking at the world. O'Donovan's theological-ethical principles on the relationship between church and state also help to bring the problem of corruption into clearer focus. As far as perspectives on theology and public policy are concerned, works by Duncan Forrester, for example, *Theology and Politics* (1988), *Beliefs, Values and Policies: Conviction Politics in a Secular Age* (1989) and *Christian Justice and Public Policy*, (1997) help in reflecting on the role of religion and the church in the public sphere and on the issue of corruption and justice with regard to policy matters. The voice of John G. Stackhouse Jr., especially in his *Making the Best of It: Following Christ in the Real World* (2008) is also crucial in light of Stackhouse's role in the development of public theology as a theological discipline and as such it has an important bearing on the problem of corruption and injustice. A number of other works and voices are also consulted on the issue of public theology, such as those of Will Storrar and South African theologians Nico Koopman and Dirk Smit. These voices challenge all in one way or another to consider corruption and in-/justice as theological issues in contemporary society deserving of the churches' serious attention. When looking at the modes of engagement of the church in the public sphere and with regard to public and private morality this study refers to works by Christian ethicists such the South African reflections by Nico Koopman on this public and civic virtues and North American theologian Stanley Hauerwas's well-known *A Community of Character: Toward a Constructive Christian Social Ethics*

(1981), his *Vision and Virtue: Essays in Christian Ethical Reflection* (1981) and *In Good Company: The Church As Polis* (1997).

Given the fact that this study has, as part of its focus, the Anglican Church in Tanzania, the input from African theologians and Anglican scholarship is important. Regarding the former, S. W. Kunhiyop's *African Christian Ethics* (2008) helps to situate corruption in the context of the challenges associated with African Christian morality. Jesse Mugambi's *Democracy and Development in Africa: The Role of the Churches* (1997) and *From Liberation to Reconstruction: African Christian Theology after the Cold War* (1995) provides a contextual perspective for looking at corruption and justice in the African context. Mugambi's so-called theology of reconstruction in Africa and his views on theology in social transformation in Africa is also reflected upon.

However, for the purposes of clarification, this study will also note a difference between Mugambi's theology of reconstruction – sometimes known as moral and social transformation – and the current perspective and understanding of transformation in countries like South Africa. In order to do so, the works of P. P. Ekeh and M. Prozesky will be briefly consulted.[17]

Another key African theological voice is that of John S. Mbiti, one of the fathers of African theology and philosophy. In his two major works, *African Religions & Philosophy* and *Introduction to African Religion,* Mbiti's points of view were grounded on the importance of morality, community and communal care, and responsibility in African societies, and of the importance of traditional leaders in African societies with regard to maintaining law and order. Mbiti offers important insights on corruption from both a theological and African cultural perspective.

Finally, on Anglicanism, the study draws on the works of former Archbishop of Canterbury, Rowan Williams's *What Is the Church? In God's Company* (2007) and *Faith in the Public Square* (2012) are important. So too are the contributions by Paul Avis – *The Identity of Anglicanism: Essentials of Anglican Ecclesiology* (2007) and *Reshaping Ecumenical Theology: The Church Made Whole?* (2010). This well-known Anglican theologian and ecumenist's work contributes not only on understanding the Anglican communion but also reminds of the need for the church to keep its theology and ethics

---

17. Ekeh, "Colonialism"; Prozesky, "Corruption as the New Treason."

together. The works of a variety of other Anglican scholars from the past, for example, John Henry Newman and recently, such as Kevin Ward's *A History of Global Anglicanism* (2006) and Richard Turnbull's Anglican and Evangelical? (2007) are valuable sources.

1.4 Possible Contribution of the Research

According to former UN Secretary General Kofi Annan, "[c]hurch organizations and their religious communities are, without question, the largest and best-organized civil institutions in the world today, claiming the allegiance of billions of believers and bridging the divides of race, class, and nationality."[18] Annan also insists that "[t]hey are uniquely equipped to meet the challenges of our time: resolving conflicts, caring for the sick and needy, and promoting peaceful coexistence among all peoples." In the case of corruption, however, its seems at first sight that it [corruption] may be receiving far more attention from secular organizations than from religious ones, that religious leaders and organizations are more engaged in the development agenda (in Africa particularly in the area of HIV and AIDS prevention and education) and that they are generally less active in the area of governance (including the area of fighting corruption).

If the above is indeed the case and if, in light of "corruption's profound moral and social justice dimensions, religious groups should be at the forefront of this struggle,"[19] this research will first of all assist the church of Tanzania, especially the Anglican church, in understanding the national contexts of corruption as well as the impact it has on the church and the country. In this sense it offers greater clarity on the churches' responsibility toward this issue. It also highlights the need for the church to understand how the discourse of faith can best apply to issues of public morality and ethics today. At the same time, this study adds to the knowledge of key Christian perspectives on theological-ethical issues in public life. As such it may inspire people to a new level of awareness of their responsibility as church and as members of the church to oppose corruption – for example, as

---

18. Speaking at the World Conference on Religion and Peace, 2001 and quoted by Julia Berger, "Religious Non-Governmental Organizations," 2.

19. Laver, "Good News," 62.

part the biblically based so-called integral or holistic mission of the church. With regard to church leaders, this research may motivate them and add to the theological language that translates the churches' responsibility to fight corruption into action. It may also contribute to efforts to challenge Christian communities in Tanzania in general to reexamine their own affairs and integrity, to get their own houses in order as a crucial step in the fight against corruption. Finally, outside of the churches, this study wishes to assist in sensitizing civil society to the fact that corruption is not only a political or economic issue and that there is a need to involve faith communities and their unique contributions in anti-corruption efforts in Tanzania.

1.5 Structure of the Study

This study comprises six chapters, which in simple terms focus on different interrelated questions:

Chapter 1 asks, in broad terms, what the study is about. As such, it provides the contours of the study. It explains the motivation and background to the study, the primary research and secondary research questions, the research design and methodology, it introduces the major conversation partners in the study and identifies possible benefits of the study.

Chapter 2 addresses the question of what constitutes corruption and in/justice and what the possible causes and consequences of the former may be – all form non-theological perspectives. It also enquires into the extent of corruption historically as well as currently in Tanzania. As such it offers a contextual and conceptual analysis of corruption and injustice in Tanzania.

Chapter 3 offers a detailed answer to the question of, on biblical-theological grounds, "Why corruption?" In other words, what makes corruption, from a biblical and theological perspective, wrong? In this chapter the theological-ethical nature of justice is thus examined in detail, but guiding principles are also identified with reference to the character of God as found in biblical texts and the thought of specific theologians as well as theological-ethical principles regarding the nature of humanity (Christian anthropology, which includes reflections on the fallen state of humanity).

In chapter 4, the leading question is "Why the church in the public sphere?" and, in light of this, a further question is raised, namely "How is the church to respond in the public sphere?" The focus is, thus, on the role of the church in public life in general and presents a critical account of not just what constitutes "the church," but also ways in which the church, Christian theology and ethics can and should appropriate the discourse on public issues in Tanzania, specifically with regard to corruption and injustice.

Chapter 5 investigates the ways in which the Anglican Church of Tanzania has participated in the past, and participates currently, in the fight against corruption. It also asks how and whether this is in accordance to the theological-ethical principles identified in the previous chapters, or how it may be aligned with these principles.

Finally, in chapter 6, the study concludes by way of a summary of the findings and suggestions toward the way forward in the Anglican Church of Tanzania's fight against corruption.

After the above introduction to the study in this chapter, the following chapter will thus offer a conceptual and contextual analysis of corruption, its manifestations, causes and consequences with a view to locate the problem in Tanzanian society specifically.

CHAPTER 2

Corruption, Injustice and Contemporary Public Life in Tanzania

By justice a king gives country stability, but those who are greedy for bribes tear it down.

Proverbs 29:4

[Tanzania] has witnessed an alarming increase in corruption activities . . . Moreover, state organs . . . have succumbed to this disease and therefore have left the people helpless.

Joseph Sinde Warioba
Chairperson, Presidential Commission of
Inquiry against Corruption in Tanzania, 1996

2.1 Introduction

In the introductory chapter, the research focus and outline of the study was presented as background to this book. This chapter offers a conceptual and contextual analysis of corruption as it pertains to in/justice. What is important, however, is that the focus will fall here on different understandings of corruption and in/justice from a variety of possible perspectives, but all are secular (i.e. non-theological) in nature as a detailed theological exposition of these concepts will only be given in chapter 4 of this study. As such, this chapter adds an important interdisciplinary perspective to the study, which will pave the way toward and will inform viable theological-ethical reflections on the need to oppose corruption as a form of injustice. At the same time, this chapter aims at finding an operational definition of corruption that will be brought into conversation with the biblical and theological-ethical understanding(s) of corruption in chapter 4.

By conceptual and contextual analyses, the meaning of the two central units of analysis, corruption and in/justice and the context in which it is investigated is given. This is necessary on the one hand to delimit the focus and scope of the research and also because, as we will see, these concepts have a variety of dimensions.

With regard to the context under investigation, this chapter also gives an overview of the United Republic of Tanzania. By doing so it traces a possible historical trend towards corruption in the country, that which makes the country historically vulnerable to the phenomenon, and it seeks to determine the current extent of the problem.

To the above ends, the chapter is divided into five main parts: *(1)* corruption and justice/injustice – a conceptual analysis; *(2)* corruption and justice/injustice in Tanzania – a contextual analysis; (3) The United Republic of Tanzania – an overview of the country; (4) a historical overview of corruption and public life in Tanzania; (5) summary and conclusion.

2.2 Corruption and Justice/Injustice – A Conceptual Analysis

According to Weithman, "justice is one of a handful of topics that has dominated philosophical ethics in recent decades."[1] Although this is a theological-ethical study and a detailed theological and biblical view of corruption and justice/injustice will be given in chapter 4, in seeking an adequate definition of corruption and justice/injustice at this stage, secular sources are consulted as this is most often where the discourse on corruption takes place. It is also in this discourse that the phenomenon is most often understood.

2.2.1 Corruption: Secular Perspectives[2]

To begin with, it should be noted that by "secular" the study does not propose to cover every field of study outside theology or theological ethics, nor

---

1. Weithman, "Nicholas Wolterstorff," 179.

2. In this study, a distinction between secular and theological perspectives is intentionally drawn for the purpose of, in the first place, showing that the discourse on corruption and injustice has for a long time been overshadowed by secular voices or has been

that it will do so in detail. What will rather be portrayed are different views on what constitutes corruption by proponents of six selected areas. These are general perspectives, philosophical, political-philosophical, anthropological, economic, and legal perspectives.

2.2.1.1 Toward a Definition of Corruption: Corruption in Traditional Discourse

The term "corruption" comes from the Latin word *corruptio* which refers to "moral decay, wicked behavior, putridity or rottenness."[3] From this etymological perspective it is already indicated that the word corruption has moral implications.

In the traditional discourse on corruption, Heidenheimer observes that "the Oxford English Dictionary gives corruption nine meanings and categorizes them under three headings."[4] These are:

(1) *Physical* corruption: the destruction or spoiling of anything, especially by disintegration or by decomposition with its attendant unwholesomeness and loathsomeness;

(2) *Moral* corruption: moral deterioration or decay; perversion or destruction of integrity in the discharge of public duties by bribery or favor;

(3) The perversion of anything from an original state of purity.[5]

In this study, in as far as the above definition is concerned, corruption will refer to the second instance mentioned. With reference to morality, values and norms, Anand, Ashforth, and Joshi speak of corruption as a "departure from accepted societal norms for personal or organizational gain."[6] In a related manner, according to Windsor, corruption reflects "a failure of moral regard on the public interest or the commonwealth in favor of illegitimate

---

receiving far more attention from secular organizations than from religious and Christian ones. This implies that, in the second place, it is critical that when a potential (public) theological approach and contribution to the discourse on corruption is considered, the language of the secular world concerning the issue be acknowledged and understood.

3. Milovanovic, *Corruption and Human Rights*, 15.
4. Heidenheimer, "Terms, Concepts, and Definitions," 3–14.
5. cf. *Oxford English Dictionary*, 1978, 1024–1025.
6. Anand, Ashforth, and Joshi, "Business as Usual," 40.

personal interest."[7] Windsor also refers to Banfield,[8] according to whom corruption is "a socially undesirable deviation (or decay) from some ideal, norm or standard."[9] Somewhat differently, Lange defines corruption as "the pursuit of individual interests by one or more organizational actors through the intentional misdirection of organizational resources or perversion of organizational routines."[10]

Based on the above, it seems that in simple terms corruption also has to do with the betrayal of trust. Moreover, to be corrupt is to destroy or pervert the integrity or fidelity of people in the discharge of their duties; to induce them to act dishonestly; the act of soliciting or offering gratification. Analytically speaking, Vito Tanzi's definition of corruption is significant as one that encompasses and gives more weight to the personal desire to commit corrupt acts or to omit acts that are required. According to Tanzi, then, "[c]orruption is the intentional non-compliance . . . aimed at deriving some advantage for oneself or for related individuals from this behavior."[11] According to Tanzi, corruption is, furthermore, characterized by unfairness and greed and manifests itself in, for example, bribery, fraud, embezzlement of public funds, misuse of authority and power, rigging of elections, tax evasion, cheating in examinations, forgery and nepotism (these manifestations will be discussed in more detail below). Bryan Evans, member of Tearfund Foundation's Public Policy Team, gives a similar list of examples of what constitutes corruption:

> It covers fraud (theft through misrepresentation), embezzlement (misappropriation of corporate or public funds) and bribery (payments made in order to gain an advantage or to avoid a disadvantage). The different types of corruption are likely to be closely linked . . . It is an act of theft (and hence an offence against human relationships), but it is a very particular kind of theft. One definition that has the virtue of simplicity (but

---

7. Windsor, "Corporate and Government Corruption," 141.
8. Banfield, "Corruption."
9. In Windsor, "Corporate and Government Corruption," 141.
10. Lange, "Multidimensional Conceptualization," 710.
11. Tanzi, "Corruption," 167.

which needs unpacking) is the act by which "insiders" profit at the expense of "outsiders."[12]

It is clear that in general terms corruption is quite a broad term with many dimensions. It is, however, also a term that is used with specific meanings within different discourses.

2.2.1.2 Corruption: Political Perspectives

According to Harvard scholar J. S. Nye, in political science corruption is defined as a "behavior that deviates from the formal duties of a public role (elective or appointive) because of private-regarding (personal, close family, private clique) wealth or status gains."[13] In this sense corruption is not surprisingly strongly related to the actions of political decision makers.

Another definition, which is widely supported by political scientists, refers to *political* corruption as any transaction between private and public sector actors through which collective goods are illegitimately converted into private payoffs.[14] It is "a form of secret social exchange through which those in power (political or administrative) take personal advantage, of one type or another, of the influence they exercise in virtue of their mandate or their function."[15] Other experts in the field define corruption in terms of its manifestations. These include fraud, which refers to false representation and prejudicing people's rights; white-collar crime, which covers non-violent crimes such as cheating and swindling; and employee deviance, which entails corporate and organizational illegality that may be manifest in a deliberate desire to and abuse of an organization's property.[16] Johnston also rightly suggests that within politics,

---

12. Evans, "Cost of Corruption," 3.
13. Nye, "Corruption and Political Development," 419.
14. cf. Heidenheimer "Terms, Concepts, and Definitions," 6.
15. Méry, cited in De Sardan, "Moral Economy," 49. The role of the concept of power and the role and responsibilities of the (politically) powerful will be often referred to in the rest of the study also from a theological perspective – cf. 3.6.2 and 4.2.3.1 below.
16. cf. Baucus and Near, "Can Illegal Corporate Behavior"; Daboub et al., "Top Management Team Characteristics"; Payne, "Organization Ethics"; Reiss and Biderman, *Data Sources*; Robinson and Bennett, "Typology"; see also Rossouw, "Defining and Understanding Fraud"; and Szwajkowski, "Organizational Illegality."

[c]orruption is understood as everything from the paying of bribes to civil servants in return for some favor and the theft of public purses, to a wide range of dubious economic and political practices in which politicians and bureaucrats enrich themselves and any abusive use of public power to a personal end.[17]

For Amundsen, political corruption not only manifests in the misallocation of resources, but also in the manner in which decisions are made.[18] Political corruption is the manipulation of the political institutions and the rules of procedure, and therefore it influences the institutions of government and the political system and it frequently leads to institutional decay.

Finally, with regard to corruption as a dereliction of duties and disregard for rules of conduct, Nye refers to corruption as "behavior which deviates from the formal duties of a public role because of private-regarding (personal, close family, private clique) pecuniary or status gains; or violates rules against the exercise of certain types of private-regarding influence,"[19] while Khan sees it as "behavior that deviates from the formal rules of conduct governing the actions of someone in a position of public authority because of private-regarding motives such as wealth, power, or status."[20]

2.2.1.3 Corruption: Economic Perspectives

Economists understand corruption within economic guidelines as well as from the nature of the dynamics of power involved in economic decision-making processes. Economics as such may be defined as the study of "mankind [sic] in the ordinary business of life";[21] or "how society decides what gets produced, how and for whom";[22] or "how men and women obtain their livelihoods."[23] In Lipsey and Stainer's broad definition of economics, it concerns the

---

17. Johnston, "Search for Definitions," 6.
18. Amundsen, "Political Corruption," 3.
19. Nye "Corruption and Political Development," 417.
20. Khan, "Typology," 12.
21. Gayer, *Basic Economics*, 1–10.
22. Fischer and Dornbusch, *Economics*, 1.
23. McCormick, *Introducing Economics*, 19.

... study of a society's use of its scarce resources with reference to (1) the extent to which they are used; (2) how efficiently are used; (3) the choice between competing alternative uses; and (4) the nature and consequence of change in productive power of the resources.[24]

It is, therefore, not strange that in economics, the understanding of corruption emphasizes the misuse of power regarding resources for the production and distribution of goods. Thus economists, such as Jain, define corruption as "acts in which the power of public office is used for personal gain in a manner that contravenes the rules of the game."[25] Similarly, Schleifer and Vishny regard corruption to be "the sale by government officials of government property for personal gain."[26] From an economic perspective, Amundsen also argues that "corruption is understood as one of the evils caused by economic underdevelopment,"[27] which according to Rose-Ackerman "tends to distort the allocation of economic benefits, favoring the haves over the have-nots and leading to a less equitable income distribution."[28] Glyn et al. also note that the "broadening and deepening of global economic integration increases the probability that the effects of corruption will spill over and resonate throughout the world economy."[29] They admit that economists have "long been baffled by the relationship between corruption and economic development and the question of how to successfully contain corruption."[30]

Importantly, these definitions again bring to light the critical issue of power and the use or misuse of power, but also of goods/property as well as the desire for personal gain. Economic definitions of corruption are also broad enough to touch on issues of poverty, development or the lack thereof, globalization, and thus on the prosperity (or not) of human beings.

---

24. Lipsey, *An Introduction to Positive Economics*, 3.
25. Jain, "Corruption: A Review," 73.
26. Schleifer and Vishny, "Corruption," 1.
27. Amundsen, "Political Corruption," 16.
28. Rose-Ackerman, "Political Economy," 33.
29. In Kimberley, *Corruption and the Global Economy*, 12.
30. Ibid.

2.2.1.4 Corruption: Anthropological Perspectives

As may be expected, the problem of corruption is understood by anthropologists in terms of the aims of the study of humanity and human societies. According to Haller and Shore, the discipline of anthropology is

> . . . concerned with understanding the rules and norms that govern social conduct, then a good way of exploring these codes is to examine instances where they are violated, how people react to such transgressions, and the strategies and tactics that actors use to negotiate between different norms and rules.[31]

Unlike "the more conventional institutional approaches and theoretical model-building that seem to characterize so much of the corruption studies literature,"[32] an anthropological understanding of corruption is based on "the key insights into socio-cultural norms, their relationship to corruption and their relevance for everyday life among humans."[33]

For anthropologists, therefore, corruption is best understood within the confines of human relations, personalization, and social networks as well as how people live as they seek to meet their material and social needs. For example, Dorle affirms that corruption "is a phenomenon that appears whenever formal or informal networks are formed."[34] In other words, "looking at corruption from an anthropological perspective necessarily draws [people's] attention towards problems of meaning and representation [reflecting social interaction]."[35] Anthropologically, therefore, perceptions regarding legitimate behavior, complexity of cultures and cultural values, contextualization, and social experience are crucial to the understanding of anthropological discourse of corruption. In this, too, the misuse of power for private gain features and has to do with corruption as "a form of exchange: a polysemous and multi-stranded relationship and part of the way in which individuals connect with the state."[36] The anthropological focus is, therefore, on the "cultural and social dimension of corruption and the way it is experienced

---

31. Haller and Shore, *Corruption*, 1.
32. Ibid., 2.
33. World Bank, The New Anti-Corruption Home Page (2002).
34. In Haller and Shore, *Corruption*, 201.
35. Haller and Shore, *Corruption*, 2.
36. Ibid., 7.

by, and its effects upon"[37] human beings and in a clear way adds the issue of relationality to the discourse on corruption.[38]

2.2.1.5 Corruption: Philosophical Perspectives

Within the philosophical discourse on corruption, different meanings, causes, forms and consequences for corruption are also identified. A basis for a philosophical definition of corruption is often traced back to the likes of Aristotle, Kant and Hobbes and their understandings of morality and human reasoning as "being true to one's own rational nature (Kant), because one aspires to human fulfilment (Aristotle), or because keeping one's contract with one's fellow citizens is necessary to prevent social chaos and warfare (Hobbes) . . ."[39] From this approach and in the philosophical discourse of corruption, therefore, an emphasis is often put on the importance of moral values intertwined with the classical emphasis on the value of reason. It is, therefore, not strange that contemporary philosophers such as Dawkins, Nichols and Dion agree and recognize that corruption "is an amoral act" or that it constitutes "moral failure," which according to them finds it source in *irrational* morality and selfishness.[40]

To unpack this further, one may say that corruption from this perspective takes place when human reasoning decides against following ethical norms. For example, Nichols argues that "ethical judgments can be explained in terms of rational standards that apply directly to conduct or to deliberation."[41] Thus, corruption occurs when human beings are not acting as moral agents. In Kantian terms, "the moral agent must have an exemplary character, one which recognizes the rational demands of duty upon him [sic] even when there are no external incentives or constraints to compel, constrain, or otherwise shape his behavior."[42] This is what Kant calls "the Moral Law within" and "imperatives of duty." In the context of avoiding corruption, Kant would

---

37. Ibid., 11.
38. As will be seen in 3.6.4 below, the issue of relationality will also be an important element in the theological rejection of corruption.
39. Lucas and Rubel, *Moral Foundations*, 116.
40. Dawkins, *Selfish Gene*; Nichols, "How Psychopaths Threaten"; Dion, "What Is Corruption Corrupting?"
41. Nichols, "How Psychopaths Threaten," 291.
42. Cited in Lucas and Rubel, *Moral Foundations*, 184.

impress upon human beings that "we are to do our duty regardless of the consequences"[43] for, according to Kant, human beings possess "a morally good will," only if we are "individuals who can be counted upon to do what we know we must and ought to do, even when there are no external forms of incentive or accountability in place."[44]

Dawkins emphasizes the selfishness of corruption. He sees corruption as a "form of innate selfishness."[45] The argument of corruption as having its origin in human reasoning and the selfish nature of humanity leading to poor rational standards is also expanded by Dion in his analysis of different levels of corruption. Dion proposes the following five levels: the corruption of principles, so-called "ontic/spiritual/axiological corruption"; the corruption of moral behavior or "moral corruption"; corruption of people, "social corruption"; the corruption of organizations or "institutional corruption"; and the corruption of states "national/societal/cultural corruption." For Dion, this analysis offers philosophers the best way to describe the deep and broad effects of corruption and it may "enhance the social relevance of philosophical discourse when dealing with corrupt practices."[46] For the purposes of this study, the philosophical emphasis on reason and greed in choosing to act in corrupt ways are important especially in light of the later discussion of human nature from the perspective of Christian anthropology.

2.2.1.6 Corruption: Legal and Judicial Perspectives

In legal and judicial circles, corruption is regarded as an attitude of disobedience to the law, the state and the functioning of society. Here corruption is also looked at from the perspective of, among others, criminal justice systems. In such systems, corruption is regarded an offence that violates rules and norms in a particular setting. This is especially true when public servants are involved in corrupt practices such as accepting, obtaining or agreeing to accept or to obtain forms of gratification for themselves or for others. From this perspective, such violations usually call for a number of legal actions or sanctions within a justice system. These actions usually imply

---

43. Ibid., 133.
44. Ibid., 161.
45. Dawkins, *Selfish Gene*, 85.
46. Dion, "What Is Corruption Corrupting?" 45–54.

the application of legislation against corruption (such as incarceration or reparation of damages suffered).

Within the legal and judicial discourse on corruption there is, however, also some ambiguity. First of all, according to Jackson et al., an illegal act may not be corrupt and vice versa as,

> . . . using law as the standard of corruption supports the assertion that everything that is not legal is permitted. The legal foundation of . . . corruption is simultaneously too narrow and too broad, excluding too much [the unethical but legal] and including too much [the illegal but not unethical].[47]

Second, according to the above authors, most comparative literature on legal or judicial perspectives on corruption admits to the commonly found existence of corruption within the judiciary as such.[48] In this case, therefore, any explanation of corruption in the judicial sense, should also be geared toward acknowledging that the problem exists within the system itself. It is not uncommon for legal practitioners and judicial public servants themselves being accused of dishonestly or fraudulently misappropriating resources or the misuse of property entrusted to them. As such, one also often finds calls for a need to increase the transparency and accountability of legal and judicial institutions themselves. What is thus especially noteworthy in the legal discourse on corruption is that it highlights the tension between that which is illegal and that which may be legal but morally wrong. For the purposes of this study, it is important to take note of this tension, even if, as will be seen later in chapter 3, the fact that something is morally wrong is the concern of theological ethics, even if it may not be "against the law." The reference to the corruptibility of the judiciary and its officials, furthermore, highlights the issue of corruption within institutions themselves, institutions that are generally expected to be the epitome of justice, fairness and moral behavior, including the church.[49]

Finally, thus far it is also clear from the above definitions of and reflections on corruption, that corruption is a convoluted phenomenon, not limited

---

47. Jackson et al., "Sovereign Eyes," 55.
48. Ibid., 56.
49. In this regard see 4.2.3.3, 4.3.1.7, and 5.7.1 of this study.

to certain spheres of society or contexts; for example, it is "an economic problem intertwined with politics" while it also "describes a relationship between the state and the private sector."[50] It takes the form of a violation of norms of duty and responsibility within the civic order and can, therefore, also be defined as the deliberate intent to subordinate common interest to personal interest.

2.2.1.7 Corruption: A Working Definition

From the foregoing discussion, a few key issues have come to light in the selected secular definitions of corruption.

First of all, it seems that finding an encompassing definition of corruption does present a challenge. In this sense, Gupta is correct in saying that "[c]orruption is an ambiguous phenomenon, often causing diverse, ambivalent, and contradictory understandings among scholars, policymakers, and practitioners alike."[51] In light of the different perceptions of corruption in Tanzania as will be seen below, Gupta is also correct in stating that, ". . . the discourse of corruption varies a great deal from one country to another, dependent as it is on particular historical trajectories and the specific grammars of public culture."[52]

A variety of scholars agree with Gupta that "[c]orruption is an elusive concept. Every definition has problems, some more so than others."[53] In fact, according to Bacio Terracino, "there is no universally accepted definition of corruption . . . [and] [t]here is a tendency to use the term 'corruption' loosely as a catch-all term. There is also considerable disagreement over which specific acts constitute corruption."[54] No wonder Johnston calls the concept of corruption "slippery and protean,"[55] because, as Scott[56] puts it ". . . each discipline [including theology] approaching corruption will see it in its own terms, positioning research questions and answers according to

---

50. Rose-Ackerman, *Corruption and Government*, 113.
51. Gupta, "Blurred Boundaries," 376.
52. Ibid., 392.
53. Uslaner, *Corruption, Inequality*, 6.
54. Bacio Terracino, "Corruption," 5.
55. Johnston, "Search for Definitions," 323.
56. M. Scott in Inge Amundsen, 1972. "Political Corruption: An Introduction to the Issues." CMI Working Paper 7. Bergen: Chr. Michelsen Institute, 1999.

its own perspectives and interests."⁵⁷ Amundsen also laments the fact that corruption is a "many-faceted phenomenon" and the concept of corruption contains "too many connotations to be analytically functional without a closer definition."⁵⁸ However, what all these scholars agree upon is the conviction that the definitional challenges should not prevent efforts to deal with the problem.

Second, there seem to be an agreement in all disciplines that corruption at least concerns the misuse of power and that it has to do with morality in society. For example, Kolstad and O'Neil suggest that "[a]t the core of the concept of corruption is a moral and ethical dimension" and that corruption "involves deception."⁵⁹ According to the World Bank, corruption refers to "the abuse of public office for private gain" and "upon this definition . . . rests a whole raft of policies concerning transparency, liberalization and 'good governance.'"⁶⁰

Third, in almost all corruption discourses, there is a general agreement not only that corruption is morally wrong, but that no society is completely free from it. According to Kolstad and O'Neil, "[c]orruption undercuts the moral fabric of society; this is reflected in the fact that societies all over the world tend to regard corruption as fundamentally wrong – even if it is accepted as a fact of life."⁶¹ This section shows that most agree that corruption is indeed an ethical problem despite the fact that definitions and solutions differ between the different disciplines. In this study the focus will fall on yet another perspective, a theological-ethical one. However, as a basic point of departure, the working definition of corruption that resonates with most definitions of corruption across disciplines is the succinct definition adopted

---

57. See also Aidt and Dutta ("Policy Compromises," 2): "While corruption is usually recognized when confronted with it, it has proved more difficult to find and agree on a precise and encompassing definition"; Kojder (quoted in Kubiac, *Corruption in Everyday Experience*, 3): "[C]orruption consists of diverse actions as well as social situations and interpersonal relations. It is therefore difficult to describe its origin, forms of occurrence in cohesive, systematized academic statements"; Miller and Blacker (*Ethical Issues in Policing*, 112): "[I]n the light of failures of analytical definitions to adequately describe corruption, it is tempting to try to sidestep the problem of providing a theoretical account of the concept of corruption by simply identifying corruption with specific legal and/or moral offences."

58. Amundsen, "Political Corruption," 6.
59. Kolstad and O'Neil, "Corruption," iv.
60. Quoted in Haller and Shore, *Corruption*, 3.
61. Kolstad and O'Neil, "Corruption," 1v.

by the United Nations, Transparency International, and the World Bank, namely that corruption is *"a misuse of public power, office or authority for private gain."* This definition does, of course, not resolve all the definitional complexities of corruption, but it is useful to apply conceptual elements of corruption with the objective of putting it at the center of a theological-ethical discourse which the purpose of this study.

What follows is a shift in focus from the conceptual to the contextual (Tanzania); first, an overview of the country, the historical trajectory of corruption in Tanzanian society, followed by an account of the manifestations and extent of corruption in Tanzania, the possible causes of corruption in the country and, finally, the consequences of corruption in Tanzania. Since the consequences as well as the study as a whole concerns the issue of corruption and in-/justice, part of the reflection on the consequences of corruption in Tanzania will include a short detour on what may then be understood (again in non-theological terms) as "justice."

2.3 Corruption in Tanzania – A Historical and Contextual Analysis

2.3.1 Tanzania: An Overview of the Country

The United Republic of Tanzania is a country in East Africa. It was formed by the unification of two sovereign states, namely Tanganyika – a German colony and later a British protectorate – and Zanzibar, including the island of Pemba, and several smaller islands. Tanganyika gained independence from British colonial rule and became a sovereign state on 9 December 1961. The country became a Republic the following year under the leadership of Julius Kambarage Nyerere. Zanzibar gained independence from Britain on 10 December 1963 and the People's Republic of Zanzibar was established on 12 January 1964 after a revolution under the leadership of Abeid Amani Karume. The two sovereign states united to form the United Republic of Tanzania on 26 April 1964. According to its constitution, Tanzania is a democratic multiparty country and is a signatory to the United Nations Declaration on Human Rights. Significant for the purposes of this study is that, enshrined in the constitution, is an emphasis on equality of all the citizens, human dignity and the rights to justice before the law and freedom of religion.[62]

Geographically, Tanzania covers a total area of 945,090 square kilometers with the Indian Ocean forming its eastern border. To the north, the country is bordered by Kenya and Uganda, to the west by the Democratic Republic of Congo, Burundi and Rwanda and to the south by Malawi, Mozambique and Zambia. Tanzania shares and borders the three largest lakes on the African continent – Lakes Victoria, Tanganyika and Nyasa. The country furthermore is not only home to the highest mountain peaks in Africa, Mt Kilimanjaro and Mt Meru,[63] but is also blessed with natural resources including tin, phosphate, iron ore, coal, diamonds, Tanzanite, gold, natural gas and nickel. The country is also known for its rich fauna and flora and has fifteen large national parks and seventeen large game reserves.[64] With a population of 4,364,541, Dar es Salaam is Tanzania's largest city and Dodoma is its political capital.

According to the 2012 Population and Housing Census (PHC),[65] Tanzania has a total population of 44,928,923 of which 51 percent are females and 49 percent males.[66] In the ten years from 2002 to 2012, the population of Tanzania increased by 30 percent. Almost half of Tanzania's population (44 percent) is below the age of fifteen years. The average age is eighteen years, and only 2 to 3 percent of Tanzanians are older than sixty-five. The life expectancy at birth is about forty-five years. Tanzanians are from a multitude of tribes with more than one-hundred thirty ethnic peoples of Bantu, Nilotic, Cushitic and Khoisan origins. Bantu people "form 90.9 percent of the population of Tanzania. The Bantu have more than 127 groups."[67] The Bantu ethnic groups are the Sukuma, Haya, Chagga, Nyamwezi, Makonde, Ha, Hehe, Nyakyusa, Bena, Nyaturu, Shambala,

---

62. See Constitution of the United Republic of Tanzania Act no. 15 of 1984, especially the section on the equality of human beings s.6.

63. URT, *National Land Policy*, 9.

64. Legal and Human Rights Center, "Public Engagement: Justice Watch Annual Report, 2007."

65. URT, *Population and Housing Census*, 9.

66. Ibid.

67. Johnstone, *Operation World*, 527; cf. Odhiambo et al., *History of East Africa*, 4.

Ruguru, Mwera, and the Rangi, and the biggest Nilotic groups are the Maasai and the Luo.[68]

Though it is socially diverse, Tanzania has in general been politically stable and has showed a large degree of national unity for the past fifty years in a region wracked by civil wars often with ethnic dimensions, for example, in neighboring Rwanda, Burundi, Uganda, Democratic Republic of the Congo and Mozambique. Despite this political stability, this "oasis of peace" on the troubled African continent is ranked as one of the poorest countries in the world by the World Bank.[69] Its per capita income is a mere USD $250 and 48 percent of the population lives below the poverty line. Only 38 percent of the population has access to safe water and 29.4 percent of children suffer from malnutrition. The infant mortality rate is high, at one-hundred seven deaths per one thousand live births.

Despite the fact that Tanzania experienced a growth period more than a decade ago with a resultant lowering of poverty levels, it remains a poor country when compared to other countries. One of the reasons for this is to be found in the structure of the country's economy, which continues to be dominated by subsistence agriculture (75 percent of Tanzanians are engaged in primary economic sectors, mostly agriculture). Tourism, fishing, forestry and mining do make some contribution to the economy, but considerable development of these resources remains necessary for them to make any considerable contribution.

2.3.2 Historical Overview of Corruption and Ethics in Public Life in Tanzania

The rationale behind this historical overview is to determine whether historically and currently corruption exists/has existed in the country. At the same time this will give some indication of the current moral state of Tanzanian society. This overview is also important as, according to Hope,[70] (2002:101), corruption is "much more socially embedded"[71] on the African continent

---

68. Ibid.
69. According to Zakia in Konrad-Adenauer-Stiftung, *Role of Faith*, 27.
70. Hope, "Corruption and Development in Africa," 17–39.
71. In his critical exploration of corruption phenomena in Africa whereby he isolates the major causes, analyses the development consequences and discusses measures to curb it as a rapidly growing crisis in ethical leadership, Hope argues that issues such as a lack

than in other regions of the world. Hope seems to suggest by this that, at least in some parts of Africa, corruption has become an everyday, socially situated phenomenon. In the same vein, according to De Sardan, in Africa's post-colonial milieu corruption has become "part of the popular know-how, at the base of good usage of administrative services, and indispensable for survival."[72] To give some historical background to allegations such as these, the following section will give an overview of corruption in Tanzania first by referring to the pre- and post-independence history of the country, and then within the latter period, to corruption and struggle against it under successive presidencies in the country.

2.3.2.1 Pre-Independence Tanzania: Colonialism, Imperialism and the Seeds of Corruption

Considering Tanzania's history from the perspective of corruption, it is generally argued that colonialism and imperialism are aspects of Tanzanian history that have, at least partly, laid the foundations for its contemporary corruption problems. According to one study, for example, in 1890 when Tanganyika (now Tanzania) was split into different areas of influence by treaties between Germany, Britain and the Sultan of Zanzibar, and when, in 1891, Tanganyika, Ruanda-Urundi (now Rwanda and Burundi) became German East Africa, and Pemba and Unguja became British protectorates, traces of corruption already existed and manifested in cultural oppression, exploitation and discrimination.[73] In fact, in the 1930s the Tanganyikan colonial administration explicitly defined the soliciting, receipt and giving of bribes as criminal offences (in this light one may also note the comprehensive definition of corruption in the colonial Act on the Prevention of Corruption of 1958). In pro-independence campaigns, corruption appeared on the lists of grievances of nationalist activists. Even today, colonialism and imperialism continue to be linked to the increasing effects of corruption. Marjorie Mbilinyi, for example, is of the opinion that "[corruption] has increased during the last twenty some years, but not in a vacuum. An

---

of ethical leadership and social cultural norms have usually contributed to the increase of corruption in across Africa.

72. De Sardan, "Moral Economy," 28.
73. *Tanzania Human Rights Report*, 4.

enabling environment was created for corruption, individualism and compradorial tendencies."[74] This "enabling environment," according to Mbilinyi, was created from colonial times and included, for example, the "neoliberal ideology and macroeconomic reforms which successfully took a dominant position in Tanzania . . . in the mid-1980s."

In pre-colonial mainland Tanzania, with its more than one-hundred twenty ethnic groups, each of these groups was more or less self-governing. Tanzanian scholar D. J. Mkude suggests that "[s]ome had what is known as a 'centralized' system of government, others had a more or less decentralized form of government."[75] In the case of the latter, there were no highly visible and systematic forms of public service. Whether or not the group was centrally governed or not, there were, nevertheless, rules that governed the behavior of those in authority and power. Violation of such rules was severely punished, sometimes by ostracizing transgressors. According to Mkude, the rules were observed because of a combination of motivating factors, namely

> the recognition and respect accorded to the individual servant and [mostly] his family for good service and fear of tarnishing the good name of one's family being ostracized. In this period, community and family bonds were sacrosanct and one derived honor and pride to be called upon to render public service.[76]

Mkunde's comments are important as they show that, with colonialism came a large-scale public service system superimposed upon the region. The norms and values that informed public service morality in pre-colonial Tanzania, such as those referred to by Mkude above, were largely ignored in favor of norms and values of governance that were imposed by the colonial ruler. "Non-conformity" to this code was ruthlessly dealt with, thus, other than in pre-colonial Tanzania, fear was the major motivation to conformity to the code, not honor, one's or one's family's good name, and other social and familial bonds.[77] In fact, many traditional norms and values came under

---

74. Mbilinyi, "Equity, Justice and Transformation," 78.
75. Mkude, "Morals for Good Governance," 1.
76. Ibid.
77. Ibid., 2.

severe strain during the colonial period. According to Mkude, this strain was caused by:

- intense interaction between Tanzanians of different ethnic groups with different background norms and values;
- a search for the means to cope with this new situation – imitation of Western norms and values was the easiest thing to do;
- a growing awareness of new and totally different styles of life including awareness of different value systems in the world;
- an influx of material goods, music and literature depicting a totally different world and tastes.[78]

These factors have at times added competing values to the already existing roles of both traditional authorities and members of Tanzanian societies. Stated differently, what used to determine people's behavior in everyday life – their social, economic and political interaction – was interrupted, sometimes for the better, but often also for worse.

Thus the highly centralized colonization system not only left a legacy of authoritarian rule that more often than not implied the misuse power for private gain, but it also interfered with indigenous cultures.[79] When referring to the reforms and neoliberal ideologies (see 2.3.2.2 and 2.3.2.3), Mbilinyi highlights the need for a reflection on the historical development of corruption in Tanzania. According to Havnevik and Isinika, "[t]he constraints of the colonial legacy for the range of political options at hand for the post-independent state are important parameters for . . . understanding post-independence [including post-independence corruption]."[80]

2.3.2.2 Post-Independence Struggle against Corruption

At independence, Tanzania inherited the intact public service structure of the colonial powers. Meanwhile, and paradoxically so, the processes of shock and alienation from traditional culture that accompanied colonialization intensified due to competing values and loss of tribal identity as mentioned

---

78. Ibid.
79. Cf. Nyerere (quoted in Legum and Mmari, "*MWALIMU*," 35): "Of all the crimes of colonialism there is none worse than the attempt to make us believe that we had no indigenous culture of our own, or that what we did have was worthless – or something of which we should be ashamed, instead of a source of pride."
80. Havnevik and Isinika, *Tanzania in Transition*, 19.

earlier. Thus, a further weakening of the traditional norms and values of good governance occurred. Furthermore, and unfortunately so, even the good and effective rules and principles of public service imposed by the colonialists were derisively referred to as remnants of colonialism. It became fashionable to reject anything restrictive or demanding as a legacy of colonialism. Slowly and quietly, a number of regulative and control mechanisms were abandoned even if not officially being struck from the book. This gave public servants an unhealthy and wide discretion in the provision of services. One example is that the systematic induction and orientation of new civil service staff was abandoned.[81] The former was important to retain as it emphasized the need for new staff to know what was expected of them from the earliest stages of their commitment to public service so that they could perform their duties with dignity.[82] Orientation also entailed the sensitization toward key issues such as transparency, responsible management, individual accountability and regular monitoring and evaluation.[83]

The situation was made worse with the politicization of the civil service. In politics, expediency is of high importance. It is a central feature of governance where the nature of the relationship between the political and administrative officials or the elected public officials and career civil servants is also determined. A study by World Bank points to the fact that the way in which governing and administrative officials work together affects government performance.[84] With the line separating public servants from politicians becoming blurred, it opened the door for vice by power-hungry politicians to "invade" the public service sector. This also occurred in Tanzania with what Makulilo calls "a state-party fusion."[85]

As will also be seen in the following section on anti-corruption measures under the different Tanzanian presidents, the devastating effect of the fusion referred to by Makukilo and of economic policies in the country, led to increased pressure towards political change in Tanzania. It grew in earnest in

---

81. Mkude, "Morals for Good Governance," 2.

82. cf. Chaliga, "Uncritical Citizens"; Mbonile, "Towards Breaking"; Iliffe, *Modern History*.

83. cf. Lerisse et al., "Vulnerability and Social Protection."

84. cf. World Bank, *Social Sector Review*, 1995; and Romzek, "Dynamics of Public Accountability."

85. Makulilo, *Annual State of Constitutionalism*, 2.

the late 1980s. Tanzanian political scientist, Mwesiga Baregu, commented that these pressures,

> ... evolved against a background of largely failed structural adjustment programs which had been put in place in the early 1980s. These programs which were supposedly intended to spearhead economic recovery on the whole had quite the opposite effects as they intensified economic difficulties precipitating popular discontent. This discontent created a crisis of political legitimacy of the state giving rise to demands which ultimately translated themselves into demands for a more open and competitive political system. The reformers' argument was, at least in part, that economic liberalization had to be accompanied by political liberalization in order to stimulate sustained economic recovery. This argument was mainly embraced by those who had lost out in structural adjustment.[86]

Part of the political change advocated was in terms of party politics, where there had been a gradual increase in political pluralism. Despite this, the CCM (Chama cha Mapinduzi), the ruling party since independence, remains dominant in government and parliament. Periodically it is accused of subverting the aspirations of opposition parties (cf. e.g. *The Citizen*, 19 January 2005). Despite lobbying, Tanzania has de facto remained a one-party state.[87] And, in the view of Makulilo "weak opposition in Tanzania is a function of lack of adequate resources, organization structure, weak social base, skewed legal guideline, weak civil societies, intra-party conflicts, and inadequate civic competence."[88]

But what has all of this to do with corruption? For one thing, it supports the continued party-state fusion. Although a multiparty system is operational in Tanzania, the weak state of the opposition in Tanzania has opened up avenues for corruption. It has done so by undermining accountability in governance, access to information, civil society and a vigilant media. The continued fusion (between the state and the ruling party) finds expression

---

86. Quoted in Havnevik and Isinika, *Tanzania in Transition*, 207–221.
87. cf. Nyirabu, "Multiparty."
88. Makulilo, *Annual State of Constitutionalism*, 2.

in, "the reliance of the ruling party on state instruments and resources to win elections, . . . [p]artisan attitudes of state officials in favor of the ruling party . . . [o]verlapping roles and jurisdictions between the state and the ruling party officials . . . and . . . [c]oerced membership and support to the ruling party."[89] In other words, "state-party fusion is still a dominant feature of the current Tanzanian political system. It is well entrenched structurally and behaviorally at the expense of [good governance], democratization and democratic consolidation."[90]

As referred to in passing above, two other significant developments drove public service morality into a deeper morass and discredit, namely the acute economic adversity of 1978 onwards and the shocking admonition to government employees to use their own ingenuity to supplement their income since the government was unable to pay them a living wage! What came to be known as "the 1978 economic crisis" was precipitated by three factors: (1) the war with Uganda which left the state with huge debt and deep psychological scars; (2) the global increase of oil prices that led to increases in the price of every other commodity; (3) an acute food shortage coupled with a slump in the price of cash crops. These created a deep sense of insecurity and forced people to search for "individual salvation" without regard for moral rules and principles.[91] It was then that in some circles the image of Tanzania changed from being a "haven of peace" to that of "a den of thieves."[92]

2.3.2.3 Post-Independence Anti-Corruption Efforts under Tanzania's Four Presidents (1961–2013)

In 2011, mainland Tanzania (the old Tanganyika) celebrated fifty years of independence from Britain. Since independence the country has had four changes of government. Literature indicates that political leadership plays a crucial role in the anti-corruption efforts of countries.[93] According to Rose-Ackerman, whenever leadership demonstrates the will – sometimes denoted as "political will" (i.e. a demonstrated credible intent or unwavering

---

89. Ibid.
90. Ibid.
91. cf. Lupogo, "Tanzania."
92. Mkude, *Higher Education in Tanzania*, 2.
93. Especially World Bank, *Governance*, 100, 103.

determination) – to fight corruption, successful anti-corruption programs becomes a reality in a particular country.[94]

It follows that, although the fight against corruption (and its success or not) cannot be linked exclusively to the attitude and priorities of leaders of governments, and although anti-corruption strategies are most effective if they are inclusive, systematic and structured (i.e. integrating all institutions and policies, prosecution, research and prevention) it is the leader, who provides the political leadership necessary to offer a vision of reforms and the political will to see them implemented.[95] As Wogau, referring to Tanzania puts it, "strong presidents, who have endorsed the fight against corruption, as one of their main presidential goals have been the main drivers of change in the fight against corruption."[96]

Against the above background, the following will be discussed below as part of the historical overview of corruption in Tanzania: the perceptions of corruption and the fight against it in the country, and the anti-corruption efforts under the four successive Tanzanian presidents to date.

Julius Kambarage Nyerere (1961–1985)

Tanzania's first president was Julius Kambarage Nyerere. Nyerere led a one-party state that nationalized key industries and created the so-called *ujamaa*, a rural, collective, village-based movement of "African socialism and self-reliance."

In 1967, a few years after independence, Tanzania also issued what was called *Azimio la Arusha* – The Arusha (sometimes Socialist) Declaration. The latter represented the country's ideological commitment to socialism and the significant role that it was to play in its political, social and economic development for decades. Part of the Arusha Declaration was its propositions regarding the leadership of the country. Legum and Mmari summarize the latter propositions as follows:

---

94. Rose-Ackerman, "Corruption and Development," 42.
95. See, Beckhard and Pritchard, *Changing the Essence*; Dalziel and Schoonover, *Changing Ways;* and Grindle, *Challenging the State.*
96. Wogau, "Transitions to Good Governance," 4.

- Every government leader had to be either a peasant or a worker and should in no way be associated with the practices of capitalism.
- No government leader should hold shares in any company.
- No government leader should hold a directorship in any privately owned enterprise.
- No government leader should receive two or more salaries.
- No government leader should own houses which he rents to others.[97]

Although later replaced by the Zanzibar Declaration of 1991,[98] some scholars and politicians continue to believe that the Arusha Declaration offered the best model for sustainable human development in Africa.[99] The Declaration has even been described as "the cradle of ethics and integrity of governance."[100]

According to many scholars, together with the Arusha Declaration, Nyerere's way of conducting government business reflected and contributed to an ethic of integrity with regard to national economic development as it followed a clear values-based model of governance. This was very important as Tanzania, like many other sub-Saharan Africa countries, "achieved its independence with a severely underdeveloped economy and extremely limited infrastructure."[101]

---

97. Legum and Mmari, "*MWALIMU*," 13.

98. This Declaration was later replaced by the so-called Zanzibar Declaration of 1991. Pro-Zanzibar Declaration politicians and some opinion leaders – mostly in the private sector – today argue that the Zanzibar Declaration came into being to address an issue of conflicts of interest that made the Arusha Declaration impractical and unachievable. Fundamentally, the Zanzibar Declaration of 1991 modified the 1967 Arusha Declaration and was meant to challenge the original objectives contained in it. The 1991 document also had great symbolic significance as the Arusha Declaration was the central document in establishing the direction of the ruling party and the country towards *ujamaa*. One notable (and in the context of this study, unfortunate) change in the Zanzibar Declaration was the fact that the new declaration lifted the key restriction on second incomes, something that is sometimes linked to corruption as some of the leaders may be tempted to use their power exactly toward this end.

99. e.g. Yansane, *Prospects for Recovery*, 15.

100. Rwechungura, "Ethics and Globalization," 76.

101. Sitta, "Integrity Environment," 5.

For Nyerere, *ujamaa* (African socialism) was meant to promote and develop a healthy society where "no person exploits another";[102] where "everybody is a worker";[103] where "people care for each other's welfare";[104] where "neither capitalism nor feudalism exists";[105] and where the state "does not have two classes of people, a lower class composed of people who work for their living, and an upper class of people who live on the work of others."[106] For Nyerere, these were the indicators of a healthy society and they suggest that ethical virtues informed each of these principles, most particularly on issues of equality, fairness, and freedom. A number of commentators remain positive about the fact that *ujamaa* succeeded in offering Tanzanians a profound experience of freedom, unity, dignity and self-respect after the degradation suffered during decades of colonial rule.[107]

However, over time, *ujamaa* faced increased popular opposition, and was slowly abandoned in the 1970s and 1980s.[108] The reasons for abandonment were diverse.[109] At first, Nyerere's *ujamaa* ideology seemed to work well and it reflected – at least in terms of the study on corruption – the desire to address social ills. The later dissatisfaction with *ujamaa* was based, however, on its inadequacies. It started to be eroded by the pressure from African countries that preferred Western capitalist systems. According to Olutayo and Omobowale:

> On the basis of the historical experience of the colonial overlords and the need to ensure a free and unfettered access to the colonies by the colonial traders and merchants, state capitalism

---

102. Nyerere, *Ujamaa*, 15.
103. Ibid., 4.
104. Ibid., 1.
105. Ibid., 15.
106. Ibid.
107. E.g., Kaiser, "Structural Adjustment."
108. Wogau, "Transitions to Good Governance," 4.
109. *Ujamaa's* communal nature or a way of life and a value system came under attack, sometimes in strong terms. According to Nursey-Bray, for example, because by it "Tanzania's economic progress was distorted and resources wasted . . . giving rise to a marginalized rural sector and a corrupt and ineffective bureaucracy" (quoted in Ibhawoh and Dibua, "Deconstructing Ujamaa," 12).

was recommended as the development paradigm for the newly independent African states.[110]

According to a United Nations Development Programme (UNDP) study on *Institutional Arrangements to Combat Corruption*,[111] under the post-1967 socialist regime, Tanzanian officials were allowed to own only one house and to drive only modest cars. At the time, the task of combating corruption was performed by the Ministry of Home Affairs, with the Police Force Department mandated to investigate and prosecute corruption offenders. However, the side-effects of the establishment of centralized economic centers of control in society under the system of *ujamaa* soon became evident – as monopolies in the economic sector, these centers provided ample opportunities, for example, for extortion. It also provided opportunities for decision making at every level, but with limited authority in terms of a line of command. All in all, this meant that the misuse of power now began to manifeste itself right up to those in leadership positions.

The fact that corruption was on the increase in the first decade after independence is reflected in the promulgation of the Prevention of Corruption Act in 1971. This act was followed, in 1975, by the creation by Nyerere himself of the Anti-Corruption Squad (ACS) under the Prevention of Corruption Amendment (PCA) Act of 1974. The ACS initially was under the authority Ministry of Home Affairs. However, in an effort to make it more independent, the supervision of the ACS was later moved to the Office of the Prime Minister and eventually to the Office of the President itself.

By the 1980s, despite the creation of the ACS, corruption had become prevalent across society – particularly in the police force! – and banditry and smuggling were widespread.[112] In 1984, the Tanzanian government promulgated the Economic and Organized Crime Control Act, by declaring offences under the Prevention of Corruption Amendment PCA as "economic crimes," as opposed to ordinary civil crimes, which again highlighted the extent to which crimes such as corruption were committed.

---

110. Olutayo and Omobowale, "Capitalism," 99.

111. United Nations Development Programme, *Institutional Arrangement to Combat Corruption*, 94.

112. Ibid.

Despite his own high moral standards and policy, and administrative efforts to curb corruption, Nyerere's presidency ended with corruption remaining a challenge. Nyerere retired in 1985, and in 1995, four years before he died, he (at a press conference on 14 March 1995) had to admit that "[c]orruption in Tanzania has no bounds. Every country I visit they talk about corruption in Tanzania. Tanzania is stinking with corruption. The country has been hit by a tremor, developing cracks which must be filled." At the same occasion, he identified pressing problems in the country as "the political union between Zanzibar and the mainland, corruption, religious tensions, tribalism, the constitutional crisis and lack of the rule of law."

Ali Hassan Mwinyi (1985–1995)

Nyerere was succeeded by the president of Zanzibar, Ali Mwinyi, who oversaw political reforms and a gradual transition to a market economy – in part due to the economic collapse brought on by *ujamaa* and centralized economic management.

During the 1990s levels of corruption continued to rise, with petty corruption (see below for a discussion on Tanzanian forms of corruption) prevalent in all sectors of the economy and social services. The higher levels of government and the public service were also affected by corruption.[113]

To address the problem, the government (in the early 1990s) launched a series of campaigns focusing mainly on promoting popular participation in the fight against corruption. One example was by way of encouraging ordinary citizens to report "wrongdoers" as well as campaigns to improve relations between the police and the public service in order to curb corruption. Incentives were also offered for reporting smuggled or stolen goods and police officers were encouraged to denounce those offering them bribes.

Although these campaigns were believed to have led to some reductions in corruption, their success was negligible at best.[114] Corruption in procurement remained high, funds from charities and NGOs continued to be funneled to private accounts, and there were constant high levels of tax evasion. In addition, court action remained slow and there were repeated failures to

---

113. Government of Tanzania, "Commission Report."
114. See Chachage, "Globalization and Democratic Governance" and Njunwa, "Combating Corruption."

bring about successful convictions. In 1991, the Anti-Corruption Squad (ACS) created under the Nyerere administration in 1974, was renamed the Prevention of Corruption Bureau (PCB), with the intention of creating an institution capable of applying a scientific and systematic approach to combating corruption.

Studies by Chachage and Njunwa, both well-known Tanzanian scholars of sociology and governance, have argued that the re-emergence of high levels of corruption in the 1990s should be understood within the context of what they call "the death of [*ujamaa*] socialism."[115] They suggest that Mwinyi's presidency was a period characterized by features and events – "some of which were externally-based" – that only deepened the corruption crisis. Njunwa lists some of the latter features and events:

- First, the country lacked adequate foreign exchange to import raw materials for the manufacturing industries. This drastically reduced industrial production of consumer goods for the local market. Commodity scarcity started to emerge and it subsequently led to bribery and racketeering.
- Second, "due to limited financial capacity, public servants remained underpaid. This created an environment for the employees to look for ways to augment their meagre salaries. One of the ways was to ask for bribes or embezzlement of public resources."
- Third, "there was an undeclared progressive departure from the principles of citizen equality . . . as outlined in the Arusha/Socialist Declaration."[116]
- Fourth, the international donor community changed its approach in giving aid to developing countries. The emphasis was now placed on channeling aid through the private sector and the need for the public service to limit its activities to creating a policy environment conducive for policy implementation to take place.

---

115. Chachage, "Globalization and Democratic Governance."
116. Njunwa, "Combating Corruption," 2; cf. also Temwende, "Tanzania."

- Fifth, "the privatization of public enterprises started, thereby increasing the momentum towards the building of peripheral capitalism."[117]

All of the above resulted in a very shaky public service, acute levels of government debt, and rampant corruption by the end of Mwinyi's first term in office in 1990.

Benjamin William Mkapa (1995–2005)

President Mkapa was elected in 1995 and corruption was one of the main issues during the 1995 election campaigns. This was the first multiparty elections in Tanzania, and Mkapa led by example in declaring his and his family's assets during the election campaign. The new president decided to establish a Presidential Commission of Enquiry against Corruption (commonly known as the Warioba Commission) as well as the Public Leaders' Ethics Secretariat.

The Warioba Commission, to which has already been referred, was appointed early in 1996 to inquire extensively into the problem of corruption in the country and to make recommendations to improve the situation. The commission produced one of most extensive analyses of corruption in African states, the so-called Warioba Report, which identified areas/environments where corruption occurs and which also revealed the mechanisms (e.g. regulations and procedures) that facilitate corruption. The report stated that both small-scale and large-scale corruption were rampant at all levels of society. Although the widespread corruption was partly explained by low salaries in the civil service, the report concluded that the worst perpetrators were actually those in higher levels of the bureaucracy with the highest salaries!

Among the Warioba Commission's recommendations to curb corruption were "the setting up of a 'Truth Commission' to prepare a code of ethics, to administer oaths, to take legal action against those making false declarations, declaration by leaders of all presents received, forfeiture of property for breaches of established rules, changes in the Prevention and Combating of Corruption Bureau (PCCB) of Tanzania. The report also recommended the

---

117. Njunwa, "Combating Corruption," 2.

improvement of government employees' salaries, the more frequent transferal of police officers and that a reduction in the size of government.[118]

Following the Commission's report, the government embarked on the formulation of a national anti-corruption strategy. The process involved government ministries, NGOs, the private sector, civic associations, donors, the media, and important for this study, it also included input by religious organizations. Resulting from this participatory process was the National Anti-Corruption Strategy and Action Plan (NACSAP), adopted in 1999.[119] The plan covered all sectors of government and set out the four courses of action in the fight against corruption, namely: (1) prevention; (2) enforcement; (3) public awareness and participation; and (4) institution building.

As was noted earlier, NACSAP was an initiative born in the wake of the Warioba Report. The Plan established tools meant to help the government mainstream and prioritize measures and reforms to fight corruption. With regard to the implementation of the program, the Tanzanian government strove to involve NGOs, private sector, civic associations, media, religious organizations, donors, etc. in an attempt to "internalize" the anti-corruption strategy by giving ownership to the various key stakeholders.[120]

Most of the new avenues of fighting corruption established by the NACSAP are still existing and functional. These include the office of a Minister of State in the President's Office with the responsibility of seeing to good governance and the oversight and coordination of all anti-corruption activities.

Another initiative taken in terms of NACSAP was the establishment in 2001 of the Good Governance Coordination Unit, which falls under the Secretary of State. This unit was tasked with administering and coordinating organizations with anti-corruption related responsibilities. The latter were the PCB, the Police, the Ethics Commission, the Commission for Human Rights and Good Governance, the National Audit Office, the Ethics

---

118. URT, *Tanzania's Presidential Commission,* Warioba Report, 96.

119. For a detailed explanation of the formation of this Plan see online: http://www.worldbank.org/socialaccountability_sourcebook/Regional%20database/Case%20studies/Africa/Tanzania%20%20Accountability,%20transparency%20&%20integrity%20project.pdf. Accessed 25 March 2014.

120. Government of Tanzania, National Anti-Corruption Strategy and Action Plan, 1996.

Inspectorate Department (located within the Public Service Management Department) and the Office of the President. It was also responsible for the enforcement of the Leadership Code of Ethics (which was part of the Arusha Declaration).

New developments were also the conversion of the Permanent Commission of Enquiry into the Commission of Human Rights and Good Governance, in 2001 – the latter commission's responsibilities include dealing with abuses of office; the speeding up of the process toward Tanzania's signing of the Southern African Development Commission Protocol against Corruption (SADCPAC) and the United Nations Convention against Corruption (UNCAC)[121]; and the strengthening of the Office of the Controller and Auditor General (CAG) via the Public Finance Act of 2001. The latter Act gave the CAG more independence in the recruitment and disciplining of staff.

The Republic of Tanzania National Anti-Corruption Forum (NACF) was established in November 2008 with the aim of providing a platform for dialogue among all stakeholders on matters of corruption in public conduct in Tanzania. The forum meets annually and includes all state-integrity institutions, local government authorities, civil society, private sector, media and development partners. In this forum all stakeholders review and discuss reports and other matters related to corruption and initiatives implemented by them during the previous year. The NACF also seeks to inform the general public on stakeholder's achievements, challenges faced by them, and the ways forward on the road to the eradication of corruption.

However, the extent of the corruption challenge is shown by the government's own admission of the limited successes of even the new measures: "the success of the Tanzanian efforts to mobilize civil society is questionable: [after the implementation of NACSAP I] there is [still] no strong civil society

---

121. The UN Convention against Corruption (UNCAC), was signed in Mérida, Mexico, on 9 December 2003. It is devoted to the prevention of corruption globally, with measures directed at both the public and private sectors. Tanzania ratified UNCAC and other international and regional conventions and protocols that bind the country to take action on preventing and combating corruption. The Southern Africa Development Community Protocol against Corruption is a regional agreement between states that shows they are committed to fighting corruption, especially by establishing an independent anti-corruption agency or agencies to deal with corruption.

network dealing with governance related issues."[122] Likewise, "insufficient enforcement of the various anti-corruption initiatives devised under previous . . . strategies appear [to have been] a significant challenge in Tanzania."[123]

In summary, with regard to the Mkapa presidency, the 521-page Warioba Report by the ten-person presidential commission is regarded as the key step in the fight against corruption in Tanzania. It helped the formation of the strategy to fight corruption which highlighted the importance of political will for the success of anti-corruption measures. It also helped to establish an institutional structure to fight corruption, but although it intensified the war against corruption, it was far from being won. The second phase of the NACSAP, called NACSAP II, which started in 2008, ran until 2011. Important to note (and this will be returned to in chapter 5 of this book), is the government's active engagement with religious institutions in both the NACSAP consultations. As was seen, however, efforts under the Mkapa administrations were also not completely successful and the struggle against corruption remained a Tanzanian reality under the next/present administration.

Jakaya Mrisho Kikwete (2005–2015)

President Kikwete was elected in 2005 and in 2010 for a second term. During the 2005 election campaign he had, like that of his predecessor President Mkapa, "a strong anti-corruption rhetoric and promised to fight against corruption."[124]

Although President Jakaya Kikwete remained popular during his first tenure of office (2005–2010), and despite his message of zero tolerance of corruption during the ruling party's (the CCM) leadership election campaign of 2007, concerns are growing over the effectiveness of the government and its political will to combat corruption. One example of this is reflected in the fact that

> the United Kingdom cut its budget support by TZS 24 billion in 2009 and expressed its worries about the lack of progress in

---

122. Tanzania's Presidential Commission of Inquiry against Corruption, Warioba Report, 1996.
123. Ibid.
124. Wogau, "Transitions to Good Governance," 20.

improving the business environment (Tanzania Development Research Group, 2011 in NSGRP Human Development Report 2011). Britain [also indicated in 2012] that it will cut its budget support channeled through the UK Department for International Development (DFID) for the financial year 2011/12 by up to thirty percent.[125]

An interesting and important fact in recent times is that Tanzanian civil society has also gradually been gaining ground in pushing for accountability and it is supported by the media in their efforts to keep the population informed.[126] These efforts have been backed by parliament where, in several high-profile cases, opposition members of parliament have challenged government officials suspected of corruption.[127] However, apart from the efforts, evidence still shows that

> the number of cases prosecuted and convictions for corruption are small fractions of the allegations received by the PCCB. Over the period from 2008 to July 2011, a total of 20,346 allegations were received by the PCCB, yet only 1,932 cases were prosecuted and 179 convictions (less than one percent of total allegations) resulted from it.[128]

From the above it is clear that neither corruption, nor the efforts at curbing it, are new phenomena in Tanzania. Before proceeding to a discussion of the contemporary extent of this corruption and the possible causes and consequences of it, one first needs some greater clarity on what exactly Tanzanians' perceptions are of corruption and the manifestations it takes.

---

125. Ibid., 2.

126. The response of civil society and the media towards corruption will be discussed in more detail later. However, this is important to note, because it shows that in some sectors of civil society there developed a clear consciousness of corruption and condemnation of it and this is where the Anglican Church of Tanzania will be brought to the stage as it works with these civil organizations as allies even though we will show that these will be working from different points of departure, that is, faith as opposed to civil action.

127. For examples see Sitta, "Integrity Environment."

128. Government of Tanzania, "National Strategy for Growth and Reduction of Poverty."

2.3.4 Tanzanian Perceptions and Forms of Corruption

In common Tanzanian parlance, two main forms of corruption are usually distinguished, namely petty corruption and grand corruption. Petty corruption is associated with small bribes, sometimes euphemistically known as "facilitation payments." These can be cash payments to, gifts to, or favors for any person in and with power (mainly government officials) in exchange for preferential treatment. The latter may, for example, be some minor business advantage or a commitment to expedite or even circumvent a routine governmental requirement, or, for example, to be moved up on a waiting list.

Grand corruption not only refers to the fact that it involves large sums of money or gifts of high value, but also that it involves high-profile political figures. A good example of grand corruption in Tanzania is what was referred to by British High Commissioner to Tanzania, Philip Parham, at the launch of Tanzania's Construction Sector Transparency Initiative (CoST) sponsored by the United Kingdom through the Department of International Development (DFID), on 22 May 2008. High Commissioner Parham spoke of the fact that "about US$ 400 billion was lost annually to corruption in the construction sector worldwide."[129] He, however, specifically indicated that in Tanzania, 90 percent of contractors pay 10 to 15 percent of the value of contracts in bribes to government officials!

Other examples of grand corruption are found in the rigging of votes during elections and in the area of tax evasion. Due to allegations of unfair election practices (rigging), Tanzania has recently "introduced electronic identification cards for its citizens as a way to prevent voter fraud ahead of its 2015 general elections."[130] The country hopes that the introduction of this identification card would "reduce fraud and ensure that only eligible citizens participate in elections."[131] With regard to tax evasion, it has been argued that Tanzania is faced with the "rising tide of corporate tax evasion and avoidance."[132] For example, Zitto Kabwe, chairman of the parliamentary committee on public accounts, recently estimated that the country is "losing about $1.25 billion a year in revenue – equivalent to five percent of its

---

129. "Corruption Out of Control," 3.
130. Cf. trust.org, 2013.
131. Ibid.
132. Ibid.

gross domestic product (GDP) – through corporate tax avoidance, evasion and corruption."[133]

The Warioba Report (1996) also classifies corruption according to two categories. The first relates to those who receive bribes to cater for their daily living needs or in day-to-day situations (in other words, what has above been referred to as petty corruption), while the other group involves high-level leaders and public officials, who are motivated by excessive greed for wealth and power (grand corruption).

Though there exists no one single comprehensive list of acts that is universally accepted as constituting corruption, the latter seeps into all aspects of life, from securing a loan or license to start a new business, to getting a passport, to preferential access to medical and other health services. It may be in the form of bureaucrats asking citizens for bribes to perform basic services, to hospital employees stealing and selling medical supplies that were meant for distribution to the poor, or to bureaucrats receiving salaries for jobs that they did not do. These acts are all also instances of corruption in terms of the United Nations Convention against Corruption as they represent

> . . . the promise, offering or giving, to a public official, or the solicitation or acceptance by a public official, directly or indirectly, of an undue advantage, for the official himself or another person or entity, in order that the official act or refrain from acting in the exercise of his official duties.[134]

Another way of distinguishing between the different forms of corruption in Tanzania is by referring to examples of acts of corruption. The most common and well-known act is the *hongo* or *kuhonga* (which means "bribery" or "to bribe"). The concept of *hongo* is also described as *kitu kidogo* meaning "something small." *Uhujumu* ("embezzlement"), on the other hand, has to do with public property. In terms of the World Bank's definition of these actions they represent,

> . . . the misappropriation or other diversion by a public official, for purposes unrelated to those for which the assets were intended, for his benefit or for the benefit of another person

---

133. Ibid.
134. United Nations, "United Nations Convention against Corruption."

or entity, of any property, public or private funds or securities or any other thing of value entrusted to the public official by virtue of his position.[135]

Embezzlement, thus, involves theft of resources by persons entrusted with the authority and control of such resources.

In Tanzania, *kughushi* ("fraud") involves acts or behavior by a staff member or other person or entity that mislead others into providing a benefit to a staff member, or other person/s or entity to whom it would not normally occur. This differs from "extortion" which involves *coercing* a person or entity to provide a benefit to a staff member, another person or an entity in exchange for acting (or failing to act) in a particular manner.[136] A further example of an act of corruption is called *upendeleo* which refers to an abuse of power (i.e. when a staff member or official uses his or her vested authority to benefit another staff member, person or entity improperly, or when vested authority is used to improperly discriminate against another staff member, person or entity).

A final act of corruption that may be mentioned is *mgongano wa maslahi*, or "conflicts of interest." This occurs when a staff member or official acts or fails to act on a matter where he or she has an interest in the outcome of the action. *Matumizi mabaya ya taarifa* may thus refer to, for example, the abuse of privileged information – when one has access to privileged information due to one's position and then one uses it to gain an unfair advantage over others or other entities.

All of these forms of corruption seem to be rife at all levels of government and in all areas of government, as the following two examples show. According to the Corruption Tracker System (CTS):

> Tanzania is facing corruption in areas such as the land sector . . . land grabbing through corruption is increasingly becoming a very serious problem both in Dar es Salaam and the country at large . . . someone should be seriously benefiting from this lucrative business.[137]

---

135. World Bank, "Six Questions."
136. cf. Argandoña, "1996 ICC Report," 134.
137. CTS, Online Newsletter 013.

In a speech delivered on 24 May 2010 in the Dar es Salaam, President Kikwete accused town and city councilors of being at the center of corruption scandals related to open spaces. Taking its cue from President Kikwete, the then Dar es Salaam Regional Commissioner, William Lukuvi, visited the Kinondoni municipality a month later and discovered numerous discrepancies relating to plot allocations and the misuse and abuse of open spaces. It is believed that plot allocations by government officials is another area where corruption is alarmingly common.

According to the CTS, the tourism and wildlife industries (the Tourism and Wildlife Department) have also not been immune to corruption allegations, but the latest reports appear to indicate that corruption players are moving away from the traditional hunting grounds towards targeting animals for shipment to foreign countries in corrupt, clandestine ways.[138] In fact, corruption and illegal exploitation of national resources reached new levels in 2010 when 130 wild animals from Tanzania's national parks were illegally exported to Doha, aboard a Qatar military transport plane!

The above examples are only two further instances that show that corruption has not only reached pandemic levels in Tanzania, but that it permeates all sectors of society.[139] It is also in agreement with the Warioba Report's findings on the wide range of spheres in Tanzanian society where corruption occurs. The report states that,

> . . . there is corruption in twenty lodges and hotels in game parks and in hotels in Dar es Salaam and Kigoma [only!]; in the offices of the Ministry of Home Affairs, the Attorney General, the ministries of education, health and lands; in the Treasury and the "Investment Promotion Centre" where tax exemptions had been given to rich businessmen; in the use of the VIP lounge at the Dar es Salaam airport; in the National Bank of Commerce (unsecured loans); in fifteen private companies (not repaying loans); in the social services (for example, demanding money for hospital beds); and especially in the police force where it was said to be deep-rooted throughout the hierarchy;

---

138. Ibid.
139. As is stated in Government of Tanzania, NACSAP II, 98.

and in the courts ("judgments are written in the streets without even a hearing"); among journalists for "cheque book" journalism – accepting bribes to write or not to write revealing stories; and so on.

2.3.5 The Extent of Corruption in Contemporary Tanzania: Comparative Statistics

The above sections all paint a bleak picture of corruption in Tanzania. But how does this compare with other countries? Is corruption on this scale a global phenomenon, or is Tanzania worse off than other countries? An answer to the latter questions may be found in the following three tables from Transparency International (TI), an NGO devoted to fighting corruption.[140] Since the 1990s, TI have been publishing a "corruption perceptions index" (CPI),[141] which measures the perceived levels of public sector corruption in countries worldwide on an annual basis. It uses a score ranging from zero (high corruption) to ten (low corruption).

According to Lambsdorff, a widely recognized scholar for his work on measuring corruption and the person who designed the Corruption Perceptions Index in 1995 on behalf of TI and oversaw its operation until 2008,

> ... [c]orruption is commonly difficult to measure. Indices that gather perceptions of business people and country analysts appear to be good proxies for real levels of corruption. The Transparency International Corruption Perceptions Index employs this approach. It is a composite index, using data from

---

140. Transparency International is a global coalition or network founded in 1993 for the purpose of exposing and raising awareness of the problem of corruption in the world and for suggesting practical way to address it. For more on TI, see online at: www.transparency.org. Accessed 30 September 2013.

141. The Corruption Perceptions Index 2012. The Corruption Perceptions Index (CPI) ranks countries according to the perception of corruption in the public sector. The CPI is an aggregate indicator that combines different sources of information about corruption, making it possible to compare countries. The 2012 CPI draws on different assessments and business opinion surveys carried out by independent and reputable institutions. It captures information about the administrative and political aspects of corruption.

seven independent institutions. The high correlation among the sources provides confidence in the validity of the data.[142]

The three tables below indicate, first, the Transparency International score for Tanzania from 2002 to 2012; second, the Transparency International score showing the three best-performing countries in the world from 2002 to 2012; third, the Transparency International score showing the three worst-performing countries from 2002 to 2012.

Table 1.1 Transparency International Score for Tanzania 2002–2012

Year	2002	2003	2004	2005	2006	2007	2008	2009	2010	2011	2012
TI Score	2.7	2.5	2.8	2.9	2.9	3.2	3.0	2.6	2.7	3.0	3.5
Rank:	71	92	90	88	93	94	102	126	116	100	102
Countries Surveyed:	102	133	145	158	163	179	180	180	178	182	174

Source: Transparency International CPI 2002–2012
Note: The index ranges from ten (highly clean) to zero (highly corrupt).

---

142. Lambsdorff, "Background Paper," 466. As possibly the best global instrument for measuring corruption, the CPI has various sources of information. For example, referring to CPI 2008, Lambsdorff ("Background Paper") comments: "[It drew] on thirteen different polls and surveys from eleven independent institutions. TI strives to ensure that the sources used are of the highest quality and that the survey work is performed with complete integrity. To qualify, the data must be well documented and sufficient to permit a judgment on its reliability. All sources must provide a ranking of nations and must measure the overall extent of corruption. This condition excludes surveys which mix corruption with other issues, such as political instability, decentralization or nationalism for instance."

Table 1.2 Transparent International Score: Three Best-Performing Countries 2002–2012

Year	Rank or Position 1 and Score	Rank or Position 2 and Score	Rank or Position 3 and Score
2002	Finland 9.7	Denmark and New Zealand 9.5	Iceland 9.4
2003	Finland 9.7	Iceland 9.6	Denmark and New Zealand 9.5
2004	Finland 9.7	New Zealand 9.6	Denmark and Iceland 9.5
2005	Iceland 9.7	Finland and New Zealand 9.6	Denmark 9.5
2006	Finland and Iceland 9.6	Denmark 9.5	Singapore 9.4
2007	Denmark, Finland and New Zealand 9.4	Singapore and Sweden 9.3	Iceland 9.2
2008	Denmark, New Zealand and Sweden 9.3	Singapore 9.2	Finland and Switzerland 9.0
2009	New Zealand 9.4	Denmark 9.3	Singapore 9.2
2010	Denmark, New Zealand and Singapore 9.3	Finland and Sweden 9.2	Canada 8.9
2011	New Zealand 9.5	Denmark and Finland 9.4	Sweden 9.3
2012	Denmark, Finland and New Zealand 9.0	Sweden 8.8	Singapore 8.7

Source: Transparency International CPI 2002–2012
Note: The index ranges from ten (highly clean) to zero (highly corrupt).

Table 1.3 Transparent International Score: Three Worst-Performing Countries 2002–2012

Year	Position 1 and Score	Position 2 and Score	Position 3 and Score
2002	Bangladesh 1.2	Nigeria 1.6	Angola, Madagascar and Paraguay 1.7
2003	Bangladesh 1.3	Nigeria 1.4	Haiti 1.5
2004	Bangladesh and Haiti 1.5	Nigeria 1.6	Chad and Myanmar 1.6
2005	Bangladesh and Chad 1.7	Haiti, Myanmar and Turkmenistan 1.8	Nigeria, Equatorial Guinea and Cote d'Ivoire 1.9
2006	Haiti, Myanmar, Iraq and Guinea 1.9	Sudan, DRC, Chad and Bangladesh 2	Uzbekistan, Equatorial Guinea, Cote d'Ivoire, Cambodia and Belarus 2.1
2007	Somalia and Myanmar 1.4	Iraq 1.5	Haiti 1.6
2008	Somalia 1.0	Iraq and Myanmar 1.3	Haiti 1.4
2009	Somalia 1.1	Afghanistan 1.3	Myanmar 1.4
2010	Somalia 1.1	Myanmar and Afghanistan 1.4	Iraq 1.5
2011	Somalia, North Korea 1.0	Afghanistan and Myanmar 1.5	Uzbekistan, Sudan and Turkmenistan
2012	Somalia, North Korea and Afghanistan 0.8	Sudan 1.3	Myanmar 1.5

Source: Transparency International CPI 2002–2012
Note: The index ranges from ten (highly clean) to zero (highly corrupt).

To avoid unnecessary confusion regarding the data presented, it must be kept in mind that the tables represent only the period time from 2002 to 2012 and that tables 1.2 and 1.3 have been designed to situate Tanzania's TI score within the global margins of best and worst-performing countries. In short, when compared to international levels of corruption, Tanzania's situation seems a dire one. According to the 2012 CPI Score Tanzania ranks at number 102 out of 174 countries with regard to the prevalence of corruption. In 2012, according to TI, the least corrupt country in the world was Denmark with a score of 9.0 and the most corrupt was Somalia, having scored 1.8 – Tanzania scored a mere 3.4. The tables also show, however, that Tanzania is not alone and that corruption remains a worldwide problem.

The above, in turn, leads to the question of what the reasons are behind these high levels of corruption in Tanzania and what their consequences may be. Some reasons and consequences have been identified in passing in the discussion on the history of corruption in Tanzania, but some need to be listed and discussed in more detail.

2.4 Corruption: Causes and Consequences

2.4.1 Possible Causes of Corruption: General Observations

Thus far and in passing, the increase in corruption in Tanzania was attributed to four main factors: neglect of the inherited traditional codes of conduct, politicization of the public service, adverse economic conditions and the permissiveness of government. However, scholars have identified and also differ on exactly what else may be behind the phenomenon of corruption.

Mkunde offers an interesting perspective on the causes of corruption by referring to Bernard Joinnet, who, almost forty years ago (interestingly enough, on the eve of the 1978 Tanzanian economic crisis) and on a philosophical note, already argued quite provocatively that "the ugly face of modern society is a product of a combination of six factors which are partly independent and partly interdependent." The factors and their influences that Joinnet identified are:

- *The development of science, technology and industry*: According to Joinnet, "people enjoy the fruits of technology and are asking for more." It is argued that this heightens what is known as the acquisitive instinct in humans, whose ceaseless quest is "to maximize pleasure and minimize pain."[143] Joinnet, furthermore,

---

143. Mkunde, "Morals for Good Governance," 3.

states that a heightened acquisitive instinct tends to overstep the boundaries of moral propriety if it is not properly controlled.
- *A pervasive liberal market economy whose basic tenet is the law of supply and demand*: The market responds to anything that people want regardless of whether what is wanted is morally good or detrimental to consumers. There are three features of a liberal market economy which also influence people's sense of morals. These are the pursuit of maximum profit, aggressive salesmanship and cut-throat competition. Each of these could be done with total regard for moral principles. Unfortunately, says Joinnet, in practice it is done with little or no regard for moral principles.
- *Preoccupation with rational explanation*: according to Joinnet, people tend to seek rational explanations for everything. Rules and laws, too, must therefore be rational and reasonable. Norms and values inherited from the past are dismissed as myths or superstitions because they, according to such a mindset, have no rational base.
- *Secularism*: Interestingly for this study is Joinnet's view that when belief in God is no longer the cornerstone of public service morality, then God is excluded from public spaces. The majority of people, then, prefer to live in a secular state. They enjoy separating their private life from their public life and tend to associate morality with their private life and not with public life with sometimes accompanying negative consequences for the latter.
- *Democracy*: People's participation in decisions affecting their lives and their ability to call to account those elected to public offices are highly valued in modern society. So too are freedoms such as freedom of speech, of the press and of opinion. These freedoms allow people to question each and everything. Though a cherished principle in many contemporary societies, it does have a down side, according to Joinnet, as this may also demean the basis of authority, including moral authority.

Mkude draws upon the above insights of Joinnet and adds to this modernization's emphasis on the individual person to the extent that it more or less excludes the family or group and may result in a lessening of care for others. Altruism has always been regarded as a major factor in building a stable and caring society. But, according to Mkude, Joinnet's five elements combined shows how a powerful weakening of the moral fabric of society may occur and may pose a challenge to the foundations of traditional morality – including those that traditionally inhibit corruption.

There are, however, also other (Tanzanian) views on the causes of corruption in that country. The Prevention and Combating of Corruption Bureau (PCCB) of Tanzania, for example, contributes corruption in the country to the following causes:

- the incompetence and inefficiencies in delivery of public service;
- legal and administrative/political guidelines that provide an atmosphere conducive to the existence of corruption;
- economic conditions that force people to merely attempt to survive;
- low salaries of public servants and rapid rise in the cost of living;
- insecurity of employment tenure, lack of transparency and accountability in executing decisions;
- and the lack of political will and an erosion of integrity of leadership.[144]

Especially interesting is the fact that one of the main causes cited by the PCCB is poor, unreliable and inadequate provision of basic services. These include ". . . education, health, water, transport, and the necessary information." These in turn affect people's ability to follow up issues in order to find solutions, for example, seeking training, employment, salary increases or promotion or even pensions in legitimate ways.

With regard to access to information, other studies have shown that corruption becomes rampant and may take on pandemic proportions where there is poor civic awareness of individual basic rights, poor or low participation in the community governance processes, and a weak or underdeveloped civil society. This may also be coupled with too rigid (or an ignorance of) bureaucratic rules, directives, regulations and procedures that induce various

---

144. Prevention and Combating of Corruption, "Causes of Corruption in Tanzania," online at: http://www.tanzania.go.tz/pcb/corruption/causes.html. Accessed 7 November 2011.

forms of corruption. Thus, inadequate and/or a lack of necessary information on policies and guidelines, transparency and accountability are also contributing factors to corruption.

Yet another perspective on the causes of corruption in Tanzania is given by the United Republic of Tanzania's (URT's) Warioba Report 1996, especially with its emphasis on the poor example of leadership in the fight against corruption. As mentioned earlier, corruption affects Tanzania at all levels of society and what is especially disconcerting is the high levels of corruption in the upper hierarchy of government. In addition, when corrupt officials at the lower levels of the bureaucracy are reported by the public, it frequently results in no action being taken as superior officers are either directly involved in the corruption or did not consider it a priority! For this reason, the Warioba Report argues that,

> [i]t has become evident that the greatest source of corruption in the country is not the poor economy and low salaries; although these too have played some part. The greatest source is the laxity of leadership in overseeing the implementation of established norms.[145]

2.4.1.1 *Tanzanian/African Cultural and Family Values and Practices and Corruption*

Cutural practices within a Tanzanian context should form part of any consideration of the possible causes and consequences of corruption in that society as these may either encourage or discourage corruption. The strengths and weaknesses of selected Tanzanian cultures and their effects on leadership and social interaction may very well have bearing on the prevalence of corruption in such cultures. For example, we noted earlier the issue of power and the level of its centralization and concentration in the hands of the leaders within most African cultures. However, other important examples may exist that suggest that these must be grounded in indigenous social values and contexts, while adapting to changing realities.

---

145. United Republic of Tanzania, *Tanzania's Presidential Commission of Inquiry Against Corruption*, Warioba Report, 1996.

This, however, does not ignore the "importance of cultural diversity, local insights and the freedom,"[146] but seeks to imply that even though it is believed that corruption is culturally determined and varies from one society to another, the fact remains that if negative cultural values are encouraged, it will lead to "moral imbalance that is detrimental to the common good of the members of a pluralistic society."[147]

Aware of the fact that "culture"[148] as reflected on within an anthropological perspective (see 2.2.1.4) and the respective differing values are important – especially those that arise from cultural experiences and expectations – in Tanzania there could be some cultures that enable or prevent moral agency from being exercised in society.[149] To understand this in the Tanzanian context, one may refer to studies on leadership in Tanzania, which show that younger people have, in recent years, tended to be critical of their leaders.[150] This growing, dynamic and critical culture has helped to some extent to change the earlier culture of silence regarding corruption. It has, for example, contributed to critiquing the misused culture of gift giving to leaders which for long has been a traditional way of showing respect to leaders.

Likewise, cultural practices or norms in Tanzania which may be detrimental include the cultures' propensity to hiding one's feelings and remaining neutral. From examples such as these, Kretzschmar's suggestions are insightful, namely that "cultures must be embarked upon if culture is to help rather than hinder in the construction of moral persons and communities."[151] On the other hand beneficial cultural values such as "communal belonging, group wisdom and an awareness of the rhythms of creation are vital" for any society, especially traditional African societies that often reflect these values as long as they are "concerned with truth and a clear perception

---

146. Kretzschmar, "Cultural Pathways," 576.

147. Ibid.

148. According to South African Christian ethicist, "culture" refers to an integral system which exemplifies the values, beliefs, customs and institutions of a particular community, or group of communities. Culture is the way a people have organized themselves to express and preserve their identity and way of life (ibid., 572).

149. cf. Hampden-Turner and Trompenaars, *Building Cross-Cultural Competence*.

150. cf. Schubert, *Christian-Ethical Comparison*, 142; Chitando, cf. "Religious Ethics," 50–56.

151. Kretzschmar, "Cultural Pathways," 585.

of the realities of life."[152] However, the issue remains complex as even a good African cultural value such as a "sense of community" (sometimes understood as "communitarianism") may in some cases lead to "nepotism (promotion of the interests of family members), "jobs for pals" (promoting the interests of friends and supporters), misplaced (blind) loyalties to clan or family members, uncritical political patronage, and an absence of personal moral accountability.[153]

Linked to the above reflections on cultural values is the issue of family values. Studies have shown growing up in an adverse family environment has detrimental effects on child development.[154] Important for the purposes of this study, is the fact that family breakdown and a lack of proper parenting has also been identified as one of the potential causes of corruption and injustice. The family is generally the space where the majority of people learn the fundamental skills for life. Physically, emotionally and socially the family is the context from which the life flows. As such, "effects of ineffective parenting on the development of self-control . . . a driver for many negative outcomes in a society" and the latter may include the absence of, or a lower sensitivity to, the moral reprehensibility of corruption.[155] This possible cause of corruption will be picked up again in chapter 5 to show that this is an area where the church has great potential as corruption is learned behavior and churches may help to reshape people's orientations and may also enable behavioral change in contexts where parental care is absent.

2.4.1.2 On Moral Decadence as a Cause of Corruption

Finally, and from a slightly different angle, scholars such as Pope, Mbaku, and Akindele have attributed moral decadence as a forgotten major cause of corruption in Tanzania.[156] These scholars argue from two main perspectives: a public service perspective and a historical perspective. Proponents of this view are of the opinion that, in order to understand the phenomenon of moral decadence in Tanzania, a historical perspective of the country is

---

152. Ibid.
153. Kretzschmar, "Christian Spirituality," 85–90.
154. cf. Kierkus and Baer, "Does the Relationship."
155. Gottfredson and Hirschi, *General Theory of Crime*.
156. Pope, *Confronting Corruption;* Mbaku, *Corruption and the Crisis;* Akindele, "Corruption and Economic Retardation."

crucial. Together with this, they emphasize that the extent of corruption in Tanzania can be best understood when the evolution of public sector service is taken as a focal point while putting special emphasis on the norms and values informing this sector.

As many of the views above suggest the close link between the moral state of a nation/country and the prevalence of corruption in it, it is worthwhile to ask what perceptions are on the current *moral state* of the Tanzanian nation. Moral decline refers to what is sometimes also referred to as moral decay or moral erosion. In simple terms this means a failure to abide by positive behavior. For instance, Turiel indicates that failure of many people "to incorporate moral values and ideals of the society are indicators of moral decline."[157]

Much has been said about Tanzania in this regard. One commentator, for example, is of the opinion that Nyerere's ideology of building a community with common political values has been torn apart by a paradigm shift from socialism to individualism characterized by an increased consciousness of ethnicity, as well as by petty rivalries, corruption (*ufisadi*) and demoralization.[158] It does seem that the general consensus is that the country is faced with a serious state what is locally referred to as "*mmonyoko wa maadili*" (moral degradation).[159] In all walks of life, it seems, the general perception is that Tanzanians must reclaim their lost morals! There is a clear cry also for moral leadership.[160] According to Hope, on the African continent as a whole, corruption is "a way of life and reflects the general, and legendary climate of unethical leadership."[161] Recent prime Tanzanian examples of such a lack in moral leadership that are often referred to are the forced resignation of the Prime Minister and two cabinet ministers (the former Minister for Minerals

---

157. Turiel, *Culture of Morality*, 2.

158. In Konrad-Adenauer, *Role of Faith*, 15.

159. Tanzanians speak of "*mmomonyoko wa maadili*" which refers to moral decay, to indicate how bad the general state of morality is in Tanzania. In the discourse on moral decay, they often refer to issues such as bad leadership, corruption, insecurity, greed, poverty, inequality, injustices, disease, hatred, discrimination, unemployment, marginalization and a host of other evils suffered by people in Tanzania (cf. Heilman and Kaiser, "Religion, Identity and Politics"; Turiel, *Culture of Morality* and Klingebiel et al., *Socio-Political Impact*).

160. See Aseka's (*Transformational Leadership*) suggestion that East Africa as a whole has had a serious deficit in moral leadership and that very little appears to be done about.

161. Hope, *From Crisis to Renewal*, 100.

and Energy and the Minister for East Africa Cooperation) in February 2008 following allegations of serious corruption levelled against them. The other, in the same year, was when the Minister of Infrastructure Development (the former Tanzanian Attorney General!) was also "forced to resign following allegations of illegal acquisition of US$2.2 million deposited in a foreign bank account in the United Kingdom."[162]

Klingebiel justifies his conviction of the moral decay in Tanzania by referring to increased tensions and conflicts.[163] According to him, Tanzania is considered a unique case of political stability in the conflict-driven region of East Africa. For a long time the country's political stability has been a constant not only with regard to its internal affairs, but also to its relations with its neighbors. Nevertheless, the country today faces various pressures on its socio-political stability and Klingebiel expressly identifies corruption as one of the major areas of potential or actual tensions. Overall, according to Ayittey,

> . . . since political independence, the twin evils of gross mismanagement of national economies and looting of national treasuries for deposit in European and offshore bank accounts became the trend in much of Africa. Even today, it continues to bite ferociously in the face of concerted calls for measures to sustainably curb it.[164]

Ayittey further acknowledges that while efforts have been undertaken in Tanzania in the past to address the levels of corruption, that the country itself needs to acknowledge that it "is faced with corruption in its public and private sectors that [have] assumed endemic proportions" and that "[t]he government views this scourge as public enemy number one."[165] However, it also is apparent that corruption has become part of daily life for ordinary citizens of Tanzania, to the extent that one may say it is almost normalized. A study conducted on Zanzibar in 2011, therefore, unsurprisingly shows that citizens of the island perceive corruption to be a relatively common

---

162. *Tanzania Mwananchi Newspaper*, 29 August 2008, 1–2.
163. Klingebiel et al., *Socio-Political Impact*, 17.
164. Ayittey, *Africa Betrayed*, 39.
165. With reference to Government of Tanzania, *National Anti-Corruption Strategy and Action Plan for Tanzania* (Dar es Salaam: President's Office, State House, 1990), 5.

day-to-day occurrence. One simply has to accept that when one delays offering a small bribe or *"kitu kidogo"* a sick relative may die in hospital, a child may fail his or her examinations, a business deal may fall through, or the best person for the job may not be employed or admitted to an academic institution.[166]

The latter comment brings us to the next section, namely, what are the consequences of corruption, especially in Tanzania? And with this we come to the promised short detour in a second conceptual analysis that is central to this study – the meaning of in/justice (as with the concept of corruption, for now, again from non-theological perspectives) as the first of a series of consequences of corruption in general and in Tanzania in particular.

2.4.2 The Consequences of Corruption (in Tanzania): Secular Perspectives

2.4.2.1 The Concept of Justice and Corruption as a Threat to Justice

Conceptual overview
One often reads about or hear of corruption by many names, all expressing condemnation of the phenomenon as a "vice," "(chronic) disease," "tragedy," "cancer," "sin," "sin that eats from within," "problem," "culture," and so forth. Likewise, condemnation of corruption is evident from the language often used to express efforts to address it: "fight," "eradicate," "curtail," "war against," "ant-corruption squads," "name and shame," "wipe out," and "crack down on" – in fact, many of these words can be found on the anti-corruption website of institutions such as the World Bank![167]

In this section, special attention is paid to consequences of corruption, and specifically to corruption as a manifestation of gross injustice. The overriding agenda is to indicate that corruption essentially entails injustice. In other words, an argument is made to indicate that the problem of corruption is a problem of justice. By examples of the consequences, the study

---

166. See in this regard the survey conducted by Tronvoll in Zanzibar in 2011, on peoples' attitudes to corruption and good governance – Tronvoll, "'Citizens' Attitude."

167. Cf. online at: www.worldbank.org/publicsector/anticorrup/. Accessed 12 April 2012.

explores the nature of corruption as a form of social injustice and seeks to tie together forms of this injustice. At this stage, however, it important to note that when referring to justice/injustice in this section, it is done with reference to justice/injustice in *non-theological terms* and from a variety of perspectives. A biblical-theological understanding of justice will be given in chapter 3 as part of the theological-ethical consideration of the nature of corruption. A grasp of justice and injustice issues in this part of the study will not only prepare the way for further discussion, but also for the later discussion (in ch. 4) on the possible responsibilities of the church toward the promotion of justice and the fight against injustice in the form of corruption. As such, this section does not attempt to provide an exhaustive analysis of justice, but rather to provide insight into some forms, associated beliefs, basic views, approaches and constructions of in/justice.

This section, however, also has to contend with the ambiguities and differences of opinion regarding the definitions of justice and injustice. As North American ethicist Karen Lebacqz argues, "[t]here is no single agreed standard for justice in our contemporary world. All the talk about justice today may not bring us any nearer to making justice a lived reality."[168] Neville agrees with this view that "the precise meaning of justice is illusive" in that,

> . . . first, . . . there are competing conceptions of justice, which compete because theorists do not agree on what constitutes justice; secondly, that discussing justice, even if full agreement could be reached concerning that which comprises justice, does not necessarily lead to justice being implemented.[169]

In a similar vein, Dukor argues that "[t]he enterprise of the analysis and elucidation of the concept [of justice] . . . seem to be very difficult one because of cluster of varying notions of it."[170] To drive his point home, Dukor refers to Greek philosopher Aristotle's (384–322 BCE) acknowledgement of the complexity of the concept justice/injustice when the latter said that, "[n]ow it appears that the words justice and injustice are ambiguous; but as the different senses covered by the same name are very close to each other,

---

168. Lebacqz, *Justice in an Unjust World*, 7.
169. Neville, "Justice and Divine Judgment," 342.
170. Dukor, "Conceptions of Justice," 497.

the equivocation passes unnoticed and is not comparatively obvious as to where they are far apart."[171]

However, despite the complexity of the concept of justice, it is clear from literature that justice is an important aspect of human life for it

> . . . weighs heavily on the moral scales not so much because it has exercised the minds of the mentally mighty but because it bears directly on pressing social, cultural, political, economic and ecological concerns. Issues that exercise our collective conscience so often comprise justice matters.[172]

The issue of justice, therefore, has understandably always been high on the agenda of the United Nations. The latter asserts that the "failure to actively pursue justice is not without consequences . . . [and a] neglect of the pursuit of social justice in all its dimensions translates into de facto acceptance of a future marred by violence, repression and chaos."[173]

So, what is justice? In its day-to-day use the word justice refers to "just behavior or treatment," and "the administration of the law or authority in maintaining this."[174] This basic definition already indicates that the concept of justice has been and is often used in different ways for different purposes and in particular situations. A common approach is when justice is used to evaluate specific situations. For example, in some situations justice could be viewed from a criminal law perspective or from a market economy perspective (sometimes known as socio-economic justice perspective) or in broad stokes in the language of the global economy and the inequalities within it. Likewise, justice is and has also been regarded as that which is used to measure standards of governance. However, despite these differences, most literature on justice seems to suggest that human beings do not live in a just world, hence the need for justice.

Often literature on justice also indicates that for a long time the concept has been equated with different philosophical theories ranging from theories on morality or ethics, to law and natural law, equality, fairness, equity and

---

171. Quoted in ibid.

172. Neville, "Justice and Divine Judgment," 340.

173. The International Forum for Social Development, *Social Justice in an Open World*, 6.

174. cf. *Concise Oxford Dictionary*, 1969, 768.

rights to mention a few. The difficulty in defining justice rests on the fact that people, times, societies, places, and the administration of justice tend to differ widely. This is why the notion has and continues to be subjected to a variety of disciplinary interpretations, including legal, political, economic, philosophical and theological scrutiny.

A good place to start any non-theological reflection on justice is undoubtedly the famous twentieth-century work, *A Theory of Justice,* by philosophical ethicist John Rawls. As is the case with any proposed theory of justice, Rawls' theory is not free of criticism, but it remains seminal in any discussion on the topic.

Rawls' analysis of justice rests on two fundamental principles:[175] (1) Each person has equal right to the most extensive system of personal liberty compatible with a system of total liberty for all. (2) Social and economic inequality are to be arranged so that they are both (a) to the greatest benefit to the least advantaged in society (so that the least well off people are made as well off as possible, which could mean giving an unequal/greater amount to the people least well off) (b) attached to positions open to all under conditions of fair equality of opportunity (so that everyone in society has a reasonable chance of obtaining the positions in society that make decisions about inequalities).[176] One of the areas in which Rawls sees injustice is that of socio-economic inequalities, that which opposes equal opportunities and beneficial results for all members of the society. From Rawls' view of "justice as fairness" one may infer that "injustice is unfairness" and what follows then is Rawls' categorization of two types of justice.[177] One is that of "fairness" and the other "equality." For Rawls, justice is to be thought of as "fairness." Here, fairness can be understood as the demand to avoid bias of any kind in people's decisions, evaluations and in the execution of justice. It is from this concept of "fairness" that this type of justice became commonly known as "distributive justice" and it is mainly concerned with the allocation of people's rights, powers (including in leadership), duties, and the challenges faced by the members of a society or group.

---

175. Rawls, *Theory of Justice*, 60.
176. National Probono Resource Centre, "What Is Social Justice?" 6.
177. Rawls, *Theory of Justice*, 303.

The distributive nature of this type of justice is, for Rawls, more important because "all social values . . . are to be distributed equally unless an unequal distribution of any or all of these values is to everyone's advantage."[178] Likewise, for Rawls, the nature of this fairness has to be regarded as "the first virtue of social institutions, as truth is of systems of thought."[179]

As far as the concept of "equality" is concerned, fair and equal opportunity is a key element in Rawls' analysis. His emphasis here concerns the fact that justice becomes evident through the elimination of all inequalities of opportunity. This argument is also linked to what Rawls would call "principles of social justice," which are central to his formulation of his "principles of justice"[180] – fairness and equality where "the appropriate division of advantages must be in accordance with principles acceptable to all parties."[181]

Rawls' thought that justice is to be viewed in terms of fairness and equality is important to this study as it serves as a helpful point of departure for further engagement when the study of corruption is explored in terms of its effects on justice. This argument can be expanded further when Rawls' original theory of social justice is taken into consideration where persons have equal rights, and where social and economic equality are to be arranged so that they benefit the whole society, especially the least advantaged.

In a context of rampant corruption, justice no longer serves as the basis of order and peace. Rawls understands the deep inequalities evident in different societies; this is the context in which he comes up with the concept of a "well-ordered society."[182] The latter is a society where "everyone is presumed to act justly and to do his [sic] part in upholding just institutions."[183] From this he concludes that the "nature and aims of a perfectly just society is the fundamental part of the theory of justice" and with it comes the

> responsibility to address systemic/structural poverty, inequality and unfairness . . . fair redistribution of resources . . . equal access to opportunities and rights . . . fair system of law and due

---

178. Ibid., 25.
179. Rawls, *Theory of Justice*, rev. ed., 54.
180. Ibid., 13.
181. Ibid., 14–15.
182. Ibid., 8.
183. Ibid.

process . . . the] ability to take up opportunities and exercise rights [toward the] . . . protection of vulnerable and disadvantaged people.[184]

Scholars often speak of a variety of forms that justice may take, including utilitarian justice, retributive justice, distributive justice, and corrective justice. With regard to distributive justice, advocates of this approach (e.g. Rawls) emphasize fair and appropriate allocation of things such as power, wealth, reward and respect among members of a particular society. Rawls also speaks of so-called *substantive justice*, which refers to the *content* of the rules of an institution and *formal justice*. The latter, for Rawls, refers to the actions of the individuals in the *application* of the above rules. In this sense it is noteworthy to look at the following quotation from the Annual Report of the Legal and Human Rights Centre of Tanzania, entitled "Public Engagement: Justice Watch," as it refers to justice in the sense of the application of law with reference to corruption in the Tanzanian judicial system:

> Solicitation of corruption in courts of law seems to be rampant and a legalized practice of providing justice. The judiciary of Tanzania has a long history of corruption, which has caused denial of access to justice to the majority of Tanzanians particularly the poor. Corruption is so manifestly entrenched and institutionalized that the judiciary, the police and the entire justice system is wallowing under the trenches of corruption. Corruption may be rated the second greatest obstacle that impedes the efficient administration of justice in Tanzania.[185]

Thus, it seems that even if government policies in Tanzania aim at and even reflect substantive justice, corruption clearly undermines formal justice in its application or when policies are contravened. Interesting for our purposes is philosopher Amartya Sen's broadened the understanding of just actions to include the "betrayal of public trust" and the breaking of the rules

---

184. Ibid.
185. Legal and Human Rights Center, "Public Engagement: Justice Watch Annual Report, 2007," 57. Corruption in the judiciary often violates the right to equality and non-discrimination which Calderisi (*Trouble with Africa*, 89) refers to this as "another millstone around [Tanzania's] neck."

to mean "violations."[186] One may say, then, that when corruption (a misuse of power for private gain) occurs, it obviously means that public officials who are expected to treat people equally and fairly do not do so. They betray public trust and violate the rules of society both with regard to its substance and its application.

With regard to the above discussion of justice, it is important to note that (unlike as it is suggested by Rawls) the principle of fairness should not only apply to public officials. It has to go beyond the latter and should include officials from private institutions. After all, do private institutions not also operate on some kind of public trust and expectations (to use Sen's terminology)? And it is also true to say that corrupt practices may involve both private and public institutions in the same act. The influence of corruption may cut both ways or may originate from the one and influence the other. In this way, for example, private or public sector corruption may affect society or government when it leads to lower investments or economic growth and the like. In studies by Mauro,[187] Keefer and Knack,[188] and Elliot, to mention only a few, it has been shown how corruption indeed negatively affects investments; Mauro, Leite and Weidman, and Mo show that it negatively affects economic growth; and Kaufmann et al. and Mo, that it affects per capita income.

Social perspectives on justice/injustice
In some circles, the concept of justice is better understood as referring to "social justice." However, again one finds different emphases with regard to this concept. Young, for example, suggests that the central concern of social justice is to eliminate institutionalized domination and oppression,[189] while scholars such as Laakso and Olukoshi broaden their understanding of the concept to include the context in which the unfair distribution of economic fruits may occur.[190] For them, it has to do with a "crisis of individual and group identity, deepening social inequality/fragmentation, weakened

---

186. Sen, *Development as Freedom*.
187. Mauro, "Corruption and Growth."
188. Knack and Keefer, "Institutions and Economic Performance."
189. Young, *Justice and the Politics of Difference*, 15–16.
190. Laakso and Olukoshi, *Challenges to the Nation State*, 7.

administrative and policy apparatuses of the state."[191] Young also gives an important possible solution to this crisis which denies fair distribution when she says that

> . . . nepotism should go, bribery should go, inheritance should go as means of attaining public office, the belief has become established that it is wrong to allow nepotism, bribery, or inheritance any sway: individual merit should be the only test that should apply.[192]

In short, this means that in the social justice discourse, inequality is one of the causes of social segmentation and social breakdown. On the other hand, the social aspect of justice is sometimes based on the sense and wellbeing of a community whereby people in a community enjoy "the freedom of others, and the chance that they give others to be themselves, and to develop their potentials."[193] This proposal signifies "a reasonable basis of agreement among people who seek to take due account of the interests of all."[194] In social justice, the "interests of all" may consist of "economic, political, moral and intellectual conditions which will allow the citizens to live a fully human life."[195]

Finally, Thomson looks at the issue of justice in "relational terms": "Justice is . . . a matter of relationship – of a better morality – and it involves all the emotions associated with being wronged."[196] From this relational perspective, Thomson also suggests that "justice includes individual accountability and social responsibility; punishment for wrong-doing and the righting of wrong relations belong within the scope of justice-making."[197]

---

191. Ibid.
192. Young, *Justice and the Politics of Difference*, 88.
193. Peperzak, "Freedom," 154–155.
194. Nielsen, "Conceptions of Justice," 86–87.
195. Pazhayampallil, *Pastoral Guide*, 878–879. This formulation of social justice by Pazhayampallil is interesting and as will later it echoes in secular terms much of the theological-ethical reflections on the concepts of human flourishing and human dignity in section 3.6.3 in chapter 3.
196. Thomson, "Satisfying Justice," 320.
197. Ibid., 335. The concept of relationality will be specifically addressed again later in the theological-ethical reflections on corruption as injustice in chapter 3 section 3.6.4 of this study.

Justice from a human rights perspective

Justice can and has also been explored from a human rights perspective by many scholars. Here it is important to note that throughout history, human rights as a concept, where it existed, like justice has been linked to customs, law, and also to religion. Although the meaning, content and standards of human rights have changed over time and according to particular contexts, their application in the context of justice has remained remarkably constant. For example, if human rights such as freedom of expression, assembly or access to information and education, are denied or restricted, then it means justice has at the same time been denied. It follows that human rights need protection in order for justice to also flourish.

Literature, such as that by Transparency International, also suggests that when justice is understood within human rights parameters, it is imperative that compelling steps toward the prevention of corruption be taken.[198] This is, among other things, because human rights also address the abuse of power, and as was seen repeatedly up to now, corruption essentially boils down to an abuse of power. In this way, a human rights analysis will also throw light on the power relations in a society because uneven power relations often leads to discrimination, undermines equity, and the removal of economic, legal and political obstacles that prevent marginalized groups from enjoying their rights.[199] If basic human rights are guaranteed, especially rights to basic necessities of life, then the incidence of corruption and related offences should at least be reduced.[200]

For the purposes of this study, an interesting voice on justice from a human rights perspective is that Nicolas Wolterstorff.[201] Wolterstorff's is a theological voice, but one that shows that even in the theological discourse on justice, human rights perspectives are also present. Wolterstorff, for example, argues that justice is "ultimately grounded on inherent rights." Wolterstorff's understanding of how human rights came to be part of the life of a human being is by virtue of "the worth of beings of their sort."[202] For him, justice

---

198. Transparency International, "Integrating Human Rights," 3.
199. Ibid., 5.
200. Ibid., 7.
201. Wolterstorff, *Justice*, 21.
202. Ibid., 10–11.

is "right order" and he goes on to expand on this by saying that "[j]ustice is present in a society . . . insofar as the society measures up to whatever is the standard for the rightly ordered society."[203] For Wolterstorff, the use of language is crucial as "the language of rights and of being wronged, . . . enables the oppressed to bring their own moral condition into the picture: they have been deprived of their right to better treatment, treated as if they were of little worth."[204] These thoughts of Wolterstorff need further unpacking, especially with regard to how they inform his theological thought. This will be done in chapter 3 (see 3.6.1), especially with regard to how a rightly ordered society is one that in theological terms is characterized by *shalom*.

2.4.2.2 Corruption as Threat to Peace, Security and Stability

Corruption not only severely affects freedom, but also peace, security and stability. This was already suggested in chapter 1 with reference to the political crises in Rwanda and Burundi in the 1990s. The term peace itself "is highly emotive" and "is often abused as a tool of political propaganda."[205] But peace is also connected to justice and injustice as, when peace is narrowly defined, it can "imply passivity and the acceptance of injustice," according to Barash.[206] And, according to Emil Bolongaita,

> . . . by weakening the effectiveness and legitimacy of public institutions, undermining economic recovery and jeopardizing international aid and foreign direct investment (FDI), corruption increases the risk of violence and undermines the well-being and political empowerment of local populations.[207]

It is, therefore, not surprising that many conflict-ridden countries are also among those perceived to be the most corrupt in the world. As was shown above with reference to Transparency International's CPI, in Africa this has been the case, for example, with Burundi and currently still in Somalia. This is probably also why corruption has recently become a major item on

---

203. Ibid., 30.
204. Ibid., 9.
205. Howard, *Problems of a Disarmed World*, 225.
206. Barash, *Introduction to Peace Studies*, 6.
207. Bolongaita, "Controlling Corruption," 679.

the international security agenda in Africa[208] and why the United Nations expressly names corruption as a major "impediment to peace building."[209] However, concerns are also found among wealthy countries about corruption and security in their own midst. These concerns have largely focused on terrorism, narcotics, organized crime and "state failure"[210] – by state failure is meant the condition whereby the state is faced with extreme situations, such as ones of violence, that lead to its inability to deliver political, social and economic goods to its citizens.

Corruption thus can and does create a further breeding ground for already existing threats to peace and security, such as poverty, ethnic and/or religious differences in Tanzania, Africa and elsewhere. No wonder that current ongoing discussions across Africa often focus on, as Le Sage puts it,

> . . . threats such as terrorism, drug trafficking, maritime threats such as piracy in the Indian Ocean and oil bunkering in the Gulf of Guinea, militia factions and armed gangs, organized criminal activities, particularly kidnapping, human smuggling and trafficking in persons, weapon smuggling, and environmental and financial crimes.[211]

At the center of this dire situation are high levels of corruption, "fueling weak law enforcement, bad governance, and poverty."[212] Le Sage is also quite clear in proposing that in order to solve the latter problems, corruption must receive a considerable public and policy level attention.

---

208. Cf. United Nations, *Corruption: Threats and Trends*.

209. Ibid.

210. In the United Kingdom, new anti-corruption and anti-bribery measures in the Crime and Security Act of 2001 were put in place as part of the anti-terrorism efforts. In the United States the same connection has been made between terrorism and corruption. See the 1998, 2002 and 2006 versions of the *National Security Strategy of the United States*; see also *Terrorism, Corruption and War*, posted by the US State Department (online at: usinfo.state.gov/products/pubs/iraq/war.htm); D. Kaufmann's, "Corruption, Governance and Security: Challenges for the Rich Countries and the World," in the *Global Competitiveness Report* of 2004/2005; William Reno's "Politics of Insurgency in Collapsing States"; and Kimberley Thachuk's "Corruption and International Security."

211. Le Sage, "Africa's Irregular Security Threats," 1.

212. Ibid.

2.4.2.3 Corruption as Threat to Basic Human Rights

Closely related to the consequences of corruption referred to thus far is its effects in human rights. Researchers in various disciplines, for example, in human development studies,[213] in political science[214] and in studies on poverty[215] have highlighted the connection between corruption and the violation of human rights. They are in agreement that although the relationship between human rights and corruption is a complex one, in practice, most acts of corruption are instances of or closely linked to violations of human rights.

Like the UN that affirms that "where corruption is widespread, states cannot comply with their human rights obligations,"[216] the International Council on Human Rights Policy expressly states that,

> [w]hile corruption violates the rights of all those affected by it, it has a disproportionate impact on people that belong to groups that are exposed to particular risks (such as minorities, indigenous peoples, migrant workers, disabled people, those with HIV/AIDS, refugees, prisoners and those who are poor). It also disproportionately affects women and children.[217]

While some certain forms of corruption clearly constitute human rights violations, the link is more difficult to see in others. Practically speaking, however, "[c]orruption may be linked directly to a violation when a corrupt act is deliberately used as a means to violate a right." An example would be when a bribe is offered to a judge and it directly affects the impartiality of that judge and hence violates the right to a fair trial. One can also note the link between corruption and human rights with regard to education and health in the following examples: ". . . when an individual must bribe a doctor to obtain medical treatment at a public hospital, or bribe a teacher at a public school to obtain a place for her child at school, corruption infringes

---

213. cf., Phillip and Robinson, *Human Rights and Development*.
214. cf. Michael, *Syndromes of Corruption*.
215. cf. Alsop, *Power, Rights and Poverty*.
216. International Council on Human Rights Policy, "Corruption and Human Rights," 23.
217. Ibid., 7.

the rights to health and education . . ."²¹⁸ A study by Ottar Mæstad and Aziza Mwisongo have shown that this is also the case in Tanzania.²¹⁹

Gruenberg offers a clear view of the impact of corruption on human rights from the perspective of access to resources:

> Corruption impacts human rights by distorting three basic rules that regulate access to resources and their distribution: (1) Rule of allocation: defines criteria for distributing public resources; (2) Rule of inclusion: defines participates, how, when and in what processes; and (3) Rule of accountability: which determines the responsibilities of each of the actors involved and the mechanisms for enforcing victims' rights.²²⁰

Gruenberg's argument is made in the context of the right to education, in the sense that, although the human right to education is supposed to be accessible to all – and it may seem to be respected when one looks at promising numbers of school enrollment, also in Tanzania – the misallocation of educational resources benefit some and exclude others in many countries.

2.4.2.4 Corruption as Threat to Human Development

According to Mauro, although corruption has always existed, recognition of the negative impact of corruption on society has broadened greatly in recent years.²²¹ He refers to the growing body of research that shows that corruption represents not just the degradation of integrity and morals, but that it is also a severe hindrance to the process of economic development. It is not the intention of this section of the study to offer a detailed analysis of the concept of human development, especially given the fact that literature and theories on human development are broad and offer an array of explanations, meanings and possibilities for it. Still, in the context of this study, the link between corruption and under- or non-development needs to be noted especially in light of the following two facts.

First is the fact that, since the 1980s, the United Nations has adopted a human development approach as a key measure that allows governments,

---

218. Ibid., 27.
219. Mæstad and Mwisongo, *Informal Payments*.
220. Gruenberg, "Corruption and Human Rights," 34.
221. Mauro, "Persistence of Corruption," 12.

the private sector and civil societies to explore and understand interlinking factors, that fuel advantages and disadvantages in societies, and create or deny opportunities for human well-being. Corruption is seen as one of the interlinking factors that may constrain human development. Corruption occurs in the way human beings do things, such as in the way they conduct business. This, together with the use or misuse of power in decision making, especially regarding a country's wealth, may create conditions in institutions that may be conducive to either development or under- (non-)development.

Second is the fact that a number of studies have shown that there is an undeniable link between corruption and low levels of human development. Akhter, for example, has shown this link from the perspective of the increased economic freedom and growing globalization.[222] In an unpublished lecture, Tran uses the concept of "human capability," developed by philosophers Amartya Sen and Martha Nussbaum, to emphasize the ability and choice dimension of human development, and points toward this link between corruption and underdevelopment when he says that "corruption, and underdevelopment mutually reinforces one another, creating a vicious cycle that traps many developing nations."[223]

According to the UN *Human Development Report of 2013*, an independent publication commissioned by the UNDP, human development is defined as "the process of enlarging people's freedoms and opportunities and improving their well-being." In earlier reports the UNDP also emphasized the importance of the freedom to choose in development: "expanding the choices people have to lead lives that they value"[224] or the freedom people have "to decide who to be, what to do, and how to live."[225] Clearly corruption limits these choices and in this way also restrains human development efforts.

Scholars of human development theories agree that the basic elements of human development are: longevity (which is measured by the life expectancy at birth); educational attainment (which includes levels of adult literacy, enrollment ratio in primary, secondary, and tertiary education, and

---

222. Akhter, "Is Globalization What It's Cracked Up to Be?"
223. Tran, "Corruption and Human Development."
224. UNDP, *Human Development Report 2001*, 9.
225. UNDP, *Human Development Report 2013*.

the standard of living which encompasses access to resources); and levels of unemployment and poverty.[226]

For the purpose of this study, it is important to note that there are a number of reasons why human development can be affected by corruption as it impacts on each of three aspects of human development (longevity, education and decent standards of living). Rose-Ackerman, for example, states that

> [c]orruption . . . tends to distort the allocation of economic benefits, favoring the haves over the have-nots leading to a less equitable income distribution. A share of the country's wealth is distributed to insiders and corrupt bidders, contributing to inequalities in wealth.[227]

Gupta, Davoodi and Tiongson also argue that corruption affects health care and education services in two ways as (1) corruption may increase the cost of these services, and (2) corruption may lower the quality of these services.[228] Mauro, too, shows how corruption influences government spending on health and education resources.[229] He expressly states that "corruption reduces government expenditure on education and health" and adds that "public officials do not want to spend more on education and health because those spending programs offer less opportunity for rent seeking."[230]

2.5 Conclusion: Corruption and Corruption as Injustice in Contemporary Tanzania

This chapter looked at the concept of corruption, especially also in the context of the Republic of Tanzania (from a historical as well as a contemporary perspective). It showed that corruption is a global challenge, as is reflected not only in statistics, but also in the variety of disciplinary discourses on the phenomenon, its manifestations, and the suggestions as to the causes and consequences of corruption. The link between injustice and corruption, and

---

226. UNDP, *Human Development Report 2001*, 240.
227. Rose-Ackerman, "Political Economy of Corruption," 33.
228. Gupta, Davoodi and Tiongson, *Corruption and the Provision*, 116.
229. Mauro, "Corruption and Composition," 265.
230. Ibid.

corruption as a form of injustice, was particularly important in the above reflections.

According to conventional wisdom, corruption undermines the rule of law, demoralizes society and inhibits economic growth. Basically, corruption makes society economically vulnerable and unfair. It also hurts those who are economically powerless, denies the poor their share of societies' wealth, and thus increases existing poverty. In fact, one of the sad and major manifestations of corruption is that it even leads to relief efforts being diverted from the poor to benefit the rich! Corruption also makes society unsafe due to a lack of, and increased competition for, food, medical supplies, and other basic sources of survival. Thus, besides being a crime in most societies, corruption fuels other forms of crime. As a result, in the extreme, it may not be going too far to say that corruption kills.

UNDP sums up the seriousness of corruption by expressly touching on the consequences of corruption for justice, human rights and the dignity of members of societies:

> Corruption causes social disintegration and distorts economic systems; it implies discrimination, injustice and disrespect for human dignity; it endangers the stability of democratic institutions, discriminates in the delivery of government services and thus violates the rights of the people, and the poor in particular. Where corruption reigns, basic human rights and liberties come under threat and social and economic contracts become unpredictable. Corruption remains thus one of the main obstacles to achieving sustainable pro-poor development in support of the MDGs [Millennium Development Goals]. A comprehensive attack on corruption remains a challenge for many countries, developing and developed alike.[231]

Likewise, according to the World Bank,

> ... corruption stymies investment and growth and misdirects public resources; corruption systematically redistributes wealth in favor of those with the connections and money to work the

---

231. United Nations Development Programme, *Institutional Arrangement to Combat Corruption*, 2.

> system; corruption acts as a regressive tax, felt most harshly by small businesses, micro-enterprise, and the poor; corruption erodes confidence in the institutions of state and is associated with organized crime; for lawful taxpayers, corruption erodes the quality of the public services upon which citizens rely and for which they pay taxes.[232]

Furthermore, according to Rose-Ackerman, widespread corruption "is likely both to retard development and to distribute the benefits of development unequal" and as such "pervasive corruption undermines . . . fairness" and "favors those with no scruples and those with connections over those who are the most productively efficient."[233] The theological interconnectedness between corruption, justice, and injustice will be pursued at a later stage, but for now should be clear that corruption and justice do not only concern diplomacy and state solutions. They is also about social goals, values and norms as well as intergroup relations.

> [V]alues and norms of the people are distorted as a result of corruption they eventually undermine moral standards and promote charlatans to the detriment of honest endeavors. This is because corruption is by nature a falsehood. It denies justice.[234]

While justice is concerned with formulating principles, creating structures, shaping institutions and providing guidelines so that people may receive their due, corruption breeds selfishness and individualism.[235] Selfishness and individualism in turn increase corruption (see again the causes of corruption listed by Joinnet and Mkunde in 2.4.1 above). Individualism in itself is not bad. However, when it takes the form of selfish individualism it becomes problematic because it ignores the welfare of others and the equality of all. Furthermore, corruption not only threatens equality, but peoples' freedom and their choices as well. Again, "freedom is an essential ingredient of justice" – referring here to freedom to or the right to act, to decide and

---

232. World Bank and the United States Agency for International Development, "Corruption in Slovakia: Results of Diagnostic Surveys," 1.

233. Rose-Ackerman, "Corruption: Greed, Culture and the State," 45.

234. Government of Tanzania, NACSAP II, 94.

235. Lorenzen, "Justice Anchored in Truth," 228.

to speak in accordance to the law.²³⁶ The effect of corruption also has severe consequences for the freedom of not only individuals but also of institutions, such as the freedom of expression of the media.

In summary, the core argument and conclusion drawn from this chapter may be expressed as follows:

- The chapter established that, although corruption existed from before the time of independence in Tanzania, "petty corruption spread to all sectors of government activity [especially] in the 1970s" and "grand corruption appeared in the mid-1980s, coinciding with liberalization of the economy."²³⁷
- The fact of the existence of corruption in Tanzania is witnessed to by the over fifty years' worth of efforts by government to establish extensive guidelines and institutions of anti-corruption laws and agencies.
- Corruption is an issue that needs to be adequately addressed because it has immense effects on Tanzanian society. For example, this chapter shows that it is acknowledged by Tanzanians (including political leaders and public servants) that there is a serious decline in standards of public service morality, which is evidenced by contemporary levels of corruption – reference was made, among others, to Transparency International's CPI of Tanzania over more than ten years.
- It was indicated that local contextual factors as well as the social-political setting within the country have also been crucial in the escalation of the incidences of corruption. For example, it emerged that when Tanzania followed *ujamaa* (the socialist path of economic development) for about twenty years and when the government was under single-party rule up until 1992, accountability was inadequate across the public sector.
- Over the last two decades, Tanzania has undergone economic and political transformations. A variety of studies agree that economic liberalization has produced a more open, transparent,

---

236. Ibid.
237. URT, *Tanzania's Presidential Commission*, Warioba Report, 1996.

and competitive economy. However, these transformations have been accompanied by the spread of grand corruption and there is evidence that this has also opened the door for new forms of politically linked corruption.

- As far as the general moral state of the nation, this chapter indicated that the ethics of public life during the *ujamaa* years has deteriorated and "there is a need to address moral decay" (see Mkude above) in broader society as well as at the level of public service.
- On examining the problem of corruption and/as injustice within secular discourse, this chapter pointed out that corruption and injustice are fundamental problems in Tanzania and that corruption has affected peoples' experiences of justice and just treatment. It was also acknowledged that corruption and justice are prone to competing interpretations that complicate any easy definition of these phenomena and "corruption" as such covers fraud (theft through misrepresentation), embezzlement (misappropriation of corporate or public funds), bribery (payments made in order to gain an advantage or to avoid a disadvantage) and theft (and hence an offence against human relationships).
- As the chapter reviewed some of the definitions of and perspectives on corruption, it also identified as a working definition of corruption for the purposes of this study the generally accepted definition of the United Nation and of Transparency International, namely that corruption is *a misuse of public power, office or authority for private gain.*
- Finally, the chapter also indicated that measures to prevent corruption have been adopted by the government of Tanzania, but the increase of the problem is evidence that these measures have not been sufficient or effective. Still there is a general consensus that anti-corruption campaigns are necessary and must be sustained. As such, punishment, reform strategies,

international cooperation and education are key areas of war against corruption.[238]

Given the sad state of affairs with regard to corruption in Tanzania, the study now turns to theology, first of all asking in chapter 3 whether and why in a theological-ethical and biblical sense, corruption is wrong. Chapter 4 will then ask whether and how the church as such should or may respond to and therefore contribute to addressing this problem.

---

238. cf. Hope and Chikulo, *Corruption and Development in Africa*; Mukandala, "State Enterprise Control"; Rasheed, "Promoting Ethics and Accountability"; World Bank, *Reform of Public Sector Management*.

CHAPTER 3

Why Corruption?

Biblical and Theological-Ethical Considerations of the Nature of Corruption and In/Justice and Corruption as Justice

> But let justice roll on like a river, righteousness like a never-failing stream.
>
> Amos 5:24

> At the core of the incidence of poverty is the issue of equity, and at the core of the issues of equity is the issue of corruption.
>
> James D. Wolfensohn[1]
> Former President of the World Bank

3.1 Introduction

In light of the seriousness of the problem of corruption and the severity of the consequences of corruption as injustice in Tanzania in chapter 2 given from a non-theological perspective, chapter 3 will focus on the question why corruption is not only a socio-political and economic issue, but also a theological one. For this reason, this chapter will ask, in simple terms: Why

---

1. James D. Wolfensohn, former president, World Bank, Address to the Ninth International Anti-Corruption Conference in Durban, South Africa, October 1999 as quoted in The World Bank, 2000. *Helping Countries Combat Corruption: Progress at the World Bank Since 1997*, Washington, DC: World Bank, 6.

is corruption "biblically and theologically"[2] wrong? Is there a dynamic link in *theological* terms between corruption and injustice, and if so, what is it? Chapter 4 will ask if and why the church as such should engage the fight against corruption (chapter 5 will apply this specifically to the Anglican Church of Tanzania) and how it may or should do so. This chapter then prepares the way for that discussion in that it seeks to identify theological-ethical guidelines and principles which may assist in answering the questions that will be raised in chapters 4 and 5.

To this end, this chapter is divided into the following sections: The first will focus on *biblical perspectives* on and forms of corruption. From this the focus will shift to the views on the *character of God* as found in Scripture and tradition. Particularly important here will be the implications of these perspectives from the Christian doctrine on God for corruption as, in terms of the title of this study, "mocking at *justice.*" The connection between the character of God in Scripture and justice will be thus be explored in light of biblical concepts and understandings of in/justice and corruption.[3]

The chapter will then indicate how justice speaks also to the issue of sin and the fallen state of humankind. In other words, as the character of God was brought into conversation with the issue of in/justice and the problem corruption, the discussion then turns to the nature of *humankind.* This will be investigated also within the guideline of understanding God's plan for humanity as attested to in Scripture. Key to this *theological-anthropological*

---

2. The phrase "biblical-theological" will be used often in this study, with no intention to equate "biblical" with "theological" but rather, as it will be discussed in this chapter and also its application in chapter 5, to emphasize the fact of the intimate relationship between theological refelction and the responsible use of the Bible; that theology cannot be divorced from the Bible. The priority of the biblical text remains paramount for understanding the theological teaching on corruption and in/justice, for identifying possible theological-ethical principles as well as providing a compass for the biblical and theological nature of the study. However, for the purposes of economy of space and in order to remain focused, the biblical approach in this study is not intended to be treated in an in-depth manner to address biblical-hermeneutical issues on corruption and in/justice. In our view, this could be the subject of an entire monograph by itself. Thus, while not everyone may agree with all conclusions, the use and analysis of the biblical texts on corruption and in/justice were chosen to highlight the ongoing validity of the need for the church to address these problems.

3. As it was indicated in chapter 1 footnote 3, the phrase "mocking at justice" is taken from Proverbs 19:28 and refers to "a dynamic theological link between corruption and injustice." As was also seen earlier, although this text speaks of "a corrupt witness" that mocks at justice, corruption is used here in general and not only as pertaining to perjury (for this and the sense of corruption "defying" or "insulting" justice, see 2.4.6.1).

analysis is a careful consideration of the biblical definition and meaning of humanity, looking at what it means to be human, as well as the importance and meaning of the link between God and humanity in terms of human dignity.

Finally, this chapter discusses what may be called *biblical visions for society*. Here issues of relationality, living together and caring for others – as it also finds expression in economic and political life – will be discussed.

3.2 Point of Departure: The Unique Nature of Biblical-Ethical Principles on Corruption and In/Justice

In chapter 2 it was indicated that issues of corruption and in/justice in Tanzania and Africa, if not worldwide, have been predominantly addressed in circles and by disciplines outside of theology and Christian ethics. Among the disciplines that play an important role in shaping the current discourse on corruption and injustice are political science, sociology, law, economics, and business studies.

An effort to identify potentially unique contributions to the discourse on corruption based on biblical-theological-ethical principles finds its origin in the fact that the latter principles concern matters of faith. In an African context, as elsewhere, the task of theology and Christian ethics in particular is to provide guidance and inspiration to the faith community to address real situations that a particular society is facing.[4] On the need for (active) faith, South African theologian Klaus Nürnberger writes:

> Realism [also with regard to corruption] is indispensable to dispel wrong expectations, but it cannot have the last word. It is precisely the role of faith to prevent realism from turning into fatalism. The human being cannot live without a hope that transcends current limitations. Hopelessness leads to paralysis. But faith is not a kind of make-believe utopianism. Faith is protest against apparent inevitabilities. It is faith which detects

---

4. Gustafson, *Theology and Ethics*, 83–100.

that fatalism is not realistic; fatalism buries sensitivities for possibilities of the future under the dead weight of despair.[5]

If theology fails to play its part, faith as a resource becomes inactive in directing and inspiring transformational visions and strategies.[6] To strengthen this argument, we find in the work of scholars in Africa the conviction that the religious context, that is, beliefs or faith, culture and customs, must be integrated in any attempt to deal with the challenges facing the continent.[7] Faith and faith communities must, therefore, also be part of the discussion and the solution to corruption. As such, phrases like "the role of religion" or sometimes the role of "faith-based organizations" (FBOs) seem to gain prominence in the discourse on corruption.

"The role of religion" is sometimes linked to organizations that are established and that work within church contexts and as such they demonstrate a clear commitment to local communities' need to stand up against social injustice, poverty, economic inequality, etc. These organizations tend to develope vital relationships with communities that are built on trust, compassion, and dedication. However, it is not always easy to articulate what exactly the theological-ethical dimensions of their dealing with corruption are. The terms "trust" and "compassion" do have theological-ethical undertones, but they do not necessarily throw light on exactly what the theological-ethical meaning and implications of corruption and injustice are and how this meaning could help the faith communities to address these challenges.

From this perspective, the concern in this section is to show that theology as a unique discipline can and should offer unique and constructive insights to understanding and addressing corruption. But where and how may one begin this theological-ethical enquiry? One way is by giving an overview of forms of corruption identified in the Bible and then by looking at corruption and injustice from the perspective of the Christian doctrine of the God of the Bible and the nature of humankind according to the Bible.

---

5. Nürnberger, *Prosperity, Poverty & Pollution*, 159.

6. cf. Ibid., 156–163.

7. cf. De Gruchy, "Of Agency, Assets and Appreciation," 34–36; Maluleke, "Rediscovery," 31; Haddad, "Theologizing Development," 16.

3.3 Forms of Corruption and Injustice in the Bible: A Short Overview

In the Bible, the most common forms of corruption were bribery and extortion.[8] Today, while bribery is understood as referring to "anything given to a person to induce him to do something illegal or wrong, or against his wishes,"[9] extortion is defined as "[t]he act or crime of getting another's money or property through force, under cover of office, fraud, forgery, intimidation, threat, blackmail, oppression or show of right."[10] In the Bible, extortion is identified as being sinful (Lev 6:2–4; Isa 30:12–13) as is bribery (Ezek 22:12; Amos 5:12). Bribery and extortion are also at several places closely associated with one another (e.g. Isa 33:15; Ezek 22:12; Amos 5:11–12).[11]

God expressly condemns bribery because it "distorts justice" (Deut 16:19). Gamble elaborates on this by stating that, "[t]here is a constant stress in the Old Testament on the dangers of bribery and its effect in destroying proper and impartial justice."[12] Like bribery, extortion is also closely connected with the denial of justice (cf. e.g. Eccl 5:8–10; Isa 59:13–14; Ezek 22:29; Mal 3:5).

The New Testament also offers "a variety of material bearing on bribes, judges, and the responsible exercise of power."[13] This is evidenced in different well-known New Testament narratives on, for example, the payment of thirty pieces of silver to Judas to betray Jesus (Matt 26:14–16; Mark 14:10;

---

8. cf. Hartley, 1992 and Gamble, "Justice."
9. Hanke, "Bribery," 653.
10. Peterson, "Extortion," 52.
11. From the New American Bible – Isaiah 33:15: "He who walks righteously and speaks what is right, who rejects gain from extortion and keeps his hand from accepting bribes, who stops his ears against plots of murder and shuts his eyes against contemplating evil"; Ezek 22:12: "In you men accept bribes to shed blood; you take usury and excessive interest and make unjust gain from your neighbors by extortion. And you have forgotten me, declares the Sovereign LORD"; and Amos 5:11–12: "You trample on the poor and force him to give you grain. Therefore, though you have built stone mansions, you will not live in them; though you have planted lush vineyards, you will not drink their wine. For I know how many are your offences and how great your sins. You oppress the righteous and take bribes and you deprive the poor of justice in the courts." See also the Hebrew equivalents: bribe – שוחד; extortion – סחיטה; usury – נֶשֶׁךְ; and unjust gain – לֹא צוֹדֵק רווח.
12. Gamble, "Justice," 217.
13. Noonan, *Bribes*, 66.

Luke 22:3–5), the payment of bribes to soldiers who were guarding Jesus's tomb (Matt 28:11–15) and the story of Peter and Simon the Sorcerer (Acts 8:18–23), which all concern bribery or attempted bribery.

Furthermore, the sinful nature of corruption is made clear by its consequences. The Bible, for example, clearly shows that bribers and all who engage in extortion may viewed as being successful in what they gain, but that these are short-term gains with long-term consequences that include ending up in poverty (Prov 22:16), turning the one who was once wise into a fool (Eccl 7:7), getting no satisfaction from what is gained (Eccl 5:10), or even worse, being testified against by God (Mal 3:5).

As far as the link between corruption and justice is concerned, in the Old Testament and specifically in the prophets, the issue of corruption, violation of human dignity, and poverty are all linked to deliberately stealing from the poor. This is why God was concerned about the situation. Israel was condemned by the pre-exilic prophets for trampling the poor and was to be punished for denying them justice (Amos 2:7; 5:11; 8:4; Isa 3:15; Ezek 22:29). The poor were forced to hand over their grain (Amos 5:11) and the people of Israel were accused of cheating in a variety of ways, such as by skimping on the measure, inflating prices, cheating with dishonest scales, defrauding and by selling even the sweepings with the wheat (Amos 8:4; Hos 12:7). The leaders of the house of Jacob and Israel were accused of despising justice and distorting what is right (Mic 3:9); justice was corrupted (Amos 5:7; 6:12; Hab 1:4) and God's courts were trampled upon (Isa 1:12); bribes were taken and the poor, orphans, widow, aliens and the oppressed were denied justice in the courts (Amos 5:12; Mic 3:11; Isa 5:23; 10:2; Jer 5:28; Ezek 22:29). Perjury was committed (Jer 7:9) and false testimony deprived the innocent of justice and made them out to be guilty (Isa 29:21).[14] As in most prophetic literature, in the biblical Wisdom literature justice predominantly reflects the character of God and it is emphasized that human beings should be concerned with fellow human beings *because of God's concerned for them* (cf. Ps 146:7–9; Prov 31:8 and Job 29:12–17).

From a New Testament perspective, divine and true justice is revealed in Christ. Christ brought justice when he inaugurated the kingdom of God;

---

14. cf. Sweeney, *Twelve Prophets*; Lonsdale, "Compromised Critics."

the kingdom of God is "grounded in the life, death and resurrection Jesus Christ" and it is *a kingdom of justice*.[15] "The kingdom of God brings deliverance from servitude and inaugurates a new covenant."[16]

In the Old Testament, justice is further given distinctive content by being linked with the Hebrew concept of *hesed* – steadfast love or loving kindness – and with humbly walking with the God of justice. Justice here is something to be *done*, not simply or primarily a matter for reflection.

In the Beatitudes (in their version in Matt 5:1–12) one hears that those who hunger and thirst after justice (*dikaiosune*) are blessed, and will be satisfied. According to Forrester,

> [j]ustice here is something about which we should be passionate, something for which we should hunger and thirst. And those people who are passionate about justice are seldom those who live in "the culture of contentment," but rather the victims, the oppressed, the forgotten and the excluded – the poor and the poor in spirit as well, those who are persecuted for justice's sake, and those who take their stand alongside those who suffer from injustice.[17]

American ethicist Karin Lebacqz offers a fitting summary for the understanding of biblical justice.[18] She writes (and this makes for a fruitful comparison with non-biblical/theological theories of justice, such as that of Rawls):

> . . . [j]ustice is not "to each according to need." Nor is it "benefit the least advantaged." Nor is it "the greatest good for the greatest number." Because justice emerges out of protest against injustice, justice is not so much a state of being as a struggle and a constant process. It is the process of correcting what is unjust. It is the process of providing new beginnings, not an ideal state of distribution.

---

15. Broughton, "Restorative Justice," 299ff.
16. Marshall in Taylor, *Justice*, 29.
17. Forrester, *Beliefs, Values and Policies*, 225.
18. Lebacqz, *Justice in an Unjust World*, 152.

3.4 On the Character of God: A Methodological Route towards Theological-Ethical Principles

This study acknowledges the fact that the nature, concepts, attributes and, indeed, as John Calvin has aptly noted, "our knowledge of God,"[19] is a very old theological question. A methodologocal "instrument" was thereful designed to help identify attributes to be used. In so doing many examples and descriptions, both old and contemporary, regarding the attributes of God were consulted. A great variety of such attributes have been identified in the process. For example, while Erickson in his *God the Father Almighty: A Contemporary Exploration of the Divine Attributes* identifies about eleven attributes, Tozer in his *Knowledge of the Holy* identifies about nineteen. Given the context of this study, African understandings of God were also consulted, such as William Brown's *Concepts of God in Africa*. This process led to two important conclusions: one is the fact that these attributes identified by scholars often overlap. Second, given the sheer number of possible attributes, a choice had to be made as to those that are most directly applicable to this study. These are God as creator, God as sustainer, God's righteousness, and God's sovereignty.

This section thus begins by asking and suggesting answers to the question: Who is God, specifically in his relation to the world? This will then form part of the guidelines within which the issues of justice and corruption will be theologically explored.[20]

Second, it will again be shown that corruption is a form of injustice and, as such, it is in itself not only opposed to who God is, but also to God's plan for human society in Scripture, for example, as Grieb suggests with reference to 2 Corinthians 5:21:

> . . . [through] Paul's soteriological metaphors of "the righteousness of God" [2 Cor 5:21] through the death and resurrection of Jesus Christ we acquire a sense of the richness of his thought

---

19. cf. John Calvin in Torrance, "Knowledge of God," 76–98.

20. It should be noted that in this section the aim is not to write or critique the complete history of reflections on the nature or characteristics of God, or to attempt to address theological or philosophical challenges associated with it. Rather, what will be shown is that some of the attributes of God identified in theological discourse may contribute to the identification of theological principles useful in addressing corruption and injustice.

with respect to how human justice might become more like God's justice, how the church might "become the righteousness of God. . ."[21]

In a sense the theological logic behind the mission of what is known as the Micah Challenge (2013)[22] sums up this "method" followed here:

> . . . *all begins with the character of God*; the shape of the story of God and the world; the nature of our creation in God's image and our growing into the image of the Son which the Spirit shapes in us as we struggle for justice and the gospel; the shape of community formed by God's saving and transforming grace; the new future towards which we head and which God seeks to form in us and through us by the power of the Spirit; the instructions that shape our view of the world and our living in it. (emphasis added)

Over the centuries many theologians have reflected on the characteristics of God in an "enterprise of thought which seeks to express conceptually . . . both the being of God and the implications of that being for human existence on earth."[23] On the "method" of looking at the attributes or characteristics of God, Duby writes:

> Patristic, medieval, Reformation and Protestant orthodox writers have appropriated certain philosophical insights and

---

21. Grieb, "So That in Him," 78.

22. The Micah Challenge is an international coalition of Christian development agencies, organizations, churches and groups that mobilize Christians against global poverty. They have launched campaigns in about forty countries around the world. See www.micahchallenge.org.

23. Gunton, *Promise*, 7. See, for example, some works on the history and recent debates and interpretations of God's attributes in McCormack (*Engaging the Doctrine of God*, 8), who suggests that a "wide range of treatments of the being and attributes of God can be shown to be compatible with the Nicene Creed [and that] Westminster Confession of Faith serves as the sole subordinate standard for determining what constitutes right teaching in this area of doctrine"; Mbiti ("Ethical Nature of God"), who emphasizes the need for the church to rethink the ethical character of God as the best way to address challenges facing the continent; for a similar conviction see Erickson (*Christian Theology*, 312): "God's perfection is the standard for our moral character and the motivation for religious practice. The whole moral code follows from his holiness." And Wolfson referring to Aquinas who ". . . thought that the attributes were actually . . . identical with God himself" (cf. Wolfson, *Religious Philosophy*, 49–52).

concepts in their contemplation of God, the works of authors such as Athanasius, Augustine, Lombard, Aquinas, Calvin . . . have been driven by biblical teaching and have taken seriously the need that sometimes arises for these insights and concepts to be modified according to the content of Holy Scripture.[24]

Torrance reflects on the modern theological approach called Trinitarian theology and the importance of and the motivation behind this approach.[25] After a careful look at what for him "displays the attributes of God" – which includes a historical survey of some of the key issues, challenges and advances in the development of the method and Trinitarian theology – Torrance writes that Trinitarian theology helps us, "in our understanding of the basic concepts and relations of God's revealing and saving activity toward us and for us of which we learn in the Scriptures of the New Testament."

With regard to Christian ethics, David S. Cunningham also reminds us that virtues are the dispositions that are part of *the nature God* and, by the grace of God, humanity freely participate in these virtues (characteristics) of God.[26] George Zachariah even refers to the importance of looking at the attributes or characteristics of God in providing alternative perspectives on public witnessing.[27] His key argument centers on the fact that "the doctrinal constructions" and "theological reconstruction" of God happens in believers' reflections on their "epiphany experiences," most particularly in the struggles of the marginalized communities for survival and to protect their commons. For Brueggemann, the character of God is "revolutionary," for "God refuses to accept the disturbing of well-being."[28] On the idea of the revolutionary character of God, Schneiders refers to "God championing Israel's cause to overturn oppressive structures."[29] Sarojini Henry refers to Isaiah and other prophets' claims, saying that it shows that

> . . . God is not to be found in the cultic practices that is unconcerned with unjust structures; rather, God is to be found in

---

24. Duby, "Classical Christian Theism," 198.
25. Torrance, *Christian Doctrine*, 168.
26. Cunningham, *These Three Are One*, 123.
27. Zachariah, "Re-Imagining God," 43.
28. Brueggemann, *Theology of the Old Testament*, 741.
29. Schneiders, *Revelatory Text*, 49.

seeking justice and goodness by implementing them in society. A true worship and adoration would become possible only by achieving justice, peace and righteousness.[30]

This process of reflection on the nature and characteristics of God is an ongoing process as Tozer suggested more than fifty years ago.[31] It is also "[t]he heaviest obligation lying upon the Christian church today [namely] . . . to purify and elevate her concept of God until it is once more worthy of Him and of her."

What follows below is a discussion of a selection of traditional attributes/characteristics of God that has particular implications for our discussion on corruption and in/justice.

3.4.1 God the Creator vs. Corruption and Injustice

The Bible tells that in the beginning God created heaven and earth and saw that it was good. Of course, creation also included humankind, but humankind was "created in God's own image" (Gen 1:27). The Bible also declares that God is perfect (another of God's characteristics) and so were human beings, precisely because they were created in God's likeness; they were "upright" (in the words of Eccl 7:29). They had no knowledge of evil. We read also that humanity's thoughts were pure and their motives were holy (Gen 3:5). The relationship between God and humankind, too, was perfect, harmonious and joyful. That is, until humanity disobeyed God and fell from their original righteousness, thereby loosing communion with God, and were eventually cast out of paradise. It follows then that if, as we will see later, corruption as a form of injustice is evil, then it is irreconcilable with the character of God, who is infinitely good and perfect. According to Charles Hodge, "[i]t is no less a doctrine of Scripture than a fact of experience that mankind is a fallen race,"[32] and one of the central Anglican doctrinal documents, the Westminster Confession of Faith (6:2), summarizes the state of

---

30. Henry, "Fair and Just," 108.
31. Tozer, *Knowledge of the Holy*, 12.
32. Hodge, *Systematic Theology*, 95.

fallen human nature: humans "became dead in sin, and wholly defiled in all the faculties and parts of soul and body."³³ According to George E. Ladd,

> [t]he prophets constantly described the establishment of God's kingdom in terms of a redeemed world (Isa 11:6–9; 65:17–25); and the New Testament shares the same theology. Creation is never viewed as something evil that must be escaped. Man [sic] as body is a creature of God. Man is not sinful because he is a creature but because he has rebelled against God. In the final consummation, the whole man and the world of which he is a part will be delivered from the curse of evil.³⁴

Brueggemann argues from a justice perspective that justice begins with God's intention for all creation to be whole in the sense of finding fulfilment in itself and in God.³⁵ Wright also states that justice on earth flows from its creator: "justice on earth flows from justice in heaven."³⁶ Corruption and injustice is therefore neither part of God's character, nor is it part of God's original creation.

3.4.2 God as Righteous vs. Corruption and Injustice

Over centuries, scholars have debated the meanings of the concepts "righteousness" and "the righteousness of God" in different ways. However, for the purpose of this study Carson's basic understanding of these terms is helpful in that "righteousness" and "the righteousness of God . . . is concerned with the way lost men and women can be right with God."³⁷ And righteousness, too, is a central element of the character of God. According to Grieb:

> Righteousness . . . is one of the most important components of any theological understanding of Scripture, especially since the biblical writers understand human concepts of justice as they are critiqued and measured by "the righteousness of God." God is manifested as exalted in justice and holy in righteousness

---

33. With reference to Jer 17:9; Titus 1:15; etc.; cf. Boettner, *Reformed Doctrine*, 73, on the use of the word "death" in the Confession as "death in its widest sense."
34. Ladd, *Theology of the New Testament*, 567.
35. Brueggman, *Theology of the Old Testament*.
36. Wright, *Old Testament Ethics*, 253.
37. Carson, *Right with God*, 2.

(Isa 5:16), the "lover of justice" (Ps 99:4) who will judge the earth with righteousness and the peoples of the earth with equity (Ps 98:9) . . . God commands the people of God to seek righteousness . . . (Deut 16:20).[38]

In order to grasp the extent of the righteousness of God it helps to reflect on the different meanings of the words used for it.[39] The fundamental meaning of "righteousness" in its several forms is derived from the Hebrew words *sedeq, sedäqäh*.[40] This is the noun that is translated as *dikaiosune* in the Septuagint. It has the general meaning of "being in the right relation with." For example, the fundamental meaning of *dikaiosune theou*, "the righteousness of God," refers to God's covenant faithfulness to Israel.

There is also a second important meaning of *dikaiosynë theou* that is derived from the context of a court of law. Contemporary scholars tend to refer in this regard to "forensic" righteousness because the court exists to "put things right," and in common parlance people are shown to be "in the right." Grieb links this meaning of righteousness with "the social aspect of God's justice," which is central to this study.[41] According to Grieb,

> God as righteous judge acts in accordance with the law to vindicate the helpless (the orphan, widow, stranger, or poor person) against the powerful oppressor. If the plaintiff brings a false accusation, God takes the side of the helpless against the powerful evildoer.[42]

God's response to the helpless – including the victims of corruption and injustice – finds clear expression in Isaiah 5:7, in the fact that God expects justice *(mispät)*, but he sees bloodshed *(mispäh)*; God expects righteousness *(sedäqäh)*, but he hears the cry (of the victims) *(secäqäh)*.

---

38. Grieb, "So That in Him," 59.

39. This should be read in conjunction to other references to the righteousness of God in this study, for example, with regard to the theological-ethical link between God's kingdom, God's commandments and God's righteousness (4.4.1.3); God's establishing God's rule of righteousness (4.4.1.3); and, later in this chapter, that God's righteousness is intrinsically connected to the well-being of the society (3.6.3).

40. cf. Wright, *On Becoming the Righteousness*, 203.

41. Grieb, "So That in Him," 61.

42. Ibid.

According to this study, there is a clear link between injustice and corruption because, among others, God's righteousness speaks to human ethical standards, moral uprightness and justice. As such, Marshall for example, argues that "righteousness" carries the sense of personal ethical purity and religious pity, while "justice" relates to public judicial fairness and equality of rights.[43] One belongs to the private, moral, religious realm, the other to the public, political legal realm. This is also true, for example, in Isaiah 6:5, written in the context of speaking the Word of God during the decline of Israel in the shadow of the Assyrian threat; and, according to Bray, when "righteousness refers to God, the term speaks of his fairness in all relationships and at times is associated with his holiness."[44]

Furthermore, God's righteousness, moral excellence and justice are interrelated in that it calls to attention the *relational character of God*. Kuyper describes the nature of righteousness as exactly that, a relational component – often in a covenant context either with God, fellow humans, or the nation.[45] This point of the relationship character of God and his righteousness applies to the day-to-day life of God's people. The covenant of God, for example, as Anthony Oliver asserts,

> . . . required the kings, leaders, and judges to seek the interests of socially and economically weak persons who were in the right. However, unrighteous kings, judges, and business persons disregarded the covenant norm when they turned their backs on God. Therefore, the poor and devout usually trusted God for deliverance and vindication of their rights.[46]

In conclusion, therefore, it can be argued that God displays God's nature in what God does, but also in what he wishes to be done by those who have been entrusted with the power to govern. But righteousness is not only demanded from those in power. According to David Peterson, God establishes God's righteousness as the standard to which *all* human beings

---

43. Marshall, *Beyond Retribution*, 40.
44. Bray, *Doctrine of God*, 215–218.
45. Kuyper, "Righteousness and Salvation," 233-252.
46. Oliver, "Righteousness of God," 36.

should conform and God will judge them accordingly.[47] This also applies to corruption as an instance of injustice. And, as Andrew Hartropp reminds us, "humanity's unrighteousness, in the face of God's universal demand for righteousness, poses the grave question of how such unrighteousness is to be dealt with."[48] He goes on to remind one that "unrighteousness – the rebellious failure to conform to God's norms, God's standard – brings the wrathful judgment of God (Rom 1:18–32; 3:9–20; 23; Eph 2:3)."

3.4.3 God as Sovereign vs. Corruption and Injustice

God's sovereignty refers to God's control over the whole universe, and references to this are found throughout the Bible.[49] Dictionaries tell us that sovereign means chief or highest, supreme in power, superior in position, independent of and unlimited by anyone else. Strauss elaborates with regard to God as being truly and perfectly sovereign, that this means God is the highest and greatest being there is; God controls everything; God's will is absolute; and God does whatever God pleases.[50] When one hears such statements, one understands it reasonably well and agrees with it until God apparently allows something that one does not like. It is here, as in the case of righteousness, that there exist protracted dogmatic debates in the history of Christian theology, most particularly on how this sovereignty of God relates to the responsibility and free will of humanity. This study does not intend to go into detail regarding these debates, but the issue needs to be taken note of nevertheless.

So, on the one hand, Tozer argues that

> sovereignty requires that He [God] be absolutely free, which means simply that He [sic] must be free to do whatever He wills to do anywhere at any time to carry out His eternal purpose in

---

47. Peterson, *Witness to the World*, xv.
48. Hartropp, *What Is Economic Justice?* 101.
49. See, for example, Gen 50:20; Deut 4:39; 1 Sam 2:1–10; 2 Kgs 19:15; 1 Chr 29:11–12; 2 Chr 20:5–6; Job 9:12; 12:13–25; 23:13; 33:12–13; 41:11; 42:2; Pss 2, 135; Prov 16:1–5; Eccl 3:14; 9:1; Isa 14:24–27; 40:12–15; Jer 18:6; 32:17–23, 27; 50:44; Lam 5:19; Dan 2:21, 37–38; Matt 11:25–26; 20:1–16; John 19:11; Acts 2:22–24; 4:24–28; Rom 8:28; 11:36; 14:11; Eph 1:11; 4:6; Phil 2:9–11; Col 1:16–17; 1 Tim 6:15; Heb 1:3; Jas 4:12; Rev 1:5–6.
50. Strauss, *Joy of Knowing God*, 114–115.

> every single detail without interference. Were He less than free He must be less than sovereign.[51]

Like righteousness, God's sovereignty is deeply rooted in God's nature and is revealed by God's mighty acts of control of the world. However, according to Pink, it is wrong to think that "divine sovereignty rules out or excludes human responsibility"[52] and, according to Zachariah, "[in] spite of our sinfulness, we are able to participate in God's creative work of allowing God's creation to flourish . . . God believes in the possibility of transformation. So sin does not deprive us of our creativity."[53] What Pink refers to as "human responsibility"[54] or Ansell as "covenantal responsibility,"[55] means that divine sovereignty is understood as the basis for human responsibility. In other words,

> . . . humanity cannot be understood apart from the sovereignty of God, but is expressed in our grateful and willing subjection to divine law. . . . In the mystery of grace, our life is our own as we are given the space to respond and initiate in our own way. Yet, this space is not neutral as it calls us to recover, maintain, deepen, and expand our relationship with God and creation from freedom to freedom.[56]

The Bible and Christian theology time and again reminds us that one of the areas in which the sovereignty of God is manifested is in God's willingness to renew humankind ("I will take the heart of stone out of your flesh and give you a heart of flesh," Ezek 36:26). By itself, humanity is unable to do so. Following House, one may thus say that to the degree that the original creation reflected God's character as righteous and just, but has fallen into sin, God's redemptive order, righteousness, and sovereign grace seeks to repair the damage.[57] And, to the extent that corruption and injustice is

---

51. Tozer, *Knowledge of the Holy*, 115.
52. Pink, *Attributes of God*, 29.
53. Zachariah, "Re-Imagining God," 47.
54. Pink, *Attributes of God*, 29.
55. Ansell, *Annihilation of Hell*, 106.
56. Ibid., 106–107, with reference to Gal 5:1.
57. House, "Creation and Redemption," 17.

contrary to God's character, to God's original creation, so too it is subject to the sovereignty of God and God's "willingness to renew humankind" to "repair the damage."

In conclusion to this section on the aspects of the attributes of God as they relate to Trinitarian theology, an additional comment from recent scholarship, namely those of Torrance and Gunton, is important. Gunton is of the opinion that the traditional doctrines of the divine attributes seem to not have been reflected upon appropriately within studies on the Trinitarian revelation of God in the history of salvation.[58] In this he joins Torrance (in his understanding of attributes of God within the realm of Reformed theology within Western theology) in believing that Trinity, which lays emphasis on the concepts of the *person* of and the *communion* between the three persons of the Trinity, constitutes fair treatment of the meaning and implication for the attributes of God. If not, it may be regarded as a prolongation of the concept of rationalism with the result that the close relatedness of Trinitarian theology and the doctrine of God's attributes will be obscured.

3.4.4 God as Faithful Governor and Sustainer vs. Corruption and Injustice

Related to the fact that God did not only create the universe good and that God is its sovereign Lord, is the fact that that God in faithfulness governs and sustains the world. In this regard, VanGemeren asserts that

> . . . [s]ince the universe not only is created out of nothing, but is maintained in its creaturely being through God's constant interaction with it, who will not let it slip away from him [sic] into nothing but grounds its existence on his eternal faithfulness, the universe is given a stability beyond anything of which it is capable in its own contingent state.[59]

VanGemeren's view is important here as it opens the door to an explanation of the link between God's governance of the universe (including humankind, despite its fallen nature which leads, among other things, to corruption and injustice) and the governance of God in terms of "God's

---

58. Gunton, *Act and Being*, 6–18.
59. VanGemeren, *Progress of Redemption*, 61.

moral governance of humankind." In contemporary terminology, one may say that from a Christian perspective it is, among other things, God's governance that reflects who and what God is and that it also sets the rules regarding "good governance" on earth. In secular terms good governance is, according to the World Bank,

> ... epitomized by predictable, open, and enlightened policy-making (that is, transparent processes); a bureaucracy imbued with a professional ethos; an executive arm of government accountable for its actions; and a strong civil society participating in public affairs; and all behaving under the rule of law.[60]

Hermes and Lensink suggest good governance should be characterized by

> ... [an] increased public accountability and transparency; respect for and strengthening of the rule of law and anti-corruption measures; democratization, decentralization and local government reform; increased civil-society participation in development; and respect for human rights and the environment.[61]

Reflecting theologically on this concept of good governance, one of course has to ask how it may be reflected in biblical terms. For one, this order or type of governance reflects what is often called the rule of the "kingdom of God."[62] For example, God wanted Israel, God's holy nation, to reflect God's rule. According to Christopher Wright, what God wanted was a "nation that would be the pattern and model of redemption, as well as the vehicle by which the blessing of redemption would eventually embrace the rest of humanity"; it was meant to be a nation "socially decentralized and non-hierarchical"; a community "geared toward the social health and economic viability"; a nation whose people comprised of the "land owning households" and not a corrupt hierarchy characterized by injustice; it was a

---

60. World Bank, *Governance*, vii. Cf. former World Bank president Barber Conable, who sees good governance as "public service that is efficient, a judicial system that is reliable, and an administration that is accountable to its public" (World Bank, *Sub-Saharan Africa*, xii).

61. Hermes and Lensink, "Changing the Conditions," 4.

62. As such the statement referenced here should be read in conjunction with the detailed and recurring references to the central theological concept of the "kingdom of God" in and its implications for this study, see 3.3; 3.6.3; 4.3.1.2; 4.3.1.2 and 4.4.1.3.

nation meant to maintain a "comparative equality of families on the land" geared toward the protection of "the weakest, the poorest and the threatened" against the rich and the powerful.[63] Clearly such a society under such governance will have no place for corruption or in fact for any form of injustice.

In substantiating this argument, as well as in linking the Old and New Testaments to it, VanGemeren emphasizes that,

> [t]he biblical teaching of God's rule established in creation correlates with God's involvement in redemption. Creation anticipates a *telos*, or end. The God who freely, graciously, and powerfully rules creation has a goal: the new creation in his Son Jesus Christ. (Gal 6:15)[64]

Likewise, VanGemeren reminds that, "[t]he absolute power of the creator [in governance] is manifested in his continued working out in an orderly, contingent, and gracious way his plan for the world and particularly for his children."[65] This is what O'Donovan calls the "moral order" that springs from the "[t]rue knowledge . . . [that is] . . . knowledge 'in Christ.'"[66]

3.5 Preliminary Conclusion: God, In/Justice and Corruption from a Biblical-Theological Perspective

Thus far, in light of the discussion of some of the traditional "attributes of God," it is clear that they (the attributes/characteristics) are not only revealed in the acts of God and in God's design for the world, but also that corruption as defined in the previous chapter and sections above, can in no way be reconciled with the character of God. The irreconcilability of corruption with the character of God is furthermore clearly due to the fact that corruption constitutes injustice. In chapter 2 of this study – where Weithman reminded that, "justice is one of a handful of topics that has dominated philosophical ethics in recent decades" – it was shown why this corruption constitutes injustice in non-theological terms.[67] This chapter shows this from

---

63. Wright, *Old Testament Ethics*, 49, 55–56.
64. VanGemeren, *Progress of Redemption*, 62.
65. Ibid., 61.
66. O'Donovan, *Resurrection and Moral Order*, 85.
67. Weithman, "Nicholas Wolterstorff's," 179.

a biblical-theological perspective and how Christian Scripture, as Reed puts it, "challenges, directs, and gives substance to critical Christian engagement with [the justice] discourse,"[68] the biblical-theological guidelines toward engagement in this discourse can, therefore, be said to find its roots in God as the God of justice. Many narratives are found in the Bible that testify towards this fact, the exodus story (Exod 2–5), perhaps the most familiar in the Old Testament where the God of justice stood for Israel's liberation from oppression. According to well-known Old Testament scholar Walter Brueggemann, "[i]n the exodus event, God refuses to make peace with powers that destroy well-being";[69] Schneiders says that the story shows how "God championed Israel's cause to overturn oppressive structures"[70] and Wright stresses that this narrative shows how "justice on earth flows from justice in heaven."[71]

From the narratives on God's acts and character, one may also already identify some biblical norms and values, including, for example, compassion for the vulnerable, marginalized and oppressed (e.g. Exod 22:22), care for the poor (e.g. Lev 23:22), the promotion of justice (for example, fairness in trade – 19:36), fairness in not charging interest (25:36), fair distribution of land (25:8–54) and paying fair wages to laborers (Mal 3:5).[72] While the above sections focused on the traditional attributes of God in the strict sense of the Christian doctrine of God, the Trinitarian theology of the likes of Torrance, Gunton, and Cunningham shows that one should not forget that biblical narratives and teaching on God in Jesus Christ and God the Holy Spirit will also reveal the Christian understanding of justice. As such, in the New Testament, love and active responsibility toward others is at the center of Jesus's ministry as he reveals the heart of the Father (cf. Matt 22:37–40). Together with love, God intends women and men to enjoy a high degree of freedom, which includes freedom to know God and to pursue a life as they choose, within the limits of their responsibilities towards others. Other values include reconciliation and peace within communities – God intends all

---

68. Reed, *Ethics of Human Rights*, 4.
69. Brueggmann, *Theology of the Old Testament*, 48.
70. Schneiders, *Revelatory Text*, 49.
71. Wright, *Old Testament Ethics*, 253.
72. cf. Gordon, "Mission of Church."

people to live in peace with each other and reconciliation (between people) is also part of the heart of God's plan for humanity (Matt 5:9). In fact, the fruits of the Spirit (Gal 5:22–23) include love and peace and can and should also be understood in light of values of fairness, justice and compassion.

In the above sections, while the nature or attributes of God were in the foreground, passing references were already made to humanity, especially in its fallen state. In the following section this and related issues are discussed in detail as the issue of corruption and injustice are reflected on from biblical-theological perspectives on humanity or in Christian anthropological terms.

3.6 On the Nature of Humankind: Christian Anthropological Perspectives in the Context of Corruption and Injustice

Thus far the study has presented some fundamental theological-ethical reasons why corruption is wrong. It has been argued that principles and reasons for this should start with understanding the character of God as a God of justice, and corruption as a form of gross injustice. The discussion now moves to *theological anthropology* as the question of the injustice of corruption is looked at from the perspective of what humanity in theological terms is, or is supposed to be.

3.6.1 Sin, Corruption as Sin, and the Fallen State of Humankind

In order to understand the interplay between God's creation, corruption and the injustice the latter constitutes, it is suggested that one begins with the biblical teaching regarding the effect of the fall upon humanity. In this section, an exploration of the meaning of sin will be undertaken with reference to the thought of specific contemporary theologians. This is necessary because, for legitimate theologically informed engagement with the issue of corruption in society one should guard against simplistic positions that ignore exactly how theologically deep the problem lies.

The two primary theological conversation partners in this discussion (in fact in the whole of the theological-anthropological discussion in this chapter) are the views of Alvin Plantinga[73] and David Kelsey.[74] Before discussing their views, however, the use of concepts in this section needs to be clarified. It is important to note that the kind of corruption discussed here refers not only to corruption as an instance of sin, but to sinfulness as such. The former (the corrupt act) is one manifestation of the latter, that is, of corruption as the fall into sin. To link this with what was said in chapter 2 on the concept of corruption: in its day-to-day understanding, corruption refers to "dishonest or illegal behavior by officials or people in positions of power, especially when they accept money in exchange for doing things for someone."[75] It also means "dishonestly using a position or power to one's own advantage, especially for money"[76] or an "impairment of integrity, virtue of moral principle; inducement by means of improper considerations to commit violation of duty."[77]

From the above definitions, and picking up on related words and phrases in them (such as, dishonest, illegal behavior, impairment of integrity), one may already say that it is logical to argue that in theological terms these words show that corrupt acts are sinful or "products of the fall and rebellion of humankind against God" – the classic understanding of sin. In the

---

73. Coming from the Reformed tradition (see his "Self Profile" in Tomberlin and Van Inwagen, *An International Series*, 3), Alvin Plantinga is believed by "[m]any scholars, from a variety of disciplines, philosophical schools, and religious orientations" to be "one of the most influential philosophers of religion writing today" (Beilby, *Epistemology as Theology*, 29). Having "written over 130 articles and twelve books during the course of his career, dealing with many of the central theistic questions" some scholars such as James F. Sennett (*Modality, Probability, and Rationality*, 112) (cf. also Timothy McGrew, "Has Plantinga Refuted," 24 and Deane-Peter Baker, "Plantinga's Reformed Epistemology," 95) argue that, "[i]n order to understand the current climate for the philosophy of religion, one must look to Plantinga." In this study, Plantinga has been chosen as one of the key conversation partners as, according to Feinberg (*Many Faces of Evil*, 63), in Plantinga's work one also finds "of the strongest formulation[s] and development[s] . . . in answering the problem of evil."

74. The choice of David Kelsey as conversation partner is linked to his seminal work, *Eccentric Existence: A Theological Anthropology*, especially as it offers a particular view on what it means to be human and, thereby, also what the dignity of human beings is about. Through his theological inquiry on central issues relating to humanity in relation to God and to creation, Kelsey's work fits well with the emphasis of the study on how to address the issue of corruption especially as it relates to discourse on justice, also in the light of the nature and the destiny of humanity, or in Kelsey's terminology, as it relates to "human flourishing."

75. Online Macmillan Dictionary, http://www.macmillandictionary.com.

76. Procter, *Cambridge International Dictionary*, 308.

77. Rotberg, *Corruption, Global Security*, 195.

creation story, Adam and Eve's transgression of the commands of God had the implication that it damaged (corrupted), among other things, the well-being of humanity. As such it fits into the bigger picture of the consequences of sin. As Plantinga puts it,

> . . . corruption both explodes and implodes creation, pushing it back towards the "formless void" from which it came . . . [when] . . . humans contradict their created status and so exercise their created freedom in rebellion against God.[78]

For Plantinga, this corruption (fallenness) is all about what he calls the "vandalism of shalom" – reflecting back on the consequences of corruption as a sinful act in chapter 2, such acts, too, as was said, demoralize society, hinder economic development, and are often found at the root of violence in society. The rich meaning of Plantinga's powerful phrase the "vandalism of shalom" becomes clear when he refers to the Hebrews prophets' understanding of shalom as

> . . . the webbing together of God, humans, and all creation in justice, fulfilment, and delight . . . In English we call it peace, but it means far more than just peace of mind or ceasefire between enemies. In the Bible *shalom* means universal flourishing,[79] wholeness, and delight – a rich state of affairs in which natural needs are satisfied and natural gifts are fruitfully employed . . . *Shalom*, in other words, is the way things are supposed to be.

Another well-known contemporary theologian, Nicholas Wolterstorff, also speaks in terms of corruption and the vandalization of shalom:

> . . . shalom which corruption vandalizes is not peace as we normally call it, it means far more than mere peace of mind or a ceasefire between enemies. In the Bible, shalom means universal flourishing, wholeness, and delight – a rich state of affairs in which natural needs are satisfied and natural gifts fruitfully employed, a state of affairs that inspires joyful wonder as its

---

78. Plantinga, *Not the Way It's Supposed to Be*, 30.

79. Note the word "flourishing" used here within the context of shalom – this concept is central in the theological anthropology of David Kelsey and others below.

creator and saviour opens doors and welcomes the creatures in whom he delights.[80]

With reference to the thought of Augustine[81] and both Luther and Calvin, Soulen and Woodhead write, "human nature is so utterly corrupted that it can do nothing on its own but contribute to its own downfall."[82] Of course, Thomas Aquinas, from a Roman Catholic perspective "offers a more positive view of human nature that is not wholly corrupted and may be perfected by grace."[83] Of course, as Plantinga also states, by God's grace all is not lost and even in

> . . . classic Protestant confessional literature, corruption — an unhappy cluster of spiritual pervasion, pollution, and disintegration — represents one of the two components of original sin (the other being guilt) . . . corruption and guilt present the problems that the gifts of sanctification and justification graciously address.[84]

In the words of prominent Dutch theologian of the previous century Henrikus Berkhof:

> When we speak of man's [sic] corruption as total inability, we mean two things: (1) that the unrenewed sinner cannot do any act, however insignificant, which fundamentally meets with God's approval and answers to the demands of God's holy law; and (2) that he cannot change his fundamental preference for sin and self to love for God, nor even make an approach to such a change. In a word, he is unable to do any spiritual good.[85]

And according to the Westminster Confession (9:3):

> Man [sic], by his fall into a state of sin, hath wholly lost all ability of will to any spiritual good accompanying salvation; so

---

80. Wolterstorff, *Until Justice and Peace Embrace*, 69–72. Note that with Wolterstorff one also finds a defence to "flourishing."
81. E.g. in Augustine, *City of God*, 14.10–11, 26.
82. Soulen and Woodhead, *God and Human Dignity*, 237.
83. Plantinga, *Not the Way It's Supposed to Be*, 237.
84. Ibid., 29.
85. Berkhof, *Systematic Theology*, 247.

as a natural man, being altogether averse from that good, and dead in sin, is not able, by his own strength, to convert himself, or to prepare himself thereunto.

In his book, *Eccentric Existence: A Theological Anthropology,* Yale Divinity School theologian David Kelsey offers some illuminating insights for the discussion on sin and the fallen state of humankind. Kelsey is helpful because he looks at how humans respond both in sin and faith to God's ways of relating to them. As Kelsey proposes to interpret what he calls his "theological anthropology" through the triune God's relating to humankind, he addresses three questions, namely: "What are we?" "How ought we be?" and "Who am I and who are we?"[86] In answering these questions, Kelsey describes the overall theme of his project is that the reality and value of human beings, their basic personal identities, and how they ought to be oriented toward their ultimate and proximate contexts, are all "eccentric," that is, as opposed to "intrinsically"-grounded, it is grounded outside themselves in the concrete ways in which the triune God relates to all that is not God, including humankind.[87] As such, Kelsey's discussion of the above three questions serves not only as a good basis for a theological understanding the nature of human beings – where he views the doctrine of creation as core to theological anthropology – but also could prove constructive for a theological-ethical perspective on corruption and in/justice.

Kelsey's approach to humanity flows from the effects of "sin, sins and evil"[88] on human beings. For him, sin has caused human failure and distortion, leaving humankind in bondage. In other words, in order to understand the state humankind finds itself in, one has to consider a theological anthropology which, as Kelsey puts it, is "systematically anthropocentric in that it is exhaustively concerned with human failure, an exclusively intrahuman defect or distortion [corruption/sin] that is in need of correction."[89] Using a biblical concept of mystery – such as the "positive" mysteries of creation

---

86. Kelsey, *Eccentric Existence,* 1–2.

87. Ibid., 501.

88. Kelsey uses these words (sin, sins and evil) together because he believes that "it is part of the logic of Christian beliefs that Christocentric accounts of how God goes about dealing with human sin, both singular and plural, entails a correlative account of sin that has a distinctive profile" (ibid., 1037).

89. Ibid., 118.

and the purpose of God, revelation of divine truth (e.g. with reference to Col 1:26) – Kelsey suggests that "[s]in [corruption] and the evil that it causes are negative mysteries."[90] He argues that, "[w]hen our practices are not formed by such a vision of our fellow creatures, the circumstances within which we act, and ourselves as agents, we risk doing violence to fellow creatures' integrity."[91] Likewise, if sin, distortion and bondage are removed, then these practices would be replaced by good practices, or in Kelsey's language, by "practicing delight," which means "an engagement with fellow creatures as they are given and self-given here and now."[92]

Furthermore, for Kelsey, "[s]in is the 'living death' of distorted personal identities" and "[t]o be in sin is to be in bondage."[93] It follows, therefore, that part of Kelsey's understanding of the fallen nature of human beings is his analysis of the damage that sin has caused to humanity. He prefers to look at this using, as previously mentioned, the concepts of "distortion" or "bondage" and identifies modes of distortions, as "distinctively Christian, theocentric concepts of sin [which] are secondary to and dependent on distinctively Christian concepts of the triune God relating [in order] to reconcile."[94] These modes, Kelsey argues, "are defined by acknowledgement of something like structural reconciliation, at least in the future, but without acknowledgement of any call to practice forgiveness now."[95] Likewise, for Kelsey, the same modes, "are defined by reference to the value of what they do," that is, the fulfillment of "moral duties."[96] Again, as indicated earlier, the kind of corruption discussed here refers to sinfulness as opposed to corruption as discussed in this study. Although the two cannot be equated, the latter is one manifestation of the former, that is to say, of the fall into sin.

Decades ago, American ethicist Reinhold Niebuhr, in his book *The Nature and Destiny of Man: A Christian Interpretation,* referred to the ongoing effect of sin in the following words:

---

90. Ibid., 410.
91. Ibid., 321.
92. Ibid., 348.
93. Ibid., 888.
94. Ibid., 872.
95. Ibid., 875.
96. Ibid., 882.

> . . . in every moment of existence there is a tension between the self as it looks out upon the world from the perspective of its values and necessities and the self as it looks at both the world and itself, and is disquieted by the undue claims of the self in action.[97]

Furthermore, according to Niebuhr,

> [i]t is in this moment of self-transcendence that the consciousness and memory of original perfection arise. For in this moment the self knows itself as merely a finite creature among many others and realizes that the undue claims which the anxious self in action makes, result in injustices to its fellows.[98]

It is to these injustices to one's fellow human beings referred to by Niebuhr that Plantinga also further elaborates on and links with sin against God by saying that

> . . . God hates sin not just because it violates law, but also because it violates trust. Sin grieves God, offends God, betrays God, and not because God is touchy. God hates sin against himself, against neighbors, against a good creation, because sin breaks the peace – in the first place between the sinner and God. Sin interferes with the way God wants things to be. That is why God has laws against it. God is for shalom and *therefore* against sin.[99]

If one considers the implications of this interpretation of the consequences of human sin, one can see that sin jeopardizes the way God planned things to be. The biblical images for sin suggest that it is not only deviant behavior, but that the heart of the sinner is also affected. The Bible teaches that when someone sins, it means he/she is guilty of transgression – Gk. *parabasis* (1 John 3:4); iniquity – Gk. *anomia* (Col 3:5–9; Mark 7:20); disobedience (Eph 5:6); trespassing – Gk. *paraptoma* (Eph 2:1; Matt 6:14); ungodliness (wickedness, impiety) – Gk. *asebeia* (Rom 4:5; 5:6); unbelief – Gk. *apistia*

---

97. Niebuhr, *Nature and Destiny of Man*, 278.
98. Ibid., 277.
99. Plantinga, *Not the Way It's Supposed to Be*, 14; cf. *Engaging God's World*, 3.

(Mark 9:24; Matt 13:58). In short, he or she is showing failure – Gk. *apotychía* (John 3:6), and is guilty (12:31; 27:4).

In order to connect these (sin and the sinful nature of humanity) with the idea of a plan and purpose of God for humankind and human society,[100] one may say that being corrupt and acting in corrupt ways makes one miss God's purpose for oneself and for human society. This is true on the basis of the fact that, biblically speaking, acts of corruption are all about missing the mark or the target, having gone astray and having lost the path one is supposed to follow. The Greek word *harmatema* (Rom 3:23) carries this meaning and this also applies to the word *parabasis* meaning to "overstep a forbidden line."[101] Accordingly, the sin of corruption occurs when people deliberately or accidentally step over the line of the law of God.

Unfortunately, the sin of corruption, implying "missing the target" and "overstepping the line," not only interferes with God's plan for humanity, but as we saw in chapter 2, it has in some contexts become a common fact of life. Or, as Plantinga states,

> . . . [t]he human problem isn't just ignorance . . . it's not just oppression; it's also corruption [and one may surely add corrupt acts]. Traditional presentations of sin, and particularly of corruption, feature a strikingly contrary pair of images . . . sin tends to despoil things . . . Sin, Christians used to hate it, fear it, flee from it, and grieve over it . . . but not anymore.[102]

Thus far, it seems beyond dispute that corruption as sin has moral implications. Within the history of the Anglican tradition, influential sixteenth-century Anglican priest and theologian Richard Hooker (1554–1600) comprehensively considers human nature in his *Lawes of Ecclesiastical Policy*.[103]

---

100. With regard to this "plan or vision for society," see 3.6.2; 3.6.3; and especially 3.6.4.

101. Reynolds, *Redeemed by God*, 66.

102. Plantinga, *Not the Way It's Supposed to Be*, 15.

103. Richard Hooker (1554–1600) is known as the great theologian and champion of the English church – the Anglican church. His life was characterized by his commitment to the church as its defender, prophet, and apologist. Gibbs ("Richard Hooker," 943–960) describes Hooker as a "Prophet of Anglicanism." This is because through his life and theology, he had and continues to have an ongoing influence on the Anglican church's life. For example, even today, his *Lawes of Ecclesiastical Polity* continue to contribute to the understanding of an identity and the role of Scripture within the Anglican church.

He does so not necessarily from the point of view of humankinds' total corruption and sinfulness (and for this he has been criticized in the past). He rather does it from the position of an innate desire for the good that draws human beings (and all living creatures) towards their creator and as they gradually grow towards God, they develop understanding through instruction, experience, and the exercise of virtue.

When Hooker does speak of sin he sees it as ubiquitous, affecting human life at every level, and that people "prefer their own private good before all things, even that good which is sensual before whatsoever is most divine."[104] The nature of human beings, their hearts and their behavior, according to Hooker, pursues their own ends; people are liable to be diverted by the desire to obtain what they want and every human being "possesses a notable capacity for self-deception . . . to be ignorant as much as may be of their own deformities, without the feeling sense whereof they are not most wretched" (1.12.2; 1:121.2–4).

Both Plantinga and Hooker's contributions are insightful because most studies on corruption (as a phenomenon and as corrupt actions) have not taken up the issue corruption as sin – as a religious concept and not only as a moral one. Since corruption is, theologically speaking sin, it is also, in Plantinga's words,[105]

> a culpable and personal affront to a personal God . . . [as] when we are thinking religiously, we view a shopkeeper's defrauding of a customer not merely as an instance of lawlessness but also of faithlessness, and we think of fraud as faithless not only to the customer but also to God. Criminal and moral misadventures qualify as sin because they offend and betray God.[106]

Furthermore, corruption as a sin finds itself within a theological-ethical and intimate nexus between it (human sin), the human heart and human

---

It provides reassurance and encouragement for those who seek to express the church's purpose and direction, especially today when there seem to be an increasingly ever-changing theological landscape within Anglicanism.

104. McGrade, *Richard Hooker: Of the Laws of Ecclesiastical Polity, Vol. 1: Preface, Books I to IV*, 74.

105. Plantinga, *Not the Way It's Supposed to Be*, 13.

106. Ibid., 12.

behavior[107] as it involves giving and the receiving of something "promising or giving of a bribe (active bribery) and the requesting, agreeing to receive or accepting of a bribe (passive bribery)."[108] This is reminiscent of Mwaura's view that

> . . . all forms of wicked behaviour of discrimination, manipulation or exploitation . . . negates the principles of equality of persons to treat people differently along certain lines [and] encompasses positive discrimination which amounts to favoritism and negative discrimination to deny others their due rights. Its moral implication includes lack of justice and fair play; suffering for certain groups, breakdown of the moral fiber of society, and loss of human dignity.[109]

Finally, in both giving and receiving (active and passive bribery/corruption) both parties use a certain power or authority, often motivated by human greed and self-interest, to complete what one may call "the circle of corruption," which brings us to the following section on the centrality of power and humankind's use or abuse of power.

3.6.2 Corruption and Power and Corruption as Abuse of Power

The focus in this subsection is on the abuse of power as a manifestation of (acts of) corruption and the latter as a consequence of corruption (in the sense of the fallenness of humankind). The correct use of power or its misuse or abuse has been referred to often thus far and will be a recurring theme in the rest of the study.

In short, power refers to "the ability to influence the actions and the opinions of people and so causes effects in affairs and people."[110] Power is central to the issue of corruption and according to Haller and Shore, "[w]e

---

107. cf. Peels, "Effects of Sin," 43 and Ochulor, "Analysis of Corruption," 474. "Man [sic], the individual man, is the origin of every moral action whether good or bad. Corruption begins first in the individual's heart, first as thoughts and then these thoughts are translated into concrete actions. When these acts are repeated over time, they become habits . . ."

108. Plantinga *Not the Way It's Supposed to Be*, 10.

109. Mwaura, "Reconstructing Mission," 35ff.

110. Zaaiman, "Towards a Third Generation Definition," 374.

should not lose sight of the fact that transactions of bribery and corruption always take place in power relationships that invariably stratify, marginalize and exclude."[111] The concept "power relationship" is broad in the sense that it has different meanings and different dimensions, positive and/or negative, depending on the situation in which it is exercised. For example, a power relationship could refer to power granted to a person or persons to command or distribute resources for the good of society. A power relationship could, however, also refer to a negative relationship, such as when political power in or of a government is centralized in the hands of a small ruling elite to the exclusion of and at the cost of others. It is this exercise of power that Jackson calls a "privilege of power" leading to "[an] attempt of the privileged powerful to take 'moral ownership' of the suffering powerless."[112] In such a context, the abuse of power – for example, in its relationship with what Olivier de Sardan calls the "abuse of the public purse" – eventually distorts the true and positive meaning of power.[113] It is also then that, according to Dougherty,

> [t]hose who have the power to grant access to resources, to give contracts, reduce taxes, help put someone else in a position of power, turn a blind eye on illegal activities etc., [which] are one part of this equation. Those who have something valuable to give in exchange are another part of the equation. Often the poorest sector of the population, who has little monetary or social capital with which to negotiate deals, are unable to partake and benefit from these informal systems of exchange and gift giving.[114]

The "abuse of power" flies in the face of the virtues of public accountability and personal responsibility. Its effects are immense and it leads to communities being socio-economically marginalized. In most African countries it is sometimes said that there is a tendency among some leaders toward

---

111. Haller and Shore, *Corruption*, 17.
112. In Zigon, *Morality*, 76.
113. De Sardan, "Moral Economy," 27.
114. In Zigon, *Morality*, 76.

"concentrating power and resources within [specific] ethnic groups,"[115] which by definition marginalizes other ethnic groups, even if the group that benefits is numerically in the majority.[116] The minority then becomes what Fraser calls the "weak public," relying on the powerful to make decisions on their behalf.[117]

Returning to the Bible and specifically to theological-ethical perspectives derived from it on power and the abuse thereof, one may again begin from the perspective of the creation narratives, where God declared God's intention to

> . . . make mankind in our image, in our likeness, so that they *may rule over* the fish in the sea and the birds in the sky, over the livestock and all the wild animals, and over all the creatures that move along the ground. (Gen 1:26, emphasis added)

It is clear that from its creation, humankind is directly linked with some idea of the exercise of power, with a command to rule and to exercise authority. God created humans and gave them power over the other creatures, says the narrative. However, it is important to note that the granting of authority was *preceded by the gift of God-likeness*. This has important theological-ethical implications. Guardini elaborates on this by explaining that

> [m]an's [sic] natural God-likeness consists in this capacity for power, in his ability to use it and in his resultant lordship. . . . Man cannot be human and as a kind of addition to his humanity, exercise or fail to exercise power; the exercise of power is essential to his humanity.[118]

Any theological reflection on power, at least as it pertains to the creation narratives in the Bible, has to begin by referring to the above mentioned two key elements of it, namely: that human beings have power because God *gave it to them,* and that having power and being created in God's image means humankind *represent* God in their exercise of this power. Wolff explains the link between the image of God and the power of human beings:

---

115. Holmquist and Ford, "Kenya," 5.
116. Abbink, "Being Young in Africa," 36.
117. Fraser, *Rethinking the Public Sphere*, 74.
118. Guardini, *End of the Modern World*, 133.

> It is precisely in his [sic – humankind's] function as ruler that he is God's image . . . Accordingly man is set in the midst of creation as God's statue. He is evidence that God is the Lord of creation; but as God's steward he also exerts his rule, fulfilling his task not in arbitrary despotism but as a responsible agent. His rule and his duty to rule are not autonomous; they are copies.[119]

Wolff's argument is important for our discussion as it raises the key issue of human beings as "responsible agents." It is to this understanding that a reflection on power has to find its meaning within the context of being ethical (i.e. accountable or responsible). With regard to power accountability and responsibility, Guardini states that it is only when viewed from the perspective of the God-likeness of humanity that the bestowal of power onto humanity by God and humanity as God's representatives

> [d]oes the phenomenon of power receive its full weight, its greatness, as well as its earnestness, which is grounded in responsibility? If human power and the lordship which stem from it are rooted in man's [sic] likeness to God, then power is not man's in his own right, autonomously, but only as a loan, a fief. Man is lord by grace of God, and he must exercise his dominion responsibly, for he is answerable for it to Him who is Lord by essence. Thus sovereignty becomes obedience, service.[120]

The abuse of power as being against the will of God finds many examples in the Bible. In the Old Testament, it was clearly believed that leaders were appointed and anointed by God in order for them to protect the weak. Whenever leaders violated the power and authority granted to them by God, God was angered because this meant acting contrary to God's will. We read that the outcome of the abuse of power led to leaders being dethroned, rebuked, punished or even killed (cf. Ps 82; Jer 22:13–14, 17 and the many instances of this in 1 Kgs). In Micah 2–3 and Ezekiel 22:27 and 34:2–5, the focus is on the accusation against the reigning parties when they are abusing their power.

---

119. Wolff, *About Philosophy*, 160–161.
120. Guardini, *End of the Modern World*, 134.

The concept "misuse of power" can be clarified further with reference to the related concept of (those in) "authority" (powerful members of society) and the poor (weaker member of society). Here too, power is not mere power, but power which is theologically understood as a gift given to a community *via* a person in power *for* those without it:

> The primary reason power is given is in order to establish ordered patterns of life together, in which those who gain advantages in the system are responsible to use their wealth and power (the advantages they accrue) for the benefit of those who become disadvantaged as a result of the operation of those patterns of common life. [In other words] *This* is what power is for in God's economy: the bringing of blessing to the community for whom it is to be exercised through the establishing of justice, through the use of power to establish, restore and maintain right relationships in the community.[121]

Time and again the Bible condemns the misuse of power: when Old Testament prophets condemned the corruption they saw in their societies, especially that committed by rulers, the judiciary and the wealthy; the powerful were accused of coveting fields and houses and seizing them (Mic 2:2); the exploitation of the poor was contrasted with the wealth of those carrying out the exploitation (Amos 5:11–12; Jer 5:27–28); rulers are directly accused of economic exploitation (King Jehoiakim, for example, is condemned by Jeremiah for forcing men to build a palace and not paying them for their labor, Jer 22:13–14); usury and excessive interest charged and unjust gains from one's neighbors (especially the poor and, therefore, powerless neighbors) by extortion is also condemned (Ezek 22:12–13; 22:29).

In the New Testament, a call to responsible exercise of power is again clearly heard. In his Letter to the Romans (13:4), Paul reminds that government is "God's servant, *to do [us] good*" (Rom 13:4), and

> ... John the Baptist, for instance, calls on those with economic and military power to use it well, not to renounce it (Luke 3:10–14); the leaders of the early church exercised their power,

---

121. Sloane, "Justifying Advocacy."

or authority if you will, for the benefit of the community both socially (Acts 6) and theologically (Acts 15).[122]

According to Macquarie, the idea of seeing and using power as a blessing, as a service to others, is furthermore theologically crucial in that

> . . . it relates to the biblical concept of *kenosis* or kenotic power, coming from a Greek term meaning self-emptying (see Phil 2:5–11). It is based on the relationship within the Trinity and is demonstrated through power that is emptied or poured out for the benefit of others. This is power at the service of others, not power for its own sake. Jesus did not seek to gain power, but emptied himself of all of his power as he came to serve and to give his life so that others may live.[123]

All of this can also clearly be linked with the foregoing discussion of humankind, its sinfulness and the implications thereof. According to Ochulor, "[m]an [sic], the individual man, is the origin of every moral action whether good or bad."[124] Corruption, for Ochulor, begins in one's heart and thoughts and then is translated into concrete actions and finally "[w]hen these acts are repeated over time, they become habits; these habits in turn become character and almost one's second nature."[125] One implication of this is that a person can be involved in acts of corruption and power abuse in different ways, for example, even by merely associating oneself in the circle of powerful and corrupt leaders or in sharing in the enjoyment of the gains of their misuse of power.

Ochulor's argument also opens the door for a discussion on virtues[126] in relation to corruption and injustice. Since, as David Carr and J. W. Steutel assert, "virtue is what enables one to perform actions that successfully pursue

---

122. Ibid.
123. Macquarrie, *Jesus Christ in Modern Thought*, 214.
124. Ochulor, "Analysis of Corruption," 474.
125. Ibid.
126. Tha the concept of virtues has always been central to ethical thought is clear in so-called virtue ethics, which refers to an ethical theory in which the notion of virtue or good character plays a central role on matters such as those of moral dilemmas. Proponents of this ethical theory believe that every virtue of character yields a positive rule of action and every vice or defect of character yields a negative rule.

good ends," it may be argued that corruption can be addressed when the ethical virtues are learned and applied by Christians.[127] However, the question is, where do Christians find these virtues and ultimately who teaches this to Christians?[128] This question will be turned to in the following chapter (see 4.4.1.3 and 4.3.2.3) on the possible role of the church in the fight against corruption, specifically with reference to the work of North American ethicist, Stanley Hauerwas.

3.6.3 God, Human Dignity and Human Flourishing

In chapter 2, it was pointed out that at the core of the problem of corruption as injustice is the dehumanizing effect of corruption. This dehumanizing effect brings this discussion to the concept of *human dignity* and a short theological-ethical reflection on it in relation to corruption. According to Vorster, even though the "concept [human dignity] originated after biblical times . . . the issue of dignity belongs to the heart of biblical message" and "[t]herefore, human dignity should be studied in the light of the of the developing line or trajectory of Scripture."[129] The best starting point in this discussion on God and human dignity, therefore, is to again turn to the Word of God.

We have seen above that in the book of Genesis (Gen 1:26–27; see also Gen 5:13; 9:6; 1 Cor 11:7; Jas 3:9) a biblical conceptualization of the human person is presented, especially with respect to the fact that humans were created in the image and likeness of God and this is also central to many theological understandings of human dignity. Groody suggests that,

> . . . [d]efining all human beings in terms of *imago Dei* provides a starting point for the discourse [on justice] . . . [The *i*]*mago Dei* names the personal and relational nature of human

---

127. Carr and Steutel, *Virtue Ethics and Moral Education*, 71.

128. Interestingly, Carr refers as far back as to Aristotle's emphasis on the importance of learning ethical virtues in this regard: Anything that we have to learn to do we learn by the actual doing of it: people become builders by building and instrumentalists by playing instruments. Similarly we become just by performing just acts, temperate by performing temperate ones, brave by performing brave ones" (Nichomacean Ethics (NE) II 1 1103a33–1103b2 in Carr and Steutel, *Virtue Ethics and Moral Education*, 59).

129. Vorster, "Theological Evaluation," 324.

existence and the mystery that human life cannot be understood apart from of the mystery of God.[130]

From this argument, it is therefore true to say that human dignity flows from a relationship with God. David Kelsey, whose theological-anthropological foci on the uniqueness of humankind's relationship with God (on which its consequent responsibilities and freedom rests), also argues that "the claims about human beings that are non-negotiable for Christian faith are claims about how God relates to human beings."[131]

Although the concept of "relational quality" and the "living together" will be discussed in more detail in section 3.6.4 below with reference to God and the biblical vision of human society, it is important at this stage to reiterate that at the center of God's relationship to humankind is the fact that God's intention for people is flourishing for all.

With regard to the concept of flourishing, in her *Tolle Lege* article, Laura Grace Alexander warns that it ". . . is not a concept that lends itself to quick and easy definition and there has been much disagreement through the ages as to what constitutes a flourishing life to its core . . ."[132] Not only is human flourishing a concept that is difficult to define, another challenge is the fact that even what exactly constitutes well-being or human flourishing is and continues to be debated. However, in this study, the concept human flourishing, sometimes described differently as "human sustainability," "human good" and/or "human goods," is chosen for the purpose of clarifying the interplay between God, the human person, human dignity and the effects of corruption and injustice.

Some trace the idea of human flourishing as far back as Aristotle. For the latter, as philosopher Martha Nussbaum reminds, "the ultimate end of human life is *eudaimonia* which he describes as the state of living well."[133] Nussbaum elaborates further that,

---

130. Groody, *Globalization, Spirituality, and Justice*, 644.

131. Kelsey, *Eccentric Existence*, 8. The issue of relationality is central to Kelsey, for whom Christian anthropology seeks to answer the question: "What is implied about human personhood by the claim that God actively relates to us?" (ibid., 46).

132. Alexander, "Human Flourishing," 1.

133. Nussbaum, *Fragility of Goodness*, 6.

[t]o the Greeks, *eudaimonia* means something like "living a good life for a human being"; or as a recent writer, John Cooper has suggested, "human flourishing." Aristotle tells us that it is equivalent to "living well and doing well."

It is important to note that the idea of "living well and doing well" itself is broad. However, it is used in relation to challenges facing humanity by philosophers such as Amartya Sen and Nussbaum, who are known for their work on the so-called capabilities approach to human development – this is about addressing the issue of poverty, inequality and seeking to see human development take priority if "living well and doing well" is to be realized.[134]

In the case of Nussbaum, her emphasis on human flourishing has been described by sociologist Des Gaper as "an evolving picture of the proposed essential components of a life that is fully human."[135] Again, the idea of "living well and doing well" is understood well by Nussbaum, when the concept of "capability" – a realization of the potential of each person – is given priority. This is why she suggests that "we believe that human life is worth living only if a good life can be secured by effort, and if the relevant sort of effort lies within the capabilities of most people."[136]

Nussbaum also suggests that, as one seeks to help people realize a good life, there should be "terms of achieving possible central human functional capabilities that indicate a life of full human functioning, or a kind of basic human flourishing."[137] The reference to "functioning" implies human participation in seeking to achieve a good life and living well. This may also imply the need for people in a given society to stand up against forms of injustices, including corruption and inequality as social ills because of the threat these pose to human flourishing.

But, what exactly is human flourishing within theological-ethical parameters? To answer this question, Alexander offers the following theological-ethical definition: "[H]uman flourishing speaks to what makes us individually and corporately fully human and what makes our lives, in every aspect,

---

134. cf. Nussbaum, *Sex and Social Justice*; Sen, "Capability and Well-Being."
135. Gaper, "Sen's Capabilities Approach," 293.
136. Nussbaum, *Fragility of Goodness*, 320.
137. Nussbaum, *Sex and Social Justice*, 40.

fully expressive of what God intended us to be."[138] This of course poses the next logical question, what exactly does God intend for us, individually and corporately?[139]

Another definition of human flourishing is given by Kenneth Loyer: "A vibrant, flourishing life occurs when we live in justly ordered relationships with God and with others by recognizing and celebrating our own God-given dignity and that of others."[140] And, in Alexander's view of human dignity one finds that echoes of the concepts of participation (in life) according to one's abilities and gifts as flourishing is shown when human beings are "fully engaging in life and bringing to bear all of our God-given gifts and abilities."[141] Another important concept within the whole of this study thus far is one of relationality and relationships, and it is not surprising that in Ian Christie's perspective human flourishing includes this as well: "Human flourishing is at heart a matter of right relationship: with God, with fellow humans, and with other creatures."[142] This is also found in Deane-Drummond's understanding of human flourishing as including elements of God the Creator, fellow humans (neighbor) and both other living and non-living things (i.e. the natural environment).[143] What is further important in the context of this study, is the express and very close link made by Ian Christie between human flourishing and justice:

> Human flourishing is bound up with justice. We are enjoined to act justly and love mercy. Injustice is the result of a forgetting of responsibilities towards one another and towards God. It is the outcome of the failure to love one's neighbour, in the fullest sense, as oneself, and to respect the integrity of common goods on which everyone's flourishing depends.[144]

---

138. Alexander, "Human Flourishing," 1.

139. This will be discussed in this section, but also has to be read together with the other sections under 3.6 as all in some sense or another also refers to God's intention for us and for our societies.

140. Loyer, "Dignity, Justice, and Flourishing," 15.

141. Alexander, "Human Flourishing," 2.

142. Christie, "Human Flourishing," 4.

143. Deane-Drummond, "Why Human Flourishing?" 24.

144. Ibid., 5.

At this point in the discussion of the concept of human flourishing, it will serve well to return to one of the key proponents of this concept of human flourishing – David Kelsey. In his seminal work, *Eccentric Existence*, Kelsey explains that human flourishing is best understood to mean both "to blossom" and "to thrive." For him, "flourishing" as "blossoming" may be used metaphorically to characterize a certain type of human life, and because for him and theologically speaking, "to blossom is to manifest the type of beauty of which a given life is capable by virtue of God's relating to it."[145] On the other hand, "to blossom" pictures the way to providing both fruit on which the others' (one's contemporaries') flourishing may depend for nurture and support, and the seeds on which a subsequent generation's life may depend. *To flourish, to blossom, and to thrive* can also be spoken of in terms of *well-being*. In Kelsey's words, "human flourishing generally is identified with the highest degree of human well-being."[146]

However, it should also be understood that for Kelsey, the highest degree of human well-being will always be determined by human beings' responding to God's call "to live in ways whose patterns are consistent with the identity we have been given in Christ"[147] and that living beings will flourish "when the patterns of their lives are consistent with their most basic identities, structurally defined by their being in Christ."[148] According to Kelsey, this a humanly appropriate love for God, that is the "desire for union with Christ, union with God-with-us here and now."[149] And this can be achieved because it is God who has given to human beings the capacity to enhance their own well-being as God continues to be part of their lives by virtue of God's relating to human being.

With regard to how the study of Christian anthropology has implications for a study of corruption, Kelsey's understanding of theological anthropology offers important insights. First, because according to Kelsey, theological anthropology becomes "systematically anthropocentric in that it is exhaustively concerned with human failure, an exclusively intrahuman

---

145. Kelsey, "On Human Flourishing," 2.
146. Kelsey, *Eccentric Existence*, 570.
147. Ibid., 702.
148. Ibid.
149. Ibid., 707.

defect or distortion [sin, corruption, injustice] that is in need of correction";[150] second, Kelsey challenges the church and ecclesial communities to respond appropriately, publicly and communally to God's relating to all living beings and all of life in faith, hope, and love.

Thus, for Kelsey, too, "human flourishing" is a central category of theological reflection and it stands in direct opposition to what he calls "living death."[151] Furthermore, for Kelsey,

> ... God is best understood in a triune way, and that the triune God actively relates to us in three interrelated but distinct ways – as One who creates, grounding our reality and its flourishing; as One who promises us an eschatological consummation and draws us to it; and as One who reconciles us in our multiple estrangements.

These words of Kelsey's contain important concepts which will be taken up in the discussion below: relationality, being created by God as human beings with human dignity, and eschatological consummation.

From the reflections on the manifestations and the consequences of corruption in chapter 2, it should be clear that corruption constitutes an obstacle to engaging in life to the full and hence for people to use their God-given gifts and abilities. As a misuse of power, corruption has implications for the "Christian vision of human flourishing [which] orients towards forms of governance that are marked by participation, service and social justice."[152] Thus corruption denies peoples' participation in the benefits of society and it denies them social justice. This participation referred to by Bain, Frost and Woolley is also key according to Sen and Dreze:

> ... [i]t has intrinsic value for the quality of human life. Indeed being able to do something not only for oneself but also for other members of the society is one of the elementary freedoms which people have reason to value. The popular appeal of

---

150. Ibid., 118.

151. Ibid., 441. For Kelsey, we live a "dying life" as we as finite beings are constantly poised on the edge of death, dependent upon God, the source of life. However, if we respond faithfully to God, we flourish. If not, our "dying life" turns into "living death" (ibid., 402).

152. Bain, Frost and Woolley, "Wholly Living," 31.

many social movements . . . confirm that this basic capability is highly valued even among people who lead very deprived lives in material terms.[153]

Deane-Drummond also directly links human flourishing with good governance in her summary of what constitutes the latter, namely:

> . . . [t]he kind of governance that makes for human flourishing is one that takes accountability, transparency, justice, fairness, equity and participation seriously. Its absence provides the breeding ground for conflict and breakdown in civil society.[154]

Similarly, Ian Christie argues that "vital for human flourishing [are] the following elements: fair economy, *just governance*, wise use of and relationship with nature, and sharing of common resources essential for a decent life."[155] When these ingredients or elements are missing, "[d]eprived people tend to come to terms with their deprivation . . . and they may, as a result, lack the courage to demand any radical change" or, one may say, corruption and injustice become the norm as "deprived groups may be habituated to inequality, may be unaware of possibilities of social change, may be resigned to fate, and may be willing to accept the legitimacy of the established order."[156] And such a situation calls for,

> . . . the removal of major sources of unfreedom: poverty as well as tyranny, poor economic opportunities as well as systematic social deprivation, neglect of public facilities as well as intolerance or over activity of repressive states.[157]

To this end, the aspects of *human responsibility* and *human freedom* again come to the fore. God gave humankind the freedom to choose to accept or reject the ongoing self-communication of God. So humanity is aware of its relationship with God and the responsibilities it brings with it.[158]

---

153. Quoted in Alkire, "Public Debate," 131.
154. Deane-Drummond, "Why Human Flourishing?" 17.
155. Christie, "Human Flourishing," 15 (emphasis added).
156. Sen, *Standard of Living*, 10.
157. Sen, *Development as Freedom*, 3.
158. cf. Kelsey, *Eccentric Existence*, 85.

The idea of the responsibility of human beings is important in the understanding of the problem corruption and if human dignity is to be respected and protected in society. Humanity is called to do so from a relational duty, as well as from a human dignity perspective. Hans S. Reinders, speaking from in the context of disability, expounds this as follows:

> . . . human beings are dignified, regardless of their state or condition, by a divine act of communion . . . In the resurrection of Christ, God the Father draws human beings into his own relationship with the Son and the Spirit and saves them from the bonds of natural necessity which means that in participating in that sacramental life, we learn to see what and how God intended us to be from the beginning.[159]

In other words, human beings are called to respond to God's grace with faith; this faith will allow God' activities to be expressed in a life free from corruption and injustice. Human beings are expected to abide and therefore participate in protecting the rest of humanity because they have been given certain abilities and these are closely related to "true and sound wisdom, [which] consists of two parts: the knowledge of God and of ourselves."[160]

A further important point needs mentioning here, namely an eschatological one. Although God accepts those who respond to God into a new relationship with God and that whoever accepts this relationship becomes part of the new humanity in Christ (meaning a changed life), the full realization of human dignity will take place only when human beings will share eternally in God's good purpose and in God's life – meaning in eternal life. This, too, has a very important implication for this study on corruption and injustice. To those who say that, given the magnitude of the problem of corruption and its corrosive effects on humanity, the transformation of social, political and economic life by making it more attentive and responsive to corruption cannot easily be achieved, Christian eschatology offers an answer and hope for ultimate success.[161] This Christian hope reminds

---

159. In Soulen and Woodhead, *God and Human Dignity*, 138, 139.

160. Kelsey, *Eccentric Existence*, 1, with reference to John Calvin's *Institutes*.

161. Compare also in chapter 4, Nico Koopman and Dirk Smit's ("Public Witness in the Economic Sphere?" 275) emphasis on "hope" as they discuss public theology as public witness in the economic sphere. For them public theology "speaks a language of hope."

one that, in the words of Douglas Meeks, "[t]he divine act of new creation is not completed until the redemptive work of God embraces the totality of humanity and the creation" and therefore the study of God in relation to the primacy of the human person and his/her dignity, begins and ends with the communal and cosmic symbol of God's reign of righteousness at the eschatological banquet where "the more than enough" of God's grace embraces all of God's creatures.[162]

In other words, God's intended purpose for human beings does not end in earthly life; the destiny of human beings is eternal. Theologically speaking, the concept eschatological consummation is about the message of hope, focusing on the future but challenging human beings amidst their suffering to continue to work towards a better today as well as a better tomorrow. For Kelsey, eschatological consummation is about the promise of transformation at the end of history, "which, in biblical language, is called the kingdom of God."[163] Kelsey also fittingly, especially for our purposes, describes this ultimate destiny of humankind as "a new age of justice and communion with God."[164]

Mindful of what has been said of the relationship between justice and good governance in this section thus far, we now turn to the issue of relationality as a biblical-theological principle in the reflection on corruption and in/justice as "[b]iblical justice is profoundly concerned about good governance as it relates to interpersonal relationships as much as it is concerned about government to people relationships."[165]

3.6.4 Relationality, Relational Justice and God's Vision of a Peaceful and Just Society

At various points in the above discussions it was maintained that God is relational as it can be seen in the triune God itself and in the latter's actions toward humankind. This will be unpacked further in this section as a key

---

162. Meeks, "Economy of Grace," 213–214.

163. Quoted from Westminster John Knox Press Radio interview with Kelsey, in 2009.

164. Kelsey, *Eccentric Existence*, 442.

165. The Micah Challenge, http://www.micahchallenge.org/beinformed/good-governance/theology-and-good-governance/338-goodness-and-good-governance, 4.

element in the discussion of the ethical-theological perspective on corruption and in/justice.

Not only God, but humankind too is relational – being created in the image of God, this is to be expected. Humankind is relational with regard to God and also with regard to one another in society.[166] In his article, "What does it mean to be human?" Paul Coulter affirms that God created human beings to live not only with God, but also with one another, as well as with the rest of creation.[167] Again, in theological terms, being human means that one is born into an unbroken line of humanity tracing its ancestry to God the Creator and seeking to live according to God's intended purpose for one's life.

But, God not only has a plan or vision for the individual human life, but also for humanity as a collective, as a society. Of course, at the heart of God's vision for society is the human person, the ones created in the image of Trinitarian God, but the fact and necessity of human common life, living together with all it entails, such as looking out for one another, also finds its origin in God himself. Human existence is *existing in communion*, first with God, and then with other human beings as well as with the rest of creation as (after all, ". . . [human beings] have more in common with the rest of the animate creation than in distinction from it . . . createdness is glory, not shame.")[168] In his book, *Being as Communion*, Eastern Orthodox theologian John Ziziolous speaks of the foundational nature of relationship for humanity and its consequences in terms of interdependency:

> To be is to be in relationship. Our independence is borne of our dependence, our rationality of our relationality. This, it will be clear, stands in very stark contrast to the idea of humans as independent, autonomous choice-making beings.[169]

---

166. According to Christoph Schwobel ("Recovering Human Dignity," 48), "relationality" has become a key word in theology in recent years, but reminds us that it is a technical term used in a variety of ways of to refer to the relationships between God, human beings and the world.

167. Coulter, "What Does It Mean to Be Human?"

168. Wright in Spencer, "Christian Vision," 5. Referring here to Nick Spencer's, "A Christian Vision of Human Flourishing," Briefing Paper of the Theos/ CAFOD/ Tearfund *Wholly Living* project which explored the different aspects and implications of a Christian understanding of human flourishing.

169. Quoted in Spencer, "Christian Vision," 5.

As referred to earlier, theologians such as Nicholas Wolterstorff (see 3.6.1) refer to God's vision of a society as one specifically characterized by shalom and this embraces the core values of peace, justice, and enjoyment *of all relationships*, centered in the relationship with God. This is reflected, for example, in 2 Corinthians 5:18–19 where one read that God in Christ has begun the work of reconciling the world to himself. Likewise, 2 Corinthians 5:19–21 refers to human participation in the work of making a society reflect God's plan as "[t]hose who are in Christ join in this marvelous work of reconciliation." Wright, also on the theme of shalom and relationality/community, reminds one that in the Bible, "shalom connotes the complete well-being *of a society or community*" and that "[w]hile shalom includes more than justice, it certainly produces nothing less than a just society."[170] In addition, God's ultimate intentions for humanity are reflected in several Old and New Testament texts that indicate God's ideal for his covenant community, a community/society in which "steadfast love and faithfulness will meet, righteousness and peace will kiss each other" (Ps 85:10).[171]

In terms of what has been said in the previous section with reference to human flourishing, society as intended by God should present a picture of exactly that, of humanity flourishing. This, according to Spencer is a society,

> . . . enabling all to have a meaningful say in the direction in which their lives travel; affording opportunities for all to be creative, productive and generous; ensuring that all share in the use of and care for our shared natural resources; making it possible for all to contribute to our common fellowship.[172]

---

170. Wright, *Knowing Jesus*, 179 (emphasis added).

171. The concept shalom implies the absence of sin, and Spencer ("Christian Vision") lists some very insightful examples of the latter in the context of the current study: [t]o "deprive the poor of their rights / and withhold justice from the oppressed of my people, / making widows their prey / and robbing the fatherless" (Isa 10:2) . . . The people do "not say to themselves, / 'Let us fear the Lord our God,' [but rather] have become rich and powerful and have grown fat and sleek . . . [failing to] plead the case of the fatherless . . . [or] defend the rights of the poor" (Jer 5:23–28) . . . "They trample on the heads of the poor . . . and deny justice to the oppressed" (Amos 2:7). Tarimo (*Applied Ethics*, 25), too, refers to the concept of shalom, equating God's intended society with "[s]halom, which is witnessed in healthy human relationships (1 Kgs 5:12), well-being (Gen 37:4), prosperity (Jer 33:6, 9) and moral character (Ps 37:37)."

172. Spencer, "Christian Vision."

Such a society is clearly far removed from those societies crippled by corruption as described in chapter 2. Such societies in no way reflect God's vision for society as a peaceful realm for human flourishing, a society that thus also reflects the relational nature of God. And, remembering what has been said in regard to the eschatological nature of human existence, "[p]olitics alone will never deliver full human flourishing. That, however, does not mean it cannot make a vital contribution."[173] As this study contends "corruption may mock at justice," but when corruption is opposed, then God's vision for the well-being of and the realization of shalom in society is witnessed to. As Gordon and Evans note, "Justice is at the heart of God's plan for humanity. God's actions in history as referred to in the Bible and God's laws demonstrate God's desire for justice and God's compassion for those who suffer."[174] Because God had a clear vision in creating human beings and for human society, it follows that God's people should also strive towards fulfilling this vision.

Writing in the context of injustice that leads to poverty and the biblical narratives and principles behind the need to reform public life, Tim Keller suggests that

> [s]ocial reform . . . seeks to change social conditions and structures. Job tells us that he not only clothed the naked, but he "broke the fangs of the wicked and made them drop their victims" (Job 29:17). The prophets denounced unfair wages (Jer 22:13) [and] business practices (Amos 8:2, 6), legal systems weighted in favor of the rich and influential (Lev 19:15; Deut 24:17), and a system of lending capital that gouges the person of modest means (Exod 22:25–27; Lev 19:35–37; 25:37). Daniel calls a pagan government to account for its lack of mercy to the poor (Dan 4:27).[175]

---

173. Ibid., 17.
174. Gordon and Evans, "Mission of the Church," 3. Cf. Wright (*Mission of God*, 96, 280): ". . . for generation after generation, century after century, the God of the Bible was passionately concerned about social issues . . . So passionate, indeed, that the laws he gave and the prophets he sent give more space to these matters than in any other issue."
175. Keller, "Gospel and the Poor," 11.

In fact, biblical teaching covers a variety of relationships, friends, family, but also the relationship between citizens and the state. All these relationships must be "right relationships," in that they must be characterized by relational justice. According to Malchow the latter means that

> [j]ustice . . . is the fulfilment of the demands of a relationship, with God or a person. There is no norm of righteousness outside of that personal involvement. When people fulfil the conditions imposed on them by relationships they are righteous. [And] [e]very relationship has specific obligations.[176]

It is with regard to this that one may say that Christ identifies characteristics of right relationships or the virtues to be displayed within right relationships to be justice, mercy, faithfulness, forgiveness, truth, generosity, compassion, respect, hope, patience and love (cf. Mark 7:21–23). On the other hand, Jesus warns that bad or wrong relationships are characterized by injustice, oppression, violence, deceit, self-centeredness, lust, irritability, envy and greed (Matt 22:34–40), of which one could confidently argue that corruption is another way of defining bad or wrong relationships and as something contrary to the biblical command to love (see Isa 51:1–8; 56:1–8; 58:6–14; 59:1–15; 61:1–11; and 65:17–25).

To put the latter texts from Isaiah in context, especially as to why they address justice as well as their emphasis on communal aspects and their importance in the post-exilic period of the history of Israel, one reads that Israel turned away from the living God, decided to serve idols and no longer lived according to the commands of the covenant. This included disrespecting justice in community. For this reason God called prophets, in this case Isaiah, to remind the people of the covenant, of their covenantal responsibilities and that the God of the covenant is not only the God of justice (Isa 30:18), but that God *loves* justice (Isa 61:8) and that this God of Israelites *delights* in justice (cf. Jer 9:23). As such, God demanded justice for and from the whole of God's people.

As was noted earlier, the relational character of God is one of the attributes of God and this is closely connected to the biblical idea of God as the God of the covenant. In the Old Testament, the covenant in essence refers to

---

176. Malchow, *Social Justice*, 18.

the fact that God decided to "relate to Israel." According to Michael Horton, this relational divine initiative indicated that, although

> [i]n the fall of humanity in Adam, recapitulated in the history of Israel, human relationships fray as a result of prior infidelity to their covenant Lord. Yet before, during, and after humankind's broken promises, the promise-making and promise-keeping God is present and will not let the web fall apart.[177]

In this covenantal divine-human relationship God kept to God's promises, but "God related" to Israel also by imposing specific obligations on them as do all the covenantal relationships. As such, God summoned Israel to be faithful to the Torah and reminded them that the norms of the covenant remain of paramount importance in the relationship – these obligations included responsibility, mercy, and truthfulness and obedience (cf. Gen 12:1–3; 17:2 and Deut 28–31).

The concept of covenant is of course not only an Old Testament concept, but is also found in the New Testament, particularly with reference to the new covenant in Christ. Under the new covenant, God again "relates" to humankind as Jesus brings a message of love from God and the obligation to love God and neighbor. However, the category of neighbor is now one without limit as *all* people are called to be members of a new covenant of love where, like in the old covenant, the new brings hope where wrong or bad relationships characterized by injustice, oppression, violence, deceit, self-centeredness, lust, irritability, envy, greed threatened justice, mercy, faithfulness, forgiveness, truth, generosity, compassion, respect, hope, patience and love.

Jesus also calls the faithful to be "witnesses" to the new covenant. One may say that Jesus called his disciples both to "gospel-messaging" (urging everyone to believe the gospel) and to "gospel-neighboring" (sacrificially meeting the needs of those around them whether the latter believe or not)! The two go together. Not only Christ's life and ministry, but also his death and resurrection attests to this. As Keller insists,

---

177. Horton, "Law and the Gospel," 9.

[t]he resurrection shows us that God not only created both body and spirit but will also redeem both body and spirit. The salvation Jesus will eventually bring in its fullness will include liberation from all the effects of sin – not only spiritual but physical and material as well.[178]

As far as relational justice is concerned, this also shows that Jesus's mission implies that his justice goes beyond punishment to include restoration of relationships and putting things right.

To sum up, then, relational justice is "about fidelity to the demands of . . . relationships. It deals with how individuals, families, communities, as well as juridical, religious, and political authorities, interact with each other, with the most vulnerable members of society, and with the Covenant God."[179] This is particularly well articulated by Keller, who contends that "true justice can only be motivated by seeing the glorious goodness of God . . . grounded in God's character and that never changes."[180] Keller continues by saying that if something "is true of God, we who believe in him must always find some way of expressing it in our own practices, even if believers now live in a new stage in the history of God's redemption."[181]

With these practices in mind, and returning for a moment to the theological anthropology of David Kelsey, the latter's phrase "God relating" strengthens the conviction of the political implications of the relationship between God and humankind. According to Kelsey, "God's creative relating to creatures is a creative blessing"[182] and part of this is that humankind as moral creatures have "capabilities" that include "freedom of choice,"[183] the "capability of transcendence,"[184] the possibility of "non-divided and wholehearted action for others."[185] This freedom of choice should be exercised with a view to enable *all* human beings to flourish. For Kelsey, anything that

---

178. Keller, "Gospel and the Poor," 3.
179. Achtemeir, "Righteousness in the Old Testament," 80.
180. Keller, "Gospel and the Poor," 21–22.
181. Ibid., 23.
182. Kelsey, *Eccentric Existence*, 479.
183. Ibid., 1024.
184. Ibid.
185. Ibid., 1025.

hampers human well-being and human flourishing is not within God's plan, but rather is a result of sin leading to broken relationships which needs rectification by "active hopeful practices." According to Kelsey, "active hopeful practices" is hoping "to overcome particular injustices in their lived worlds and to liberate them from particular kinds of oppression"[186] leading them to the "new age of justice and communion with God."[187]

Thus, *living together* is about God the Creator; it is about God divinely relating. The implication of this divine relating "is central to every creature's integrity and to the integrity of the everyday world as a whole."[188] As such, despite the importance of freedom of choice, according to Ruston, justice "is derived from the essential conditions of human flourishing, rather than from the single value of sovereign individual choice."[189]

3.7 Conclusion

In chapter 2, it was shown why in secular thought corruption is morally wrong. It will be remembered that this was based on the understanding of corruption as "the abuse of power for private benefit or private gain," a definition proposed by the United Nations Convention against Corruption (UNCAC)[190]. The latter convention, it was said, laid the foundations for international cooperation in fighting corruption and came into force on 14 December 2005. Tanzania ratified it in 2005 and the Prevention and

---

186. Ibid., 569.
187. Ibid., 442.
188. Ibid., 322.
189. Ruston, *Human Rights*, 11.

190. Section 38 of UNCAC observes that there is need for cooperation between national authorities and Section 39 talks about cooperation between national authorities and the private sector. Sections 11 and 12 of the African Union Convention on Preventing and Combating Corruption also emphasize the participation of private sector, civil service and the media in combating corruption. Section 19 speaks of international cooperation for member countries. All these efforts have been undertaken because of UN and its members' declaration of corruption as a universally unacceptable and constituting universal crisis. In the same spirit, in November 2008, Tanzania established its National Anti-Corruption Forum (NACF) under the National Anti-Corruption Strategy and Action Plan- Phase II (NACSAP II). The aim of this was to provide a platform for dialogue among all stakeholders (including churches and faith-based organizations) on matters of corruption and its effect on society. For further details see the *Joint Evaluation of Support to Anti-Corruption Efforts Tanzania Country Report 6/2011 – Study, Norwegian Agency for Development Cooperation* (NORAD, "Joint Evaluation of Support").

Combating of Corruption Act of 2007 was enacted to take forward the UNCAC commitments.

This chapter set out to answer why, in biblical-theological terms, corruption is wrong, especially in light of the fact that corruption constitutes injustice, or, in the words of Martha Kirkpatrick, in light of the "indissoluble link" between corruption and injustice.[191] In order to do so, a variety of themes were addressed based first on the implications of the traditional biblically based doctrine of God – specifically with reference to understandings of the characteristics or nature of God, the nature of humanity (especially the fallenness of human nature), God's purpose for human life (for example, with reference to human flourishing) and Gods vision for human society (especially in its just, peaceful and relational nature as it also reflects the just, peaceful and relational character of God). It was also indicated that the themes of corruption and justice are clearly spoken of in Scripture as keys to the understanding who God is and what God wishes humanity to be.

Contemporary studies in Tanzania suggest that corruption prevents government from meeting its obligations to act justly toward its citizens and in terms of our biblical and theological reflections in this chapter,[192] corruption is not only exploitative,[193] but it also exacerbates the pain of injustice and oppression. One may say that corruption, at least in Tanzania, constitutes the foundation for unjust social conditions or for treatment that keeps people in poverty (similar situations are referred to in the Bible, e.g. Ps 82:1–8; Prov 14:31; Exod 22:21–27). Without drawing easy or superficial comparisons, what is happening in the terms of "corruption mocking at justice" in Tanzania is, therefore, not dissimilar to much of the oppression and corrupt social systems in biblical narratives in the favoring of the powerful (Lev 19:15), the exploitation of the poor (Exod 22:25–27; Eph 6:8–9; Jas 5:4), etc.

In as far as biblically and theologically, corruption constitutes "the abuse of power," it was shown that a corrupt person with the capacity to abuse

---

191. Kirkpatrick, "Incarnational Ecology," 41.
192. cf., e.g. the Government of Tanzania, *National Anti-Corruption Strategy*, 65.
193. Tanzi, "Corruption around the World," 45.

power turns God's gifts away from their intended purpose.[194] For this reason, concept of power, and the relationship of power and corruption was discussed theologically in the above sections.[195]

Of course, the Tanzanian context also differs widely from the biblical one – for one, as we saw in chapter 2, with regard to the sometimes expressly "modern" forms of corruption such as the misallocation of disaster or humanitarian aid; the looting of funds intended for the medical treatment of citizens; the delaying of the judicial process and unfair judgments; substandard public works and stalled public projects; irregular and illegal acquisition of public land, property and utilities; a rise in other forms of crime and insecurity, to name but a few. In short, this chapter in this sense showed that by denying people justice, corruption also denies them

> everything necessary for leading a life truly human, such as food, clothing, and shelter . . . the right to education, to employment, to a good reputation, to respect, to appropriate information, to activity in accord with the upright norm of one's own conscience, to protection of privacy and rightful freedom.[196]

---

194. As an aside, this argument may also be informed by the theological thought of, for example, the liberation theologian Gustavo Gutiérrez. Gutiérrez and fellow proponents of this kind of theology – such as Juan Luis Segundo and Jon Sobrino – agree that this "largely Latin-American movement (a) is inspired by the exodus, prophetic calls for justice, and Jesus' proclamation of the kingdom, (b) reads the Bible in the key of integral liberation, and (c) has struck deep roots where structures of injustice and economic dependence oppress great masses of poor people" (O'Collins and Farrugia, *Concise Dictionary*, 139–140). This strand of theology is "deeply concerned with the public function of theology in encouraging social change" (ibid.). His book, *A Theology of Liberation,* pictures the effect of the abuse of power. He discusses it in terms of selfishness, unjust structures, and therefore lack of freedom. He states, "For freedom Christ has set us free" (Gal 5:1), St Paul tells us. He refers here to liberation from sin insofar as it represents a selfish turning in upon oneself. To sin is to refuse to love one another's neighbors, and therefore, the Lord himself. Sin – a breach of friendship with God and others – is according to the Bible the ultimate cause of poverty, injustices, and the oppression in which men live" (Gutiérrez, *Theology of Liberation*, 35–36).

195. In fact, throughout this study thus far this connection has been made – in chapter 2, for example, with reference to the concept power from a secular anthropological perspective; the meaning of power in relation to a Tanzanian understanding of corruption; Amartya Sen's (*Development as Freedom*) broader definition of corruption based on the misuse of power, or in his terminology, the "betrayal of public trust" and "violation of public trust" (2.4.6.1); also the effects of misuse of power on human development and on justice from a human rights perspective. In this chapter, it formed the focus of section 3.6.2.

196. Groody, *Globalization, Spirituality,* 644 quoting from the papal encyclical *Gaudium et Spes*, 1965.

In theological terms, in the view of scholars such as Kelsey, Alexander and Spencer and others, by denying people justice, corruption denies them the necessary conditions conducive to what they call human flourishing. Corruption, with its exclusivity and obsession with "private benefit or gain," denies participation and empowerment of citizens towards working for the realization of a prosperous, healthy and fulfilled citizenry. And, according to Neville, "[s]ince justice is a central scriptural concern, it can hardly be marginal to Christian witness in public"[197] for

> [j]ustice weighs heavily on the moral scales not so much because it has exercised the minds of the mentally mighty, but because it bears directly on pressing social, cultural, political . . . concerns. . . . In biblical terms, justice might be said to be the moral equivalent of "holy ground."[198]

The head of Transparency International, Huguette Labelle, reminds us that in poor countries corruption often means the difference between life and death, having food or not, having access to clean water or health services and medication or not.[199] And according to Ochulor,

> [i]f we go by the simplest understanding of justice as giving someone his [sic] due, then we will easily see that since corruption deprives people of their due, their due in terms of the good roads and other facilities the money corruptly embezzled would have provided for them, *then corruption is morally wrong*.[200]

In light of the findings in this chapter, the following chapter will ask: If corruption therefore constitutes injustice and as such is biblically and theologically wrong, (1) why should *the church* as such, on theological grounds, participate in the fight against corruption and, if it should, (2) again on theological grounds, how may it do so? This will in turn prepare the way for chapter 5 of this study in which the focus will fall on the anti-corruption efforts or the lack thereof of the Anglican Church of Tanzania and the theological-ethical grounds these efforts are or may be based on.

---

197. Neville, "Justice and Divine Judgment," 356.
198. Ibid., 340.
199. Labelle, Opening Speech.
200. Ochulor, "Analysis of Corruption," 473 (emphasis added).

CHAPTER 4

Why the Church... and How?

The Public Role of the Church in the Context of Corruption

God's intent was that now, through the church, the manifold wisdom of God should be made known.

Ephesians 3:10

The church rediscovers her certainty as the church of Christ when she takes theology seriously and makes use of it in her daily life.

Attributed to Jürgen Moltmann

4.1 Introduction

In the second chapter of this study, a conceptual analysis of corruption and a contextual analysis of the phenomenon both in the history of and in contemporary Tanzanian society, were considered. The chapter ended by stating that not only is corruption rife in Tanzanian society, but that efforts to curb it thus far have been neither sufficient nor successful. It was also shown, in non-theological terms, what the possible causes and consequences of corruption are, especially as it not only leads to injustice, but how, in fact, it is itself a form of injustice. In chapter 3 the same issue was addressed, but from a theological-ethical and biblical perspective. It was shown that, as in the case of secular views on corruption, there can be no doubt that on theological and biblical grounds, corruption is wrong, sinful, and a manifestation of injustice. The focus now turns to the Christian response to corruption, in other words, the question of what may be done about corruption and how. One possibility is that the church engages in the fight against corruption. However, the background of this is first the issue of what is understood as "the church" and the broader issue of whether the church, on theological grounds, has a role to play in the public sphere at all. Only then can one ask how it may or should play this role with regard to corruption. In short, after having established what is meant by "the church," the chapter will consist of two parts, addressing two questions, namely "Why the church in the fight against corruption?" and "How?" In chapter 5 it will be asked, given the extent of corruption in Tanzanian society, whether and how the Anglican Church of Tanzania has been involved in the fight against corruption, or is currently doing so and, why or why not this is the case and whether it has been successful in any anti-corruption efforts.

In order to answer the latter two questions (why and how), this chapter will focus on public theology as it is this theological discipline in particular that seeks answers to the interrelated questions of "how [as a church] we should speak, to whom we should speak, when we should speak, about what we should we speak, what we should say and with what kind of authority we can speak in our own efforts to be Christian in public."[1] The most important contemporary conversation partners for this section will be public theologians – such as Duncan Forrester, Max Stackhouse, Dirk Smit and Nico Koopman, Will Storrar, etc. – but reference will also be made to a selected number of theologians in the history of the church whom are not necessarily thought of as public theologians. As the study progresses, reasons behind the choice of these scholars will be given. In light of the African and Anglican church focus of this study, reference will also be made to selected African theological voices and Anglican voices, although the exclusive focus will fall on the Anglican tradition only in chapter 5.

---

1. Koopman and Smit, "Public Witness in the Economic Sphere?" 272, with reference to Keith Clements.

4.2 Point of Departure: What Is "The Church"?

Although it is impossible within the scope of this study to give a comprehensive reflection on the nature of the church, it is important to note that if one is to appreciate the role of the Christian church and its value to society, a basic understanding of what constitutes "the church" is required. Again, as in the case with other key concepts in this study such as corruption and in/justice, to define the church is not an easy task and any such definition will be at least multifaceted.

4.2.1 The Church: Basic Biblical and Theological Considerations

Since Christ established the church, there has been and continues to be many descriptions of what constitutes the church. However, the meaning of "the church" can best be defined by looking at Scripture and its interpretation. This prepares the way of understanding the church's origins, nature, essence, and function/role in the world.

The Greek word *ekklēsia,* derived from *ek* (meaning "out of") and *klèsis* (meaning "a calling" – *kaleò,* to call), was used among the Greeks to refer to a body of citizens gathered to discuss the affairs of the state.[2] This word (*ekklēsia*) has also been traditionally regarded as the classic point of departure when biblical and theological scholars sought to define what the church is. It was a word used by New Testament communities themselves to designate who and what they were, albeit also in different ways. While Peter, for example, uses the word *ekklēsia* to demarcate a group of individual persons, who are depicted as the chosen people of God (1 Pet 2:9), Paul qualifies this group (the *ekklēsia*) as a special one, to the degree that it may be called the "body of Christ" because of its union with Christ (Eph 1:22–23).[3]

An emphasis on the concept of "calling" or "being called out" means that the church is definitely not the building in which people meet, as is often commonly understood, nor does it refer to the leadership of the institution,

---

2. Vine, *An Expository Dictionary*, 83.

3. The Letter to the Ephesians, with its exalted view of the church in God's plan of redemption, (among other things) was written in around 61–63 CE within a context of a struggle for unity within the Ephesian faith community and in order to remind it that the church should be seen in cosmic terms by emphasizing its unity in the metaphor of the body of Christ, with Christ as the head.

but rather it is the gathered people, those who become or form this specific community. This community responds to God's call in Jesus Christ. In fact, in biblical terminology, the church comes to existence, as Jesus explained, when "two or three are gathered in my name" (Matt 18:20). Again, from a biblical perspective, although during his lifetime Jesus himself was the physical focal point of this gathering of his followers, after his death, resurrection and ascension, the church continued to gather around Christ, who is seated at the right hand of God the Father (cf. Heb 12:22ff). In other words, every local church is a manifestation of this heavenly gathering.

Ferguson and Wright offer a good explanation of the church as both "a people called" and a "visible assembly":

> The church may [therefore] be defined as God sees it, the so-called "church invisible." This is composed of all whose names are in the Lamb's book of life (Rev 21:27). The "church visible," on the other hand, is the church as we see it, the family of believers. This distinction guards against equating membership in the church visible with salvation, or, on the other hand, disregarding public identification with God's people.[4]

From the above discussion and theologically speaking, Jesus Christ is central to the understanding of the church. Christ is the center of the church and is present with his people in the power of the Holy Spirit that dwells in and sustains the church. This idea is emphasized by many contemporary theologians including, for example, Jürgen Moltmann, according to whom "[w]ithout Christ, [there is] no church. There is only a church if and as long as Jesus of Nazareth is believed and acknowledged as the Christ of God."[5] This is understanding is expanded by, Möller, who observes that,

> [the church] is not an institution which is established and in which it is endeavored to bring people to Christ. . . . In this regard we should particularly note the expression: "Of Christ." Christ is there first and foremost, and then instituted the church

---

4. Ferguson and Wright, *New Dictionary of Theology*, 141.
5. Moltmann, *Church in the Power*, 66.

for himself as his body. That is why the church is known as the body of Christ.[6]

According to John Howard Yoder, the church to be a distinctive minority community,[7] marked out from the rest of society by its confession of faith, but a specific faith, that of the Lordship of Christ. The definition of the whole of human society, as opposed to the church, is exactly the absence of this confession.[8] For Charry, the church is an institution and is thus given a particular honorable identity and high calling by virtue of its "owner," who determined the corporate culture into which its members are acculturated.[9] Here words and phrases such as "by virtue of her owner," "corporate culture," and "acculturation" refer to the institution as having its own particular essence – which in turn is the fundamental nature of something apart from which the thing would not be what it is.[10] Essence, then, is the core of what makes something what it is without being something else; in the case of the church it is its head, Christ. Furthermore, linked with the idea of morality, are the concepts of "following Jesus" and "bearing testimony," which are central to Christians as the church. This will be so particularly with regard to the issue of corruption – as, for example, in Stassen and Gushee's view of "Jesus as manifesting the character that we are to imitate and the purpose of life we are to pursue."[11]

Other aspects of the essence of the church are the Word and the sacraments. In one of the classic works of Reformed theology, *The Institutes of the Christian Religion*, John Calvin defines the church exactly in these terms: "Wherever we see the Word of God to be purely preached and heard, [and]

---

6. Möller, *Kingdom Of God*, 75.

7. Likewise, Yoder emphasizes the membership of the church as those who have been visibly identified as "other" by "baptism, discipline, morality and martyrdom" (Yoder, *Royal Priesthood*, 56).

8. Yoder, *Politics of Jesus*, 108.

9. Charry, "Sacramental Ecclesiology," 201.

10. According to Grenz, Guretzki and Nordling, *Pocket Dictionary*, 46.

11. Stassen and Gushee, *Kingdom Ethics*, 59. Paeth (*Exodus, Church and Civil Society*, 161–64) refers to a "messianic ethic," i.e. to Jesus's teaching that offers the church a model, a norm and a mandate towards prophetic witness.

the sacraments to be administered according to the institution of Christ, there we cannot doubt that a church exists."[12]

Furthermore, according to the New Testament, the term "church" refers also to a meeting of Jesus's followers or, indeed, any gathering of people who believe in God or all people who are Christians *in a particular area*. This emphasis on locality thus applies to people who belong to a group of believers even when they are not gathered together. This also implies that believers in a particular locality may be under the special oversight or care of a group of elders or leaders. However, the church can also refer to all believers everywhere, to the worldwide church of God. Edmund P. Clowney and Gerald Lewis Bray write on this nature of the church as a worldwide communion, that of its catholicity.[13] In their words, "Catholicity is found in the church's identity [which is, according to him, founded on its relationship to the triune God], not simply in geography, numbers or sociological statistics."[14]

To summarize, in the above basic understanding of the church, two concepts are crucial: one is that the church consists of a group of people that are followers of Jesus Christ, and the second is that the church is also the community in which God lives by his Spirit. Moltmann offers a fitting description of the latter when he observes that the church is the fellowship of believers who follow the one Lord and have been laid hold of by the one Spirit.[15]

This community lives by following biblical practices and beliefs, professes faith in the living God, and bears testimony in word and deed to the reality of salvation through Jesus Christ according the Scriptures. This community is, furthermore, described in the New Testament not only as the body of Christ (1 Cor 12:12–31), but also in other telling ways, such as the "family of God" (Eph 3:14), a "community of covenant people" (1 John 4:21), and a "gathering or assembly of citizens" (Heb 12:23). In influential twentieth-century Protestant theologian Karl Barth's words (which includes all the elements of call, community and the triune God): "The Church is a summoning forth of God's people, the community of men [sic] of faith,

---

12. John Calvin, *Institutes of the Christian Religion*, Vol. 4, 1.9.
13. Clowney and Bray, *Church*.
14. Ibid., 93.
15. Moltmann, *Theology of Hope*, 106.

created through Christ on the foundation of the Covenant between God and man [sic], and awakened by the Holy Spirit."[16]

To return to the etymology of the word *ekklēsia* as referring to the "ones called out," Grenz argues that early Christians saw themselves as a people belonging to God, those called out by God in Christ for the purpose of the proclamation of the gospel and that has important implications (for the purposes in this study as well) as it already determines something of the nature of the church's role *in public*.[17] This role is summarized by John Calvin to mean an actual type of responsibility to be, in the classic formulation, "God's people as priestly, prophetic, and kingly" (a detailed public-theological understanding and the implications of these three concepts will be discussed in section 4.3.2.3 below as they feature in the theology of, especially, Nico Koopman).[18]

4.2.2 The Many Faces of the Church: Dirk Smit on the Social Forms of the Church

In preparation to the discussion that follows later, on what the church may or should do in the fight against corruption, at this stage and following the broad background given above to what constitutes the church, South African theologian Dirk Smit's understanding of "the social forms of the church" is particularly useful.

Based on the concepts of witness and service within denominations and church institutions, Smit posits six social forms of the church.[19] For Smit, these forms are meant to be and should be viewed as concrete and visible forms and refer to the church as: (1) the worshipping community, (2) the local congregation, (3) the denomination (4) the ecumenical church (5), individual believers, and (6) voluntary initiatives and activities by members of the church in society.

Where the church exists as *local congregations* and as *worshipping communities*, it is meant to be first and foremost a community that honors God. In other words, the first duty of believers is to put God first. The church is

---

16. Quoted in Johnson, *Mystery of God*, 138.
17. Grenz, *Theology for the Community*, 464.
18. Quoted in Heath, "Church and Ministry," 328.
19. Smit, "On Learning to See?" 55–77.

to bring to God the prayers and the honor due to God's name (1 Pet 2:5). However, for Smit, this duty is also broader in that worship and congregations also entails life in local congregations, their policies and the practices of respective *denominations*. Within this social form, a clear relationship exists between liturgy and life, and worship and ethics are key to how the church can and should seek, as a worshipping community, to witness and give service to the community. Smit acknowledges that the style of how this becomes functional may not be the same, as denominations and congregations differ. However, he maintains that the dynamics of social processes would be almost the same in that they are set within the worshipping community which forms a unique identity, be it collectively or individually. It is within these communities that characters are formed which shape the community at large.

As far as the *denominations and the ecumenical church* are concerned, Smit suggests that it is here where "the dramatic effects of the radical social transformation processes are already most clearly to be seen."[20] The focus here is on role of the church played in united efforts within different denominations and ecumenical churches. Smit, for example, identifies and gives examples from a South African perspective on such initiatives in the work of the "National Religious Leaders' Forum, who regularly meets with the president and other government officials." Especially relevant to this study, is Smit's reference to the work of the "[South African] Moral Regeneration Movement, focusing on moral issues, like corruption and moral formation."

As a *voluntary organization,* Smit sees churches, like other organizations, in terms of their structures and systems of governance and continuity. He looks at the roles of *individual believers or Christians* by putting an emphasis on spirituality, witness and actions of individual believers. Here Smit applies the metaphor of "salt of the earth" and "light to the world" to show that the way in which the believer lives and acts has gospel implications in the sense that a follower of Christ has and is required to live according to the teaching of the head of the church, Christ himself. In other words, this means

---

20. Smit, *Essays on Being Reformed*, 403. Other scholars have also defined the church by looking at it from an ecumenical point of view, that is to say the church as ecumenical body, which refers to churches entering into meaningful partnerships in which, according to George (*Called as Partners*, 35), a "first concern [is] to get to know one another and [to] cultivate relationships by observing, listening, and asking questions."

an individual believer is called to be and to manifest to the world, through the church, a model of a society that reflects biblical values. This can also be achieved in the effective use of gifts. For example, Anglican theologian Rowan Williams sees the individual believer in the context of what an individual believer could and is supposed to offer to the service of the church. He says that, "[t]he New Testament sees church as a community in which each person has a gift that only he or she can give into the common life."[21]

For some scholars, latter forms of the church are sometimes expressed in terms of the church as a "missional church." This means, that the mission of service and witness occurs where the church, in the power of the Holy Spirit, with integrity, in obedience and in following Christ with compassion and in humility but also in boldness, serves others and witnesses to God's love for the world. In reaching out to all people, new borders are continuously crossed and service and witness are not to be separated. Examples of proponents of such a view includes Bosch, Hunsberger and Van Gelder, Guder, and Newbigin.[22]

With this in mind and moving in the direction of the discussion of the possible role of the church in the public sphere, it is also interesting to see how Duty's views echo that of Smit's in the formers statements that local

> [c]ongregations are called to public life. The lives of congregations are inherently public. When congregations live the life to which they are called they both invite people to faith in Jesus Christ as members of his public community and form and shape the faith of their members for public witness and service in the world.[23]

Duty also echoes Smit with regard to his view on the local congregation and its worship services where "congregations help to form the character and conscience of individuals who become Christian actors in the public sphere."[24] In fact, "the more Christians participate in public life the more

---

21. Williams, "Challenge and Hope of Being an Anglican Today."

22. Bosch, *Believing in the Future*; Van Gelder, *Church*; Guder, *Missional Church*; and Newbigin, *Gospel*.

23. Duty, "Congregations and Public Life," 271.

24. Ibid., 279. This idea will again become very important in 4.4.1.3 with regard to kingdom values and the church as community of character.

they develop attitudes and behavior that contribute to their public moral agency as both Christians and as actors in civil society."²⁵ With this in mind, the role of the church in the public square moves directly into focus in this chapter.

4.3 The Fight against Corruption: Why the Church?

4.3.1 The Church in the Public Square – A Centuries-Old Question

The next crucial question that has to be attended to is whether the church has a place or role in the public sphere or in public life at all. Within this study, the question, of course, has consequences for the question of whether the church has a role in public sphere and public life in *the fight against corruption*.

A good starting point for this discussion is the acknowledgement that the question of the place of the church in the public sphere is a centuries-old question, in fact, it is as old as the church itself. According to Ringer and Glock:

> [h]istorically, the role of the church in society has been a subject arousing considerable controversy. The controversy is about as manifest today as at any time in history [and it] centers around the question of what areas of life properly fall within the authority and responsibility of the church. Particularly at issue has been and continues to be the church's responsibility in social, economic, and political affairs.²⁶

The persistence of the issue of the place of the church in the public sphere will be reflected below with reference to a few selected theologians from four main periods of the history of the church: the early church, the scholastic Middle Ages, two from the Reformation and one Protestant representative (probably the most famous one) of the twentieth century.

---

25. Ibid., 283.
26. Ringer and Glock, "Political Role," 338.

These are: Augustine of Hippo (354–430), Thomas Aquinas (1226–1274), Martin Luther (1483–1546), John Calvin (1509–1564), and Karl Barth (1886–1968). This will help to give some idea of the breadth of the discussion on the subject.

The second reason for this historical detour is that some of the key ideas of these theologians carry with them important insights to usher in reflection on the development of the contemporary discourse as well as establishing foundations on how the church can contribute to the fight against corruption and injustice.

4.3.1.1 Augustine's The City Of God: *A Separation of the Church and State?*

Arguably the greatest of the (Western) early church fathers, Augustine of Hippo, lived at the end of the fourth century and the beginning of the fifth century CE. He lived in the time traditionally known as the era of the emergence of Christian political world.[27] Augustine's view of the role of the church in the public sphere is found mainly in his major work *The City of God*, a work that was written when he became the Bishop of Hippo in 396 CE. In this work Augustine was responding to, among other things, immoral tendencies he saw in the churches, among its members and leaders under his jurisdiction. As Giles puts it, Augustine saw people living unregenerate lives as "the covetous, the defrauders, the robbers, the usurers and the drunkards."[28] In doing this, Augustine identifies two types of cities defined by Knowles as follows:

> The earthly city [which was] was created by self-love reaching the point of contempt for God, [and] the heavenly city that by the love of God carried as far as contempt of self. In fact the earthly city glories in itself, the heavenly city glories in the Lord.[29]

At first glance, such a dualistic point of departure makes Augustine seem set against any public role for the church. However, it may be that as the

---

27. cf. Fortin, *Political Idealism*.
28. Giles, *What on Earth Is the Church?* 190.
29. Augustine, *City of God*, 593.

church seeks to claim a place in the public sphere, it simply has to bear in mind that the two cities are different. However, the same cities also have the ability to influence each other either positively or negatively. Webber, for example, suggests that "[f]or Augustine, the state is a human society . . . and as such it contains members of both the city of God and the city of man."[30] He goes on to indicate how important individual believers can play their part more fruitfully by saying, "[i]f those who control the state have at the same time a final commitment to God, their influence will be felt in the social order." This is not to say that Augustine outright opposes the state, nor is he against the involvement of Christians in the government. But rather, Webber insists, for Augustine, "God is 'now' ruling his world through the church" and at the same time "the church assumes the shape of the society."[31]

From the perspective of the two central issues of this study, namely corruption and in/justice, Augustine's thought is useful. As a churchman he condemns the human lust for power. As was shown in the previous chapter, the lust for power often leads to its abuse and this often lies at the root of corruption. Augustine, for example, rightly asks whether "[i]s it reasonable, is it sensible to boast of the extent and grandeur of empire when you cannot show that men lived in happiness, as they passed their lives amidst horrors of war?"[32]

On the theme of justice/injustice, Augustine is not silent either. For him,

> [j]ustice, not power is the essence of the state . . . [r]emove justice . . . and what are kingdoms but gangs of criminals on a large scale? What are criminal gangs but petty kingdoms? A gang is a group of men under the command of a leader, bound by a compact of association, in which the plunder is divided according to an agreed convention.[33]

Augustine's position on justice is that "ideal justice cannot be realized in political society."[34] This argument is elaborated on by Webber, who inter-

---

30. Webber, *Secular Saint*, 140.
31. Ibid., 142.
32. Augustine, *City of God*, IV.3.138.
33. Ibid., IV.4.139.
34. Weithman, "Augustine's Political Philosophy," 244.

prets Augustine's position by including the idea of the role of church and Christians in public sphere.³⁵ Webber writes that,

> [w]hile no society on earth can fully express this justice, the one that is more influenced by Christians and Christian teaching will more perfectly reflect a just society. For this reason Christians have a duty toward government.

Conclusively, it is reasonable to suggest that the overriding approach of Augustine to the place of the church in the public sphere concerns the effort to change any unjust society. Augustine contends that the church's role could be in teaching and worship where values such as justice can best be experienced whenever God is truly worshipped.³⁶

Finally, Rowan Williams offers a summary of what transpired in the discussion above on Augustine's contribution to bringing a particular Christian understanding of human beings and the nature of reality into political life:

> . . . at one end of that spectrum stands, very clearly, a world in which the citizens are living for one another because of their love of the infinite, the limitless, endless good and beauty that is God: because they are torn out of their selfishness by that love for the divine beauty. They are instinctively generous to one another and able to live by bearing each other's costs and burdens.³⁷

4.3.1.2 *Thomas Aquinas and the Principle of Cooperation between Faith and Power*

Thomas Aquinas, for many the greatest Roman Catholic theologian of all time, was without doubt the most influential thinker of the High Middle Ages, a time that saw the rise of the medieval political world and the height of what is known as Scholasticism. Aquinas's theological legacy is found, according to Kerr, in his "ability to equip the church with the intellectual weaponry necessary to rethink Christianity in terms of modern thought."³⁸

---

35. Webber, *Secular Saint*, 140.
36. cf. Pinsent, *Second-Person*, 108ff.
37. Williams, "Relations between the Church."
38. Kerr, *Thomas Aquinas*, 116.

To explore Thomas Aquinas's views of the role of the church in the public sphere, one has to look at his most famous work, the *Summa Theologiae*. In it, Aquinas lays down principles of his understanding of, among other things, God and world. In this work he also focuses on the importance of the church, laws, human actions, justice, human social and spiritual condition, human nature and the common good, and the necessity of a relationship between civil and religious authorities.[39]

The principles Aquinas lays down are based on (for him) the sources of knowledge. Aquinas understand there to be two such sources: the mysteries of Christian faith and the truths of human reason.[40] For Aquinas, sound philosophical thinking would help individual Christians and the church to recognize the "essential order of life in societies." The mysteries of Christian faith, on the other hand, help the church to understand and work under the biblical "notions that sin is an action which goes against reason, [therefore], mankind needs laws to govern behavior."[41]

However, Aquinas also goes beyond the notion of sin and views the church an institution that cares for souls, and he also believes that the very church that cares and the state are ultimately complementary. His further thoughts linked to the possible role of the church in the public sphere and public life centers on the necessity to understand the nature of human beings and their well-being, or in his words, the "common good" and the necessity of government.[42]

For Aquinas, human beings require political rule for their social survival. The survival he talks about concerns human life as a whole: "*totius humanae vitae.*"[43] "Human life as a whole" has to do with knowing and relating appropriately according to God's purpose for humanity in the world – the so-called "transcendent cause of all being."[44] Aquinas sees kings or governments as institutions whose purpose is, among others, to prevent chaos. He also sees political institutions as key to fostering knowledge, culture and virtue.

---

39. cf. Weithman, "Complementarity and Equality."
40. Sigmund, *St. Thomas Aquinas*, 80–89.
41. Kerr, *Thomas Aquinas*, 115.
42. Murphy, "Consent, Custom," 323.
43. Thomas Aquinas, *Summa Theologica* I–II, Q. 2, Art. 2, *ad* 2.
44. Aquinas, Sum I–II, Q. 94, Art. 2, *ad 3*.

Through this fostering of knowledge, Aquinas argues, human beings are enabled to pursue their ultimate end themselves – the enjoyment of God. If this is not made possible by the political institutions, governments or kings, says Aquinas, it is *the church* that should seek to make it possible because the church "has the authority of curbing secular rulers."[45]

In the public sphere and public life Aquinas, however, believes that there are critical limitations. He believes that "spiritual goods" (whose source is Scripture) excel other goods, but in order for these spiritual goods to become a reality, secular goods of peace, order, justice, protection of the family, and the freedom to practice the Catholic faith must be made available in any society. Unfortunately, according to Aquinas, these goods cannot be sustained unless *Christian faith* and not only reason are applied. In other words, the church is a key player in public life because political rulers' natural capacities have limitations.[46]

4.3.1.3 Martin Luther and the Principle of "Two Kingdoms"

The time in which the Reformers Luther and Calvin lived is also traditionally referred to as the era in which the basis of modern political thought was established. While Augustine's antithetical thoughts are based on the "City of God" versus the "City of Man," and Aquinas' on spiritual goods versus secular goods and natural versus revealed knowledge, Martin Luther's view of the life of the Christian and the church in the public sphere may be conceived as also rooted in a basic dualism by some. Ebeling summarizes this issue as follows:

> Luther's thought always contains an antithesis, tension between strongly opposed but related priorities: theology and philosophy, the letter and the spirit, the law and the gospel, the double use of the law, person and works, faith and love, the kingdom of Christ and the kingdom of the world, man [sic] as a Christian

---

45. Aquinas, Sum II–II, Q. 12, Art. 2, *ad* 1.

46. This argument, is contrary to some scholars' view that Aquinas shows a "lack of interest in politics and his few comments on the relationship between church and State" in the *Summa Theologiae* is evidence of this. See Kerr (*Thomas Aquinas*) and Luscombe ("State of Nature," 757–758).

and man in the world, freedom and bondage, God hidden and God revealed.[47]

For our purposes, the focus on Luther's thoughts is due to the fact that it is to this aspect that Luther tends to identify his approach regarding the role of the church in the public sphere and public life. For Luther, as Webber puts it, "God works in the world through the state and the church," which also means that church and Christians are called to live according to this dual commitment.[48]

It follows, therefore, that "since [a Christian] is under God both in state and in the church, he [sic] is constantly caught in the tension between these spheres in matters of time, talents and energy."[49] According to Mueller, Luther's "concept of secular authority" is that "civil order is ordained by God" and the concept of church as "a spiritual entity that is being built, as it were, from above."[50] William J. Wright recently commented that "[u]ntil the mid-nineteenth century, Luther's ideas on the two kingdoms had not been greatly politicized, even though the concept had been absorbed into the state-church constitutions of the German territorial and dynastic states."[51]

Although the two entities, church and state, can naturally coincide, Luther's fundamental argument thus seems that government rules in secular affairs and the church rules in with regard to spiritual matters.[52] In his famous phrase, Luther seem to say that Christians live in "two kingdoms" that are differentiated by what Christians are expected to experience from each of the two kingdoms. While in one kingdom they hear the gospel and experience the love of God in Jesus Christ, in the other kingdom, they listen to the secular or political authority, state or government and, therefore, experience and obey the law. Christians are expected to do this because it is God who ordained political authority. Christians are, therefore, called to obey, honor, respect and pray for their rulers (with reference to 1 Tim 2:12; 1 Pet 2:13–17) and are required to also pay their taxes (Rom 13:7).

---

47. Ebeling, *Luther,* 25.
48. Webber, *Secular Saint,* 133.
49. Ibid.
50. Mueller, *Church and State,* 7.
51. Wright, *Martin Luther's Understanding,* 20.
52. cf. O'Donovan and O'Donovan, *Bonds of Imperfection.*

In turn, the state is expected to promote the good – such as peace, justice and rights – and it is the duty of the state to punish evil in earthly life (with reference to Rom 13:34). Luther observes that,

> [t]herefore, care must be taken to keep these two governments distinct and both must be allowed to continue their work, the one to make people just, the other to create outward peace and prevent evil-doing. Neither is enough for the world without the other. Without the spiritual government of Christ, no one can be made just in the sight of God by the secular government . . . And equally where the spiritual government rules over a country and its people unaided, every sort of wickedness is let loose and every sort of knavery has free play.[53]

It is important to indicate that Luther's theology was perhaps not as dualistic as it at first glance seems. Even if Luther distinguished between the two "kingdoms" this does not necessarily imply separating them. In his thinking on the kingdom of God (*regnum Dei*), the latter is opposed to the kingdom of the world in the sense of the fallen world or the kingdom of the Devil (*regnum diaboli*). Despite this, however, God is *not* simply in opposition to the world, because the world includes both the *regnum diaboli* and the *regnum terrena*, the rule of God over the earth. The church is to have nothing to do with the *regnum diaboli*, but the church should participate in the affairs of the world, because God is concerned with the world that God has created and seeks to save. The over-emphasis of dualism in Luther's thoughts is probably related to the distinction drawn by Ulrich Duchrow and Dorothea Millwood between Luther's own theology and subsequent Lutheran theology.[54] In this way there exists today a view of Luther's take on the role of the church in the public sphere as being much more compartmentalized and it may also be what one finds behind Stackhouse's comment on the "kind of social implication of the law/gospel dichotomy [that are] characteristics of Lutheran thought."[55]

---

53. Luther, "On Secular Authority," 12.
54. Duchrow and Millwood, *Lutheran Churches*.
55. Stackhouse, *Making the Best of It*, 27.

4.3.1.4 John Calvin: The Public Gospel, the Christian Faith and Public Duty

John Calvin was a major theological thinker of the Reformation. He is known for his loyalty to the truth as he saw it in the Word of God. The insights he provides in his major work *Institutes of the Christian Religion* provides one with the biblical and theological keys to help the church's engagement in public sphere and public life.

Calvin, for example, proposed the form in which the Christian faith is related to church-state relations. He believed that the church should not be subject to the state or vice versa, because church and state are both subject to God's law and consequently he insists that the two institutions have their own God-ordained and separate spheres of influence. He thus warns that the state should not interfere on the day-to-day work of the church.

Calvin's view of the role of the church in the public sphere is a consequence of his brand of Reformed faith. The heart of his presuppositions, especially on issues such as the relationship church and state, rests on key foundations of his thinking. These are the sovereignty of God, the authority of Scripture and his views of humanity, sin and salvation. As these foundations determine Calvin's thinking, we shall explore them somewhat further to come to an understanding of what Calvin is saying regarding the place of the church in the public sphere and public life.

To understand what Calvin's *sovereignty of God* implies to the public sphere and public life, Henry van Til observes that

> God's sovereignty is the atmosphere in which the Calvinist lives, the milieu in which he [sic] acts as a cultural being. It means that religion is not a life of things apart, but the end-all and be-all of man's [sic] life under the sun.[56]

Van Til's observation suggests that, according to Calvin, religion is not limited to a particular space to the extent that it leaves others outside of it. It does extend and encompasses every sphere of human life. It not only concerns a person's personal belief and private devotion, but all of life and works. God is sovereign over God's entire creation. This sovereignty of God has implications for both the role of the church and the role of the state.

---

56. Van Til, *Calvinistic Concept*, 53.

First, as Mueller observes, "[t]he church and the state are both subject to the *regnum Dei et Christi*. The authority of both spheres inheres in the will and purpose of the living God."[57]

Regarding the authority of Scripture, humanity, sin and salvation, Biéler and Wolterstorff see the link between what Calvin sees in humanity, sin and salvation and a Christian message of salvation found in the Word of God, in that the message could become futile unless its implications are extended throughout the whole of human life (i.e. also into political and social structures).[58] Arguably this is why, for Calvin, faithful teaching of the Word of God is to be at the helm of the ministry of the church. As referred to earlier, in his *Institutes*, Calvin defines the church as "[w]herever we see the Word of God purely preached and heard, and the sacraments administered according to Christ's institution."[59] Again, what is brought to the fore is the primacy of the Word of God for Calvin. If the church is understood in this way, then it has tasks to perform with regard to the state, and Graham identifies four such tasks as per Calvin's enumeration:

> [t]o pray for the political authorities, to encourage the state to defend the poor and weak against the rich and powerful, to ensure its own status by calling on the political authorities for help in promoting true religion and even enforcing ecclesiastical discipline and to warn the authorities when they are at fault.[60]

In summarizing, the four tasks above indicate that, for Calvin, the church has a particular role to play towards the state. Thus, Webber affirms the fact that

> [i]n Calvinistic thoughts, the origin and purpose of the church, points to the necessity of Christian involvement [in the public sphere] . . . If the Christian submits to what he understands the will of God to be in the state, the order of society will be stable and sin will be held in check.[61]

---

57. Mueller, *Church and State*, 127.
58. Biéler, *Calvin's Economic*, and Wolterstorff, *Until Justice and Peace Embrace*.
59. Calvin, *Institutes*, 1023.
60. Graham, *Constructive Revolutionary*, 61ff.
61. Webber, *Secular Saint*, 149.

For Calvin, "[i]nvolvement in government is therefore a calling"[62] and, as we shall see later in this study, Calvin's ecclesiological insights have contributed considerably in the church's engagement in modern secular democracy in Africa and beyond.

4.3.1.5 Karl Barth and the Church Called to Partnership with the State

Karl Barth is in all probability the most influential Reformed theologian of the twentieth century. Much of the significance of his contribution to the Christian faith and theology in relation to the role of the church in the public sphere is to be found in the way he applied theology to day-to-day life. He is known for his ability to dig deeply into Scripture and for his interaction with context. For Karl Barth, "theology . . . [has] to converse with context."[63]

Although Barth should not be expected to give answers to each and every theological challenge that faces the church as it engages the public sphere and public life, his influential theological work, *Church Dogmatics,* reveals not only his christological theology and his christological point of departure in his theology, but also his understanding of key issues pertaining to the role of the church in the world.

Barth believes that "Dogmatics tests the Church's speech about God."[64] This is because, at the disposal of the church are two sources that test its listening: Scripture and tradition.[65] Barth's insight helps us to appreciate Scripture as a fundamental tool/resource in public engagement. For Barth, it requires the church to measure its ability to speak about God in truth.[66] This can best be achieved if the church lives with the expectation that it hears the Word of God afresh.[67]

---

62. Ibid.

63. cf. Hordern, "Barth as Political Thinker," 412; Busch, *Karl Barth* and Jehl, *Ever Against the Stream,* 80.

64. Barth, *Church Dogmatics,* 781.

65. Ibid., 816, 822.

66. Ibid., 270.

67. Ibid., 810.

In the light of the church's mission, Barth goes on to describe the twofold function of dogmatics in the church.[68] The first requires the church to be a hearing church.[69] Barth describes this function in the following way:

> Dogmatics invites the teaching church to listen again to the Word of God in the revelation to which Scripture testifies. It can do this only if for its own part it adopts the attitude of the hearing church and therefore itself listens to the Word of God as the norm to which the hearing church knows itself to be subject.[70]

Furthermore, Barth articulates the nature of public engagement of the church by pleading that "[a] silent community, merely observing the event of time, would not be a Christian community."[71] He strongly asserts that "Christians are not called to be passive observers of their situation."[72] According to Hordern, this insight makes Barth unique among theologians of his time. Hordern writes,

> [a]ll the great 20th-century theologians started out as political radicals who attacked the status quo. But as the years passed they became conservatives who supported the status quo. All except Karl Barth; he remained a radical to the end.[73]

It is also believed that Barth "helped the church to rediscover the Bible [and] called the church to social and political responsibility."[74] As he strived to demonstrate the meaning, function, and modes of engagement of the community of Christian believers – the church in public sphere and public life – Barth did not, as Green puts it, "construct or write his theology in isolation from the rest of the world . . . his theological views speak directly to the heart of human experience."[75]

---

68. Ibid., 797–884.
69. Ibid., 797.
70. Ibid.
71. Karl Barth quoted in Jehl, *Ever Against the Stream*, 80.
72. Barth, *Church Dogmatics*, 711.
73. Horder, "Barth as Political Thinker," 412.
74. Hunsinger, *Karl Barth and Radical Politics*, 82.
75. Greem, *Karl Barth*, 98–113.

Based on his principle of church's partnership with the state, Barth outlines different roles that both institutions (church and state) should play. For example, while the church can dedicate its mission to the state largely as one of intercessory prayer,[76] the church is called to testify a message of hope, and in so doing the state receives a similar call, but this time a call that directs this instrument to oversee and promote the well-being of its citizens.[77] So, for Barth, the state has a responsibility to look after its citizens and to promote a sense of community.[78]

From the perspective Karl Barth's ecclesiology, the church is understood in terms of its relationship with different parties: God, religions, people and institutions outside the Christian faith, the state. However, unlike other parties, the church's main perspective arises from the call to be in partnership with the state.[79] The church, therefore, has to carry a responsibility both as people of faith and as faithful citizens to engage with the powers and to facilitate discussion on the basis of morals and principles of the Christian faith.

4.3.2 The Church's Role in the Public Sphere: From History to Contemporary (Public-Theological) Perspectives[80]

The foregoing discussion is a clear demonstration that theologians over the centuries struggled with the question of what it means to be the church in

---

76. Barth, *Community, State and Church*, 135.
77. Barth, *Ethics II*, 445.
78. Ibid.
79. Barth, *Community, State and Church*, 144.

80. Care must be taken that the discussion of the views and emphases of different contemporary public theologicans does not necessarily mean that there exists total agreement among these scholars. Due to limits of space, the study took an approach, as Jacobsen suggests, of "mapping and grouping similar contributions" (Jacobsen "Models of Public Theology," 8) from selected public theologians. Technically speaking though, it is also worth noting that "[s]uch mapping will not be able to do justice to the [detailed] specificity of thought, but it has its value in providing a systematic view of the different perspectives that are presented in the name of a 'public theology'" (ibid., 8). It is important to remember, as we have already indicated in our abstract, this study falls within the field of Christian ethics, but also on an intradisciplinary level it finds itself within the relatively new field of "public theology." With regard to the latter, Smit rightly insists "there exists no single and authoritative meaning of public theology and no single normative way of doing public theology" (Smit, "Notions of the Public and Doing Theology," 443). That said, it is critical to note that each selected public theologian focuses on "addressing different audiences, such as the academy and the church (model of the audience); articulating itself through a style

the public sphere and in public life. In spite of the fact that the detailed arguments in the examples vary, they share some significant characteristics. None of them were silent on or required silence from the church in the public sphere. In fact, when looking at the above historical perception, they identify certain key issues that are all important to this study.

First, all of them to some degree allude to the need for the church *to be aware* of the social, moral and cultural concerns of their time. This suggestion is substantiated by some commentators, such as Webber and Graham, who suggest that the views of these theologians could be regarded as referring to "a transformational approach or model" with regard to the church's role in public sphere.[81] To summarize the latter point, Webber observes that a

> ... transformational model sees the church as that social context in which the redeemed reality is to be modelled. The church is more than a mere collection of believers. It is a new community called to exemplify the principles of the kingdom and thus to have a saving effect on all the structures of life.[82]

Second, all the historical examples given in the previous section agree that an important aspect of the role of the church in the public sphere concerns *the way individual Christians live in society.*[83]

Third, all show some consciousness of a *connection between the secular and sacred, public and private* in what is sometimes referred to as "dualistic thought." As already noted, the church lives both in this world and in the kingdom – meaning that both governments/States and the church are ordained by God, but the church and Christians do point toward the ultimate kingdom of Christ.

---

and an accessible form of argument (apologetic model); addressing contextual challenges (contextual model)" (Jacobsen "Models of Public Theology," 7). See also Tracy's audiences; "the wider society, the academy, and the church" (Tracy, *Analogical Imagination*, 3, 5) all of which shows, as we have earlier on stipulated, each public theologian has a different concern and emphasis in his approach. The indicative possible points of conflict sufficiently highlighted in this study justifies the fact that "theology is . . . incarnate in the pains, faith and hopes of people . . . and is not an empty and irrelevant discourse" (Jacobsen, "Models of Public Theology," 22).

81. Webber, *Secular Saint,* and Graham, *Constructive Revolutionary.*
82. Webber, *Secular Saint,* 164.
83. cf. Barth, *Church Dogmatics,* 711, and Rousseau, *Social Contract,* 206.

Fourth, it is clear that these theologians affirm the fact that there has been and continues to be *more than one way or approach* for the church and Christians to live and participate in a responsible relationship with and in the world – the public sphere. This includes the concept of the church being "public" – that which is marked, as Duty puts it, "by a concern for the public order of society and for the common life among people"[84] – to Berger and Neuhaus, who contend that the church is public in that it "is a primary agent for bearing and transmitting the operative values for our society."[85] In fact, some scholars, such as Berger and Neuhaus and Habermas – especially in his seminal work *The Structural Transformation of the Public Sphere* – have concluded that for centuries the church has either attempted to transform, or, in fact separated itself or identified with the public sphere. Duty believes that history has shown that

> [t]he more Christians participate in the public life of their congregations and in the public life of the larger society, whether as part of their congregation's ministry or not, the more they develop attitudes, values, knowledge, skills, and behaviour that contribute to their public moral agency as both Christians and as actors in civil society.[86]

Today, this ongoing debate (i.e. on the role of the church in the public sphere) is central to what some scholars such as Forrester, Stackhouse, Smit, Koopman, Storrar and Williams and others call the discipline of public theology.[87] To this end, the study now turns to contemporary public-theological reflections. The focus will be on the views of a series of theologians as they speak on *why* and *how* the church has a role to play in the public sphere as

---

84. Duty, "Congregations and Public Life," 281.
85. Berger and Neuhaus, *To Empower People*, 30.
86. Duty, "Congregations and Public Life," 283.
87. Contemporary definitions of public theology include that it is a "kingdom of God theology." As such it "intervenes critically and prophetically in the public affairs of a given society, and draws public attention, not to the church's own interests, but to 'God's kingdom, God's commandment and his righteousness,' as Thesis 5 of the Barmen Theological Declaration says" (cf. Moltmann, *Church in the Power*). According to Clive Pearson, "public theology is that theology which seeks to provide resources for people to make connections between their faith and the practical issues facing society. It does not seek to 'convert,' but is concerned with the secular well-being of society" ("What is Public Theology?" 1).

it seems indeed to be the case that, in the words of Anglican Bishop Michael Nazir-Ali, "[we] are now . . . in a context where we will not be able to escape the problems raised by faith for public life. The question . . . is not 'should faith have a role in public life?' but 'what kind of role it should have?'"[88]

4.3.2.1 Duncan Forrester: Public Theology as Conversation in an Unsystematic and Fragmented Context

Duncan Forrester's contribution to contemporary theology flows from his interest in theological reflection on the relationship between Christianity, ethics and society. It is embedded in and forms part of a strand of public theology from a Presbyterian perspective.[89] With regard to the relationship between Christianity, ethics and society, Forrester is passionate about the articulation of theology from practical, public and political perspectives. Like North American theologian, David Tracy,[90] Forrester is convinced that the foundation for fruitful theological discourse is based in the fact that theology must be understood as conversation.

With the latter in mind, Forrester considers forms of discourse as a way of doing public theology and ethics. At the same time, in this way theology should remain sensitive to other voices within the public square, but without forsaking the fact that *Christian* public participation should be informed by God's revelation. As such, for Forrester, the best theology should on the one hand always begin with a genuine knowledge and experience of "the concrete, the particular, the person, or the issue" and, on the other hand, should then proceed to seeking "insight from Scripture and the tradition,

---

88. Nazir-Ali, "Breaking Faith with Britain," 45.

89. Forrester is emeritus professor of Christian ethics and practical theology at the University of Edinburgh. He has been a well-known voice in public-theological circles for many decades. In 2004 a publication by fellow scholars from across the world titled *Public Theology for the 21st Century* was published in Forrester's honor. In this book, Forrester's journey and commitment to public theology is clear (see, e.g. Storrar and Morton, *Public Theology*, 1–7). He is also the founder of the Centre for Theology and Public Issues at the University of Edinburgh and its director from 1984 to 2000. Some of the themes in the Centre and Forrester's work include the welfare state or welfare society, ethics and economics of the distribution of income and wealth, education and community, finances and ethics, the renewal of social vision, justice, guilt and forgiveness in the penal system, security, solidarity and peace-making, work, worth and community, responding to the crisis of work and exploring the increased risk of suicide among young men (ibid., 3–4).

90. Tracy, for whom *all* theology constitutes public discourse/conversation depending on the "public" theologians address – *Plurality and Ambiguity*, 114.

and also attends to God speaking to us through the 'secular' sciences and their theories."[91]

There are various reasons why Forrester believes that the church has a role to play in the public sphere. One of these is that the church should witnesses to the truth. By "witnessing to the truth," Forrester believes that the church's role in the public sphere is to "speak out a confessional vision" in "plain language."[92] This "speaking out a confessional vision," Forrester is "[talking] about God, which claims to point to publicly accessible truth, truth that is relevant to the pressing issues which are relevant to the pressing issues which are facing people and societies today."[93] This truth "[has to be] relevant to what is going on in the world," according to Forrester.[94]

As the church talks about God, Forrester wants the Christian believer to live in and impact today's secular, global and pluralistic society in effective ways. For example, in his *Christian Justice and Public Policy* Forrester seeks to answer the question, "What kind of Christian voice is appropriate in the public realm in relation to debates about public policy, and how might it be most appropriately articulated today?"[95] In this work, Forrester therefore also challenges the church to bring back religion to the public square because the common trend in the modern world today seems to indicate that religion "has been domesticated and deprived of public relevance and is no longer capable of feeding into public discussion disturbing memories or distinctive insights into the human condition."[96]

Forrester finds another reason for the church's public role in the message of the church.[97] He contends that "[the church] has a gospel to share, good news to proclaim" and that this proclamation could be fruitful if the church is "to understand the Christian faith as an ongoing story, a narrative, rather than a theory or a system."[98] Forrester thus proposes what he calls "unsystematic Christianity" in this narrative way as a methodological alternative

---

91. Forrester, *Theological Fragments*, 4.
92. Forrester, *On Human Worth*, 21.
93. Ibid., 127.
94. Ibid., 21.
95. Forrester, *Christian Justice and Public Policy,* 9.
96. Ibid., 21.
97. Forrester, *On Human Worth*, 127–128.
98. Ibid., 16.

to typical understandings of religious belief. He also speaks of "theological fragment" as a means of expressing the mode of theological discourse needed today.[99] This implies and cautions one not to expect a single way, model or approach in theological discourse of the church (as a community of believers). Forrester, in *Theological Fragments: Essays in Unsystematic Theology*, calls on the church and public theologians to understand the "fragment nature" also of the public and the subsequent need to adopt "fragment" as a form of theological discourse and expression. In other words, he sees the need for the church to make use of Christianity's internally fragmentary character within the fragmentary nature of the public sphere.

What Forrester is considering with the latter argument is also the fact that, as the church faces the public, it should be aware that the public itself is already fragmented and therefore needs a "fragmentary form of engagement," which can be constructed from various approaches to theologies as a collection of a unique tradition's fragments. To explain this further, Forrester chooses the public understanding of two important public issues, namely justice and public policy as examples of the fragmentary nature of the public. On justice, Forrester notes that,

> [t]he problem is that too many people and groups have too many differing and often contradictory accounts of justice. Too many people think that they know what justice is, and usually they understand justice in a way that suits their individual or collective interests. In such a context we have not so much a vacuum as an arena, or even a battlefield.[100]

Likewise, on public policy, Forrester argues that,

> [t]here is increasing confusion and uncertainty about the bases for public policy. Some argue for a pragmatic ad-hoc approach; others seek a popular consensus around some theoretical core; others again appear to support any policy they believe likely to win votes.[101]

---

99. Forrester, *Theological Fragments*, 1–24.
100. Forrester, *Christian Justice and Public Policy*, 40–41.
101. Ibid., 10.

The above two examples leads Forrester to conclude that "[t]here is an important place today for a modest and unsystematic theology, consisting of 'theological fragments' rather than some grand theory."[102] On this fact, Forrester converses with Alasdair McIntyre on, among other public issues, the fragmentation of the moral fabric of our society and he argues that "[w]hether fragmentation is a predicament or an emancipation, the gospel can be proclaimed in a fragmented age."[103] Forrester's emphasis on the multifaceted (or fragmented) nature of both public theology as a conversation and the fragmented nature of the societies in which it is practiced is an important insight to remember in the consideration of the role of the church in the public sphere. It has already been shown with regard to examples of the fragmentary understandings of justice and corruption in the secular sphere, and what chapter 3 and this chapter also hopes to show, is that there are indeed a variety of (equally legitimate) theological perspectives on the issues of justice, corruption and the role and modes of engagement of the church in the public sphere.

Some further reflection on Forrester's thought is also important for the purposes of this study, especially as it may impact on the issue of corruption, human worth,[104] human destiny and human fellowship – which were discussed in detail in the previous chapter with reference to the concepts of human flourishing, human destiny in relation to the plan of God for humankind and fellowship, or relationality. In light of the suffering caused by corruption, it seems that the church should, in the first place, seek to establish the extent of the damage that corruption is causing to those who suffer, to the victims of corruption. Part of the "fragments" that should inform the theological reflection on justice, corruption and the role of the church need to be the willingness to listen to and the content of the voices of the victims. Forrester puts this idea plainly when he says that "the voice of the victims should be treated as a primary and privileged insight into the nature of injustice, which must not be pushed aside."[105]

---

102. Forrester, *Theological Fragments*, ix.

103. Ibid., 10–11.

104. For further reflection see an extensive discussion on in his book Duncan Forrester, *On Human Worth: A Christian Vindication of Equality*.

105. Forrester, *Christian Justice and Public Policy*, 57.

According to Forrester, understanding victims of injustice can be achieved precisely by doing *public* theology. For him, theology has the task of engaging with the underlying assumptions of society and culture about the nature of human beings, about human flourishing, about human destiny and human fellowship, about relations of the social order and the transcendent order, and about the way a community allocates worth and chooses its goals.[106]

The concept of human flourishing that Forrester refers to as opposed to a "fractured, stressed, relationally broken and spiritually empty" type of life, is explained well by Miner, Dowson and Devenish's description of the concept:

> [human] flourishing describes both the journeying and arrival that turns broken hearts and homeless minds into purposeful pilgrims whose journeys are engaged in living life on a *grand scale*, and are subsequently filled with hope, expectation and the sense of something "more."[107]

For (public) theology to contribute towards this goal, Forrester insists that it therefore also ". . . must cease to be just an academic activity. Public theology must be a church theology that has values and goals in her ecclesiastical mission taking the gospel to the rest of the nation."[108] Forrester is of the opinion that it is important that theology engages in critical questions of what the church is able to offer, the challenges and the opportunities to be confronted over time. His issues a strong warning against the tendency for the church to work under the dichotomy of what he calls the "public realm and private realm":

> This confinement of religion to the private realm should be a major concern for public theologians. When Christianity is assigned to the private realm it lacks the potentiality for prophetic importance because it tends to engage in an easy-going validation of the values of the society, influencing personal morality and accepted values . . . This lays great responsibility

---

106. Forrester, *Beliefs, Values and Policies*, 36–37; note also in "Working in the Quarry," 431–438.

107. Miner, Dowson and Devenish, *Beyond Well-Being*, vii.

108. Forrester, *Beliefs, Values and Policies*, 13–15; note also Forrester, "Working in the Quarry," 432.

upon Christian theology in that it has to fulfil its function as "civil religion"[109] while holding on to Christian truth. How to develop and support all that is good while concurrently addressing a prophetic word to the nation is the main challenge.[110]

Furthermore, with regard to why the church should be involved in public life, for Forrester, Christ is pivotal for "theology in principle is concerned with the wholeness of life as a consequence of belief in the universal lordship of Jesus Christ."[111] As will be seen in what follows, the emphasis on the centrality of Christ, especially his example of engagement in society is one that is universally shared by public theologians.[112] Forrester's argument is also useful when it comes to challenging the church to encourage theologians to engage in crucial issues facing the public in the sense that he strongly believes that public theologians should be those who keep alive the vision of the ending of worldwide human despair and speak in public deliberations in ways that are prophetic, passionate and yet obtainable. As

---

109. The term "civil religion" is quite loaded term. Scholarly opinion, for example, sometimes suggest that, since the term was coined for the first time by Jean-Jacques Rousseau in his book, *The Social Contract*, it has led some scholars to reject it for reasons that, as Spillers (Martin Luther King, Jr," 44) puts it "vary across a range of misgivings, from what they would consider the distastefulness of the very idea, to definitional objections." Some definitions of civil religion include those of Kessler (*Tocqueville's Civil Religion*) and Branch (*At Canaan's Edge*). While Kessler (*Tocqueville's Civil Religion*) understands civil religion as that which refers to "to a religion [or elements of religious belief and practice] which purports to be theocentric, but in fact is designed to serve secular, as opposed to transcendent or other worldly ends," Branch (*At Canaan's Edge*) understands civil religion as a "kind of faith" which "make the individual, rather than divine revelation, the ultimate arbiter of duty and truth." According to Couto (*Political and Civic Leadership*, 505) that "civil religion, not unlike sacred religion, conveys a sense of being part of something much bigger and more important than just oneself or one's immediate social group." From this understanding Rousseau enters the conversation again. Rousseau believes that civil religion has a role to play in societies as it "would encourage people to behave in moral ways as they had historically been directed through religious teachings. It would reinforce the value of faith-based beliefs without religious doctrine" (in Couto, *Political and Civic Leadership*, 506). Likewise, "[c]ivil religion has liturgical expression in rites such as holidays, re-enactments, inaugurals, and national anthems and symbols. These symbols and rites call forth a common set of beliefs that provides citizens with a cohesive identity and binds them to each other despite differences" (Couto, *Political and Civic Leadership*, 505). In is worth noting that in other circles, civil religion has been termed as "public religion" (see for example Casanova, *Public Religions*; and Mazuwaza in Watling, *Ecological Imaginations*).

110. Forrester, *Beliefs, Values and Policies*, 7, 8–9.

111. Ibid., 12.

112. cf. Koopman's use of the threefold office of Christ in 4.3.2.3 below as guideline in public theology.

such, he also calls on public theologians to "Work hard and humbly in the quarry of the rich resources of the Bible; to follow the Christian tradition; and to produce the fragments of insights, challenges and the truth that may help to pave way in the coming of God's reign."[113]

Finally, one element of Forrester's views, one that will again and again resurface in the discussions that follow, is his view of public theology as conversation which "requires learning the language of the secular world in such a way that Christian discourse relates to it without losing its particular insights and contribution to the discussion."[114]

4.3.2.2 William Storrar and the Importance of Interdisciplinary Public-Theological Inquiry

Like Forrester, William Storrar – Director of the Center of Theological Inquiry at Princeton Theological Seminary and founder member of the Global Network for Public Theology – approaches public theology from his Presbyterian tradition.[115] For Storrar, public theology should first and foremost be understood within the context of an opportune time for practicing it. And Storrar believes that the church and theologians now live in an era defined as a "kairos opportunity" which offers or demands the possibility of interdisciplinary inquiry. For Storrar, this kairos opportunity therefore is "a moment of opportunity for theologians and other scholars working in the emerging field of interdisciplinary theological inquiry into contemporary public issues."[116]

According to Storrar, "the task of public theology is to call Christians out of that world of mutual incomprehension into the world of public citizenship in the company of strangers."[117] The idea of Christians as public citizens is important as we will see, has a variety of implications, among others with regard to Christian civil virtues that need to be taught and nurtured as part of a Christian response to corruption and injustice (see 4.4.1.3 and 4.3.2.3). Storrar backs his observation with the likes of Osmer and Schweitzer, and

---

113. Forrester, "Working in the Quarry," 437.
114. Forrester, *Beliefs, Values and Policies*:61.
115. Storrar, "Kairos Moment for Public Theology," 5.
116. Ibid., 5.
117. Ibid.

Dreyer, who suggest ways in which public theology can be practiced by Christians as they engage in the world.[118] For them (Osmer, Schweitzer and Dreyer) the task of public theology is threefold: to include the public subjects in the practicing of theology; to include everyday matters as objects of theological reflection; and to facilitate dialogue between theology and contemporary culture. A similar view can be found in Cady's understanding of the task of public theology, namely:

> [t]he task of public theology is to elicit a recognition of and commitment to the common life within which we exist. In and through the appropriation of religious symbolism, public theology seeks to nurture, deepen, and transform our common life that, while obscure and damaged, is never totally eroded. Thus public theology is not simply proposing a utopian communal vision that flies in the face of what we know about cosmic and human life. It is, rather, offering a constructive agenda that grows out of discernible features of our individual and corporate experience.[119]

Storrar is also aware of the importance of what one may call the "art" behind the practice of public theology. Although he emphasizes the "question of how we understand Christian identity [as] central to doing public theology in a global era,"[120] like Forrester[121] and Tracy he also acknowledges the need for the proper use of the "language" and especially for a specific style of engagement, namely "conversation" in the process. For example, as Christians engage in the "world of public citizenship,"[122] Storrar asks, "Do Christians only speak their own strange language or can they learn the language of strangers and find in the conversation mutual understanding, common ground, a common humanity and the possibility of making common cause in public issues?"[123]

---

118. Osmer and Schweitzer, *Religious Education,* 218; Dreyer, "Pastoral Response."
119. Cady, *Religion,* 92.
120. Storrar, "Kairos Moment for Public Theology," 4.
121. Forrester, *On Human Worth,* 21.
122. Cf. in this regard also Mathewes's (*Theology of Public Life,* 17) understanding of "faithful Christian citizenship."
123. Storrar, "Kairos Moment for Public Theology," 5.

Another area that Storrar, like Forrester – and, as will be seen later, also Koopman – emphasizes is the participation of Christians in public *policy* discourses. Here one finds a good example of Storrar's understanding of the role of the church in public life when the church, as he puts it, works towards respecting "shared beliefs and related ethical principles of Christianity, and the very specific decisions and judgments that Christians as policymakers, practitioners, citizens and voters must be free to make on often complex economic, social and political matters."[124] According to Storrar and Morton, again pointing towards interdisciplinary issues, this can be approached under an "ecumenical and interdisciplinary study of public issues dealt with both the Christian and ethical perspectives, on the one hand, and the relevant empirical evidence, on the other hand."[125]

Furthermore, in practicing public theology Storrar suggests that Christians' participation should be a humble approach and he warns that "if we only participate in the public sphere to assert the superiority of our Christian viewpoint and to dismiss all others, then we make no constructive contribution to the renewal of our local and global public life."[126] Here one finds echoes of the humility required from public theologians in light of Forrester's recognition of the "fragmentary" nature and variety of insights both in theology and in society.

4.3.2.3 Nico Koopman's Trinitarian Model of Doing Public Theology

South African Christian ethicist and public theologian Nico Koopman finds the foundation for his views on public theology in the Reformed tradition and, as such, he strongly bases it on biblical concepts.[127] Koopman sees public theology as that theology which works within the context, first of all, of "reflection upon the content of Christian faith as Trinitarian faith,

---

124. See also, Storrar and Morton, *Public Theology*, 38. This is again especially important for this study in light of its implications for norms and values that the Christian church may bring to the public discourse on corruption and injustice.

125. Ibid., 39.

126. Storrar in Venter, *Theology and the (Post)Apartheid Condition*, 4.

127. Koopman, "Churches and Public Policy Discourses."

[then] second upon the rationality of this faith, and third on the impact and implications of this faith":[128]

> Public Theology helps us to rediscover the inherent public content, thrust and focus of our faith. God's Trinitarian love which is expressed as the creative and caring love of our heavenly Creator and Parent, as the saving and reconciling love of Jesus Christ our Saviour, as the renewing and perfecting love of the Spirit our Guide and Comforter, is a love for the cosmos, for humans in all walks of life – marriage, family, circles of friends, culture, work, church, society (which includes political life, economic life, ecological life, civil society, public discourse), and for all of creation.[129]

For Koopman, there is no doubt that the church has a role to play in issues of public importance. Christ, the head of the church, is central in the reasons behind this conviction. In this sense Koopman argues that church's role can best be understood from a christological perspective with the church as those called and elected, justified and sanctified by the triune God to participate in his mission in the world (the *missio Dei*) and this can in turn be described in terms of the threefold office of Christ. Therefore public theology as Christian theology is a reflection of the confession of the threefold office of Christ as a prophetic, priestly and royal-servant theology.[130]

Expanding on his argument that public theology is a prophetic, priestly and royal-servant theology, Koopman first identifies five roles of *prophetic public theology*, which "firstly spells out the vision and contours of a new world of dignity, freedom and justice for all." Being prophetic, public theology is also critical in that it "exposes contemporary wrongs and employs the notion of empire to describe these wrongs." Prophetic public theology is, at the same time, a narrative theology in that it "tells the stories of pain and suffering, and of hope and liberation." Fourth, prophetic public theology is technical (here one finds clear echoes of the views of the interdisciplinary

---

128. Koopman, "Public Theology and the Public Role," 52; cf. "Some Contours for Public Theology," 48.

129. Koopman, "Public Theology and the Public Role," 54.

130. Ibid.

nature and conversation nature of public theology as emphasized by Storrar and Forrester). As such, prophetic public theology

> . . . engages in technical debates about contemporary challenges. With the help of experts from various appropriate disciplines it engages in detailed scientific and technical discussions about the complex challenges that we face.

Finally, prophetic public theology is engaged in policy discussions. Especially important for this study is the fact that Koopman acknowledges the importance of "broad visions," but emphasizes that these are not enough, although "[d]etailed policy blueprints should also not be offered." What is needed, according to Koopman, is that "between these broad principles and detailed blueprints ethical parameters for policymaking should be developed."[131]

According to Koopman, *priestly public theology* seeks to overcome "various forms of alienation, exclusion and brokenness in local and global contexts." While the royal-servant public theology "advances an ethos of servanthood, hope and responsible and ethical global discipleship and citizenship."[132]

In short, for Koopman the church has a role to play in the public sphere by way of doing public theology as it ". . . calls and challenges, illuminates and inspires, reminds and re-awakes churches – to act Christianly amidst the current global challenges."[133] A final observation that Koopman makes should also be noted, namely that the church needs to understand the local and global contexts in which it lives today. In his own words, the church needs to understand that it lives in the world where

> . . . [s]ocieties hunger for people of public and civic virtue: public wisdom in contexts of complexity, ambiguity, tragedy and *aporia* (dead-end streets); public justice in context of inequalities and injustices on local and global levels; public temperance

---

131. Koopman, "Churches and Public Policy," 1.

132. Ibid. On the topic of service, it is interesting that Beisner ("Justice and Poverty," 22), for example, uses the concept of "practical righteousness" links service directly with justice: "practical righteousness or justice . . . requires graciously serving the poor – and not only the poor but all people with all kinds of needs. Believers, individually and corporately owe God this gracious service to the needy as a matter of obedience."

133. Koopman, "Some Contours for Public Theology," 54.

in context of greed and consumerism amidst poverty and alienation; public fortitude amidst situations of powerlessness and inertia; public faith amidst feelings of disorientation and rootless-ness in contemporary societies; public hope amidst situations of despair and melancholy; public love in societies where public solidarity and compassion are absent.[134]

4.3.2.4 Rowan Williams's Mutuality Approach to Public Theology

To begin this section, speaking from an Anglican perspective, former Archbishop of Canterbury William Temple (1881–1944) may be viewed as an Anglican public theologian (though the term did not exist with the same meaning in Temple's time as it does today). Temple's *Christianity and Social Order* may be regarded as a classic of public theology which shaped modern Anglican social thought. It also informs and affirms Rowan Williams's argument on the role of the church. For Temple the church is meant to "pass on to Christian citizens, acting in their civic capacity, the task of reshaping the existing order."[135] Dackson elaborates on this statement saying that it shows that the "public role of the church is to equip those called by virtue of the citizenship bestowed on them by a secular democracy to exercise a public vocation."[136]

A more recent Anglican voice than Temple and equally highly respected is that of another former Archbishop of Canterbury, Rowan Williams. Williams's understanding of the "why" of public theology begins with his view of the need for a clear understanding of why all Christian theology, including public theology, exists. For Williams, theology

> . . . represent[s] a "separate" frame of reference, one that does not at all depend on how things turn out in this world for its system of values. That is why it is not in competition with other sorts of discourse . . . [theology] recalls us to the idea that what makes humanity human is completely independent of anyone's

---

134. In Cole, *Theology in Service*, 152.
135. Temple, *Christianity and Social Order*, 58.
136. Dackson, "Archbishop William Temple," 239ff.

judgments of failure or success, profit or loss . . . [theology] is sheer gift – sheer love, in Christian terms.[137]

Williams also argues that theology does not solve specific questions.[138] However, what it does is to offer a definition of human well-being and it gives a rationale for a life well-lived in common which of course has important implications for our common and public life. This common life is characterized by (and at the heart of Christian theology), and is the concept of, "mutuality" – "[c]entral to what Christian theology sets before us is mutuality":

> The Christian Scriptures describe the union of those who are identified with Jesus Christ as having an organic quality, a common identity shaped by the fact that each depends on all others for their life.[139]

At this juncture one may identify three central themes in the above view of Williams, namely *identity and quality*, *nature*, and the *duty or role* of the church. We shall look at Williams's understanding of these, more specifically by focusing on his definition of the church as "a political body, a place for education on civic questions and human dignity, as a prophetic community, a citizen assembly."[140] According to Williams, in an address on the relationship of church and state and the role of the Christian today,

> [t]he Christian church presents itself in its very origins as a political body, a polis, a kind of city. And its members therefore are citizens before anything else. To belong in the body of Christ, to use the other great metaphor in the New Testament, is to have the dignities of a citizen. Civic liberty, civic dignity is one of the favored ways of expressing what it is to come into the community established by Jesus Christ.[141]

---

137. Williams, "Theology and Economics." 615.
138. Ibid., 607.
139. Ibid., 610.
140. Williams, "Relations between the Church."
141. Ibid.

Thus, Williams's understanding of the church in relation to its practice of public theology challenges the church to understand that by its very nature, existing as a community and in communities, it has the responsibility "to be a place where people [are] educating one another about civic questions and human dignity, where people [are] educating and being educated about liberty, responsibility, the creation of a sustainable human environment."[142] However, in order to perform this role more productively, the church has to set itself aside as a unique body. Williams calls this "the church's first business." He elaborates on this as it means, according to him, that the church

> . . . is to live differently, to be the kind of learning community where civic dignity is all the time being developed and explored. And that civic dignity, as it is developed and explored, becomes the organ, or the motor by which people are stimulated to go out into the wider society and talk about, argue about, what is good for the community.[143]

To live differently has implications. Like Nico Koopman,[144] who speaks extensively on the prophetic role of the church, Williams also uses the concept of the church as a prophetic community. However, he is critical of the meaning and use of the phrase "to be prophetic," unless it is used in a very specific sense. For example, he says, "to be prophetic is not making radical noises" but rather

> . . . it is about trying to identify the truths that lay beyond party squabbles and short-term advantage, about trying to identify what it is that lies beyond winning and losing in the secular political game. It is about being politically and civically virtuous.[145]

Williams's view of public theology can be summarized, in the words of Skinner, as "public theology addresses the possibility of utilizing the resources of the Christian faith to speak publicly into contemporary discourse."[146] Faith is, therefore, an important agent for any society towards its flourishing

---

142. Ibid.
143. Ibid.
144. Koopman, "Public Theology as Prophetic Theology," 117–130.
145. Williams, "Relations between the Church."
146. Skinner, "Going Public," 17.

and the church is called to draw on its members' faith for the wider public good. This is because the church is

> . . . a community where we argue about what's good for the human race. And we do so in the light of what God has shown concerning the calling and the dignity of humanity overall; because of course this is a city, a polis, which has no ethical or local boundaries, a political community which is in principle open to the whole of humanity.[147]

4.3.2.5 Max Stackhouse's Normative, Constructive and Apologetic Role of the Church

Max Stackhouse is another prominent contemporary public theologian and ethicist from the Reformed tradition. For Stackhouse, public theology "points towards a wider and deeper strand of theological reflection rooted in the interaction of biblical insight, philosophical analysis, historical discernment and social formation."[148] Stackhouse's contribution to contemporary public theology rests on a number of convictions, three of which make his understanding of public theology and how best the church can play its role in addressing contemporary issues, especially clear.

First and foremost is Stackhouse's understanding of the *public and private realms of religion and theology*. As was seen in the case of Forrester and the other public theologians referred to above, for Stackhouse religion is not supposed to be a matter of merely personal or private devotional life, it has to be part of all aspects of a believer's life, including those related to the "public life domain," covering other areas of life, beyond spirituality, such as economics, civil society, the state and culture. In this concept of public and private, Stackhouse affirms the public significance of theology when he says that,

> . . . theology, while related to intensely personal commitments and to a particular community of worship, is, at its most profound level, neither merely private nor a matter of distinctive communal identity. Rather, it is an argument regarding the way

---

147. Ibid.
148. M. Stackhouse, "Public Theology," 230.

things are and ought to be, one decisive for public discourse and necessary to the guidance of individual souls, societies, and, indeed, the community of nations.[149]

Second, Stackhouse asserts the *constructive tasks of public theology* as that it "must show that it can form, inform and sustain the moral and spiritual architecture of a civil society so that truth, justice and mercy are more nearly approximated in the souls of persons and in the institutions of the common life."[150] More emphatically, Stackhouse summarizes these tasks of public theology to be "defining the operating values and norms that dominate a social or cultural ethos . . . determining 'what values and norms are right' as well as 'calling upon people to enter into the reconstruction of the social or cultural ethos.'"[151] In other words, according to Hogue, these are the normative, constructive and apologetic modes of doing public theology one finds in Stackhouse's thought.[152]

Thus, for Stackhouse, theology will become public theology, if and only if it indeed goes public, and again the issue of language and conversation are important:

> . . . if a theology is to be trusted to participate in public discourse it ought to be able to make a plausible case for what it advocates in terms that can be comprehended by those who are not believers . . . It should be able to articulate its core convictions in comprehensible terms across many modes of

---

149. Stackhouse, "Public Theology and Ethical Judgment," 165). It is to this public dimension of religion and theology that Stackhouse's fellow public theologians, for example, Doak (*Reclaiming Narrative*) and Hollenbach ("Public Theology in America") also speak. While Doak (*Reclaiming Narrative*, 9) identifies two main objectives of public theology to be that of "defining and defending a public role for theological discourse in a religiously pluralistic society" while at the same time promoting "societal commitment to maintaining the quality of our public life and to pursuing a common good," Hollenbach ("Public Theology in America," 299) argues, not unlike Stackhouse, that public theology "attempts to illuminate the urgent moral questions of our time through explicit use of the great symbols and doctrines of the Christian faith."

150. Stackhouse, *God and Globalization*, 107.

151. Ibid., 231.

152. Hogue, "After the Secular," 362.

discourse, explaining its symbolic and mythical terms . . . in ways that expose their multiple levels of meaning."[153]

Third, Stackhouse emphasizes the *vocational dimension of public theology*.[154] Hogue describes Stackhouse's work as "tradition-based apologetic public theology."[155] In other words, for Stackhouse, public theology as Christian apologetics justifies the normative task of public theology. This approach is especially important in that it opens the door for public theology to be practiced at the grassroots level of the church, for example, when applied to rural setting of most African churches. The approach implies that, if public theology is applied to the discipleship style of ministry, it can eventually challenge church members to see the need for building up their own theological knowledge toward faithful engagement in the public sphere and toward eventually enabling them to become active citizens.

Finally, what make Stackhouse's contributions important for this study are two suggestions. The first suggestion is his emphasis on the need for the church – especially some of its members who find themselves in what Stackhouse calls a "fideistic paradigm" – not to confine itself within its own boundaries or to separate itself, but rather to reach out. Such a church and such members of the church ". . . do not give a public account of their convictions because they believe that one should not; the content and quality of faith is and must be entirely self-authenticating . . . it seems so to them."[156] Stackhouse sees the church as, and reminds the church to be as, "those who receive the vision of the promised reign of God" and that they "are to employ every means to make it actual . . ."[157] This is because the church is not an institution working in abstract, but rather it has the mandate to and therefore "is convicted to instill . . . integrity, honesty, diligence, fairness, and stewardship. [And] [o]f additional importance is the encouragement of a sense of responsibility to contribute to the social and economic development of their communities."

---

153. Stackhouse, "Reflections," 112.
154. Stackhouse, "God and Globalization," 16.
155. Hogue, "After the Secular," 362.
156. Stackhouse, "Public Theology and Ethical Judgment," 175.
157. Stackhouse, "Public Theology," 180.

Stackhouse's second suggestion is his emphasis (again, like that of Forrester, Koopman, Storrar and Williams), on the use of fitting *language* in doing public theology. These two emphases, non-separation and the use of language, is also well put by Bedford-Strohm:

> . . . public theology that does not separate itself from the world into a self-sufficient counter-community with its own religious language, but knows how to speak the language of the world and how to be in dialogue with the world; a public theology that . . . is grounded in Christ and therefore challenges the world to make God's way for the world visible, a prophetic theology that leads the world beyond its worldly ways.[158]

In summary, then, the above discussion offers insights into the contemporary discourse on public theology. The views expressed are those of a selected group of public theologians and has highlighted, albeit by way of sometimes different approaches and emphases, that the church undoubtedly has a role to play in public sphere. We saw this in the *conversational approach* of Duncan Forrester, the *interdisciplinary theological inquiry* of William Storrar, the *prophetic, priestly and royal-servant model* of Nico Koopman, the *mutuality approach* of Rowan Williams and the *normative, constructive and apologetic* approach of Max Stackhouse. In the latter's words, they all would agree that the church and theology have the task to fulfil as, "[w]e need a theology wide and deep enough to interpret and guide [the] public."[159] As we conclude the contemporary public-theological reflection on the role of the church in public sphere, it is important to link the outgoing discussion with our acknowledgement (in ch. 2), that corruption takes place at different levels and involves individuals, groups and organizations, for example, businesses and governments. From what has been central to our discussions in this chapter thus far, the church is also an institution and a community, as well as a sum of individuals. In the next section we indicate that there are clear reasons not only for the church's participation in the public square in general, but *specifically with regard to the fight against corruption.*

---

158. Bedford-Strohm, "Tilling and Caring for the Earth," 36.
159. Stackhouse, *God and Globalization*, 33.

4.3.3 Corruption and the Church: Baseline Biblical-Ecclesiological Considerations

It has been shown from the perspective of history and from the perspective of a series of contemporary public theologians *why* the church has to be involved in the public square. Before the study moves on to the second primary question to be answered in this chapter, namely *how* it may do so, this section offers three baseline biblical-ecclesiological insights into the nature of the church as an institution which need to be kept in mind when reflecting on the role in the public square – not only in general, but specifically also with regard to the challenge of *corruption*.

The first insight is that the efforts by the church to fight corruption and injustice needs to be grounded in God for its power, authority and mandate. The second insight is that the efforts by the church to fight corruption and injustice need to draw its wisdom and knowledge from and understanding of Scripture. The third insight is that the efforts by the church to fight corruption and injustice will only be effective if church leadership is inspired toward the responsible exercise of its leadership function.

4.3.3.1 God's Power and the Power of and in the Church

In her essay, "Power, Knowledge, and Authority in Public Theology," Elaine Graham quotes Stephen Sykes, who argues that issues of power concerns theologians in three ways.[160] First, there is what Sykes calls the "power of God," which relates to the "imagery of the character of God and God's action in the world." Second, the "power of the church" concerns the ways in which church as a "political institution" engages with or intervenes in wider society. Third, the power in the church concerns "the distribution and exercise of power by various members of the church and how internal relations of authority, decision making and participation are exercised."

Building on Sykes's argument, the church not only has the authority, a mandate, but also the power to carry out its mission. The authority, power and mandate are all rooted in the fact that the church is the church of *God*. As noted earlier (4.2.1), the word *ekklēsia* refers to the gathering together of the assembly of Christians "by" God himself (Acts 20:28; cf. Ps 74:2). The church is of God. There are other assemblies and organizations in the

---

160. Graham, "Power, Knowledge," 42–62.

world that deal with corruption and injustices, but by belonging to or being "of God," the church is distinguished from other secular forms of *ekklēsia* (in the sense of "gatherings"). Furthermore, when the church attends to the issue of corruption while at the same time being empowered by the Spirit, it proclaims the gospel and bears witness to Christ in the world (Acts 1:8). Speaking from a Trinitarian perspective, regarding how God's power, authority and mandate works for and within the church, one also needs to emphasize that the church depends on the intercessory ministry of Christ for its grace (Heb 4:14–16), interceding also by the Spirit for a suffering world (Rom 8:26). This makes the church a unique institution. For Dirk Smit, this nature of the church is what would be described in his six visible social forms of the church, especially in the church as a "worshipping community" and as "individual believers."[161]

In considering the answer to the question of what the church is doing as far as the war on corruption is concerned, the suggestion of understanding God as a source of power, authority and mandate for the church contributes to the meaning of the church and offers a rationale for its engagement in addressing the problem of corruption. Linked to this analysis are both the primacy of scriptural wisdom and the quest for ethical leadership in the church.

4.3.3.2 The Church and the Primacy of Scriptural Wisdom

Throughout the history of the mission of the church, the source of truth as it carries out its mission has always been the Bible. The church has maintained that the Bible is God's authoritative and trustworthy Word containing its objective and the truth (2 Tim 3:15–17). Biblical truth thus also serves as key, not only with regard to knowing God, humanity and morality, but also the fundamental realities behind the tragic dilemma of corruption.

The late Steve de Gruchy once referred to the critical role that the Bible plays when the church engages in issues of the society saying that, "if we as church have anything special and specific to offer the public debate, then it will come from the wisdom of the Scriptures."[162] De Gruchy continued,

---

161. Smit, "On Learning to See?" 55–77.
162. De Gruchy, "Engaging," 1.

[t]here is no point in the churches simply saying what other people can say, because they can normally say it better than us! Our unique voice is the ability to bring centuries of wisdom about human life in the Bible to bear on our context.[163]

As was seen, Forrester likewise urges theologians to work hard and humbly in the quarry of the rich resources of the Bible, to follow the Christian tradition, and to produce the fragments of insights, challenges and the truth that may help to pave way in the coming of God's reign.[164]

On the uniqueness of the Bible, Indian philosopher, writer, lecturer and social reformer, Vishal Mangalwadi, sees the Bible as a library in which the books give an expanding, progressive, yet coherent view of life and the world; it presents the human situation; it gives purpose to an absurd-looking life, meaning to a human quest for morals, and hope in the face of awful evil; it inspires life in God, in a universe that seems to be governed by random chance, if not capricious fate or fortune.[165]

For the purposes of this study, besides the many biblical insights into the sinfulness of corruption given in chapter 3, one of the primary biblical considerations behind the need for the *church* to become involved in the fight against corruption is that this serves as an affirmation of God's redemptive purposes.

According to Hans Küng, this essence of the church is "God's salvic act in Jesus Christ."[166] These theologians regard the church as the family of faithful fulfilling the mission of Jesus Christ. However, this concept of salvation is not limited to the "winning of souls." It has a much broader meaning in the sense that it has implications for how communities of believers are supposed to live with other people. This salvation is relational. Biblical salvation is meant to affect the whole of humanity. In Paul's word, salvation is "cosmic" (cf. Rom 8:18ff.). God's salvation in Jesus Christ is not limited to the

---

163. Cf. also Koopman ("Public Theology as Prophetic Theology," 127): "[T]he church has the role to play in public policy discourse not only by providing motivation, goal and meaning, but also by making a unique indispensable input regarding the contents of the debate."

164. Forrester, "Working in the Quarry," 437.

165. Mangalwadi, *Book That Made Your World*, 211.

166. Küng, *The Church*, 15; for a similar view, see Moltmann, *Church in the Power of the Spirit*, 1–65.

salvation of individual human beings; it is not even limited to the church (the new community of redeemed humanity); it is extended to the whole creation and it is meant to bring hope. With regard to the latter, Beker, for example, explains the scope of this salvation in terms of the hope it brings: "the hope in the dawning victory of God and the imminent redemption of the created order, which he has inaugurated in Christ."[167] One may thus say that this cosmic nature of salvation has meaning to whoever is working towards curbing corruption in that, by doing so, one participates now in God's redemptive activity that extends to the world (i.e. the community, society as a whole, and all of humankind). On the "cosmic nature of salvation," Wright reminds of what he calls God's "cosmic ownership" and "cosmic sovereignty."[168] It is God who owns the process of saving people from all nations and God is control. Likewise, Wright warns us that "[w]e can be so accustomed to thinking of salvation in purely individualistic terms that we neglect this fully biblical dimension of it."[169]

This redemptive purpose of God also serves as the basis for church's involvement in addressing corruption and injustice. This purpose was revealed by God himself through Christ who died and rose from the dead. From the risen Christ, the mission of the church finds its meaning, that is to work with God to bring about God's kingdom. This kingdom is characterized by the "good news" of Jesus Christ and as such it includes "a bigger picture of justice," which surely includes the absence of corruption.[170]

Furthermore, as was seen in chapter 3, the Christian faithful and the church draw moral guidelines from the life of Jesus. It was also seen that for Jesus the primacy of human dignity, the necessity of justice and care and concern for others were at the center of his mission on earth. Jesus not only modelled servant leadership, but he was also willing to suffer for the sake of humanity. Jesus was concerned about corruption, and he stood firm against corruption, hypocrisy and injustice in Jewish society – Jesus's testimony when he entered the temple in Jerusalem is witness to this (cf. Mark 11:15–17). As was seen, also with regard to injustice, Jesus time and

---

167. Beker, *Paul the Apostle*, 363–366.
168. Wright, *Salvation*, 140.
169. Ibid., 146.
170. Gordon, "Mission of Church," 16.

again acted or spoke out against it. From these examples the church should also draw her concern for corruption.

With regard to the meaning and application of the concepts of the church as a being "called out" and as a community "bearing witness," the role of the church in fighting corruption has its roots in the understanding, obeying, accepting, and responding to God's biblical commandments. The church can also appropriate her involvement in fighting corruption as a witness to the authority of God-in-the-world. That is to say, any authority the church claims to possess derives ultimately from God and is manifested through Jesus the Christ (Matt 28:18). When the church does witness in the public square, and seeks to speak out against corruption, one might say it is responding and faithfully following Jesus Christ "into the public commons, and enables [it] to humbly but decisively offer a public witness to the public truth of the gospel."[171]

Looking forward toward the next section on the importance of ethical leadership, one is reminded by Mangalwadi[172] that in history the Bible has also acted as a force that freed entire nations from corruption while simultaneously giving them also political freedom, even if his assertion that ". . . empirical data says that countries most influenced by the Bible are the least corrupt" is questionable.[173] Be that as it may, one may still hope that the knowledge, wisdom and the moral decision-making guidelines found in the Bible may change leaders toward becoming and remaining ethical and not corrupt. As another South African public theologian, Clint Le Bruyns states:

> The issue of corruption and unethical conduct in all sectors of life today does not necessarily imply that leaders and people at large are not interested in ethical living. It is more realistic to acknowledge that their dilemmas simply overwhelm them and that they do not always have *a knowledge base for moral decision-making resources to draw from,* which more that often results in unethical acts. Leaders require such knowledge empowerment in order to strengthen their capacity and in turn the capacity of

---

171. Pfrimmer, "What Do Canadian Politicians," 199.
172. Mangalwadi, *Book That Made Your World*, 255.
173. Ibid., 256.

those they serve toward the broader realization of a more ethical society . . . A knowledge base envisaging a morally transforming society requires a developing pool of resources and examples that motivate improved action.[174]

4.3.3.3 The Importance of Ethical Leadership in Society and the Church's Location and Experience in Society

In light of the above discussion, it is quite clear that power and authority is one of the avenues for service and responsible stewardship. This stewardship involves accountability, honesty and mutual control of power. This also sets the context and draws attention to the importance of leadership in the church when it comes to the church claiming and performing a participatory role in fighting corruption. Moral leadership in the church is critical in this endeavor.

This moral leadership within the church is not only, as Dames puts it, "a critical element for the realization of a morally transforming society" but also one that is "capable of transforming institutions and society, and envisioning new possibilities for a more humane society through reciprocal expressions of the 'common good life.' So [the church is] challenged to contribute to the constructive task of healing the world and building a new society" for it is ideally positioned to facilitate "the deepening and nurturing of moral vision of society."[175] To do this, church leadership needs to be credible. It has to be clothed in service with a sense of care and compassion, integrity and dignity.

The need for ethical leadership in the church is even more pressing in light of two further considerations. These two considerations are the facts of the church's unique location and experience in meeting human needs and the shift in public opinion on the significance of faith values.

Regarding the first consideration, the church has a role to play in the fight against corruption, especially in Africa, because of its position in many African societies. In many African countries, the church constitutes the largest social institution. In almost every small rural town and city suburb one finds a church.

---

174. Le Bruyns, "Ethical Leadership," 51 (emphasis added).
175. Dames, *Ethical Leadership*, 9.

To explain this phenomenon better, Bedford-Strohm refers to the church to as the "public church."[176] He argues that "with roots in local parishes all over the world, and at the same time, being universal in the fullest sense makes the church an ideal agent of a global civil society." This argument is in line with what the church in many places is already doing with regard to various contemporary public issues. Likewise, apart from the fact that many of these churches have well-developed social programs and projects, they also have a wealth of potential in their members with a variety of passions and gifts.

Apart from the strengths of the church due to its geographical location and infrastructure (in some African contexts the only existing infrastructure), is what may be called its long-time practical acquaintance with meeting human needs. Reference was made in section 1.8 of this study of former UN Secretary General Kofi Annan's view that

> [c]hurch organizations and their religious communities are, without question, the largest and best-organized civil institutions in the world today, claiming the allegiance of billions of believers and bridging the divides of race, class, and nationality. . . . They are uniquely equipped to meet the challenges of our time: resolving conflicts, caring for the sick and needy, and promoting peaceful coexistence among all peoples."[177]

This is, for example, seen in the impact the church has had

> on modern and postmodern society . . . as a result of [her] strong focus on world relief, aid, and human as well as economic development. This can be seen today through medical services, AIDS care, community development, water purification, orphan services, economic aid, shelter, food provision, educational opportunities, as well as a host of other contributions.[178]

With regard to the second consideration, namely the fact that there is an apparent growing appreciation of the significance of faith values in society,

---

176. Bedford-Strohm, "Tilling and Caring for the Earth," 232.
177. In Berger, "Religious Non-Governmental Organizations," 2.
178. World Vision, *About Us: Who We Are*; cf. Evans, "Campaign for Human Development."

is the following statement: Despite the fact that societies are increasingly becoming more secular[179] and despite of the increase of global religiously plurality, hence raising the question of whether Christianity still has the role to play in the public square, some secular bodies, such as the international organizations as well as governments, have over the last decade or so begun to understand and appreciate the unique role which the church can play in society and also in the fight against corruption.[180]

The above is exemplified in the UN Convention against Corruption (UNCAC) to which has been referred previously. This internationally agreed upon guideline for combating and preventing corruption at global and national levels calls for a comprehensive and multidisciplinary approach to preventing and combating corruption effectively. This includes the efforts of governments as well as individuals and groups outside the public sector. According to Article 13 of UNCAC, under the heading "Participation of Society," the Convention calls on governments to

> take appropriate measures, within its means and in accordance with fundamental principles of its domestic law, to promote the active participation of individuals and groups outside the public sector, such as civil society, non-governmental organizations and community-based organizations in the prevention of and the fight against corruption and to raise public awareness regarding the existence, causes and gravity of and the threat posed by corruption.[181]

Although the church is not expressly mentioned, the fact remains that "religious communities are increasingly challenged to relate and apply their beliefs, rituals and symbols to the constructive task of healing the world and building a new society."[182] Those, such as Petersen, who assert this believe that within faith communities we typically find a network of people formed

---

179. That is, "[t]he process by which sectors of society and culture are removed from the domination of religious institutions and symbols" (Berger, *Social Reality of Religion*, 107) or "[t]he process whereby religious thinking, practices and institutions lose their social significance" (Wilson, *Religion in Secular Society*, 108).

180. Transparency International, "Integrating Human Rights."

181. United Nations, Statement by the General Secretary, 1.

182. Petersen in Le Bruyns, "Ethical Leadership," 56–57.

on the basis of trust and respect on a foundation of common beliefs and shared values; faith communities "provide value guidelines"; and in the fight against corruption,

> faith traditions can serve as a critical partner with government, business, labour, education and civil society. These partnerships are essential for any envisaged improvement in condition of life for all, and thus nullify any modes of engagement that are self-seeking, competitive and uncooperative.[183]

For Keith Vermeulen, "religion unites us in goodness and in the belief to discern, understand and share life in the world."[184] Thus, although for many years when there may have existed what may be called a spiritual vacuum in the global anti-corruption effort, in recent years the church, other religions and religious communities in many countries are no longer marginalized. This is true for Africa as well. In fact, the efforts of churches to emphasize corruption as a critical moral issue is what seems to have contributed greatly to this shift. Therefore, in some parts of the world the church is becoming a key player in the war on corruption.

What then are the implications to this plea with regard to the role of the church in combating corruption? A clearly notable implication of this is that the church is being challenged to be aware that it is *expected*, both biblically and from the side of secular society, to play its part as a partner in the fight against corruption. This is a challenge that goes hand in hand with the quest of the church to understand how to respond in the public arena not only to issues of corruption, but also the manifold challenges facing societies today. Likewise, the church is being reminded that because of its proximity to vulnerable communities throughout the developing world, as well as its ubiquity within many contexts, it is placed in a strategic position to be able to address these challenges.

---

183. In Le Bruyns, "Ethical Leadership," 57.
184. Quoted by Le Bruyns, "Ethical Leadership," 57.

4.4 The Church in the Fight against Corruption – How?

Up to now this chapter has focused on the questions of what the church is, why the church has a role to play in the public sphere, and why this is so specifically in the fight against corruption. In this final section of the chapter the next logical question that needs to be addressed is *how* it then may do so.

4.4.1 The "How" of the Church's Engagement in the Fight against Corruption: Nature, Contours and Modes of Engagement

In the sections below seven concepts or theological-ethical considerations are discussed which will clarify exactly what the nature, contours and modes of engagement the church may consider in answering the question of how it is to understand, approach or implement its unique role in the fight against corruption.

4.4.1.1 *The Centrality of* Holistic Mission *in the Church's Engagement in the World*

The church exists because of its mission, as it was first called to be involved in mission.[185] As African theologian Jesse Mugambi argues, "the major business of the church is to be in mission" and this mission remains the backbone of the church's activities since its inception.[186] And, when the church contributes to anti-corruption work, one may say it is also "doing mission." Why may one say this?

Because the word "mission" can have a broad meaning, David Bosch warns that one should be careful not to "incarcerate it in the narrow confines of our own predilections."[187] In the context of this study, mission includes the fight against corruption if one understands it, as Mugambi does, namely that mission is "an activity whereby God calls his disciples and sends them as salt and light to add flavour and shine to the world . . . [referring] primarily

---

185. Jürgen Moltmann (*Way of Jesus Christ*, 358) understands the church's obedience to God to be a vital "apostolic characteristic," central to the carrying out of the apostolic proclamation and missionary charge, in essence, the church's foundation and commission.

186. Mugambi, *Biblical Basis*, 13.

187. Bosch, *Transforming Mission*, 9.

to *missio Dei* (God's mission) and it has to do with transforming or changing the world."[188]

The above view is related to the popular contemporary reference to mission as something that ought to be "holistic" or "integral." The latter means it is a type of mission that envisions that the church does not settle for communicating the faith separate from social involvement.[189] As Bulmer and Hansford argue, "justice and justification by faith, worship and political action, the spiritual and the material, personal change and structural change belong together."[190] Or, as the Micah Network defines holistic mission,

> Integral Mission or holistic transformation is the proclamation and declaration of the gospel. It is not simply that evangelism and social involvement are being done alongside each other. Rather, in integral mission, our proclamation has social consequences, as we call people to love and repentance in all areas of life. And our social involvement work will have the evangelistic consequences as we bear witness to the transformation grace of Jesus Christ.[191]

For Jesus Christ, this integral or holistic mission was about the fullness of life. He makes a powerful declaration of his mission on earth in John 10:10: "I have come that they may have life and have it abundantly." This is what he came to do and he called upon his disciples [also as church] to continue doing this after his ascension. "As the Father sent me, so I send you" (John 20:21). Christ came to give life – fuller life – to both spiritual and social dimensions of all human life. He ministered to the spiritual

---

188. Mugambi, *Biblical Basis*, 13.

189. Clearly what is being said here in a different way reflects what public theologians have been warning against in the preceding sections (see 4.3.2.1 and 4.3.2.3), namely the unacceptability of withdrawal from the world, from withdrawal of faith into the spiritual sphere of life leaving it with little or no contribution to make in the public and material spheres of life.

190. Bulmer and Hansford, *Local Church*, 12.

191. The Micah Network is related to the Micah Challenge referred to earlier in this study and is the name of a coalition of evangelical churches and agencies from around the world. Individual organizations are drawn together because of their passion and commitment for integral mission. Underpinning all that Micah does around the world is the inspiring verse from Micah 6:8: "He has shown you, o mortal, what is good. And what does the Lord require of you? To act justly and to love mercy and to walk humbly with your God." (http://www.micahnetwork.org/. Accessed 19 January 2014.

needs of humanity, which included forgiveness of human sin, and deliverance, but also to the social needs of human beings.[192] It is to this model of Jesus Christ that the church has to aspire, also in its response to the tragic contexts of corruption.

There is, therefore, a strong resonance between the vision of a corruption-free society and the vision of the fullness of life, that is, the kingdom of God or the reign of God. A corruption-free society may therefore be seen as one element of the manifestation of the coming of God's kingdom – bringing the good news, putting things right, bringing redemption and reconciliation. Central to this good news is the idea of putting things back to how God originally intended, redeeming things for their original purpose (Col 1:20; 2 Cor 5:19).

Moltmann, who bases his view of public theology on the concept of the kingdom of God – he even calls public theology "kingdom of God theology" – is especially helpful and will again be referred to below. According to Moltmann, "kingdom of God theology intervenes critically and prophetically in the public affairs of a given society, and draws public attention, not to the church's own interests, but to God's kingdom, God's commandment, and his righteousness."[193] The implications of a kingdom of God theology includes calls for critical and prophetic intervention by the church – including addressing the issue of corruption. This idea is summarized well by Tinder: "To anticipate the coming of the kingdom of God is merely sentimental . . . unless one seeks ways of reshaping society according to the form of the immanent community."[194] The kingdom of God, therefore, concerns more than individual salvation. It is also about human well-being and human flourishing, which are both denied by corruption, an insidious plague that has a wide range of corrosive effects on societies. In the words of former Secretary General of the United Nations, Kofi Anan, corruption "undermines democracy and the rule of law, leads to violations of human rights, distorts markets, erodes the quality of life and allows organize crime, terrorism and other threats to human security to flourish."[195]

---

192. Mugambi, *Biblical Basis*, 13.
193. Moltmann, *Church in the Power*, 20.
194. Tinder, *Political Meaning*, 155.
195. United Nations, Statement by the General Secretary.

Corruption as we have seen, is found in all countries – big and small, rich and poor – the extent of corruption may differ greatly, but it is in the developing world that its effects are most destructive. "Corruption hurts the poor disproportionately by diverting funds intended for development, undermining governments' ability to provide basic services, feeding inequality and injustice."[196] The first point here is, thus, that regarding the nature of the church's participation in anti-corruption efforts, it is integral to its mission, its holistic mission to the world. It is part of the church's call to proclaim hope, hope rooted in the gospel, in God's good news about our human condition. As such, the church has "to explore the challenges as well as the opportunities of being the church specifically in promoting moral renewal."[197] This brings us to the next concept of how the church may be involved in the fight against corruption.

4.4.1.2 Moral Transformation as a Defining Matrix for Church's Fight against Corruption

Closely connected to the importance of ideal of holistic nature of the church's mission is the issue of the church's role in moral transformation is paramount.

From what has been seen repeatedly in this study thus far, corruption is caused to a large degree by irresponsible and immoral behavior of those who have been entrusted with power (see 3.3.6.2). Furthermore, it was seen that corruption tends to manifest and operate, not only on an individual level, but also to a higher degree in society and public affairs (see 2.2.3.3 and 2.2.3.4); for this reason, it has both private and public implications. Therefore, the underlying call for the church to speak out has to be on the question of public morality. One may thus say that the church's function is, among others, to guide and enable society to affirm the Christian values and norms for governance within the social and political structures – or in the words of Stackhouse above: "[The church] must show that it can form, inform and sustain the moral and spiritual architecture of a civil society so that truth, justice and mercy are more nearly approximated in the souls of persons and in the institutions of the common life."[198]

---

196. Ibid.
197. Goba, "Role of the Church," no page number.
198. Stackhouse, *God and Globalization*, 107; see also 4.3.2.5.

In light also of what has also been said in this and the previous chapter with regard to the concept of human dignity (i.e. that although it originated after biblical times, it belongs to the heart of the biblical message),[199] it is again from Scripture that the church draws its vision of service and ministry to humanity. The Christian conviction of the dignity of human beings, after all, is usually traced back to the creation narrative, especially to the phrase that all human beings are made in God's own image and likeness (the *imago Dei*) (Gen 1:26–27).

Corruption denies dignity because it is a source of structural impediments that deny people access to the spiritual and material goods that belong to the community in which they live. Vorster affirms this saying that "When the human is prohibited from taking part in inter-human interaction, his [sic] dignity is impaired."[200] In conjunction with the view in chapter 2 that corruption threatens peace, freedom, justice and equality, Vorster also argues that a "human's creation as a social being presupposes a right to freedom and equality . . . [one] can only realize himself [sic] within social relationships when [he/she] has a certain freedom that includes the right to self-realization, association, and expression."[201] Corruption thus denies relationship. It destroys the avenues that "maintain human dignity [that] finds shape in love that acts as an instrument of justice. Love and justice are the regulative ideals in the light of which human dignity ought to be made."[202]

When the issue of public morality is addressed, then the image of God is respected for the human person is the most central and clear reflection of God in the church and society. Human dignity is an essential part of every human being and is an intrinsic quality that can never be separated from other essential aspects of the human person. Belief in the dignity of the human person is the foundation of morality and therefore a core element of the church's vision for society. The church's obligation to participate in shaping the moral character of society is a requirement of faith. It is a basic part of the mission which the church received from Jesus Christ, who offers a vision of life revealed to us in God's holy Word.

---

199. Vorster, "Theological Evaluation," 324.
200. Ibid., 327.
201. Ibid.
202. Ibid., 334.

It has also been argued that the kingdom of God is the central tenet of Jesus's teaching and is essential to his ministry.[203] In the Gospel of Mark, for example, Christ begins his ministry by proclaiming the immediacy of the kingdom (Mark 1:15). His emphasis was on pointing out that the healing of the sick and casting out of demons was not only the manifestation of, but also a reality of, the kingdom of God (Matt 12:28).

As far as moral transformation is concerned, an understanding of the church of the kingdom of God and the rule of Christ now and thereafter is also important. To this point Moltmann's concept of "anticipation" provides one with some useful theological insights.[204] When the church is working towards transforming the world, its work concerns not only the kingdom of God now, but also the future kingdom of God. On the concept of anticipation, Richard Gibb argues that ". . . human activity in the present [is] building the kingdom of God, the hope of a new reality arouses activity in the present, which anticipates the eschatological kingdom."[205]

Beyond "anticipation" – the eschatological echo of the kingdom of God, another implication for the kingdom of God, is understood in the context of and links it with the church doing mission or the church's mission in the world. In this understanding, the kingdom of God is thought to be manifested through human beings who are members of the church and therefore the missionary activity (broadly or holistically understood) is connected with the purposes of the kingdom.

If to be church is to be the "salt of the earth" (Matt 5:13) and "light of the world" (Matt 5:14),[206] this is what has to be done if the Spirit of Christ, active in each member of the church, is to produce the "good works" which will lead to reconciliation, justice and peace in the church and society in Africa (cf. Matt 5:16). The Lausanne Theology Working Group speaks of this as a special calling with particular advice on what constitutes this calling: "[missional] calling demands more careful and critical . . . prophetic denunciation, advocacy for and mobilization of the victims of world injustice."[207]

---

203. cf. Beasley-Murray, *Jesus and the Kingdom*, x.
204. Moltmann, *Church in the Power*, 24–26.
205. Gibb, *Grace and Global Justice*, 68–69.
206. cf. Smit in section 4.2.2 above.
207. Lausanne Theology Working Group, "Whole Church."

Thus, the role of the church is to stand at the side of Jesus Christ and, as Moltmann puts it "to continue the mission of Christ to combat all contradictions to the freedom and brotherhood of mankind [sic]."[208] Moltmann also sees the church as the community which seeks correspondence to the kingdom of God in history. It is to this view that he calls for the church to "encourage the forms of government which best serve human fellowship and human rights and dignity, and it must resist those forms which hinder or suppress these things."[209] As the church plays an important active role in this, it is also helping in the formation of a social-political order that overcomes the suffering due to corruption and ministers to the new life of the kingdom of God. In the establishment and maintenance of political order, faith then becomes a critical ingredient. In clarifying this ingredient, and by taking his cue from Moltmann, Richard Bauckham writes, "for Moltmann Christian political engagement is no substitute for Christian faith, but one of the forms which faith must take in action; and political theology is no substitute for dogmatic theology, but theology's critical reflection on its own political function."[210]

Finally, and very importantly, also is the fact that the kingdom of God means that God is sovereign (see 3.3.4.3). As the Lausanne Theology Working Group puts it, "God owns the world, rules the world, reveals himself through the world, watches all that happens in the world, and loves the world."[211] The kingdom of God also means "God's acting in his sovereign power to deliver man [sic] from the destructive powers that enthrall him."[212] So what does this imply for the nature of the church's role in the fight against corruption? First of all, the church is called to participate in the building of the kingdom of God. The church manifests itself when, as an agent of transformation, it becomes active in enabling and keeping society as a place where human beings can live justly and peacefully. As the church addresses the issue of corruption it is doing "kingdom work" or "kingdom mission." Oliver O'Donovan says that truth "represents God's kingdom,

---

208. Moltmann, *The Church in the Power*, 176–177.
209. Ibid., 178.
210. Bauckham, *Theology of Jürgen Moltmann*, 99.
211. Lausanne Theology Working Group, "Whole Church."
212. Beasley-Murray, *Jesus and the Kingdom*, 1.

before which the authorities and powers of this world must cast down their crowns, never to pick them up."[213] What may be called the pursuance of kingdom values therefore forms a guideline for the faithful and the church in how they should seek to promote the moral transformation of society, also with regard to issues of corruption and injustice.[214] The reference here to values opens the door to the discussion in the following section on the role of values or virtues and the way that society may be transformed by the church by being "a community of character," a character which reflects kingdom values and norms. After all, one of the tasks of the church, as Nyiawung reminds is ". . . to define and maintain societal standards in accordance with the prescription of kingdom principles preached by Jesus."[215]

4.4.1.3 Kingdom Values/Virtues and Norms and the Church as Community of Character

What exactly are kingdom values and norms, how do they inform the fight against corruption and injustice and how are they taught and learned?

It will be remembered that Koopman spoke earlier (4.3.2.3) of virtues in the context of public theology as public and civic virtues:

> public wisdom in contexts of complexity, ambiguity, tragedy and *aporia* (dead-end streets); public justice in context of inequalities and injustices on local and global levels; public temperance in context of greed and consumerism amidst poverty and alienation; public fortitude amidst situations of powerlessness and inertia; public faith amidst feelings of disorientation and rootless-ness in contemporary societies; public hope amidst situations of despair and melancholy; public love in societies where public solidarity and compassion are absent.

---

213. O'Donovan, *Ways of Judgment*, 292.

214. cf. Vorster, "Theological Evaluation," 333. Time and again in the course of this study reference has been made especially to the centrality of the scriptural importance of the values of justice and righteousness – e.g. Col 4:11: "Jesus, who is called Justus, also sends greetings. These are the only Jews among my co-workers for the kingdom of God, and they have proved a comfort to me"; Rom 14:17: "For the kingdom of God is not a matter of eating and drinking, but of righteousness, peace and joy in the Holy Spirit . . ."; Matt 5:10: "Blessed are those who are persecuted because of righteousness, for theirs is the kingdom of heaven."

215. Nyiawung, "Prophetic Witness," no page number.

Max Stackhouse refers to the church as "those who receive the vision of the promised reign of God" and those who are "convicted to instill . . . integrity, honesty, diligence, fairness, and stewardship"[216] (4.3.2.5). Rowan Williams is convinced that the church is "to be a place where people [are] educating one another about civic questions and human dignity, where people [are] educating and being educated about liberty, responsibility, the creation of a sustainable human environment" (4.3.4.2). In chapter 3, section 3.6.4 (Relationality, Relational Justice and God's Vision of a Peaceful and Just Society), it was said that with reference to Mark 7:21–23 that Christ identifies characteristics of right relationships or the virtues to be displayed within right relationships to be justice, mercy, faithfulness, forgiveness, truth, generosity, compassion, respect, hope, patience and love, mercy, faithfulness, forgiveness, truth, generosity, compassion, respect, hope, patience and love.

All of the above represent what one may also call "kingdom values or virtues." In his article, "The Kingdom of God in the Teaching of Jesus," New Testament scholar G. R. Beasley-Murray explains that "[t]he expression 'kingdom of God' has itself been the subject of a great deal of discussion [and] that is not surprising in view of the breadth of meaning often attributed to it."[217] Since it is not our intention to explore various meanings, but rather to establish a general picture which reflects the kingdom of God in relation to its values and norms, we adopt the Beasley-Murray's definition, according to which,

> in the NT as a whole, the kingdom of God has specific reference to the fulfilment of the promises of God in the OT of the time when God puts forth his royal power *to end injustice and oppression* by this world's evil powers and to establish his rule of *righteousness, peace and joy* for humanity – in a word, *to fulfil his purpose in creating the world.*[218]

According to Carl Henry,

> [t]he kingdom of God is proclaimed in prophecy, intrudes its signs and wonders, is historically present in the sinless and

---

216. Stackhouse, "Public Theology," 180.
217. Beasley-Murray, "Kingdom of God," 19.
218. Ibid. (emphasis added).

suffering servant's coming, is hastened toward its universal climax by his resurrection in anticipation of an eschatological judgment of mankind and universal *victory of righteousness*, and is extended by the new regenerate society's *containment of injustice and unrighteousness*.[219]

These perspectives, which emphasize God's exercising his royal power to end injustice and oppression or to ensure justice, salvation, peace and righteousness on earth, forms the background to the important concepts of "values" and "norms" in the kingdom. First of all, these "norms and values have but one source: the Bible . . . and are spread wherever social reform takes place so that injustice is rolled back. [It is a] kind of kingdom-expectation Jesus considered of central importance."[220]

Kingdom values and norms calls for the church to focus her public role as working towards building God's kingdom here on earth. However, it should be clear that God's kingdom should remain *God's* kingdom and that the church is only *participating* in extending that kingdom. The church, the human fellowship cannot at all determine the direction of the said kingdom, but it has the mandate to perpetuate it. In the words of Bradley Pace: "The kingdom of God is not a result of human action, but the fulfilment of God's purposes on earth. Nonetheless, Christians are called to work toward God's kingdom – we might say to work in the trajectory of the Kingdom."[221] As such, Pace strengthens this argument as he quotes Temple: "The loyalty of the disciple is still to Christ and his absolute demand; but that demand is to be fulfilled, not by isolation from the world but by the life of consecration in the world."[222] And, as Gordon and Evans summarizes:

> [t]he kingdom of God is central to God's overall plan for humanity. Focusing on the kingdom of God enables us to understand the wider implications of Jesus' life, death and resurrection. He has come to restore all things to how they should be, to tackle the effects of all sin, which includes offering individual

---

219. Henry, "Reflections," 45 (emphasis added).
220. McKenzie, "Christian Norms," 421.
221. Pace, "Public Reason," 282–283.
222. Pace quoting Temple, *Citizen and Churchman*, 283.

salvation as well as restoration of our society. Followers of the King are required to work with him in bringing this good news to all people. . . [*for*] The kingdom is characterized by '*shalom,*' which includes social justice, peace and personal integrity. It is based on love and grace, submission and service.[223]

On the need for ethical and moral renewal as a prerequisite to fighting corruption, there is a need to first understand that when corruption is rampant in any society, it distorts the existing values. So renewal of values and norms has to be an important part of the process of fighting corruption by the church. Though this process can complex and the church needs to be careful in order not to compromise its call, Forrester advises that,

> in seeking a renewal of values . . . in challenging rather than conforming to the conventional values of our society, we are seeking to confess the faith and make that contribution which only Christians can offer. All down the centuries Christianity has generated and sustained values, but this has for the most part been done as a by-product or spin off from the endeavor to proclaim the gospel and live the life of the kingdom.[224]

In the context of corruption, when the church is doing this (working toward moral regeneration), it means it is conforming to God's call and that it should also attend to the fact that

> theology has the task of engaging with the underlying assumptions of a society and culture about the nature of human beings, about human flourishing, about human destiny and human fellowship, about the relation of the social order and a transcendent order, about the way the community allocates worth and chooses its goals.[225]

It is clear that from a theological-ethical perspective and in line with our purpose in this study (i.e. to establish what role can the church play in

---

223. Gordon and Evans, "Mission of the Church," 3. See again the relationship between justice and shalom and sin as the absence of shalom in the discussion on the thought of Plantinga, Wolterstorff and Wright in 3.6.1.

224. Forrester, *Beliefs, Values and Policies,* 40.

225. Ibid., 38.

the fight against corruption), that the source of virtues to be "generated" or "regenerated" is of course the Bible and the example and teaching of Christ. But is it the church, say for example in its sermons, parents, and members (as a manifestation of "the church" in everyday life [Smit]) – that may play a key role in teaching ethical virtues. For centuries, it has been the role of the church to teach believers to obey God's laws. The focus of the church's teaching has for long been on the "development of habit" which "requires consistency of conduct, or conduct that is consistently shaped in all its details toward what is desirable."[226] If this done properly by the church, it will have a long-term effect. In this regard Carr refers to Aristotle:

> By doing the acts that we do in our transactions with other men [sic] we become just or unjust, and by doing the acts that we do in the presence of danger, and being habituated to feel fear or confidence, we become brave or cowardly. . . . It makes no small difference, then, whether we form habits of one kind or of another from our very youth; it makes a very great difference, or rather all the difference.[227]

At this stage, it is helpful to bring into the discussion some of the insights of North American ethicist Stanley Hauerwas, whose ecclesiology emphasizes the fact that the church should be viewed as a unique community that can sustain ethical life in societies. Hauerwas believes that a good society needs a more substantial ethic to survive, and that through its very nature the church can play its social role more effectively – this role is in character formation which should be at the heart of ethical living. In Hauerwas' words,

> to reassert the social significance of the church as a distinctive society with an integrity peculiar to itself . . . the truth of whose convictions cannot be divorced from the sort of community the church is and should be.[228]

The social significance of the church, is also expounded by Hauerwas in terms of service by the church as a community, and one may add, to

---

226. Carr and Steutel, *Virtue Ethics and Moral Education*, 70.

227. NE II 1 1103b17–25 in Curren, Randall R., *Aristotle on the Necessity of Public Education*, 154.

228. Hauerwas, *Community of Character*, 1.

the community. Again the uniqueness of the church remains crucial in his argument. For example, writing in collaboration with William Willimon, Hauerwas affirms:

> [t]hus the power and truth that make Christian service possible are intrinsic to the church's character and correlative interpretative skills which enable Christians to name what is happening and to discern what to do thereafter.[229]

A particularly relevant concept for our purposes and used by Hauerwas is that of "story telling" as the mode of engagement as the church seeks to influence public and political policy.[230] Before story telling is applied, however, Hauerwas suggests two crucial points. First, he is of the opinion that the church "must be trained" in certain virtues. According to Hauerwas, a "tangible and trained character rather than theoretical belief is the sign of the church, for it is the story of the love of God in Christ crucified that we must be trained in." Leonardo Boff refers to "Hauerwas' emphasis upon practices and performance as exposers of truthful living rather than simply ideas."[231] Boff chooses the term "practice" (the actual doings of the church) and "performance" (the task accomplished and standard level of the church) to be important if one wishes to understand Hauerwas. The idea of training suits our argument in that it portrays the fact that if the church is

---

229. Hauerwas and Willimon, *Resident Aliens*, 146.

230. Interestingly the idea of biblical narrative used in the biblical-theological assessment of in/justice has been referred to earlier in this study as well, for example in 3.6 with reference to Gordon ("Mission of Church") and proponents of Trinitarian theology: "From the narratives on God's acts and character one may also already identify some biblical norms and values, including, for example, compassion for the vulnerable, marginalized and oppressed (e.g. Exod 22:22), care for the poor (e.g. Lev 23:22), the promotion of justice (for example, fairness in trade – 19:36), fairness in not charging interest (25:36), fair distribution of land (25:8–54) and paying fair wages to laborers (Mal 3:5) . . . The Christian doctrine of God, the Trinitarian theology of the likes of Torrance, Gunton, and Cunningham shows that one should not forget that biblical narratives and teaching on God in Jesus Christ and God the Holy Spirit will also reveal the Christian understanding of justice." Also noteworthy is some theologians' emphasis on the role of narrative within public theology – e.g. Koopman: "Prophetic public theology is, at the same time, a narrative theology in that it 'tells the stories of pain and suffering, and of hope and liberation'" (4.3.2.3) and Forrester (4.3.2.1), who reminds one that "the Christian faith is an ongoing story, a narrative, rather than a theory or a system" and then "proposes what he calls 'unsystematic Christianity' in this narrative way as a methodological alternative to typical understandings of religious belief."

231. Boff, *Church, Charisma and Power*, 109.

not knowledgeable enough in contemporary public issues such as those of corruption, it will not be effective in its mission of constituting, as Hauerwas puts it, a "socio-political ethic."²³² What Hauerwas wants to do is to challenge the church to understand "what kind of community [it] must be to rightly tell the stories of God?"²³³ – even if the church may know very well that "discipleship displays the story of the kingdom which Jesus embodied and which is embodied among his followers [and] [i]n so being church, [it is] the organized form of Jesus's story."²³⁴

Second, as referred to above, in addition to training, Hauerwas is of the opinion that "story telling" as a mode of engagement by the church is to be understood in the context of the church understanding its message – the gospel and ethics. For Hauerwas, the gospel is about the nature of the self. By "self" he emphasizes the concepts of virtue and character in his understanding of Christian ethics. To explain this interplay between the gospel, virtue, character, and self, it is worth quoting Hauerwas once more:

> [t]he nature and moral determination of the self, vision and virtue again become morally significant categories. We are as we come to see and as that seeing becomes enduring in our intentionality. We do not come to see, however, just by looking but by training our vision through the metaphors and symbols that constitute our central convictions. How we come to see therefore is a function of how we come to be since our seeing necessarily is determined by how our basic images are embodied by the self, i.e. our character.²³⁵

To Hauerwas's insights and bringing the discussion squarely within an African context is the thought of paramount African theologian, John S. Mbiti, known as the father of Christian theology in Africa.²³⁶ Mbiti's par-

---

232. Hauerwas, *Community of Character*, 51–52.
233. Ibid., 4.
234. Ibid., 50.
235. Hauerwas, *Communiy of Character*, 2.
236. See one of his major works, *African Religions and Philosophy*. This work is most commonly regarded as a small compendium on the meaning of life in traditional and modern African society. The fact that emphasis is here placed on the thought of Hauerwas and Mbiti, this does not mean that similar convictions are not subscribed to by other (public theologians). One finds, for example, in Forrester (*Beliefs, Values and Policies*, 7)

ticular contributory relevancy rests on his sharp emphasis on the importance of morality, community and communal care and responsibility in African societies.

Mbiti describes morality in African contexts by using the word "morals" as an ethical description of principles that not only constitute African morality, but that need to be upheld in an African society. In his words, Mbiti asserts that

> [m]orals deal with the question of what is right and good, and what is wrong and evil, in human conduct. African peoples have a deep sense of right and wrong. In the course of the years, this moral sense has produced customs, rules, laws, traditions and taboos which can be observed in each society. Their morals are embedded in these systems of behavior and conduct.[237]

Most importantly is the way that for Mbiti, ethics and morality are seen as standard setters in Africa to test and perhaps approve any member of a community's quality of life. Mbiti therefore observes: "To say, in African societies, that a person is 'good' or 'bad' has extremely profound connotations, for it summarizes the whole image or picture of the person in the context of his [sic] actions."[238] As it pertains to this study, a corrupt member of community is expected to be aware that by offering or accepting a bribe, he or she is automatically a bad person. For Mbiti, according to African moral or ethical life and teaching,

> [t]here are many things held to be morally wrong and evil, such as: robbery, murder, rape, telling lies, stealing, being cruel, saying bad words, showing disrespect, practicing sorcery or witchcraft, interfering with public rights, backbiting, being

---

an emphasis on "personal morality and accepted values"; in Stackhouse ("Public Theology and Ethical Judgment," 105) a focus on the need to understanding what he calls "realms [. . .] personal or individual and communal morality personal/individual and communal morality"; in Lamin Sanneh (*Abolitionists Abroad*, 119) a plea to church and society to seek to show and act on the "[. . .] commitment to establishing a new society based on public morality, freedom, human dignity, integrity, the rule of law, and justice"; and in Kunhiyop's *African Christian Ethics* a placing of corruption and injustice within the context of the challenges associated with African Christian morality.

237. Mbiti, "Ethical Nature of God," 175.
238. Mbiti, *African Religions and Philosophy*, 215.

lazy or greedy or selfish, breaking promises, and so on. All these and many others are moral vices in the eyes of the community. Whoever does them is considered to be a bad or evil person.[239]

By being corrupt, a "bad" member of an African society, says Mbiti, justifies the seriousness of said state when he says:[240] "African morals lay a great emphasis on social conduct, since a basic African view is that the individual exists only because others exist" and he further pleads: "[i]t is morals which have produced the virtues that society appreciates and endeavors to preserve, such as friendship, compassion, love, honesty, justice, courage, self-control, helpfulness, bravery, and so on." Contrary to morals and virtues is to welcome the "moral evil," which for Mbiti "pertains to what man [sic] does against his fellow man."[241]

Important for us, too, is the fact that Mbiti brings to the stage the important concept of good governance in an African context (on good governance see 4.4.1.5) as "[t]raditional chiefs and rulers, where these exist, have the duty of keeping law and order, and executing justice in their areas."[242] In addition, for Mbiti, if injustice is not adequately addressed, then African communal "sense of security and unity [will be] shaken and undermined. [Then] Africa must now search for new values, new identities and a new self-consciousness."[243]

In conclusion to this section, Luke Bretherton, scholar at and convener of the Faith and Public Policy Forum at King's College, London, draws insights from the likes of Hauerwas, O'Donovan and also from Pope John Paul II, when writing in the context of his understanding of ecclesiology and the political mission of the church. He reminds us that "faithful Christian witness necessarily reframes every aspect of human life, including its political ordering, through the prism of church order which is an icon of the Christ-event."[244] This means that the church as an institution with its offices and principles of government, doctrine, authority of creeds, discipline, and

---

239. Mbiti, "Ethical Nature of God," 178.
240. Ibid., 175.
241. Mbiti, *African Religions and Philosophy*, 213.
242. Ibid., 211.
243. Ibid., 271.
244. Bretherton, *Christianity and Contemporary Politics*, 55.

sacraments all set within the guideline of scriptural truths, has the potential play its role in public through manifesting the implications of the death of Jesus Christ to it. Ultimately, though, Bretheron reminds us that theology should go

> beyond our church circles to the point of engaging with leaders in the public domain . . . as . . . [o]ur present situation, conveniently called 'post-Christendom,' requires us to address especially the challenge of the society; it has as its backdrop those centuries-long engagement with government which we call "Christendom."[245] The church's one project is to witness to the kingdom of God. Christendom is response to mission, and as such a sign that God has blessed it. It is constituted not by the church's seizing alien power, but by alien power's becoming attentive to the church."[246]

This means that the success of the church's influence will depend on how it effectively deploys its biblical-theological arguments in the public square as responses to contemporary issues, in "speaking the truth to power."

4.4.1.4 Speaking the Truth to (Political) Power and the Issue of Language

Because this section reflects on the church engaging the state as prophetic witness, it is important to first briefly clarify the understanding and the relevance of the word "politics" here. For this purpose, the study adopts Roger Overton's definition of politics:

> Politics concerns the legitimate exercise of state power through laws. All legitimate state power is concerned with protecting every citizen equally through law, submitting every citizen equally to the law, and securing citizens equally against the "bad guys" inside and outside the borders – all by laws that should promote

---

245. O'Donovan says he uses the term "Christendom" (in keeping with the good deal of current discussion) to refer to a historical idea: that is to say, the idea of a professedly Christian Secular political order and the history of that political idea in practice. Christendom is an *era*, an era in which the truth of Christianity was taken to be a truth of secular politics See O'Donovan, *Desire of the Nations*.

246. O'Donovan, *Desire of the Nations*, 193.

virtue and punish vice. Legitimate state power is concerned with justice, peace and security.[247]

As we noted earlier, it is often in the political realm where corruption is rife. It is also in the world of politics where governance, standards of decision making, justice, the application of the rule of law, democracy and the well-being of the state are generally determined.[248] In order to tackle corruption by restoring trust and embracing a culture of transparency in public life, Oliver O'Donovan's idea of political theology embedded in justice, church and state, and Christian moral theology fits well. For O'Donovan,

> [t]heology must be political if it is to be evangelical. Rule out the political questions and you cut short the proclamation of God's saving power; you leave people enslaved where they ought to be set free from sin – their own sin and others.[249]

The phrase "speaking truth to power" came about as one of the ways in which the church could be encouraged to engage the state in the long-standing debate on the relationship between the church and state.[250] This tension is sometimes regarded historically as "a fight which portrayed the enmity between the church and the state as the two centers of power and authority."[251]

Again the main thrust of speaking the truth to power is grounded on the idea of the church seeking to engage in the enterprise of moral and social transformation. South African theologian Charles Villa-Vicencio broadens this to include not only the prophetic, but in fact also "priestly roles of the church in relation to its political responsibility"[252] (cf. again Koopman's ex-

---

247. Overton, *God and Governing*, 117. Note how the concepts of justice, peace and security, but also virtues all features in this definition.

248. Political corruption is also that which "points to lack of accountability, authoritarian styles of leadership and abuse of power. Its remedies typically include democratization, a strong media, and legislative oversight of the executive, codes of conduct governing the behavior of politicians, campaign finance legislation and a mobilized civil society ready to bring politicians to account" (Mulgan et al., "Corruption and Anti-Corruption," 9).

249. O'Donovan, *Desire of the Nations*, 3.

250. cf. Sloane, "Justifying Advocacy."

251. De Gruchy, "Christian Witnessing," 66.

252. Villa-Vicencio, Towards a Transformed Society, 6.

planation of prophetic, priestly and servanthood nature of public theology in 4.3.2.3 above). Villa-Vicencio makes some cautionary remarks which further highlights exactly what speaking the truth to power is about. He argues that the

> . . . church needs to be more than the purveyor of what the "prophet-turned-politician" [offers, namely] "naïve and unrealistic" niceties in the face of hard political realities. Without surrendering the importance of the prophetic and priestly voice, both prophet and priest have a responsibility to speak to the real world in promoting concrete possibilities for resolving of the social problems facing the nation. The church cannot afford to speak only at the level of principle, absolute standards and what would be nice in an ideal world if it is to promote real transformation.[253]

In this study, the concept "speaking truth to power" is called an "art" to indicate that there is more to it than the mere uttering of words – albeit critical words – to the state. It is a skillful execution, a careful and well-articulated activity in which speaking the truth to power (or, as it is known in some circles, "public witnessing") results from a dialogue between Scripture and the realities of the society. In other words, for the church truthful speaking must never be divorced from, and must in fact flow from, its most authoritative source, Scripture, albeit in conversation with political, economic and social realities.[254]

Koopman calls on the church to participate in addressing public issues by and through courageous criticism, storytelling, conscious technical analysis, and participating in policy making. As such, the work of the church should be characterized by a "prophetic vision, prophetic criticism, prophetic storytelling and prophetic analysis." Quoting Hauerwas, Bretherton calls this work a "true gift of the church to society," a gift in a form of the church's ability "to open new horizons, provide new languages of description, and embody alternative practices."[255]

---

253. Ibid.
254. cf. Sloane, "Justifying Advocacy," 4–5, 11.
255. Bretherton, *Christianity and Contemporary Politics*, 54.

Bretherton's reference to "new languages of description" opens the door to a core argument in this section, namely that the church also has to learn "secular language" to partake in the struggle against corruption, while remaining faithful also to the language of faith.[256] As was seen, this requirement was emphasized repeatedly by several of the public theologians referred to above.[257] One example of this in the context of this study may be the use of UNAC's definition of corruption often referred to in this study, namely, "The abuse of public power for private benefit." In the secular sphere, it has been shown that the discourse on corruption has been "as an area of multifocal inquiry." This has been shown by the increased number of endeavors

> to explain context-specific instances of corruption through various models, approaches, studies and analyses . . . various understandings of corruption [which] render it a field of much contention marked by lack of consensus on its meanings, causes, and a theoretical inconclusiveness as to its remedies.[258]

While no theologian would disagree with the importance of the traditional biblical, theological, and ethical definitions of corruption as sin or lawlessness (1 John 3:4) and our "lacking the godliness demanded,"[259] in order for the church to address the issue of corruption, the church also needs to understand and engage secular understandings of corruption, its causes and effects and ways to address. In light of this, one may call this a shift from a secular political to a theological-ethical language. The change could also

---

256. cf. Koopman and Smit quoted in Hansen, *Christian in Public*, 9.

257. Cf. Forrester public theology as conversation "requires learning the language of the secular world in such a way that Christian discourse relates to it without losing its particular insights and contribution to the discussion" (Forrester, *Beliefs, Values and Policies*, 61), (4.3.2.1); Stackhouse: ". . . if a theology is to be trusted to participate in public discourse it ought to be able to make a plausible case for what it advocates in terms that can be comprehended by those who are not believers . . . It should be able to articulate its core convictions in comprehensible terms across many modes of discourse, explaining its symbolic and mythical terms . . . in ways that expose their multiple levels of meaning ("Reflections," 112), (4.3.2.5); Bedford-Strohm: ". . . public theology . . . does not separate itself from the world into a self-sufficient counter-community with its own religious language, but knows how to speak the language of the world and how to be in dialogue with the world ("Reflections," 36), (4.3.2.5).

258. Pavarala and Malik, "Religion, Ethics and Attitudes," 10.

259. Schreiner, *New Testament Theology*, 510.

be understood as a process to "theologize the universally (internationally) endorsed and widely used understandings of corruption."[260]

The above considerations again show that the church must learn the language of secular discourse *and* at the same time remain conscious of its own unique language of addressing public issues. This is a task *par excellence* of public theology. For example, Katie Day suggests that, "in the production of public theology the community of faith needs to find a language and an agenda which is meaningful to those both inside and outside the tent, persuasive to both communities and finally contributing to the social good."[261] This has been part of the aims of this study thus far as well in understanding the secular perspectives and language on the issue of corruption (ch. 2) while remaining true to the language of faith as it concerns corruption and in/justice (ch. 3).

4.4.1.5 The Church as Prophetic Witness toward Good Governance in "Critical Solidarity"

In several instances thus far, the concept of (good) governance has been explored with reference to different contexts, for example, "God is the creator, [and God of justice] and the world that he created is good (Gen 1:1, 21, 25) (see 3.4.3 and 3.4.4). Clearly the church has ". . . a mandate to be concerned with how God's world is governed."[262] It was shown that God's governance of the universe acknowledges the importance of human freedom, within defined limits (3.6.3). Human responsibility is dependent on being able to choose between right and wrong. One may therefore say that governments also have a limited role in trying to dictate human behavior, but should allow for significant freedom and responsibility.[263] To this argument, Wayne Grudem asserts that "government cannot save people or fundamentally change human hearts" because "personal salvation is a work of God, not government . . . [C]ivil government – even a good one – cannot

---

260. Ibid.
261. Day, "Construction of Public Theology," 356.
262. Stott in Kunhiyop, *African Christian Ethics*, 26.
263. Gordon and Evans, "Mission," 18.

save people from their sins, for that can come about only through personal faith in Jesus Christ."[264]

Furthermore, God is sovereign over *all* nations and *all* people are accountable to God (3.4.3) – "God also holds unbelieving nations accountable for their actions (see Isa 13–23; Jer 46–51; Ezek 25–32; Amos 1–2)."[265] Of course, theologically speaking, governments too are accountable to God and "should serve the people and seek the good of the people, not the rulers"[266] because the "use of government power for self-enrichment of the leader and his family and friends betrays the fundamental purpose of government to serve people" (cf. 4.3.1 above).[267] Corruption is, therefore, also a symptom of weak human governance and it is manifested in oppression, neglect, marginalization, instability and the betrayal of promises and hope. Corruption is "a resultant effect of poor governance, excessive discretionary powers, lack of checks and balances in the government institutions and high levels of inefficiency."[268] This clearly does not echo the picture of the kingdom of God painted in the previous section. God wants to see governance done properly for the well-being of humanity. According to Nyiawung, "[t]he suffering imposed on humanity by egoistic systems and individuals, in both government and private sectors, is such that the Christian heart and conscience cannot ignore it."[269]

Equally important is for the church to know that "inwardly transformed people are needed to see a transformed society. Merely passing good laws and having good government will never be enough to change a society." We need to "affirm that government policy and laws do have an immense influence on a nation for good or for evil."[270] The relevance of prophetic witness by the church as a possible mode of public discourse, therefore, remains important for this study. According to Goba, this prophetic witness is

---

264. Grudem, *Politics*, 96.
265. Ibid., 85.
266. Ibid.
267. Ibid., 87.
268. The African Executive, "Corruption," 1.
269. Nyiawung, "Prophetic Witness," no page numbers.
270. Ibid., 96, 99.

> . . . aimed at liberating the good news of God's salvation that has, to date, been confined within the four walls of the church and directing the church's attention towards the public and its needs. It is an attempt to enable the church to review its strategy and its impact in the market place of the cry for social justice. It is a topic that tickles and awakens the church's awareness and its responsibility towards another important but neglected dimension of its prophetic mission, which is that of prophetic witnessing to the public.[271]

Other scholars, such as Knight, reminds that the church's prophetic witness in the public sphere is part of the legacy of Jesus Christ himself, and Knight refers, for example, to Jesus's words in Luke 4:43: "I must preach the good news of the kingdom of God to the other cities also; for I was sent for this purpose," and Luke 2:38 with regard to Jesus's public witness about the liberation of Jerusalem.[272] In this regard, Paeth refers to a "messianic ethic" (i.e. to Jesus's teaching) that offers the church a model, a norm and a mandate towards such prophetic witness.[273]

In the context of what has been said in this section and in light of the historical and contemporary theological perspectives on the church's role in the public sphere, in the acknowledgement of the role of both church and state and the prophetic role of the church as prophetic witness to good governance, what has been called "constructive engagement and critical solidarity" are other useful dimensions of a description of the church's prophetic witness. This is a more common approach adopted by the church as it seeks to continue to be an effective instrument or agent of moral transformation.

Without entering into a too deep discussion on the dynamics involved when the church uses this approach,[274] a common meaning of it concerns a relationship whereby the church seeks to work with the state by supporting its efforts to rebuild and transform society, yet at the same time, it continues to reserve the right to criticize government in areas where this may be

---

271. Goba, "Choosing Who We Are," 66.
272. Knight, *Luke's Gospel*, 85.
273. Paeth, *Exodus Church*, 161–164.
274. For more detail on the concept of critical solidarity, also see Le Bruyns, "Theological Perspectives."

necessary. It is also done in light of the church's understanding of its own identity. In the words of Kumalo,

> A prophetic role in this situation means that the church affirms government when it is addressing the needs of all people especially the poor, but also criticizes and distances itself from it when it is ignoring them. In this case the church never stands with government but with the poor, it is government who joins the church and the poor and it benefit from the affirmation and praises of the church, but as soon as it leaves the poor, it has left the church and risks the ruthless criticism and denunciation of the church in the name of God.[275]

This task may sound easy, but Setiloane's understanding of critical solidarity reminds the church to be careful and vigilant to not succumb to extremes as this

> . . . means that the church supports initiatives, which promotes justice, peace and democracy whilst continuing to protest against unjust policies and protecting the interest of those vulnerable and minority groups. This means that a new approach to church-state relations needs to be developed which moves away from the dominant models in which the church is either absorbed by the state or it regards the state as an enemy.[276]

As such, H. Russel Botman also reminds that,

> the challenge for the church is to be provocative – to be political, without being bound by loyalty to a specific political party; to analyse economic systems and their consequences, without adhering to one economic theory or ideology; to challenge and question policies that exclude or marginalize specific sections of society; and to challenge the priorities of public spending.[277]

---

275. Kumalo, "Prophetic Church," 5.
276. Setiloane, *Introduction*, 33.
277. Botman, "Good Governance," 4.

4.4.1.6 Reconstruction and Public Policy Advocacy as Reconstructive or Transformative Prophetic Action

In this section the focus falls, first on the church's mode of engagement in the public sphere as it pertains to corruption and injustice as a form of transformative public policy advocacy, and second, on the issue of reconstruction with the help of the views of African scholar Jesse Mugambi.

One often hears appeals on the church in its engagement in the public sphere to be involved in "public policy advocacy." Advocacy, too, "is notoriously difficult to define and is used by different people to mean different things. In some ways this is helpful since it demands that the concept evolves, changing over time and being shaped by different contexts and understandings of power and politics."[278] Given the volume and scope of material existing the subject of advocacy, for the purposes of this study, advocacy is understood to refer to *speaking up on behalf of those who have been treated unfairly*. This approach could also entail engaging with the general public to raise awareness on an important issue as well as influencing policymakers towards desired solutions.

In this study thus far, it has been suggested that churches, more than ever before, are called to participate in analyzing government policies that impact on the lives of people. This calls for theological-ethical analysis of social issues and problems. In order to do so the church is also challenged to learn about, understand and to speak on behalf of the people with regard to the prevailing policies, dominant cultural values and institutional power structures that affect their lives. To do this effectively, the church is challenged, as was seen, to uphold the tenets of the gospel in its advocacy which means it has to "to define and maintain societal standards in accordance with the prescription of kingdom principles preached by Jesus."[279] This task has implications for the advocate (or, in this context, the prophet). The critical nature of the prophet's task requires that he/she steers away from partisan politics, for the prophet is a representative of the values, principles and presence of the reign of God.[280] "[T]he church must be conscious of the

---

278. Gibbs and Ajulu, *Role of the Church*, 11.
279. Nyiawung, "Prophetic Witness," no page numbers.
280. Botman, "Towards a World-Formative Christianity," 74.

fact that 'what the world waits to see is whether what we (the church) have is better than what they have.'"[281]

Goba also raised concerns about a careful approach to advocacy as an ethical task of the church:

> This means we [the church] need to be very clear about what we are proclaiming because we stand under judgment if we proclaim something that is less than hope or is shown to be a false hope. That is why we need as a church to be very careful about proclaiming a particular policy of a human government or political party to be the hope of the poor. We need to subject it to biblical scrutiny, so that we can be assured that what we are proclaiming is in fact rooted in the gospel, the good news of what God would want us to say today.[282]

The reference to public policy advocacy as transformative prophetic action, opens the door for some further reflection on the issue of transformation or, in the terminology of African theologian Jesse Mugambi, reconstruction. Mugambi's theological explanation of the role of Christian theology rests on his views for the need for transformation/reconstruction of the whole of Africa. This need is well articulated in his works *God Humanity and Nature in Relation to Justice and Peace; The Church and the Future in Africa: Problems and Promises*, and *From Liberation to Reconstruction: African Christian Theology after the Cold War*.

Mugambi understands the need for reconstruction at three major levels. First, reconstruction is personal, in that *individual reconstruction* is the starting point. The intentions and motives of the individual must be changed to reflect the direction of the appropriate social change. Recalling our previous discussion on human nature and human behavior in the context of corruption, Mugambi's first level of reconstruction is useful in that corruption can be addressed by the church because its focus is in soul winning – meaning in this sense the effect of the gospel on human beings when personal lives are changed for better, that is to say when the hearing of the gospel results in a life-changing experience.

---

281. Lewis and Wilkins, *Church*, 48.
282. Goba, "Role of the Church," 6.

Second, there is a need for *cultural reconstruction*. Such cultural components include politics, economics, ethics, aesthetics and religion. Each of these must go through a kind of reconstruction for appropriate social change to happen. It also includes acknowledging, appreciating and cultivating traditional African values such as giving, generosity, hospitality and mutual care. This second level of reconstruction serves as yet another entry point for the church to engage politics and governments in seeking to address injustices of corruption in society.

Third, Mugambi argues for *ecclesial reconstruction*. This includes reconstruction in the areas of management structure, financial policies, pastoral care, human resources development, research, family education, service and witness. This third level of reconstruction brings a clear challenge for the church to be concerned about her reputation in wider society (see in this regard, 4.3.1.7). The war on corruption will be successful if carried out by an accountable church – a church which understood itself as that which is made up of believers will give an account of themselves and fellow human beings to God (with reference to Rom 14:12). Reputation as a social construct is also a church's public image, so the church must pay some attention to its reputation, where failing to correct a negative impression would be harmful to the success of its message.

Mugambi's view of reconstruction is very important because it includes not only social but also personal, cultural and ecclesial transformation. Mugambi holds strongly that theology in the twenty-first century will be most effective if the social and physical reality of the continent and its people are accurately understood and reinterpreted. He also suggests that the fundamental themes of Christian theology should be treated in relation to African culture, history and situation. Arguably, this suggestion is valid because it is useful in the wider approach, for example Mugambi's concept of reconstruction which in his view should take a multidisciplinary perspective – he advises that reconstruction is the most useful concept for reflection in Africa now and in the future.[283]

Mugambi furthermore warns that for theology and the church to play a role in public square and in order bear fruit there it must

---

283. Mugambi, *From Liberation to Reconstruction*, 5.

be reconstructive, rather than destructive; inclusive rather than exclusive; proactive rather than reactive; complementary rather than competitive; integrative rather than disintegrative, programme-driven rather than project driven; people-centered rather than institution-centered; deed-oriented rather than word-oriented; participatory rather than autocratic; regenerative rather than degenerative; future sensitive; rather than past-sensitive; cooperative rather than confrontational; consultative rather than imposition.[284]

Mugambi's proposal for *ecclesial* reconstruction in the context of what he calls the characteristics of African religiosity is also important. The specific characteristics he refers to are African spirituality, the Bible and lay participation as keys to the hope for ecclesial transformation.

Mugambi regards African spirituality as synonymous with African religiosity because in the African context, religion is and has to be at center of life. In other words, ecclesial reconstruction necessarily means and involves the study of the total or full appropriation of the Christian faith. Talking about the Bible as the central book in Christianity, it is from his strong evangelical background that Mugambi emphasizes the authority of Scripture. As far as lay participation is concerned, Mugambi argues that lay leaders, regardless of gender, are key people because they sustain the daily life of congregations and these would play a major role in ecclesial reconstruction especially in this era of secularization in Africa. If religion is to be relevant to Africa, Mugambi asserts, it must make qualitative changes in the lives of people. This again echoes earlier reflections on human well-being and flourishing that should be found in a corrupt free society. In short, for Mugambi intensification of religious commitment should lead to positive social reconstruction and not passive piety and this is necessary in Africa.

---

284. Ibid., xv. Mugambi's views clearly also reflect something of the likes of Forrester and Kelsey (3.6.3) and their views on human flourishing and well-being as referred to in this and the previous chapter, with the former's focus on the human person. Mugambi asserts that "[t]he well-being of a nation's people must be in some way connected with the ability of the people to control their immediate and long-term destiny within history . . . A socially healthy nation should consume what it produces and exports any surplus . . . Thus the goal should be self-sufficiency" (ibid., 158). Mugambi's discussion here implies that when human capacity is reduced by the challenges facing humanity, say corruption, self-sufficiency cannot be achieved.

It will be difficult, also, to disagree with Mugambi's prioritizing for African churches of scholarship and fellowships for Africans to train and improve their skills within Africa to deal with the challenges facing Africa. He also makes a connection that this should go hand in hand with evangelization, which is supposed to be helping in the social reconstruction of people's environment and the improvement of quality of life. To do this, there should be a shift in focus and Mugambi suggests that,

> [t]he church's essential task is evangelization. Since the old frontiers on the missionary agenda of Christian churches till now have been geographical, cultural and ritual, the new frontiers should be theology, knowledge, technology, pastoral care, ecumenical unity, healing and management.[285]

Unfortunately, Mugambi's vision for the church of the future in Africa is silent specifically on the scourge of corruption. However, his views are helpful in that they may be applied to different challenges, among them corruption. He challenges the church to understand and appreciate the aspirations of the afflicted people of Africa to be the plight of refugees and displaced persons; reconciliation between culture and nature, reconciliation between peoples, especially by creating programs of conflict resolution within and between denominations and nations; more focus on the active roles of women in ecclesiastical affairs; taking the disabled as one of the church's priorities; and finally to contribute for the improvement of food production, diversification, preservation and storage. All of these are burning issues on the African continent and can best be dealt with by the valuing the gospel to be sources of help as Africans seeks to regain their confidence and hope. But corruption is an equally formidable challenge and threat to human flourishing on the continent and has consequences for or contributes to and exacerbates many of the above challenges – we have seen how it does so with regard to peace and security and development (and, among others, food production and distribution) (2.4.6). In the words of Stückelberger, writing from concrete experiences of churches, aid agencies and missionary societies in Africa, corruption

---

285. Ibid., 167–173.

undermines values that are vital for the coexistence within a society: injustice instead of justice; inequality instead of equal rights also for the poor; lies instead of the truth; extortion instead of freedom; theft instead of performance; unpredictability instead of rationality and efficiency; non-transparency instead of co-determination and participation; manipulation instead of human dignity; self-interest instead of general welfare; irresponsible use of power instead of power used with responsibility.[286]

As such, Mugambi's call for the role of the church as an instrument of reconstruction and transformation of society must include it being involved in the fight against corruption; this this reconstructive and transformational nature of the church's role in with regard to the individual, culture and the church itself, is part of the nature and mode of the church's involvement in the fight against corruption. Finally, it must again be reiterated that, all of these prophetic, transformational and reconstructive activities of the church and its policy advocacy have to be undertaken in what David Bosch calls a mode of "bold humility," which for him means "not as judges or lawyers, but as witnesses; not as soldiers, but as envoy of peace; not as high-pressure salespersons, but as ambassadors of the Servant Jesus."[287]

Before concluding this subsection, and as was referred to in the third section of chapter 1, there exists a difference between the meaning of the word "transformation" as used in Mugambi's theology of reconstruction and the current use of the word by other scholars, such as Ekeh and Prozesky. While Prozesky emphasizes that transformation as it relates to understanding corruption in African context should take on board what can be called "an ethic of cultural sensitivity," taking into consideration facts about "Africa's Moral wisdom,"[288] Ekeh suggests that Africa should understand corruption within the context that it "arises directly from the amorality of the civic public and the legitimation of the need to seize largesse from the civic public in order to benefit the primordial public."[289] For Ekeh, Africa's "post-colonial present has

---

286. Stückelberger, *Corruption-Free Churches*, 183.
287. Bosch, *Transforming Mission*, 489.
288. Prozesky, "Corruption as a New Treason," 7.
289. Ekeh, "Colonialism," 110.

been fashioned by our colonial past. It is that colonial past that has defined for us the spheres of morality that have come to dominate our politics."[290]

From the above discussion, an emphasis on African moral wisdom, an ethic of cultural sensitivity, as well as its post-colonial present having been fashioned by its colonial past, should enrich Mugambi's proposal on the church's mode of engagement in the public sphere as it pertains to corruption and injustice as a form of transformative public policy advocacy.

4.4.1.7 Corruption and the Integrity of the Church: Brief, but Important Considerations

It was made clear thus far that church does indeed have a clear, relevant and specific role to play in the public square. The church has authority in executing this role because it has been sent by God. It also has rich, unique perspectives and insights which, for many centuries, have impacted lives of multitudes.

However, despite the power and authority of the church and God's mandate upon the church that has shaped it for centuries of attending to human needs, before bringing the argument to a close, one critical issue the church had to face over the centuries, and increasingly has to face today, and which affects its testimony in the public sphere, needs to be brought to the scene. This is the problem of the integrity of the church or church's credibility with regard to corruption. It is a well-known and a sad fact that over the centuries the church has often been complacent to, and at times even complicit in, acts of the violation of human dignity, of greed, of misuse of power, and indeed of corruption itself. The latter may occur at any level of the church, from the misuse of church property to unfair labor practices with regard to church employees; from "embezzlement of funds meant for church projects" to the "unauthorized sale of church-owned land for private gain, at a price which is below market value"; to influencing of the awarding of "tenders for the construction of church buildings."[291]

In this regard, one may indeed echo the challenge and sentiments of issued by the Lausanne Theology Working Group for the Third Lausanne Congress on World Evangelization (Cape Town 16 to 25 October 2010)

---

290. Ibid., 111.
291. Stückelberger, *Corruption-Free Churches*, 67.

that whenever the question of church's credibility is introduced, it is usually regarded by many as an uncomfortable question. But this is the reality which the church should continue to contend with. The church will continue to face challenges unless it retains its own integrity.[292] In light of this caveat to the church, four areas of importance may be considered.

First, is the importance of acknowledging evidence regarding the problem of the integrity of the church, as well as the acknowledgement of its consequences for the witness of the church.

Second, the acknowledgement that the church is to offer, in all humility, an apologetic response to skeptics and doubters of the church's role in the public sphere, especially concerning corruption. That the church in some quarters is faced with an integrity crisis and that, therefore, its legitimacy in dealing with a number of contemporary public issues is questioned, has been voiced by a host of contemporary commentators. Some commentators have indicated that the differences in theological, ethical and ecclesiological perceptions, "informed by different theological traditions, historical contexts as well as practical considerations"[293] across churches is one of the areas in which the general public asks whether the church has a place in addressing issues of a public nature – in fact, some churches themselves subscribe to the belief that the role of the church should be one of non-involvement and that it should, therefore, steer clear from participating in public discourse. According to Goba, this "fragmentation [of views leads to], spiritual fatigue, and lack of zeal for prophetic social action."[294] Fortunately, there remain the voices of those who remind the church that

> Christian teachings on Trinity, Creation and God's Household, do not exclude any sphere of life from the influence and rules of faith. Thus Christianity perceives the whole of the constellation of creation as interconnected and Christian life as a holistic participation in all spheres of life. Christianity has a role.[295]

---

292. cf. Lausanne Theology Working Group, "Whole Church."
293. Goba, "Role of the Church," 6.
294. Ibid.
295. Vellem, "Towards a Transformed Society," no page; cf. again 4.4.1.1 above.

Third, is the challenge of moral leadership in many churches. Goba sees the major problem here as being "the promotion of ecclesiological self-interests of denominations promoting the privatization of our faith. The ecumenical imperative that informed our prophetic stance [has been compromised]."[296] Or, as Villa-Vicencio argues "the root cause of our failure lies deeper. The cause of our failure lies within the soul . . . reaching inter alia, into the inner sanctuaries of faith communities."[297]

The fourth aspect of the integrity and legitimacy of the church in the public sphere concerns the churches' capacity to withstand the massive challenges society faces. Again Goba sees this as "a serious difficulty" in the sense that the "church exists in a dynamic environment confronted by numerous challenges (e.g. the conspiracy of postmodernism/globalization) creating a high level of uncertainty about traditional ways of knowing and doing theology."[298] In short, the church exists in the midst of a hermeneutics of suspicion.

Other scholars, too, like Wessel Bentley, who speaks from a South African perspective, have argued that a legitimate role played by the church in the public sphere is also challenged by changes in wider society and culture. The church works in an increasingly intensive competing environment, among a variety of voices, from the media, government to economic structures and other faiths. According to Bentley, in South Africa, for example, "[t]he adoption of the South African Constitution meant that the voices of different religions now carry equal weight. Christianity is now on par with other religions."[299] In addition, "the religious perspective is now but one of many different perspectives in a secular democracy." Growing secularism and pluralism in South Africa and indeed in the rest of Africa, including Tanzania, affect people's thinking, their values, and activities in ways that previous eras and generations could not have envisioned.

All of this, but especially the issue of the integrity of the church, brings one back to the importance of an honest apologetic discourse on the possible role of the church in the public sphere. Quoting St Augustine, Moltmann

---

296. Goba, "Role of the Church," 6.
297. Villa-Vicencio, *Towards a Transformed Society*, 1.
298. Ibid., 7.
299. Bentley, "Defining Christianity's," 261–273.

reminds us of a fundamental insight in this discourse, namely that the church is not a society of saints, but a "mixed body" of "saints and sinners."[300] His main point lies in the fact that,

> though transformed by Christ, members of the church sometimes act contrary to their identity – as if they belong to the fallenness of the world. Whenever these members organize in institutional forms, they can therefore participate in and perpetuate systemic evil. [But] [a]s the body of Christ, empowered by the Spirit however, the church [also] transcends the world and therefore has an alternative to offer.

Fundamental to the church's mission in the world, grounded as it is in the good news of Jesus Christ, is the need for the church to remember the importance of its own integrity, the importance of "behavior worthy Christians calling" (Phil 1:27). If the church is not careful, it may strengthen an environment of uncertainty with regard to a legitimate place and role for the church in the public sphere. In this, according to Hauerwas, the first task of the church is to exhibit in its common life the kind of community possible when trust rules our lives.[301]

4.5 Conclusion

In chapter 3 of this study the question was asked whether and why, from a biblical-theological perspective, corruption especially as it constitutes injustice is wrong, or in theological terms, why it is sinful. Once this has been established, this chapter (4) set out to answer whether and why, on theological grounds, the church should be concerned about corruption to the extent that it should do something about it and how it should go about it. What theological-ethical reasons are there that the church should become involved and, seeing as there are many secular institutions and organizations that are fighting corruption, what is the unique contribution the church may make to this process?

---

300. In McGrath, *Christian Theology*, 479.
301. Hauerwas, *Community of Character*, 85.

Given the variety of understandings of what constitutes "the church," this chapter first needed to come to some conclusion of what the church is for the purposes of this study. This was done with reference to biblical and theological insights into the meaning of the word *ekklēsia* and then specifically to systematic theologian Dirk Smit's view of the encompassing social forms of the church, which includes among others the church as local congregation, worshipping community, institution (also in the ecumenical sphere) and the individual believers in their day-to-day life in society.

Once clarity was established regarding what "the church" is, a twofold "Why the church?" question was asked. First of all, whether and why the church should at all be involved in the public sphere – why should the church not be concerned only with matters of faith, with spiritual matters? It was shown that this is a question as old as the church itself and that over the centuries many theologians have struggled with this question. However, with reference to prominent theologians in different eras of the church's history (Augustine, Thomas Aquinas, Luther, Calvin and Karl Barth), it was shown that for the most part, even if clothed in a variety of terms, they all gave a positive answer to this question. Of course, one cannot remain in the realm of Christian history and, therefore, the same question was asked to a selection of contemporary theologians, particularly those who one may call public theologians. Again it transpired that among these scholars (Forrester, Storrar, Koopman, Stackhouse, Williams) all agree with Forrester that when "Christianity is assigned to the private realm it lacks the potentiality for prophetic importance" and that theology is "talk about God," but *public* theology contributes to "public discussion."[302] They agree that when someone is practicing public theology, as Jürgen Moltmann says, such a person is "involved in the public affairs of society"[303] and that in the words of John de Gruchy, the nature and substance of public theology is that of being "confessional and evangelical. It has a gospel to share, good news to proclaim . . . [and is] concerned with the public affairs of society in the light of hope in Christ for the kingdom of God."[304]

---

302. Quoted in Storrar and Morton, *Public Theology*, 1.
303. Ibid.
304. De Gruchy in Storrar and Morton, *Public Theology*, 1, 21.

For the sake of the logical flow of the argument it was then asked why it is then necessary for the church to be concerned specifically about corruption and injustice in society. Since the whole of chapter 3 was dedicated to answering the question as to the biblical-theological moral rejection of corruption, the discussion here focused on only three baseline considerations, namely the fact that corruption is a manifestation of the misuse of power and is contrary to the Bible's and the church's understanding of power as coming from God to be used in way fitting such gifted power; an reiteration of the all-important guideline for individual believers and the church of scriptural wisdom with regard to corruption and injustice; and the centrality of ethical leadership in the church to the background of the church's pursuance of ethical leadership in society. In the discussion of these three considerations reference was also made, for example, to the fact that there is currently, despite increased secularization in societies worldwide, also an ironic increased appreciation of the role in society of faith and religion and that part of this is due to the historic locality of the church in many societies in the meeting of human need.

The third broad question that this chapter wished to answer was, if one then says that the church has a role to play in the public sphere and especially in the fight against corruption, what are the modes of engagement, the nature of the churches' engagement with this issue? In short, how does the church play a role in the public sphere – specifically where it concerns corruption? If Elaine Graham is correct, public theology has to "speak about God-in-the-world to the world" – how does it do so and how does the church do so? To do this successfully, Graham suggests that public theology will "need to adopt a functional and sacramental role"[305] meaning the church exercising its role in gathering, leading, and teaching or taking functional initiative, be it in its liturgical, pastoral or prophetic roles.

The "how" question was answered by looking at a series of interrelated theological concepts or theological considerations that give some clue as to how the church may fulfil its task with regard to addressing corruption and injustice. To this purpose reflections were offered on the nature of the holistic mission of the church beyond the spiritual sphere; on the role of the

---

305. See Elaine Graham in Storrar and Morton, *Public Theology*, 385–403.

church in moral transformation of society; on the church as a community of character and as such the locus of character formation and of instilling kingdom values and norms; on the fact that and the ways in which the church should speak the truth to those in power in language that is understandable to those outside of the church, while remaining true to the uniqueness of the church and its message; on the prophetic witness of the church, specifically as it pertains to good governance; on the role of the church as agent of reconstruction and change, among others by way of public policy advocacy; and, finally, on the need to acknowledge and address corruption in its own ranks if the church wants to be credible outside its own walls in its efforts to fight corruption in society.

In these and possibly other ways as well, (public) theology as practiced by the church reflects conversation and God's commitment to speak for and act through the church on behalf of victims of injustice. In this way, to tie what has been said here with the previous chapter, the church may help to maintain an environment that allows human beings, made in God's image, to flourish and to live in such a way as to exercise their human gifts of creativity and productivity in order to participate in and contribute fully towards common life.[306] Or, in Martin Marty's understanding of the aims of public theology, how the church may "bring the wisdom of the Christian tradition into public conversation to contribute to the well-being of society."[307]

This brings us to chapter 5 of this study (and back to the Anglican and Tanzanian context) with an exploration of the role of the Anglican Church of Tanzania and the interrelated questions: In its discourse of faith on corruption in Tanzania, what has the Anglican church done in the past? What is it doing at present? Has its efforts at all been successful? And what are the theological grounds on which it has acted (or not) on the issue of corruption? Is the church aware of theological-ethical principles for combating corruption and do these principles offer it a guideline or constructive strategy for public discourse of faith in combating corruption?

---

306. cf. Spencer, "Christian Vision," 18.

307. Quoted in Hansen, *Christian in Public*, 98.

CHAPTER 5

The Anglican Church of Tanzania and Its Response to Corruption

But you are a chosen people, a royal priesthood, a holy nation, a people belonging to God, that you may declare the praises of him who called you out of darkness into his wonderful light.

1 Peter 2:9

A church that doesn't actually say to the world, this is the new creation, this is an order of justice, reconciliation, and a countercultural movement, that is not really a church.

Rowan Williams
Former Archbishop of Canterbury, 2008

5.1 Introduction

Reflecting back on the previous four chapters, chapter 1 gave an introduction to the study and explained its general structure of the study. In chapter 2 a conceptual and contextual analysis of corruption, justice and injustice was given with reference to their meaning, typology, and manifestations. Regarding the former (conceptual analysis), it was also showed at an interdisciplinary level what corruption and justice/injustice means for scholars in different fields or disciplines. In a contextual analysis the forms, extent, history of and possible reasons and implications of corruption in Tanzania was discussed. Chapter 3 asked the question whether and why corruption in its many forms is wrong on biblical and theological-ethical grounds and chapter 4 asked – again on biblical-theological-ethical grounds – why and how the church should be involved (1) in the public sphere and by extension, and (2) in the fight against corruption not only in the church, but in society at large.

With regard to chapter 3, it was shown that, according to biblical teaching and theological perspectives on corruption and injustice that (a) corruption is a form of injustice and, as such, it is in itself not only opposed to who God is (being irreconcilable with the character of God), but also to God's plan for human society and to what biblically speaking humankind should be. For these reasons both corruption and injustice are not only wrong, but there also exist a dynamic link between the two. Likewise, in chapter 3, it was contended that failing to imitate the character of God, the sinful human condition and the abuse of power are contributing causes to corruption. In this chapter, suggestions will be made as to how these are to be combated by the Anglican Church of Tanzania (ACT) alongside other key proposals for a comprehensive programme of, for example, theological renewal, personal discipleship and leadership formation, gospel clarity and integrity, accountability, spiritually formation, education and empowerement. In chapter 6 how this may be done will be further explained.

Chapter 4 made it clear, with reference to a variety of theologians, that (a) the church must be aware of the social, moral and cultural concerns of its time; (b) the church has a place in the public sphere and this can be made more evident in the way the church – as individual Christians or as a community, a denomination, an institutionalized or ecumenical church – live and act in society; (c) that there is a connection between the secular and sacred, public and private; (d) that there has been and continues to be more than one way or approach for the church and Christians to live and participate in a responsible relationship with and in the world, in other words, that the history of the church has followed no single approach as it sought its place in the public sphere; (e) that in contemporary discourse theologians often refer to this endeavor with reference to the relatively new discipline of public theology; (f) that within public theology itself there exist different approaches, emphases and suggestions as to the modes of public engagement open to the church.

This chapter (5) returns to the Tanzanian context and asks whether and how ACT has been or is engaged in combating corruption and thus in promoting justice in Tanzanian society. At first glance there seems to be little doubt that ACT accepts a responsibility to act in the public sphere. In fact, according to its website, the involvement in public life of ACT is based on the aim of, in Kiswahili, *kuutangaza ufalme wa Mungu* – meaning "to announce the kingdom of God." This already is an important statement in light of what has been said in the previous chapters and the prominence the theological concepts of the kingdom of God and kingdom values and norms have played in the discussion of the theological rationale behind the "why and how" of the church's role in the public arena (see 3.3; 3.6.3; 4.3.1.1 and 4.4.1.3). But, what other reasons does ACT offer for its participation in the public sphere? Does this apply to and is this reflected in ACT's anti-corruption efforts if such efforts indeed exist. And if they do not exist, why do they not?

However, to begin with, a brief historical overview of Anglicanism and ACT will be given, also with regard to its place within the worldwide Anglican community.

5.2 The Anglican Communion and the Origins of Anglican Church of Tanzania

The Anglican Church of Tanzania is that part of the worldwide Anglican Communion with its seventy-seven million members. This Communion, according to Hassett, is one of

> national or regional Anglican churches, united by their roots in the Church of England; their common loyalty to the Archbishop of Canterbury; their common faith and praxis embodied in their prayer books, all based upon Cranmer's Book of Common Prayer; and their common participation in the decennial Lambeth bishops' conference and other occasions which bring together leaders from all over the worldwide Communion.[1]

According to Jacob, as part of this Communion, ACT functions according to its "common faith consisting of adherence to the catholic faith as

---

1. Hassett, *Anglican Communion in Crisis*, 34.

contained in the Scriptures summed up in the Apostle's creed, as expressed in the sacraments of the gospel and in the rites of the primitive church."[2] That said, however, it is important to realize that ACT is also an independent institution in terms of its theology and administration and that,

> . . . in spite of all this shared heritage, Anglicanism today is far from a uniform tradition globally. Local cultural, political, and economic factors, and particular histories of missionization and revival, have created significant diversity among the provinces of the Anglican world.[3]

ACT's independence and the acknowledgement of the importance of its own context is important for the purposes of this study as, as will be seen, it has influenced the church in determining its position in Tanzanian society and in setting its own agenda, also in the public sphere.

Formerly part of the Church of the Province of East Africa (which included both Kenya and Tanzania), the Church of the Province of Tanzania was established in 1970 as an independent province with its headquarters in Dodoma. It has grown steadily in terms of geographical area and numbers, from the initial eight dioceses when the independent province was established to the current twenty-six dioceses. The twenty-six dioceses represent both Evangelical and Anglo-Catholic streams in Anglicanism.[4] Currently, ACT has about 3,225,000 members and it represents the third biggest of Christian denomination in Tanzania.

With regard to ACT's leadership structure, one finds at its head an archbishop, who is elected every five years by his fellow bishops while he also

---

2. Jacob, *Making*, 300.

3. Hassett, *Anglican Communion in Crisis*, 34.

4. There are two streams within Anglicanism, which reflect much of the diversity within the tradition to which Hasett refers to above. The evangelical tradition emphasizes the significance of the Protestant aspects of the Church of England's (Anglican church) identity, stressing the importance of the authority of Scripture, preaching, justification by faith and personal conversion. The Anglo-Catholic or the Catholic tradition within the Anglican church, strengthened and reshaped from the 1830s by the what is known as the Oxford movement, emphasizes the significance of the continuity between the Church of England and the early church and the church of the medieval period. It stresses the importance of the visible church and its sacraments and the belief that the ministry of bishops, priests and deacons is a sign and instrument of the Church of England's catholic and apostolic identity.

remains the incumbent bishop of his own diocese. The current head of ACT is Rt Rev Dr Jacob Chimeledya. The archbishop is ATC's highest authority and leads the church as *primus inter pares,* first among equals. Bishops are the highest authority in the respective dioceses of the province. The administration of Anglican affairs in Tanzania is the responsibility of the Provincial Office, situated in Dodoma, and is headed by a General Secretary. The Provincial Office is also responsible for coordinating the management activities of provincial institutions. At a national level, the government of the church is in the hands of the Provincial Synod. This synod is divided into a House of Bishops, a House of Clergy and a House of Laity. Policy changes need to be agreed to by a majority in all three houses. This broad consultation across hierarchical borders should be applauded, but as may be expected, the fact that all three houses need to agree to policy changes and that these changes have to be supported by a majority in all three Houses, also represents a challenge, sometimes in terms of ACT's involvement in public life. This was again seen, for example, in recent times in the preparation policies regarding HIV and AIDS, the national constitution review, and issues of education.

With regard to the origins of Anglicanism in Tanzania, this study does not intend to trace in detail the missionary history of the church in Tanzania. However, for the purpose of understanding the role of the church in Tanzania, some historical background needs to be given in order to trace the extent of the development of public involvement of ACT in Tanzanian society.

The earliest origins of ACT can be traced to the work of two British missionary societies in the mid-nineteenth century, namely the Universities' Mission to Central Africa (UMCA, now USPG), and the Church Missionary Society (CMS, now Church Mission Society). The history of the church in Tanzania starts in 1844, with the work of the Church Missionary Society (CMS).[5] In his book, *The History of the Church in East Africa*, Anderson covers a wide range of missionary endeavors, including the work of CMS and other mission societies, as well as the growth of the Anglican church and its impact on socio-political upheavals. According to Anderson, the

---

5. The CMS is an English missionary agency founded by Anglicans in response to the evangelical revivalism in the Church of England at the time.

earliest missionaries in East African were Johann Ludwig Krapf and his wife Rosine, who arrived at the harbor of Mombasa in May 1844. They were later joined by Rev Johan Rebman and, in July 1844, these missionaries built the first mission station at Rabai near Mombasa. From there, their missionary activities spread over the next twenty-five years to reach other areas such as Mpwapwa in Dodoma and Mwanza. Krapf also visited Kilimanjaro and Usambara areas in Tanganyika, contemporary Tanzania.

Together with CMS, missionaries from the Universities Mission to Central Africa (UMCA) were among the first in Tanzania. UMCA was formed as a result of Livingstone's famous speech at Cambridge University in 1857, when he made the following appeal:

> I beg to direct your attention to Africa. I know that in a few years I shall be cut off in that country, which is now open; do not let it be shut again. I go back to Africa to make an open path for commerce and Christianity; do you carry out the work which I have begun. I leave it with you.[6]

This statement also "appealed for missionaries to tackle the ills of central Africa, especially the disruptions of the slave trade."[7] As will be seen, the Anglican involvement in efforts to end this evil system serves as the example *par excellence* of its involvement in the public sphere.

In 1861, the first UMCA group, led by an *Anglican Bishop* Charles Frederick Mackenzie, landed in Cape Town and journeyed north up to the Shire Highlands in Malawi. In 1862, Bishop Mackenzie died and William George Tozer succeeded him. In 1864, Bishop Tozer moved the UMCA station to Zanzibar.

5.3 The Church's Engagement in Public Life: The UMCA and CMS Missionary Methods

According to Turnbull, Anglicanism in its various expressions and forms has always embodied the claims of the Christian gospel upon the transformation

---

6. Quoted in Odhiambo, et al., *History*, 102.
7. Ward, *History*, 159.

of society.⁸ During the earliest stages of East African Anglicanism, a good example is found of its legacy of public engagement in the region. According to Ward, history suggests that "Anglican engagement with Africa coincided with British involvement in the Atlantic slave trade."⁹ Likewise, Ward emphasizes that,

> UMCA was . . . activist . . . in the struggle against the slave trade in 1873, [it] made possible the treaty for the abolition of the Zanzibar Slave Market. This treaty was signed by the Sultan [of Zanzibar]. Bishop Steere bought part of the slave market site and built a church there, which presently is the Cathedral of the Anglican Diocese of Zanzibar.[10]

The role of both CMS and UMCA on and outside of the mission field in East Africa strongly shaped and influenced the later approach of ACT of engagement in issues of public life, partnership with the government in addressing public issues, and its establishment of projects such as health care, various types of educational initiatives and other development programs. The model of missionary outreach and work in Tanzania of the CMS and UMCA was anchored in evangelism, education, medical work, and small enterprise projects. Although evangelism – in the sense of preaching, teaching and baptizing – stood at the center of all the activities, an emphasis was also placed on communicating the good news, the message of Jesus Christ, by way of acts of service as part of Christian witness. In light of what has been said in the previous chapter with regard to a holistic understanding of mission and the mission of the church (see 4.3.1.1), it seems that historically ACT has been and is in agreement with this understanding of mission. This approach has also been at the core of ACT's ministry since its establishment in 1970.[11] At the same time, this opens the door for public-theological reflection or discourse in ACT on corruption and injustice. Public theology is,

---

8. Turnbull, *Anglican and Evangelical?* 145.

9. Ward, *History,* 112.

10. Ibid., 164.

11. By way of example, ACT's medical and educational work in Tanzania has been historically grouped together and termed as "provision of social services intended for the welfare of the people." In Tanzania, therefore, there remain church-owned and managed hospitals, schools, colleges and other higher learning institutions. Hospitals under the management of the Anglican Church of Tanzania include, for example, St Augustine

after all, as Moltmann calls it, "kingdom of God theology" which "intervenes critically and prophetically in the public affairs of a given society, and draws public attention, not to the church's own interests, but to God's kingdom, God's commandment, and his righteousness."[12]

5.4 Reflections on Anglican Theology, Identity and Spirituality

This subsection is important in that it may be expected that elements and the nature of Anglican theology, identity and spirituality in general should have played and should continue to play a role in determining ACT's approaches to engaging in public life.

First and foremost, it should be pointed out that ACT is a human association characterized by structures and offices that are maintained by authority institutionalized in the form of offices (reminding one of Smit's social form of the church as institution in 4.2.2),[13] but that for the Anglican church, this authority expressly finds its source firstly in Scripture, but also tradition and reason.[14] Martha Kirkpatrick summarizes what these theological characteristics, Anglicanism's "threefold appeal to Scripture, tradition and reason," mean.[15] By using the words of Livingstone and Fiorenza, Kirkpatrick expounds further on the meaning of this as a theological method that is "correlative in that it seeks to explain the contents of faith through existential questions and theological answers in mutual interdependence."[16] With regard to Scripture, statements of Anglican doctrine called *Thirty-Nine Articles of Religion* affirms under article VI that:

> Holy Scripture containeth all things necessary to salvation: so that whatsoever is not read therein, nor may be proved thereby, is not to be required of any man [sic], that it should be believed

---

Hospital, Muheza Designated District Hospital and Murgwanza Designated District Hospital in Ngara.

12. Moltmann, *Experiences in Theology*, 20.
13. cf. also Brueggemann, "Rethinking Church Models," 129.
14. cf. Atkinson, *Richard Hooker*.
15. Kirkpatrick, "Incarnational Ecology," 193.
16. Ibid.

as an article of the faith, or be thought requisite or necessary to salvation.

With regard to its doctrinal and theological foundations, ACT has been operating as part of a theological tradition that, as Ian Markham puts it, has the following characteristics:

> First it is creedal. The Apostles and Nicene creeds are properly foundational. These express the triune character of God and make the story of Jesus central . . . In the creeds we learn of the self-disclosing God. In the creeds we learn of the second person of the Trinity being made flesh. In short, the creeds are our epistemology.[17]

One may thus say that in light of the biblical reflections on and reasons given for the unacceptability of corruption, it being contrary to the nature of God (3.4), and a Trinitarian understanding of public theology and the church (4.3.2.3), the extent to which these are also reflected in the Apostles' and Nicene Creed should provide yet another theological base for ACT's public engagement in issues of corruption and injustice.

The second foundation of the Anglican tradition, according to Markham, is its liturgical and engagement characteristics.[18] In this he suggests that the liturgical side is seen in "[t]he logical flow of the service of Holy Eucharist in the Book of Common Prayer." It is exactly here that one hears echoes of Smit's explanation of the church as a worshipping community (4.2.2). It is here, as we have seen where, according to Smit, "a unique identity, be it collectively or individually" is formed, where the community is shaped. And the extent to which the service of Holy Eucharist and the Book of Common Prayer in Anglican thought reflects the church's understanding of its role in public and with regard to injustice, it should also inform its understanding of corruption as injustice and the responsibility of ACT to respond to it, also outside of the walls of the church.

The third, and for the purposes of this study, very important characteristic is a "commitment to engagement" as "Anglican theology is intrinsically engaged with all the main trajectories of human knowledge and

---

17. Markham, "Theological Education," 160.
18. Ibid.

understanding."[19] This does imply an openness to other non-theological disciplines and knowledge and, as was seen in the discussion on public theology, the latter demands such an openness and engagement if the church wants to have any influence in the public sphere, even if only to be able to speak and be understood within it (see 4.4.1.4 as well as the various views on the need for this as expressed by public theologians in 4.3.2). Markham's comment also implies socio-political and civil engagement. Although it is not directly part of Markham's understanding of engagement, other studies such as those by Hansen and Twaddle, Kalu, and Branch and Cheeseman expressly emphasize the role of Anglican church among other mainline churches in socio-political and civil engagement, for example, in the democratization processes and the provision of social services.[20]

However, while we continue to look at further theological underpinnings of Anglicanism worldwide and ACT in particular, Jacob's further comment is worth noting:

> . . . like the early church, the Anglican church is not a church of fixed structures and systematic theologies. It has maintained that its doctrines are the doctrines of the whole church, believed by everybody, everywhere and at all times, not the doctrine of a particular tradition . . . It derives its teaching, which is proclaimed in its daily liturgy, from scriptures and tradition. Scripture should be accessible to all people, and requires an analytical and critical approach.[21]

For Cerar this means that "Anglicanism is a home for all legitimate, faithful and biblically justifiable expressions of the Christian faith, whether Catholic, Evangelical or Charismatic."[22]

While someone like Mark Chapman argues – on the basis of a series of conflicts in the history of the Anglican church (on authority of the church and of the Christian), the interpretation of Scripture, theological pluralism in the church's understanding of mission and of recent disagreements

---

19. Ibid.

20. Hansen and Twaddle, *Religion and Politics*, Kalu, *African Christianity*, and Branch and Cheeseman, "Democratization, Sequencing."

21. Jacob, *Making*, 299.

22. Cerar, written essay in "Why Anglicanism?" 18.

over homosexuality) – that there is no such thing as "Anglican theology,"[23] former Archbishop of Canterbury (1961–1974), Michael Ramsey, understood Anglican theology in terms of the Evangelical and Catholic nature of the church as that which constitutes Anglican identity.[24] For Ramsey, the Evangelical and Catholic unity of the gospel that is found in the teaching of the Anglican church is at the heart of the Anglican theology.

Michael Petty finds Anglican theological identity in its Reformation roots:

> Anglicanism has a coherent theological identity, the main outlines of which can be discerned in the primary texts of the English Reformation and after, while also embracing the central doctrinal distinctive of the Reformation: *sola scriptura, sola gratia, sola fide*.[25]

This means once again, according to Petty, that Anglican theology is rooted in the primacy, clarity and sufficiency of Scripture. As such the canonical Scriptures of the Old and New Testaments are regarded as the final source of authority in the church. This has important implications for ACT in this study as it means that in Scripture it is to find its final and authoritative principles with regard to corruption and addressing it (some of which has been identified in chapter 2 of this study – cf. especially 3.3; 3.4 and 3.5). The *sola gratia, sola fide* in Anglican terms are explained by Witt as follows:

> The person and work of Jesus Christ in his incarnation, life, death and resurrection are the means by which God has redeemed sinful humanity. One's right standing before God depends entirely on Jesus Christ's atoning work, and not on one's own meritorious works of any kind, not even on the sincerity of one's appropriation of that work. Justification by faith alone means that one trusts in Jesus Christ and Jesus Christ alone for salvation.[26]

---

23. Chapman, *Anglican Theology*, 138.
24. Ramsey, *Gospel*, 208.
25. Petty, "Introducing Anglicanism," no page.
26. Witt, "What Is Anglican Theology?" no page numbers. The doctrinal emphases on *sola scriptura, sola gratia, sola fide* applies to both Evangelical and Catholic traditions found in Anglicanism. According to Michel Ramsey (*The Gospel*): "To understand the Catholic church and its life and order is to see it as the utterance of the gospel of God; to understand

In a more elaborate Anglican theological discourse on salvation, Baucum writes that the Anglican church,

> ... has three defining doctrinal emphases, which together constitute the full power of Christian salvation: original sin (everyone needs a Saviour, not just a coach), justifying grace (such a Saviour and His salvation has been given to us without our merit) and sanctifying grace (the salvation that is offered to us is transformational, not merely transactional. That is, it must be personally and continually appropriated).[27]

Baucum explains the nature of living and proclaiming salvation in the context of Anglican spirituality as follows: "Authentic Anglican spiritual life is very much centered on Jesus, the unique Word of God made flesh and blood, who suffered and died to make God's salvation available to all who call upon His name."[28] In a theological discussion on corruption, all the above points made by Baucum with regard to Anglican belief may be easily linked with what has been said in the Christian anthropological reflections in this study – especially with regard to corruption as sin, the sinful nature of humankind and God's gracious response to this in Jesus Christ (see 3.6 in this study).

---

the gospel of God is to share with all the saints in the building up of the one Body of Christ. Hence these two aspects of Anglicanism cannot really be separated. It possesses a full Catholicity ... it is fully Evangelical in so far as it upholds the church order wherein an important aspect of the gospel is set forth. To belittle the witness of the Reformers and the English church's debt to the Reformers is to miss something of the meaning of the church of God; to belittle church order and to regard it as indifferent is to fail in Evangelical insight since church order is of the gospel. Hence 'Catholicism' and 'Evangelicalism' are not two separate things which the Church of England must hold together by a great feat of compromise. ... A church's witness to the one church of the ages is a part of its witness to the gospel of God." Cf., for interest's sake, Barth (*Evangelical Theology*, 5): "[T]he expression 'evangelical' ... cannot and should not be intended and understood in a confessional, that is, in a denominational and exclusive, sense. This is forbidden first of all by the elementary fact that 'evangelical' refers primarily and decisively to the Bible, which is in some way respected by all confessions. Not all so-called 'Protestant' theology is evangelical theology; moreover, there is also evangelical theology in the Roman Catholic and Eastern orthodox worlds ... What the word 'evangelical' will objectively designate is that theology which treats of the God of the gospel. 'Evangelical' signifies the 'catholic,' ecumenical (not to say 'conciliar') continuity and unity of this theology."

27. Baucum, written essay in "Why Anglicanism?" 15.
28. Ibid., 28.

Despite the above constants, it must also not be forgotten that the Anglican church, like other mainstream churches, has over centuries also undergone significant changes based on the geographical, cultural, social and historical settings since the Reformation. Petty has identified some of these significant changes as ranging

> [f]rom inter-church polemic within a Christian culture to a divided church within a post-Christian culture; from a European church to a "Global South" church; from doctrinal polemic to ecumenical reconciliation; [and] Evolution of the Anglican Communion: the goal of the church is communion not denominationalism.[29]

Petty's caveat reminds one that all has not necessarily been said with regard to corruption and injustice, also not from an Anglican theological-ethical perspective. Therefore, what has been said thus far, also in this study, requires a degree of humility and the acknowledgement that social, geographical, cultural and historical settings may always challenge current understandings also of corruption and injustice.

5.5 The Anglican Church of Tanzania's Public Witness in the Context of Church-State Relations

In principle, this section continues the description of the historical developments in ACT, but now from the perspective of its relationship with the state, which of course forms an important context for its public witness – also against corruption. This is done in order to understand how this relationship influences the current work and also to determine the future work of ACT in its prophetic ministry and its views on "Christian faith in political engagement."[30]

It has been referred to above that in colonial Tanzania, the Anglican mission societies established the church through evangelism which sought not only to meet peoples' spiritual needs, but also their material needs. As such,

---

29. Petty, "Introducing Anglicanism," no page.
30. Kunhiyop, *African Christian Ethics*, 100.

missionaries established, for example, health and education institutions and these were also maintained after independence.[31]

In order to achieve their goals, missionary societies and churches from the beginning needed to establish some sort of relationship with the colonial powers. According to Lonsdale et al.[32] and Sabar[33] the church in that situation operated mainly within the ideological guidelines of the colonial government and also "emerged as an extremely important and well-respected actor both pastorally and developmentally."[34]

The influence of the Anglican Church of Tanzania *during and following independence* cannot be discussed without referring to Julius Kambarage Nyerere, a key role player in the Tanzanian struggle against colonial rule.[35] As will be remembered from chapter 2 (2.3.2.3), Nyerere, who was also the first president of the United Republic of Tanzania and "father of the nation," was a devout Roman Catholic whose views and example have had an impact on the life of the nation and the nature of church-state relationship since Tanzanian independence in 1961. Nyerere's views on society also reflected his faith perspectives. He is, for example, quoted as saying that:

> We say man [sic] was created in the image of God. I refuse to imagine a God who is poor, ignorant, superstitious, fearful, oppressed, and wretched – which is the lot of the majority of those whom He created in his own image. Men are creators of themselves and their conditions, but under present conditions we are creatures, not of God, but of our men.[36]

Unlike in some of the countries in Africa, where states at independence openly declared themselves to be entirely secular – with, as subtext, that religion should not play any or only a minimal role in such states – Nyerere

---

31. cf. Chambers, *Rural Development*, 46 and Deheragora, "Impact of Globalization," 12.
32. Lonsdale et al., "Emerging Pattern," 269.
33. Sabar, *Church, State and Society*, 27.
34. Lawson and Rakner, "Understanding Patterns," 15.
35. See, for example, Fashole-Luke et al., *Christianity in Independent Africa*, 267–284.
36. In Legum and Mmari, "*MWALIMU*," 6. It is interesting to note that in this example of Nyerere's political rhetoric, he uses a theological concept to which has been referred to several times in this study as one of the theological grounds on which corruption is rejected (see 3.6.2; 3.6.4 and 4.4.1.2).

was not of the same mind and church-state relations in Tanzania still draws on Nyerere's legacy. The influence of Nyerere's view on this issue extended even beyond Tanzania itself. One finds an acknowledgement of this, for example, in an essay by Steve de Gruchy on theology and development.[37] In it De Gruchy argues that "the Christian concern for development must be rooted in the 'vocation of the poor,' rather than in the compassion of the non-poor" and he refers to Julius Nyerere as one of the key African leaders who represented the view that "Christian faith is not just about intellectual assent, but about a life lived in compassionate service to others, especially the vulnerable."[38] De Gruchy also uses an extended quote by Nyerere in the latter's "The Church and Society" in *Freedom and Development*:

> I am suggesting to you that unless we participate actively in the rebellion against those social structures and economic organizations which condemn men [sic] to poverty, humiliation and degradation, *then the church will become irrelevant to man and the Christian religion will degenerate into a set of superstitions accepted by the fearful. Unless the church, its members and its organizations, express God's love for man by involvement and leadership in constructive protest against the present conditions of man, then it will become identified with injustice and persecution.* If this happens, it will die and, humanly speaking, deserve to die-because it will then serve no purpose comprehensible to modern man.[39]

Likewise, long-standing friend of Nyerere's, Bishop Trevor Huddleston reiterates Nyerere's vision on the church's role to shape what he called "political philosophy and its impact on governance, social and economic development, international relations and, the role of sub-Saharan Africa in the world."[40] Part of this was also, of course, Nyerere's views on the importance of equality and justice:

---

37. De Gruchy, "Of Agency, Assets and Appreciation," 20.
38. Ibid.
39. Nyerere, *Freedom and Development*, 215 (emphasis added).
40. Legum and Mmari, "*MWALIMU*," 1; cf. Mwakikagile, *Nyerere and Africa*.

> We have agreed that our nation shall be a nation of free and equal citizens, each person having an equal right and opportunity to develop himself, and to contribute to the maximum of his capabilities to the development of our society. We have said that neither race nor tribe, nor religion nor cleverness, nor anything else, could take away from a man his own rights as an equal member of society. This is what we have now to put into practice.[41]

The point that needs making here, is that, unlike in many other African countries, Tanzania historically and in principle had in its first president a proponent of cooperation between church and state for the benefit of society, or in other terms, it has a history and legacy of the acknowledgement of a role for the church in the public sphere. As such, this should have made it possible for ACT to contribute to the public discourse on corruption in Tanzania. Nyerere led the country for twenty-three years. Thus it may not be incorrect to state that, long before Nyerere retired and died, the country was already rooted in part not only in his political and economic ideals, such as his *ujamaa* socialism, but also in his ideas on religion and church and his views on the moral and social fabric of the country. After Nyerere, the Tanzanian public in general continued to welcome the church in the public sphere.

However, there has also been changes as "after independence the influence of the church was and continues to be analyzed within a seemingly absurd, fast-changing society."[42] In light of the latter, over time, the church needs to revisit the ways it engages in public discourse on various social ills. In Tanzania and elsewhere, we find ourselves now in a time, as Villa-Vicencio's theology of reconstruction suggests, of the church being challenged "to engage in serious dialogue with democracy, human rights, law making, nation building and economics in order to improve quality of human life."[43] It is a time, according to Mugambi, when that African states are "undergoing rapid social transition with new beliefs, norms and values introduced from outside

---

41. Nyerere, in Kaniki, "TANU," 17.
42. Chambers, *Rural Development*, 46.
43. In Maluleke, "Half a Century," 492.

[so] the church needs leaders who can adequately handle these changes."[44] One of the social ills that still needs to be considered more adequately is corruption. As was indicated in chapter 2 of this study, corruption already existed in the time of Nyerere and before it, but after Nyerere corruption increased and over time it became clear that it threatened Christian principles such as fairness, equality and justice.[45] Despite the fact that, as was seen, Tanzania was and remained politically stable,[46] but with the growing concern regarding increases in corruption, the country is now left vulnerable.

The changes referred to by Mugambi and others above have challenged ACT and consensus suggests that, while "[t]he international community has been paying increasing attention to corruption and how to control it,"[47] churches in Tanzania and elsewhere in Africa were paying little or far too little attention to it and for this reason various bodies, including governments themselves, called on churches to become involved in issues of national reconstruction and social development and with it the issue of addressing corruption.[48] In what follows, some examples are investigated of the ways ACT has responded to this call.

5.5.1 Strategic Planning: A Popular Contemporary Approach in the Church's Public Engagement

A good source for finding an indication of ACT's understanding of its involvement in the public sphere, the motivation for it and forms it takes or may take is by looking at its so-called Strategic Plan, as accepted by the Provincial Synod in 2010.

It has been indicated above that as a mainline church in Tanzania, ACT has functioned as an important force in development in the country long before independence in 1961. Most of its involvement has mainly been in the areas of education and health care and was aimed at uplifting the lives of the people by, as Mathewes puts it, offering "imaginative alternatives to the fallen

---

44. Mugambi, *From Liberation to Reconstruction*, 26.
45. Luanda, "Christianity and Islam," 180.
46. Barkan, *Beyond Capitalism*, 9.
47. USIPE, *Governance, Corruption, and Conflict*, 4.
48. cf. Agbasiere and Zabajungu, *Church Contribution*; Koegelenberg, *Transition and Transformation*; Pityana and Villa-Vicencio, *Being the Church*.

social structures."[49] This involvement of the church in development projects is equated with ACT's priority of evangelism for all Christians in response to the great commission of Jesus Christ,[50] also understood as an encounter of a people with the good news of God's love proclaimed by Jesus Christ.

The growth in the church also went hand in hand with the use in church circles of the concept of "strategic planning," an important modern tool to guide the work of organizations.

In his article, "The Theology and Practice of Strategic Planning," Zigarelli explains in theological terms the concept of strategic planning.[51] He writes that "God is a planner. He planned the whole storyline of Scripture from the beginning. He had it laid out, down to the very last person (e.g. Jer 1:5)." Zigarelli adds that, as God is a planner, "[a]nd since the imitation of God glorifies God, we are to be planners, too." From a New Testament perspective, Zigarelli, suggest that, "Jesus also affirmed the enterprise of planning."[52] To justify his arguments he quotes Luke 14:28–30:

> Suppose one of you wants to build a tower. Will he not first sit down and estimate the cost to see if he has enough money to complete it? For if he lays the foundation and is not able to finish it, everyone who sees it will ridicule him, saying, "This fellow began to build and was not able to finish."

From this brief reference to the "theology behind strategic planning" it is understandable that ACT adopted this "tool" for the purpose of consolidating its work by linking dioceses through departments such as those of Development and Community Services, the Mother's Union, Youth, Evangelism, and Communication. It seems that this would also be a good way of addressing corruption in a unified strategy or with unified programs across dioceses and departments of the church. In principle, the strategic plan, both as tool and process, is meant to carry out ACT vision and mission based on its statement of faith. For the theology behind ACT's strategic plan one, therefore, has to turn to the latter.

---

49. Mathewes, *Theology of Public Life*, 216.

50. See Pobee, "Lord, Creator-Spirit," 55; and World Council of Churches, "Nature and Mission of the Church," 11.

51. Zigarelli, "Theology," 4.

52. Ibid.

5.5.2 ACT's Strategic Plan: Theological Principles Allowing for a Public Engagement with Corruption

The ACT Strategic Plan is informed by the church's mission goals and actions that cut across or transcend the boundaries of dioceses, the entire machinery of the church, and it is coordinated by and from the church's headquarters. The reasoning behind the 2010 Provincial Synod's decision was that ACT should and can take even greater advantage of its distributed strengths, while also reinforcing those strengths and facilitating the bottom-up blossoming of what it understood to be the innovation and creativity characteristic of the current twenty-six dioceses. In short, as was said above, the strategic plan, both as tool and process, is meant to carry out the ACT vision and mission based on its statement of faith. ACT's vision, mission and statement of faith reads:

> *Vision*: The Anglican Church of Tanzania (ACT) envisions a sustainable church working together effectively for the growth of God's Kingdom through prayer, worship, preaching, teaching, pastoral care and social services.
>
> *Mission*: ACT's mission is to proclaim the Kingdom of God through spiritual and socio-economic transformation and empowerment of individuals and communities to experience the fullness of life in God.
>
> *Statement of Faith*: We affirm our belief in historic Christianity as revealed in the Scriptures and summarized in the three Creeds (the Apostles, the Nicene, and the Athanasian) and the Thirty-Nine Articles.[53]

When one looks at the above statement some things immediately stands out in light of the study thus far:

1. With regard to its *vision*, ACT expressly acknowledges that one of the root metaphors in its vision for itself and society is that of the kingdom of God. As such it opens the way for a discourse on how this should be understood and its implications. As was

---

53. The Anglican Church of Tanzania. http://www.anglican.or.tz/. Accessed 14 March 2015.

seen in chapter 4, the concept of the kingdom of God opens the way for discussing the characteristics of this kingdom and how it and the people of the kingdom would reflect the virtues and norms expected from it. With reference to the likes of Forrester (see 4.3.2.1), Koopman (4.3.2.1) Hauerwas (4.4.1.3) and Smit (4.2.2), the congregation was shown to be the primary place where this happens, and echoes of an acknowledgement of this is found in ACT's vision that the growth of God's kingdom is and will be through "prayer, worship, preaching, teaching, pastoral care and social services."

2. Regarding its *mission*, ACT again links it with the theological concept of the kingdom of God, but places it squarely within the understanding of the church's mission as a holistic one of "spiritual and socio-economic transformation," a view that, as was explained, by the very nature of corruption and its unjust consequences would require the serious attention of the church in its mission (see 4.3.1.1) and its efforts at transformation of society and the world (4.3.1.2 and 4.3.1.6). The goal of ACT's mission of ensuring "individuals and communities to experience the fullness of life in God," also sounds familiar when compared to what has been said in this study. It presents an opportunity to reflect on humanity and human societies in the grips of corruption from the perspective of the relational nature of the triune God and of humanity and God's vision of human society as one of peace and justice, one in which people can "flourish" (3.6.4; cf. 3.4; 3.6.1; 4.4.1.6, etc.).

3. Finally, ACT's Statement of Faith acknowledges the primacy of Scripture as summarized by the Creeds and Thirty-nine Articles, in accordance to the whole point of departure of this study, namely that "[t]hroughout the history of the mission of the church, the source of truth as it carries out its mission has always been the Bible. The church has maintained that the Bible is God's authoritative and trustworthy Word . . . Biblical truth thus also serves as key, not only with regard to knowing God, humanity and morality, but also the fundamental realities behind

the tragic dilemma of corruption" (4.3.2.3; see also 3.2; 3.3; 3.5; 4.2.1).

Given the overwhelming biblical witness to the moral reprehensibility acts of corruption and of corruption as manifestation of injustice, of the nature of God, humanity and the church and its role in society, the admission that Scripture is at the base of all it believes, clearly should also find expression in a concern for and in engaging in the fight against corruption by ACT in Tanzania.

Apart from the vision, mission and statement of faith, the ACT Strategic Plan also emphasizes that the relationship between dioceses to the central administration of the Anglican Church in Dodoma should involve an ongoing dynamic cooperation between dioceses, provincial centers and projects. Reading the plan, it is quite clear that there is a recognition of the challenges and opportunities for the ACT in Tanzania's changing environment. It acknowledges that it is working in a different setting and, therefore, it has to prepare itself to face new challenges. However, unfortunately no express reference is made to corruption anywhere in the plan. Despite of this unfortunate lack of acknowledgement of the challenge of corruption, how does ACT engage in practice in the public sphere and with the issue of corruption?

5.5.3 ACT's Public Engagement as Part of Global Anglican Communion

As was explained in section 5.2 above, ACT has a connection not only to a local/national, but also to the international community of fellow Anglican followers of Christ. This means that the nature of ACT's engagement in the public sphere also needs to be reflected upon in the context of a worldwide Anglican communion.[54]

From this perspective, the argument is that ACT's public engagement is also related to the mission of Anglican Communion and hence this helps not only to justify its involvement in issues such as political justice and democracy, provision of health and education services, but also its involvement in influencing policy as well as working against corruption.

---

54. cf. Ward, *History*; Turnbull, *Anglican and Evangelical?*; Avis, *Identity, Reshaping Ecumenical Theology*.

As far as the vision and mission of the Anglican Communion is concerned, the Communion developed its "Five Marks of Mission" to indicate the church's focus in mission. These are:

- To proclaim the good news of the kingdom,
- To teach, baptize and nurture new believers,
- To respond to human need by loving service,
- To seek to transform unjust structures of society, and
- To strive to safeguard the integrity of creation, sustain and renew the life of the earth.[55]

The above "Five Marks" are also a clear admission of the Anglican acknowledgement of the holistic nature of the mission of the church to which was referred in detail in 4.3.1.1 above. It will be remembered that such holistic mission requires the church to "not settle for communicating the faith separate from social involvement" and that "justice and justification by faith, worship and political action, the spiritual and the material, personal change and structural change belong together."[56] The Anglican "Five Marks of Mission" have been developed over several years. As contemporary challenges arise and impinge on the mission field of the Anglican Communion worldwide, the Anglican Communion has been proactive in creating a plan to address these issues so that its mission may continue to be successful. For example, the fifth mark was added at the eighth meeting of the Anglican Consultative Council in Cardiff, Wales, where

> . . . [t]he report of "Section II: Mission, Culture and Human Development" stated: There has been a consistent view of mission repeated by the Anglican Consultative Council, the "Lambeth Conference," the Primates' Meeting and others in recent years, which defines mission in a four-fold way . . . We now feel that our understanding of the ecological crisis, and indeed of the threats to the unity of all creation, mean that we have to add a fifth affirmation: to strive to safeguard the integrity of creation and sustain and renew the life of the earth.[57]

---

55. References to the Anglican "Five Marks of Mission" can be accessed on the Anglican Communion Website. *www.anglicancommunion.org.*

56. Bulmer and Hansford, *Local Church*, 12.

57. See *http://archive.anglican.ca/v2019/mm/mm.htm.* Accessed 30 May 2012.

As indicated in the above extended quote, the Anglican Consultative Council additional mark of mission is linked to, as Avis reminds us, "the 1988 Lambeth Conference [when] a resolution was passed to initiate a Decade of Evangelism in the final years of the second millennium."[58] That resolution reads:

> This Conference, recognizing that evangelism is the primary task given to the church, asks each province and diocese of the Anglican Communion, in cooperation with other Christians, to make the closing years of this millennium a "Decade of Evangelism" with a renewed and united emphasis on making Christ known to the people of his world.[59]

Thus, ACT's process of reviewing its work and mission in its Strategic Plan is in line with what has been happening in the worldwide Anglican Communion as the former calls for each entity of the Anglican Church of Tanzania – departments, dioceses, bodies – to clarify its vision and mission which will help to stipulate strategies that are meaningful and intentional within its given context. It is from the strategic plan initiatives that a theology of public engagement is beginning to be made much more relevant today. For example, currently most dioceses agree that the most critical contemporary issues in Tanzania are social-economic disparities, growth of prosperity gospel, interreligious tensions, the gap in the integration of faith with day-to-day living.[60] From these contemporary issues, and in the context of ACT, fighting corruption clearly falls within its mission and the mission of the Anglican Communion as it pertains to "transforming unjust structures of society."

In light of the discussion of the theological unacceptability of corruption and injustice in with reference to the nature of God, ACT's actions (in public engagement and fighting corruption) as part of the Anglican Communion also echoes what is found in the statement in the Lambeth Conference Resolution II, that "[a]ll our mission springs from the action

---

58. Avis, "Catholicity Outweighs Autonomy."

59. See *http://www.anglicancommunion.org/ministry/mission/commissions/missio/b_doc.cfm*. Accessed 14 May 2014.

60. cf. Mbogo, "The Anglican Church," 14.

and self-revelation of God in Jesus Christ. . . [and] our call to mission and evangelism [is] grounded in the very nature of the God who is revealed to us."

Another example of a clear statement of the role in the public sphere was issued in 2008 – and with it express references to injustice and corruption with theological principles in support of its position on these matters. What is referred to here is the Jerusalem Declaration of 2008. In June 2008, about 1,200 Anglican leaders, bishops, clergy, and laity from twenty-seven provinces of the Anglican Communion gathered in Jerusalem for the Global Anglican Future Conference (GAFCON).[61] After the conference, the GAFCON Primates' Council commissioned the Theological Resource Group to prepare a commentary on the Jerusalem Declaration's Clause 10, which includes the following statement:

> *Our God is a God of justice* and He commands His people to "act justly and to love mercy and to walk humbly with your God" (Mic 6:8). Throughout the Scriptures God insists on honesty and integrity at all levels of our dealings with one other (Exod 23:6–7; Prov 11:1; 17:15; Mic 6:8). *God is also the ruler of the kings of the earth. Christians are called to be loyal citizens of their country.* They are also called to be loving critics and critical lovers of their country. *Corruption needs to be dealt with appropriately.* In mixed societies, Christians have a responsibility to demonstrate just dealings *in their own lives,* and to do all they can to promote justice *on the larger scale. The church must engage with, and prophetically challenge, political and community leaders, in order to bring about change in society that will benefit all* (Jer 29:7). Of particular concern will be the persecuted minorities, where love and justice call for prayer and protest on their behalf (Gal 6:10).[62]

---

61. The Global Anglican Future Conference (GAFCON) is a global Anglican spiritual movement with the aim of "preserving and promoting the truth and power of the gospel of salvation in Jesus Christ as Anglicans have received it. GAFCON cherishes the Anglican heritage and believes that, in God's providence, Anglicanism has a bright future in obedience to our Lord's Great Commission to make disciples of all nations and to build up the church on the foundation of biblical truth."

62. GAFCON, *Jerusalem Declaration*, 58–59 (emphases added).

The above statement is crucial for understanding and appreciating the global Anglican Communion's theological stance on corruption and injustice. Clearly both the issues of justice and corruption are part of the major challenges that this global Anglican gathering acknowledges. Important too is the theological basis for this, according to the Declaration, which offers ACT theological principles to support efforts in fighting corruption and injustice, many of which have been identified as part of this study. There is an acknowledgement of the nature of God as a God of justice (see 3.4.2), but also of the sovereignty of God (see 3.4.3). In the Declaration one also finds a theological acknowledgement, with reference to the prophet Jeremiah, that "[t]he church must engage with, and prophetically challenge, political and community leaders, in order to bring about change in society."[63] This view clearly speaks to the reflections in chapter 4 not only on the church as a prophetic witness toward good governance (4.3.1.5) and this witness as one of the modes of public engagement open to the church, but also to the theological-ethical and biblical mandate of the church towards the transformation of society – what has been referred to as moral transformation (4.3.1.2), or in Jesse Mugambi's terms the (moral) reconstruction of society (4.3.1.6) and policy advocacy as transformative prophetic action.[64]

Furthermore, the Jerusalem Declaration also clearly acknowledges not only the role of the church in these endeavors, but also that of the individual believer in the sense that they "have a responsibility to demonstrate just dealings in their own lives, and to do all they can to promote justice on the larger scale." This reminds not only of Smit's formulation of the various social forms of the church as both institution and individual believers in their daily lives and as part of civil society (4.2.2), but also that the church as an institution and as a community of individual believers are "communities of character," which have a mandate to teach and exemplify Christian virtues (4.4.1.3).

With the above background of a possible theological rationale for ACT to engage in the fight against corruption and injustice in the public sphere, both from a national and international perspective (independently and as part of the global Anglican Communion), we now first turn to the broader

---

63. The Global Anglican Future Conference (GAFCON).
64. Ibid.

issue of ACT's record of public engagement on issues of in/justice and, due to the link between injustice and corruption or corruption as injustice (cf. 3.1 and 5.1 above), to the narrower issue of the anti-corruption work undertaken by and opportunities open to ACT.

5.5.4 ACT and the Public Discourse on In/Justice

5.5.4.1 Colonial *Injustices as a Source of ACT's Public Engagement*

From the outset of this study, the focus has been on corruption as it relates to justice from the perspective of Christian theology, in other words, the focus has been on a theological-ethical reading of corruption and justice. This has also been the case in this chapter. Now that biblical and theological perspectives have been brought to bear on the problem of corruption and injustice (from ACT and the Global Anglican Communion's perspective), it is important, to pay attention to the extent to which ACT has enacted its prophetic role on justice (and corruption) issues.

This study has already noted that the history of the Anglican church's public involvement with the issue of in/justice may be traced back to the latter part of the nineteenth century and that, at the time, it was linked to the work of UMCA missionaries. In his book, *A History of Global Anglicanism*, Kevin Ward aptly affirms this:

> The UMCA's most formidable missionary was Frank Weston, who first arrived in Zanzibar in 1898, and became bishop in 1908. He was as willing to campaign against colonial injustice as against ecclesiastical fudges, most famously protesting against forced labour in British East African possessions in The Serfs of East Africa – policies which affected his own diocese as well as Kenya, since German East Africa had just come under British administration.[65]

Weston's campaign against colonial injustice flowed from two important sources, namely his personal and "deep commitment to see Christianity engaging with the social and political realities of [colonial Tanzania]"[66]

---

65. Ward, *History*, 173 (emphasis added).
66. Ibid., 184.

and, second, to his understanding of the theological-ethical foundation of the Anglican tradition, which "[speaks] of humanity being called into relationship with God and that human purpose and destiny is fulfilled in relationships of mutuality, love and justice."[67] It was this foundation that missionaries such as Weston felt called to not only to preach, but to live out according to the message of the gospel and the church. They saw this in relation to kingdom of God, as a new polity of justice and peace, and its role principally to realize the full establishment of the kingdom by living out the story of Israel and Christ.[68]

It is thus clear that Weston and his fellow Anglicans in East Africa knew that they had to stand firm and had to live in accordance with the hallmarks of the early Christ-followers, namely in service, humility, and opposition to injustice. As Varughese reminds, "[t]his non-negotiable standard of faith is the characteristic mark of a genuine Christian community. And this Christian community exists to offer hope to the world."[69] This argument is also in line with the teaching of the Anglican social theology based on the Anglican traditions – both *evangelical* and *catholic* (or *high church*), which "[speaks] of humanity being called into relationship with God and that human purpose and destiny is fulfilled in relationships of mutuality, love and justice."[70]

Reflecting back on earlier discussions on God, church and humanity, there seem to be something of the relationality of God, humankind and the church that stands to the background of this. What early Anglican missionaries did in the discourse on justice in Tanzania in fact seems similar to what Boesak talks about in the context of challenging the church's silence in South Africa: "[T]o reject human injustice,"[71] to participate in "radical demands for justice" and to show "God's passion for justice and God's anger against injustice,"[72] was the result of missionaries "[learning their] commitment to justice and the poor . . . from the Torah, the prophets, and Jesus

---

67. Ibid., 173.
68. cf. Hauerwas and Willimon, *Resident Aliens*, 45–48.
69. Varughese, *Discovering the New Testament*, 353.
70. Turnbull, *Anglican and Evangelical?* 176.
71. Boesak, *Tenderness of Conscience*, 73.
72. Ibid., 91.

of Nazareth."[73] The Anglican missionaries were thus challenged and stood up for what Sanneh calls "[the] public cause in the sense of commitment to establishing a new society based on public morality, freedom, human dignity, integrity, the rule of law, and justice."[74]

5.5.4.2 ACT's Engagement in Justice Issues in Post-Colonial Times: *A Renewed Emphasis and the Role of the CAPA*

The missionary engagement with injustice during colonial time has continued to inform the post-independence discourse on justice by ACT and the latter's social ethics, but as Chapman puts it, "[w]orking against injustice [also] became increasingly important."[75] However, the role of the church as an institution that engages with government on justice issues has for long in the post-colonial period focused more on addressing inequalities by way of the provision of social services (particularly in education and health care) despite the fact that "[c]hronic corruption, economic mismanagement, human rights violations, injustice, and oppression" has increased in the country and that these weaknesses "have all been cited as a result of poor governance in leadership."[76] This focus on the provision of social services, particularly in education and health in recent times, has been and continues to be viewed as part of ACT's efforts to address injustice (and indirectly, one might venture to say, the adverse consequences of corruption) (see 2.2.3 and 2.2.4).

Moreover, as part of ACT's public engagement on justice, cognizance needs to be taken of social services provision and ecumenical involvement/activities over the last decade by the Council of Anglican Provinces of Africa (CAPA). This Anglican regional organization was established in 1979 in Chilema, Malawi, by the Anglican Primates of Africa, and it coordinates and articulates issues affecting the church and communities across Africa. According to the CAPA's vision, it is aimed at "[a] unified and self-sustaining Anglican Communion in Africa, providing holistic ministry to all and fulfilling God's promise for abundant life" and its mission is "[t]o effectively

---

73. Ibid., 166.
74. Sanneh, *Abolitionists Abroad,* 119.
75. Chapman, *Anglicanism*, 124.
76. Ibid., cf. Ilo et. al., *Church as Salt and Light,* and Okumu, *African Renaissance.*

coordinate and provide a platform for the Anglican church in Africa to celebrate life, consult and address challenges in the continent in order to fulfil God's promise for abundant life."[77]

The CAPA's vision, in addition to constituting in itself a further articulation of the theological basis for its members' (including ACT) involvement in the public sphere, what is especially important here are the practical ways of doing the latter as identified by the CAPA. Among the CAPA's duties are the coordination of "advocacy, lobbying, networking, collaborations and partnership building." According to CAPA's own Strategic Plan 2010–2014 (entitled *Called to a Life of Faithfulness*), it wishes to lead "its members in their advocacy, lobby for good governance and justice."[78] Especially important for the purposes of this study is the explicit recognition here of one of the modes of doing public theology that was referred to in chapter 4 of this study, namely that of a public advocacy role of the church (see 4.4.1.2 and especially 4.4.1.6).

To add to ACT's and other provinces' efforts to engage in issues of public life, CAPA's approach to facilitate the contribution of faith communities and leaders, has purposely broadened the issues of justice as that which should be understood within the context of analyzing key challenges in the prevailing situation of Africa today.[79] An emphasis on the prevailing situation deserves quoting at some length as it focuses on:

> *Political environment* characterized by weak and often poor national governance structures, politically instigated conflict, **corruption** and repetitive cases of flawed elections; *Economic environment* indicates that Africa's economy has severely deteriorated over the past decade due to a multiplicity of factors including import/export restrictions, harsh lending conditions, skyrocketing unemployment, rampant poverty, HIV and AIDS, donor fatigue and rapid globalization; *Social* environment is characterized by infiltration of negative dominant foreign culture, HIV and AIDS scourge and its effect on productivity,

---

77. See http://rowanwilliams.archbishopofcanterbury.org/pages/the-council-of-anglican-provinces-in-africa-capa.html. Accessed 12 July 2015.

78. CAPA, "Called to a Life."

79. Ibid, 9–10.

retrogressive cultural practices such as female circumcision and wife inheritance; *Technological environment* is characterized by lack of technical expertise, poor power supply and use of outdated technology within a fast-changing information communication technology (ICT); *Ecological trends* is recognized as major environmental problem facing the globe; *Religious environment* where the concern is on ecclesiastical issues, such as those of pastoral care for those infected and affected by HIV and AIDS; reconciliation and mediation among those affected by conflict and war; evangelism among millions of poor people; polarization with the western church regarding issues of human sexuality; and within Africa an acute need for pastoral care for those affected by HIV & AIDS and victims of poverty, conflict and war.[80]

Importantly, among the challenges to churches in Africa listed above one not only finds an express mention of corruption, but also many of its consequences of challenges that are exacerbated by corruption as listed in this study – such as its threat to peace, security and stability (2.4.2.2), to basic human rights and equality (2.4.2.3), and as economic threat and threat to human development (2.4.2.4).

5.6 ACT's Anti-Corruption Efforts

In chapter 4 of this study, reference was made to Koopman's understanding of public theology with a view to a vision and contours of a new world of dignity, freedom, and justice for all. Koopman also offered his understanding of the importance of the Word of God in public engagement in a practical sense (the Word not only nourishes faith and sustains ministry of the church, but also gives criteria for working for justice); and his reasons for the church's public engagement, most particularly when emphasizing the biblical affirmation of God's redemptive work, moral transformation, prophetic witness and the cry for social justice (4.3.2.3). This section identifies, examines and locates the availability of practical ACT strategies and

---

80. As in http://rowanwilliams.archbishopofcanterbury.org/pages/the-council-of-anglican-provinces-in-africa-capa.html. Emphasis added. Accessed 12 July 2015.

work on public engagement in the war on corruption – also with regard to existing mandates, processes, styles and content in order to pave the way for suggestions on how ACT could, if needed, extend its role and be more relevant to Tanzania.

Returning again for the moment to Smit's social forms of the church (4.2.2), it will be seen that some of ACT's activities below find themselves within the social form of the church as institution and denomination, others as it acts in the ecumenical sphere, and yet others have to do with the social form of the Christian church as individual believers in their daily lives in society or as members of associations, such as NGO's in society.

A final issue to remember before proceeding is that it will be realized that the question of language looms large in all the examples listed below. This was emphasized by most public theologians in their views on the modes of public engagement of the church, for example Stackhouse (4.3.2.5), according to whom:

> . . . if a theology is to be trusted to participate in public discourse it ought to be able to make a plausible case for what it advocates in terms that can be comprehended by those who are not believers . . . It should be able to articulate its core convictions in comprehensible terms across many modes of discourse, explaining its symbolic and mythical terms . . . in ways that expose their multiple levels of meaning.[81]

The above may be especially relevant in all interfaith or civil society initiatives and dialogue on corruption, as will be Forrester's conviction that such collaboration "requires learning the language of the secular world in such a way that Christian discourse relates to it without losing its particular insights and contribution to the discussion,"[82] and Bedford-Strohm's view that the church needs to know "how to speak the language of the world and how to be in dialogue with the world."[83]

---

81. Stackhouse, "Public Theology and Ethical Judgment," 112.
82. Forrester, *Beliefs, Values and Policies*, 61. See also 4.3.2.1.
83. Bedford-Strohm, "Tilling and Caring for the Earth," 36. See also 4.3.2.5.

5.6.1 ACT and the Government of Tanzania

In 4.2.3.3 reference was made to Petersen's view that "faith traditions can serve as a critical partner with government, business, labor, education and civil society,"[84] and that "[t]hese partnerships are essential for any envisaged improvement in condition of life for all, and thus nullify any modes of engagement that are self-seeking, competitive and uncooperative."[85] It will also be remembered that in expanding on his argument that public theology as a prophetic, priestly and royal-servant theology, Koopman identifies five roles of *prophetic public theology*, one of which was public theology's engagement in policy discussions, by offering guidelines somewhere "between . . . broad principles and detailed blueprints" in the form of "ethical parameters for policymaking,"[86] advancing "an ethos of servanthood, hope and responsible and ethical global discipleship and citizenship."[87] Again, for Stackhouse, one of the constructive tasks of public theology is that it "must show that it can form, inform and sustain the moral and spiritual architecture of a civil society so that truth, justice and mercy are more nearly approximated in the souls of persons and in the institutions of the common life."[88] It will also be remembered that the concept of "critical solidarity" is one that is often referred to by public theologians when reflecting on the public role of the church and that it entails "a relationship whereby the church seeks to work with the state by supporting its efforts to rebuild and transform society, yet at the same time, it continues to reserve the right to criticize government in areas where this may be necessary."[89] How has this been, and does it or could it happen in the life of ACT today?

a) A Consultative Role via the International Donor Community

The sad fact that ACT currently does not have its own coordinated program against corruption has already been mentioned above (5.4.2). However,

---

84. In Le Bruyns, "Ethical Leadership," 57.
85. Ibid.
86. Koopman, "Churches and Public Policy," 1.
87. Ibid.
88. Stackhouse, *God and Globalization*, 107.
89. See also 4.4.1.5.

reflecting on the vision, mission, faith and belief statements, it is clear that it such a program may well fall within ACT's self-understanding of its role in the public sphere. Despite the non-existence of its own program against corruption, in recent years, ACT has had invitations to *collaborate* with other key players in the fight against corruption either directly with government or via other role players with government. One example is efforts initiated by the United Nations Development Programme, specifically its Partnership Strategy, whereby the latter seeks to partner not only with the government of Tanzania but also other partners in civil society, including churches. A major focus here has been on election fraud and "the civic and voters education, and participating in monitoring elections." For example, in from 2012 to 2014, ACT was involved in the "constitutional reform process" under the auspices of the UNDP in order to "to increase [churches' and FBOs'/CSOs'] capacity to conduct . . . democracy and elections education and also contribute to conflict mitigation and peace building."[90] Clearly, as far as political corruption is concerned, FBOs and churches such as ACT have been acknowledged and given the chance to participate in the struggle against corruption as it pertains to free and fair elections.

Another example is that of Norwegian Church Aid (NCA). Tanzania is characterized in the NCA Country Plan 2011–2015 as follows: "Tanzania is often characterized as a peaceful and united society. There is political stability and a sound macroeconomic performance. But we also find incomplete transitions in its political and economic systems and a structural lack of accountability."[91] It is in this spirit that Norwegian Church Aid Tanzania aims to increase the capacity of civil society, especially FBOs, to address poverty and inequality and to advocate for justice and accountable governance.[92]

Again, there seems to be a clear recognition of churches as key institutions in meeting the needs of the people. For the NCA, what justifies this recognition includes; ". . . long established networks of grassroots congregations and organizations that date back to the pre-colonial era"[93] and experience in service provision. NCA affirms that "[c]urrent estimates show that FBOs

---

90. UNDP, Democractic Empowerment Project.
91. Norwegian Church Aid, "NCA Country Plan 2011–2015," 4.
92. Ibid., 10.
93. Ibid., 8.

provide almost 50% of services in the education and the health sector."[94] The nature of ministry by the church is also regarded as important, especially with regard to moral regeneration and the transmission of values. For example, NCA strongly believes that,

> [f]aith offers hope and courage in overcoming fear and powerlessness . . . [t]he church is a custodian of moral values for large groups of the population. Values and attitudes rooted in faith can be mobilized for transformational development. Faith actors often have access to large constituencies. Even in the poorest and most remote areas, people organize themselves for religious practice. Religious leaders are listened to and represent institutions with the potential to challenge and counterbalance injustice.[95]

These views of donor organizations are important and offer current and future opportunities for ACT to collaborate, often via these organizations, with government in the fight against corruption.

b) *The Christian Social Services Commission (CSSC) as Platform for ACT's Public Policy Dialogue with Government*

The importance of public policy dialogue and the church's role in it has been referred to at various points in this study. Examples includes Forrester's view on theology and public policy,[96] Koopman's emphasis on public policy discourse (4.3.2.3),[97] Hauerwas' views on public and political policy and debate,[98] Mugambi's work on government policy, social transformation and reconstruction and public policy advocacy as a mode of transformative prophetic action.[99] What is alluded to by the above scholars is mirrored in the role ACT plays as facilitator in public policy dialogue, most particularly as

---

94. Ibid.
95. Ibid.
96. Forrester, *Theology and Politics, Beliefs, Values and Policies, Christian Justice*. See also 4.3.2.1.
97. Koopman, "Human Dignity."
98. Hauerwas, *Resident Aliens*. See also 4.4.1.3.
99. Mugambi, *From Liberation to Reconstruction*. See also 4.3.1.6.

a member of the Tanzanian Christian Social Services Commission (CSSC). CSSC is a cooperative initiative among Tanzania churches with overseas civil partners on matters regarding social services provided by Tanzanian churches. The CSSC core functions include:

> [t]o participate effectively in the formulation of policies and/or present comprehensive policy proposals to the Government, which may assist the Government in the formulation of gross policies in all matters related to the provision, improvement, expansion and maintenance of education, health and other social services provided by the churches and its organs for the Tanzania people, and in so doing observe the policies for such services as outlined by the Government and to harmonize or reconcile church policy relevant to provision and support of social services in education and health sectors and other social services.[100]

In its participation in the CSSC, ACT, as Allen puts it, is working towards "an effective and streamlined state, ensuring legitimacy, accountability and transparency . . . preference for reform, and strategies for social and political change based upon dialogue [and] consultation."[101] The CSSC plays an important advocacy and lobbying role

> . . . [t]owards the government of Tanzania and the churches on relevant social issues and for maintaining or even improving a conducive environment for the provision of the churches' social services. *Advocacy work which is the central core function of CSSC* shall be extended to district and local levels as a response to the social sector and local government reforms. *CSSC seeks to influence legislation through a dialogue with lawmakers in a manner that is fair and compatible with democratic principles.*[102]

---

100. See: http://www.cssc.or.tz/about_us/corefunction.php.
101. Allen, "Who Needs Civil Society?" 330–331.
102. CSSC, http://cssc.or.tz (emphases added).

Other areas of the CSSC's work include addressing issues of education, health, capacity building, research and dissemination of information, consultancy, and support services.

5.6.2 ACT's Christian Ecumenical and Interfaith Collaboration

Recalling references to the nature of the church in chapter 4 of this study, especially to its *servant* nature as a church called by God called the church to service (2 Cor 4:5),[103] it will be remembered that this call concerns more than announcing the coming of the kingdom of God, but includes the ministry of "justice, transformation and healing."[104] Its role consists of its dedication to the transformation of the world into the kingdom of God[105] and keeping alive the hope and aspiration of all human beings for the kingdom of God. ACT also recognizes the need to proclaim the good news in this broad understanding, reaffirming in its vision, mission and statement of faith:

> ARTICLE V *The Christian Church*: The Church as the Body of Christ, whose members belong to the new humanity, are called to live in the world in the power of the Spirit, worshipping God, confessing His truth, proclaiming Christ, supporting one another in love and giving themselves in sacrificial service to those in need.[106]

In a variety of places ACT participates in working towards this goal – in ecumenical forums and even interfaith forums, and also as it pertains to the promotion of justice and the fight against injustice and corruption.

a) ACT as Member of the Christian Council of Tanzania (CCT)

In addition to collaboration with the government of Tanzania via donors, the international community and the CSSC, ACT is also involved in anti-corruption work via its collaboration with other ecumenical organizations.

---

103. cf. McGrath, *Justification by Faith*, 393. See also 4.3.2.3.
104. Dulles, *Models of the Church*, 98.
105. Ibid.
106. http://friendsofsaintjohns.org/docs/ACT-vision_mission_faith.pdf. Accessed 14 May 2014.

A good example of this ecumenical involvement is its membership of the Christian Council of Tanzania (CCT). The latter was founded in 1948 and seeks to be "a committed, faithful, transparent and accountable instrument for promoting ecumenical unity and community development."[107] It also wishes "to facilitate and coordinate the united witness of member churches and church-related organizations by building their capacity in evangelization, networking, *advocacy and socio-economic development* for the benefit of the community."[108] Once again one finds here an emphasis on and opportunity for ACT to participate in advocacy and development in this ecumenical platform.

The CCT's engagement in public affairs goes back to before Tanzanian's independence. According to Ludwig, the CCT,

> [b]ecame particularly important in relations between church and state by the establishment of the office of a General Secretary in 1961. The CCT coordinated [and continues to do so] the interests of the Protestant churches and usually the General Secretary negotiated with the government.[109]

The work of the CCT is organized across seven programs, namely (1) ecumenism and interfaith relations, (2) graduate volunteer program, (3) health and HIV/AIDS, (4) women development, children and gender, (5) climate change, environment and food security, (6) media and communication, and (7) the program on peace, socio-economic justice and good governance. It is under the latter program that the problem of corruption is mainly addressed as

> [t]he goal of this programme is to enhance and sustain peaceful coexistence, respect for human rights and equitable participation in managing and sharing social, economic, political and cultural life among the communities. The purpose will be the enhancement of the capacity of CCT members and communities to engage in fostering peaceful coexistence and respect

---

107. Lugongo et al., "Let's Not," no page number.
108. Christian Council of Tanzania, http://cct-tz.org/. Accessed 28 September 2012 (emphasis added).
109. Ludwig, *Church and State in Tanzania*, 230.

of human rights at all levels. This will be achieved through four outputs: increased capacity of communities to understand current issues related to civic affairs, public policies, political parties' manifestoes, and human rights; and enhanced collaboration and networking among CCT members, other FBOs and the wider CSOs community.[110]

Through its participation in this program, ACT engages with communities, parishes and people from various denominations and faith traditions also on the issue of corruption.

b) ACT in Dialogue and Collaboration with Interfaith Bodies

The concept of dialogue or conversation (also as, for some, constituting the essence of public theology) has often been referred to in this study (among others as a mode of doing public theology, see 4.3.2.1 and 4.3.2.5). As can be seen, ACT's involvement in the public sphere and in anti-corruption work also often happens through collaboration based on dialogue. This is also the case in its dialogue at the level of multifaith initiatives and action on issues of common interest. As was seen, this model of engagement has a theological foundation. For example, Stott sees dialogue as "a token of genuine Christian love, because it indicates [believers'] steadfast resolve to rid [their] minds of prejudices and caricatures which [they] may entertain about other people."[111] Samuel and Sugden understand dialogue as "being open to other religions, to recognize God's activity in them, and to see how they are related to God's unique revelation in Christ."[112] From such theological justification, ACT has over the past decade or so participated in shared activities across different religious communities. This participation tends to bring together religious leaders and experts from different faiths mainly to discuss and deliberate on issues of common interest such as those of corruption and injustice.

---

110. Ibid.
111. Stott, *Lausanne Covenant*, 81.
112. Samuel and Sugden, "Dialogue," 128.

For Nicholls this dialogical approach not only gives another definition of dialogue as "working together in harmony for the good of all people,"[113] but it encourages the church, not only as institutions or denomination, but also in its form as *individual members* (cf. again Smit, see 4.2.2), to faithfully participate in civil organizations and institutions, NGOs or FBOs because dialogue, spoken in this context means "a way of life, an attitude of mind as well as verbal defense and proclamation of the gospel" and therefore it has to be "a way of life for all men and women of good will."[114] By so doing, each believer will have a duty to defend societal ethics and denounce unethical behavior such as those of corruption and build a sound democratic Tanzanian society. For example, under the support of donors such as UNDP and NCA, ACT has in recent years worked with at an interfaith level with organizations such as Baraza Kuu la Waislam Tanzania (BAKWATA), the Muslim Council of Tanzania), the Hindu Council of Tanzania (HCT), the organization of Tanzania Muslim Professionals (TAMPRO), and Tanzania Youth Interfaith Network (TYIN).[115]

By way of example, Norwegian Church Aid (Tanzania) was referred to above as a key partner in ACT's collaboration with government on corruption. However, NCA also supports ACT's dialogue and collaboration with the interfaith bodies in its efforts to increase the capacity of civil society, especially FBOs, to address poverty and inequality and to advocate for justice and accountable governance.[116] Thus, there seems to be a clear recognition from NCA (referred to in 5.6.2 (b) above as well) and other organizations that the religions are and have been key institutions in meeting needs of the people. In fact, the NCA strongly believes that,

> [f]aith offers hope and courage in overcoming fear and powerlessness. . . [t]he church is a custodian of moral values for large groups of the population. Values and attitudes rooted in faith can be mobilized for transformational development. Faith actors often have access to large constituencies. Even in the poorest and most remote areas, people organize themselves for

---

113. Nicholls, "Witnessing Church," 62.
114. Ibid., 60–61.
115. See Konrad-Adenauer, *Role of Faith*.
116. Norwegian Church Aid, "NCA Country Plan 2011–2015," 10.

religious practice. Religious leaders are listened to and represent institutions with the potential to challenge and counterbalance injustice.[117]

Together with international donors such as NCA, ACT conducts training on social accountability monitoring, for example, via its involvement in the CCT and in collaboration with other religions. The issue of corruption and good governance looms large in these training programs. With cases of misappropriation of public funds at the grassroots level, the NCA in Tanzania, in collaboration with her core partner the CCT, has gone out to create awareness of this. The Public Expenditure Tracking System (PETS);[118] is one of the successful stories.

5.6.3 Anti-Corruption Clubs in Schools and at Universities: An Opportunity for the Teaching of Virtues

One other area that ACT has been involved in fighting corruption has been in accepting the government of Tanzania's request to assist the younger generation of Tanzanians in secondary schools and universities to form "anti-corruption clubs." Through these clubs, ACT assists the youth to improve their ethical knowledge base as it relates to the issue of corruption. The need for "ethics training" among the youth in Tanzania may be linked to the arguments regarding virtue in the previous chapters. The importance of ethical virtues in the fight against corruption has been highlighted, for example, with reference to: the thought of Julius Nyerere (2.3.2.3); the virtue of fairness and justice in the thought of John Rawls (2.4.6.1); the virtues as "the dispositions in God's nature"(3.4)[119]; Hauerwas' view of the church as locus of the teaching of virtue as "communities of character" (4.4.1.3); and Koopman's explanation (4.3.2.3) of "public and civic virtue" as,

---

117. Ibid., 8.

118. *A Public Expenditure Tracking Survey* (PETS) tracks the flow of public funds and material resources from the central government level, through the administrative hierarchy, and out to the frontline service providers. The aim is to improve the quality of service delivery at the local level, and the key question that a PETS sets out to answer is: *Do public funds and material resources end up where they are supposed to?* If they don't, the survey may go further and ask: *Why are those funds being diverted?* Such surveys are typically implemented at the sector level, usually in health or education. For more on this Survey see: www.http://.u4.no/themes/pets/main.cfm.

119. Cunningham, *These Three Are One.*

public wisdom in contexts of complexity, ambiguity, tragedy and *aporia* (dead-end streets); public justice in context of inequalities and injustices on local and global levels; public temperance in context of greed and consumerism amidst poverty and alienation; public fortitude amidst situations of powerlessness and inertia; public faith amidst feelings of disorientation and rootless-ness in contemporary societies; public hope amidst situations of despair and melancholy; public love in societies where public solidarity and compassion are absent.[120]

One may also refer back to Stackhouse's view that the duty of the church includes "to instill . . . integrity, honesty, diligence, fairness, and stewardship. [And] [o]f additional importance is the encouragement of a sense of responsibility to contribute to the social and economic development of their communities,"[121] or Rowan Williams's view that churches and faith communities have "to be a place where people [are] educating one another about civic questions and human dignity, where people [are] educating and being educated about liberty, responsibility, the creation of a sustainable human environment."[122]

A good practical example of ACT's involvement in teaching virtues in the fight against corruption in anti-corruption clubs, is at St John's University of Tanzania, an ACT institution where several anti-corruption clubs have been established. Again, the issue of collaboration looms large as it is through Tanzania's National Anti-Corruption Strategy and Actions Plan (NACSAP, see 2.3.2.3), and the United Nations Development Programme,[123] that the establishment of anti-corruption clubs in tertiary institutions and the provision of support for these clubs was made possible. According to the SCCCT, these clubs have been highly effective in raising public awareness on anti-corruption.[124]

---

120. In Cole, *Theology in Service*, 152.

121. On the understanding of Rowan Williams's mutuality approach to public theology as disussed on section 4.3.2.5.

122. Stackhouse, "Public Theology and Ethical Judgment," 112, as discussed in 4.3.2.4.

123. Cf. UNDP 2013 – Tanzania Success Stories Fighting Corruption and its project entitled "Strengthening Capacities to Combat Corruption in Tanzania" (SCCCT).

124. See UNDP Tanzania Success Stories Election Support 2010.

5.7 ACT's Anti-Corruption and the Discourse on Justice: A Failure or Success?

The evaluation of the impact of ACT's involvement in the fight against corruption is very difficult to determine. However, it seems that thus far ACT has acted according to its conviction that it does have a role to play in the public sphere, but that when it comes to issues of justice, it often does so in collaboration with other secular or religious role players. This is even more so in the case of its (often indirect) response to corruption. In fact, this seems to be the single greatest reason for the apparent lack of success of ACT in the public square with regard to the fight against corruption: the lack of an own self-initiated program of action. All the above examples of ACT's involvement have been in collaboration with other denominations, civil organizations, government or even other religions. However, a single (or multiple for that matter) effort to theologically reflect on the issue of corruption and from there to proceed to formulating a theological and practical response to corruption is still sorely lacking.

The latter does not mean that there is no consciousness of the challenge and dangers of corruption among individuals in ACT, even among its leadership. Recently it was reported, for example, that during the 2015 Easter services, several Tanzanian church leaders called "for sobriety in debates on the envisaged new Constitution [see 5.8 below] and war on corruption, warning that any segments of the society seeking to use the availed platform to gain political mileage could plunge the country into anarchy."[125] This fear and warning was expressed not only by Roman Catholic Auxiliary Bishop Eusebius Nzigilwa in the Diocese of Dar es Salaam, but also by Bishop Renard Mtenji of the Lutheran Church in Ulanga, Kilombero and Bishop Valentino Mokiwa (the former primate of ACT) and Bishop Godfrey Mhogolo of the Central Diocese of ACT.

In the wake of another recent corruption scandal, the Tageta Escrow accounts scandal in 2014 comes to mind. It involved several high-ranking government ministers and officials as well as the Tanzanian Prime Minister, who were implicated in the transferral of between 250 million and 400 million USD from the Bank of Tanzania for alleged distribution among

---

125. Lugongo et al., "Let's Not," no page number.

government officials. Again church leaders joined in the outrage and disappointment at the situation and among these voices were individual Anglican bishops, such as the bishop of the Central Tanganyika Diocese, Dr Dickson Chilongani, and Bishop Michael Hafidhi of the Zanzibar Anglican Church.[126]

In the sections that follow, some possible reasons for this lack of a concerted and focused effort by ACT will be reflected upon. As will be seen, these reasons will also be brought into conversation with the theological-ethical concepts and considerations regarding the nature of the church and its role in the public sphere – both regarding the theological reasons behind the latter and the forms or modes of its engagement in that sphere.

5.7.1 Corruption within the Church

It has been maintained that in order for the church to be successful in its mission, it has to maintain its own integrity and its leadership needs to be especially credible (4.3.1.7). It has to be "clothed in service, a sense of care and compassion, integrity and dignity."[127] Not only this, but it is very unfortunate that too often the church itself as well as other religious institutions are afflicted by corruption. This has its consequences. The church's witness is being undermined in the public arena as one finds a situation which reminds of the biblical metaphor where "the speck in the government's eye" is emphasized at the cost of "the plank in the eye of the churches." As Avis reminds us, the church needs to keep its theology and ethics together as,

> . . . theologians as ostensibly different as Thomas Aquinas and Karl Barth have insisted, doctrine and ethics must go hand in hand; ethics cannot be separated from dogmatics. So it is a matter of theological integrity that ecclesiology should have an ethical dimension.[128]

Or, as Stückelberger, University of Basel ethicist and founder of the Geneva-based global network on ethics Globethics.net puts it:

---

126. cf. "Escrow Saga Dominates Sermons on Christmas."

127. On the role of ethical, competent, committed and effective leadership in the church in the fight against corruption as discussed on section 4.3.1.7 of this study.

128. Avis, *Reshaping Ecumenical Theology*, 159.

> Corruption in religious institutions is especially disturbing because these institutions and their representatives are seen worldwide, even in secular societies, as moral authorities. If even pastors and bishops are corrupt, who else can set benchmarks of truth and transparency? But not only is the credibility of individual believers at stake. The gospel itself is discredited because more and more people start to doubt if faith can help to overcome this cancer of society.[129]

ACT is growing in membership numbers across its twenty-six dioceses. There is an increase in vocations, in the number of local clergy, educational, health and pastoral institutions and development projects and programs aimed at uplifting the lives of people. In this sense, its missionary activities in terms of gospel proclamation and witness seem to be successful. However, despite this growth, in some sectors of ACT, as in most churches, traces of corruption scandals do occur.[130] After reporting on "[a] successful Tanzanian minister [who] built a multi-million religious empire by encouraging the faithful to give a chunk of their wealth as a sign of commitment,"[131] Mfumbusa uses the example of two cases from the mainstream churches "to indicate the pervasiveness of the reality of corruption,"[132] one being from ACT! It regards a long-time problem in the Anglican Diocese of Victoria Nyanza, where poor leadership, infighting, self-centeredness, and disunity have weakened the local churches and marred its ability to be effective ministers of the gospel. According to Mfumbusa, in the diocese,

> [a] bishop was accused by the faithful of abuse of office, nepotism, and embezzlement of funds. . . . the bishop was relieved of his responsibilities. The case had two dimensions: the bishop accused of corruption in terms of accumulating wealth for private interests and the claim that ethnic sentiments were behind

---

129. Stückelberger, *Corruption-Free Churches*, 16.
130. cf. Mfumbusa, "Church Is Growing," no page numbers.
131. Ibid.
132. Ibid.

the eviction as the bishop didn't belong to the most prominent tribe in the area.[133]

An even more upsetting instance of allegations of corruption within ACT was that of election fraud during the election of the present primate of ACT in 2013.[134] This resulted in speculations and accusations in the media, and although the election results were approved by twenty-five ACT bishops, the issue clearly shows how vulnerable the image of the church is to such allegations. In a statement that acknowledged and regretted this, the General Secretary of ACT explained that,

> The Special Electoral synod of the Anglican Church of Tanzania met on 21 February 2013 in the Cathedral of the Holy Spirit, Dodoma to elect the sixth Archbishop of the Anglican Church of Tanzania. Since then some unfounded accusations of corruption, bribery and tribalism surrounding the election of our new Archbishop have been made on the internet. The internet can be used to develop relationships, but it can also be used to spread gossip and destabilize the church. None of those writing these false stories sought to confirm them with us. It is very sad that someone who did not attend the election would spoil what was confirmed by all our bishops as a fair and transparent election.[135]

An important insight referred to earlier (see 4.3.1.7), with reference to St Augustine and Jürgen Moltmann, is that the church not a society of saints, but a "mixed body" of "saints and sinners" and that,

> . . . though transformed by Christ, members of the church sometimes act contrary to their identity – as if they belong to the fallenness of the world. Whenever these members organize in institutional forms, they can therefore participate in and perpetuate systemic evil. [But] [a]s the body of Christ, empowered

---

133. Ibid.
134. cf. Haley, "Charges of TEC-Related Fraud"; Geoconger, "Tanzania Church."
135. Quoted in *Thinking Anglicans*, "News Items."

by the Spirit however, the church [also] transcends the world and therefore has an alternative to offer.[136]

Like all people in power, the leadership of ACT is not immune to the temptation of corruption through enrichment and other failings that compromise the church's integrity and its ability to do what is right and just. Therefore, when the church speaks "truth to power" (4.3.1.4) and to all who exercise power and authority, it is required to tackle corruption from within before dealing credibly with external corruption.

When speaking of corruption in the church, Stückelberger identifies different forms or levels of corruption (some of which are unfortunately also been prevalent in some quarters in ACT),[137] namely:

- the misuse of church properties;
- unfair labor standards for church employees such as failure to pay competitive salaries and pension fund contributions of church staff;
- payment of bribes by church members so that they are elected as bishops, elders and heads of hospitals, schools and colleges run by the church;
- appointment of church leaders because they are founders of the church but lack any theological training;
- embezzlement of funds meant for church projects;
- unauthorized sale of church-owned land for private gain, at a price which is below market value;
- influencing the award of tenders for the construction of church buildings; and
- punishing whistleblowers who report corrupt activities instead of protecting them.

Thus, although the church is made up of human beings who are members of one body of Christ and is open to the activity of the Holy Spirit, in its

---

136. Cf. Mfumbusa, "Church Is Growing," no page numbers. "The church is both human and divine. Its members are naturally capable of saintly as well as sinful acts. The cases cited are only indicative of the fact that the church is besotted with problems. Still the church is also a community of grace capable of immense good. A lot of good has been done and continues to be done in the name of the church. The association of dominant Christian values and institutions in the post-colony have sometimes reflected badly on the church."

137. Stückelberger, *Corruption-Free Churches*, 67.

human condition it is still subject to the conditions of the world[138] and it is "a human institution" both "holy and sinful"[139] and in continual need for repentance.[140] Therefore, ACT and all other churches in addressing corruption in society need to be conscious of and need to do all in their power to guard their own integrity in all its different social forms,[141] as worshipping community, local congregation, denomination and institution, ecumenical role player and individual believers.

5.7.2 Fighting Corruption from the Pulpit: A Theological Disagreement

ACT is, in Smit's terms, a "worshipping community" and as such it is also a kerygmatic community. This means that as a church ACT is constituted where the faithful gather to worship God and wherever the Word of God is proclaimed and accepted.[142] Worship is the "heart of the life of the church, in such a way that in and through this common worship the believers are called to serve one another and the world."[143] This worshipping community also "contribute[s] to the embodiment of the commitment to unity, reconciliation and justice" for its worship serves also to "strengthen the believers in their faith and to prepare them for their service to each other and the world."[144] The heart of the message the church articulates is the justice of God which effects transformation.[145] However, there exists theological disagreement in some parts of ACT specifically on whether the pulpit is meant to be used for addressing only "sacred" and not "secular" issues. It remains a fact that some church leaders have tended to hold on to the dualistic theology of a sacred-secular divide, as discussed in paragraph 4.3.2.5 above with reference to Stackhouse. Stackhouse, namely affirms the public significance of theology when he says that,

---

138. Mwaura, "Reconstructing Mission."
139. Healey, *Church, World and the Christian Life*, 28.
140. cf. Dulles, *Models of the Church*, 53–54.
141. Smit quoted in Hansen, *Christian in Public*, 9.
142. cf. McGrath, *Justification by Faith*, 404, with reference to Calvin.
143. Smit, *Essays on Being Reformed*, 449.
144. Ibid.
145. Cf. Marshall, *Little Book of Biblical Justice,* and "Meaning of Justice."

> . . . theology, while related to intensely personal commitments and to a particular community of worship, is, at its most profound level, neither merely private nor a matter of distinctive communal identity. Rather, it is an argument regarding the way things are and ought to be, one decisive for public discourse and necessary to the guidance of individual souls, societies, and, indeed, the community of nations.[146]

It will also be remembered that, according to Forrester (4.3.2.1), "when Christianity is assigned to the private realm it lacks the potentiality for prophetic importance because it tends to engage in an easy-going validation of the values of the society, influencing personal morality and accepted values."[147]

For some church members and leaders to maintain that issues such as those of corruption and injustice are of the world and thus only a problem for governments or civil society to address is clearly in opposition to what has been shown in an extended way in chapters 3 and 4 of this study. Fighting corruption and its accompanying injustices is part of the mandate of the church. As such, it follows that to condemn it also from the pulpit is among the unique ways in which churches and ACT can be involved in addressing the issue of corruption.

Coupled with this, ACT has to be cautioned not to heed the warnings and threats of politicians to stay out of issues government and to concentrate on "spiritual matters," on matters of faith. As has repeatedly been shown in this study, corruption and injustice are not only socio-political and economic issues. They are also, to a profound extent, a matter of faith. As emeritus Anglican Archbishop of Kenya, David Gitari, speaking at Kenyatta University observed:

> [t]here are some sections of the church which have stressed the utter hopelessness of this world and called upon the individual to concentrate solely on preparing his soul for the world to come. By ignoring the need for social reform, religion is divorced from the mainstream of human life. Christianity is not just meant for the soul it is for the whole person . . . The

---

146. Stackhouse, "Public Theology and Ethical Judgment," 165.
147. Forrester, *Beliefs, Values and Policies*, 7.

church must seek to transform both individual lives and the soul situation that bring to many people anguish of spirit and cruel bondage.[148]

In a similar tune, Villa-Vicencio, though not specifically mentioning corruption, strongly "appeals for a post-Cold War theology for Africa to engage in serious dialogue with democracy, human rights, law making, nation building and economics in order to improve the quality of human life."[149] If this is understood by leaders and members of the church, it is not only going to help in addressing the problem of corruption, but also other social ills afflicting Tanzania. This will also help the church to continue, as Ka Mana puts it,

> engaging in a mission to teach Christian communities alternative ways by living an active and genuine faith in Christ without falling into types of religiosity that develop feelings of enchantment about the invisible at the expense of public involvement in public affairs.[150]

5.7.3 A Divided and Fragmented Church Fighting Corruption?

In the previous chapter in section 4.4.1.7, it was mentioned that differences in theological, ethical and ecclesiological perceptions, "informed by different theological traditions, historical contexts as well as practical considerations"[151] across churches is one of the areas in which the general public asks whether the church has a place in addressing issues of a public nature. In fact, some churches themselves seem to subscribe to the belief that the role of the church should be one of non-involvement and that it should, therefore, steer clear from participating in public discourse. According to Goba, this "fragmentation [of views leads to], spiritual fatigue, and lack of zeal for prophetic social action."[152]

---

148. Gitari, *In Season and Out of Season*, 32.
149. In Maluleke, "Half a Century," 492.
150. Ka Mana cited in Deji, *Reconstruction and Renewal*, 122.
151. Goba, "Role of the Church, 6.
152. Ibid.

Reference has been made to ACT both as part of the worldwide Anglican community and as "an independent institution in terms of its theology and administration."[153] Although diversity can be enriching, it can, however, lead to a lack of unity and divisiveness especially on theological and/or ethnic grounds which can be detrimental to the public witness of the church, also with regard to corruption and in/justice. This is an additional factor to what we saw earlier, that is, corruption in its own ranks. Unfortunately both these factors also exist in ACT and limits its credibility in fighting corruption.

With regard to the lack of unity and divisions in the global Anglican Communion, former Archbishop of Canterbury, Rowan Williams, is on record saying that:

> Clearly the division is very real. Nobody is denying that. The question is how we cope with it, how we argue with one another, whether we are still able to sit in the same room and argue the case, and that's why I'm sorry that there are not those here to continue that argument among us.[154]

In this regard, the Jerusalem Declaration referred to in 5.4.2 is a timely statement for the church not only as it grapples with the issue of corruption, but also because it acknowledges that the church has to deal with enormous changes in society, culture, and the question of her identity, as well as its desire to fulfil a constructive role in society. GAFCON laments the fact that in these endeavors, it is unfortunate that the Anglican church is faced with the serious problem of being "divided and destructed."[155] Although the extent of this division may differ in different regions, and may be less in the case of ACT than in other parts of the church, it is in opposition to the biblical image of the church as one body where, when one part of the body suffers, it affects the whole body (1 Cor 12:26). In other words, it compromises the integrity of the Anglican church's worldwide mission and has jeopardized the identity of Anglicanism.

---

153. Hassett, *Anglican Communion in Crisis*, 34. See 5.2 "The Anglican Communion and the Origins of Anglican Church of Tanzania."

154. Quoted in Lyle, "Re-establishing Relationships," no page numbers.

155. GAFCON, *Jerusalem Declaration*, 3.

On 20 April 2010, in a video address by Anglican Archbishop Rowan Williams to the Fourth Global South to South Encounter meeting in Singapore, he emphasized that it is the work of God's Spirit that can heal the tensions within the Anglican family "in the light of confusion, brokenness and tension within our Anglican family – a brokenness and a tension that has been made still more acute by recent decisions in some of our Provinces."[156] Again, although this situation is facing the global Anglican world, its effects extend to Tanzania because the crisis under discussion, has "torn the fabric of the communion."[157] It has also "affected the whole church in terms of her desire to encourage each other,"[158] and in the view of this study, this means that the wider Anglican Communion struggles to continue to be boldly and joyfully true to its mission. This is the mission which the church has for many years been faithful and effective especially in upholding and advocating justice in society and to seek relief and empowerment of the poor and the needy. Likewise, while ACT is hailed for the joy it expresses in community life according to the values of solidarity, mutual caring, reverence for God, and a dynamic engagement with the government, it is suggested that if the issue of divisiveness and the lack of unity is not addressed, it will jeopardize the witness of the church with regard to its ecumenical cooperation on the issues of corruption and injustice.

5.7.4 ACT, Theological Education and the Challenge of Effective and Competent Leadership

Earlier in this study, the role of ethical, competent, committed and effective leadership in the fight against corruption was discussed (see 4.2.3.3 and 4.3.1.7). According to Dos Santos, a major problem facing the church in Africa is a lack of sufficient and competent leaders.[159] A decade before Dos Santos, John Mbiti expressed the same view, writing that "in spite of the rapid growth experienced by the African church, the church continues to suffer due to lack of theologically well-grounded natives to lead it."[160] Mbiti

---

156. Williams, "Archbishop's Message."
157. Ibid.
158. Ibid.
159. Dos Santos, "Planning Theological Education," 1–2.
160. Mbiti, *New Testament Eschatology*, 177.

referred to the church in East Africa and Africa as a whole as a church that "has come into existence and has grown evangelically and not theologically."[161]

Although Dos Santos's and Mbiti's views are more than a quarter century old, in Tanzania ACT continues to face the same challenge today. While Emmanuel Ngara asserts that "theological colleges need to have a contextualized curriculum which addresses itself to the needs of local [Tanzanian] people . . . this will lead to church leaders getting proper training so as to understand what their job entails and how they should go about doing it,"[162] theological education nationally has been and continues to be in line with the secularly popular method characterized by clear teacher direction, syllabus or curriculum and class outlines, learning in groups and through discussion with clear feedback on progress, all of which are unfortunately rarely accessible in most theological institutions.

Furthermore, most syllabi were developed in the 1980s and were based on the reigning English model of the period. In light of this, ACT needs to ask itself whether its current training produces church leaders relevant to the current Tanzanian situation. Writing from the perspective of leadership training for mission in East Africa, Bowers in 1982 already called for a theological training system which is "relevant and viable."[163] He posed the challenge that, given the prevailing situation, there is a need of having curricula designed with deliberate reference to the context rather than one being imported from overseas. Years later, Bowers would again remind the East Africa churches that training must produce graduates that have a strong biblical foundation and are "engaged with the dynamic realities of their cultural context."[164]

One cannot disagree with the likes of Downs that there is a need to "change the quality of life of . . . students, raising them to a higher measure of obedience to God and higher level of holiness"[165] and that those who are trained become ministers "required to be matured spiritually, grown in Christian faith, academically excellent, theologically balanced, loving

---

161. Ibid.
162. Ngara, *Christian Leadership*, 14.
163. Bowers, *Evangelical Theological Education*, 113.
164. Bowers, "Theological Education in Africa," 149.
165. Downs, *Teaching for Spiritual Growth*, 33.

and approachable and ethically committed to service."[166] However, what is especially needed is what Collins calls "theological soundness,"[167] which is synonymous to contextualized theology that will enable church leaders "to meet the challenges of the society" – in the case of this study, especially corruption and injustice, after the completion of their studies. Proper theological training is vital in that, "[i]t encourages prophetic voices and courageous stances."[168] Roy and Jan Stanford support Collins's proposal and, therefore understandably, emphatically call on theological training institutions to address with vigor, scholarship and practical action "present issues of the impact of world poverty, social injustice and the widening gap between the rich and the poor."[169] Surely, one may add corruption as injustice to this list.

To conclude this critical assessment of ACT's lack of adequate efforts to fight corruption and the possible reasons for it, one may heed the words of Koopman. In his essay, *Prophet for Dignity? A Theological Perspective,* in which he portrays the work of Adam Small[170] as a prophetic work, Nico Koopman offers suggestions, advice and hope as he encourages the church to understand the need for self-criticism when speaking prophetically. This is also important if the church is not to lose hope in the war against corruption, even in the face of a number of obstacles that inhibit a successful prophet stance. Koopman clearly states that

> [p]rophetic discourse as prophetic criticism also entails self-criticism. For various reasons churches should engage in constructive self-criticism. We should, however, guard against a form of self-criticism that does have pacifying effects, a self-criticism that serves as excuse to terminate public involvement, because we are ourselves so very imperfect. What is required is self-criticism, which shows that we are aware of our sinfulness and fallibility as human beings. Because we are imperfect,

---

166. Jeyaraj, *Christian Ministry-Models,* 333.
167. Collins, "Models of Training," 92.
168. Eleanor and Clark, *Anglicans in Mission,* 58.
169. Standford and Standford, "Poverty and Inequality Report," 174.
170. Adam Small is one of South Africa's foremost poets and philosophers. He provided a voice to the struggle of the so-called colored people during the apartheid years. He is regarded as one of South Africa's leading intellectuals and is former professor of English literature at the University of the Western Cape.

sinful beings even our best efforts as churches might be contaminated. Without constructive self-criticism we cannot speak legitimately in the world.[171]

5.8 A Final Word: Appreciating a Societal and Political Context Conducive to an Anti-Corruption Public Role

Before concluding this chapter it is important to reiterate the importance for ACT to appreciate the social and political context it finds itself in and the opportunities this holds for an anti-corruption public engagement for it in Tanzania.

To begin with, with reference to the Tanzanian Constitution, ACT should appreciate the freedom it guaranteed in Section 19 subsection 1, according to which,

> 19. – (1) every person has the right to freedom of thought or conscience, belief or faith, and choice in matters of religion, including the freedom to change his religion or faith. (2) Without prejudice to the relevant laws of the United Republic the profession of religion, worship and propagation of religion shall be free and a private affair of an individual; and the affairs and management of religious bodies shall not be part of the activities of the State authority. (3) In this Article reference to the word "religion" shall be construed as including reference to religious denominations, and cognate expressions shall be construed accordingly.[172]

Current president, Jakaya Kikwete, has on several occasions promised to abide with the constitution. For example, in his speech on *Religious Diversity in a Democratic Environment: The Tanzanian Experience,* which he delivered at Boston University, USA, on 25 September 2006, he stated that,

---

171. Koopman, "Prophet for Dignity?" 137.

172. Tanzanians adhere to different religions which have a particular history of their own and Tanzania's constitution promotes no state religion but rather provides religious freedom for all its citizens (Tanner 2002).

[t]he constitution of independent Tanganyika, and subsequently of a united Tanzania, after the union with Zanzibar in 1964, entrenched the freedom of worship for citizens.[173]

As was stated earlier in the contextual analysis offered in chapter 2 of this study, it was said that Tanzania is often referred to as a country of democratic rule that respects diversity of opinion and that it has a tradition of constitutionality and respect for the rule of law – at least when compared with most African countries. Throughout the study, it has also been indicated that the government of Tanzania has always opened the door for and invited religious institutions such as ACT to assist in addressing a number public issues such as the provision of education and health services, including anti-corruption work. It is important that ACT should appreciate and act on goodwill from the side of government toward religious organizations as expressed, for example, in Kikwete's promise at his coming to power that "as a government, we have supported such initiatives from the religious organizations themselves. We will continue to be supportive and cooperative. It serves our national interests well."[174]

Over the years since independence, the church and state relationship in Tanzania has been stable even though there have been some aspects of a changing relationship. In principle, however, the government of Tanzania respects people's religions. Koopman refers to such an attitude of government as "government hospitality."[175] Although Koopman is writing in the South African context, his argument on religion being accepted in public domain applies in the Tanzanian context as well. Koopman writes that in South Africa "religion is . . . not relegated to the private spheres of life. In all public spheres there is a high level of hospitality to religion. Religion is welcomed in political life, economic life, ecological matters, civil society, as well as in the processes of public opinion formation and public policy formulation."[176]

---

173. Quoted in Mesaki, "Religion and the State in Tanzania," 93.

174. Ibid.

175. This attitude and the invitation to participate in the building of the nation has always been extended by the government of Tanzania to churches and other religious institutions by all heads of states as was seen in 2.3.2.3 of this study, from the first president of Tanzania Julius Kambarage Nyerere to the fourth and current president, Jakaya Kikwete.

176. Koopman, "Public Theology as Prophetic Theology," 118.

Such a good relationship remains one of the key opportunities for the church for addressing the problem of corruption.

It was also shown that, unfortunately, despite the "hospitality" shown to religious institutions by the Tanzanian government, critically speaking, it did not seem to have had any significant influence on ACT's engagement specifically on corruption in the public sphere. In the previous section (5.7) four areas of concern were highlighted as possible reasons for this state of affairs, namely the challenge of internal integrity, theological disagreement, division and distraction, and the challenge of sufficient and competent leadership. ACT needs to works towards addressing these concerns otherwise as the silence of the church in matters of public concern, such as corruption, may have serious consequences. As such, South African theologian, Allan Boesak warns of four such dire consequences if churches become silent:

> (1) the state will underestimate its limitations and lapse into greed and corruption; (2) the state will fail to acknowledge the role of faith and spirituality in moral regeneration; (3) the state will elevate its leaders to a god-like status; (4) the state will deprive the powerless and voiceless.[177]

Religion has been and remains to this day one of the most powerful forces contributing to the shaping of Tanzania.[178] The government clearly recognizes this and acknowledges the church and Christian faith as a fundamental part of the culture of integrity and at the root of human rights and ethical principles in the country. While the platform given to religion in the country is cherished, Kikwete shows that there is not yet, in the church in general, a comprehensive understanding of the fundamental nature of corruption as a cause of social issues such as poverty, justice, and human rights. It may thus be argued that ACT has not yet laid down a comprehensive plan to address the problem of corruption because church leaders in general are still blind to the denigrating effects of corruption.

With regard to specific opportunities for public engagement, the following example comes to mind. In spite of the high praise for the constitutionality and democratic nature of contemporary Tanzania, it was also indicated

---

177. Boesak, *Tenderness of Conscience*, 169.
178. Perkinson, "John S. Mbiti," and Herstad, *Role of Religious Communities*.

that in recent years the country has experienced traces of a constitutional crisis (see 2.3.2.3). The Open Society Initiative for Southern Africa (OSISA), for example, states that "Tanzania has been an example of half-hearted attempts by the government to garner public participation in the constitutional reform process, yet the underlying political will has been absent, resulting in widespread discontent among civil society."[179] That said, the current 2010–2015 constitutional review process in Tanzania as an opportunity for ACT in possible efforts to address the issue of corruption and injustice in the country. The opportunity is promising, not only because there is an increasing demand for a comprehensive constitutional review process, but also because other key role players in the process have started to "critically analyse the process of constitution making to ensure 'inclusivity, credibility and acceptability' of the different bodies involved in the process."[180]

The question is how ACT will make use of this opportunity. To use Wessel Bentley words (cf. 4.3.1.7), ACT needs to ask itself what it means to be a church in a secular constitutional democracy. To answer this question it is worth revisiting, among other sources, John Rawls's *Political Liberalism*. Rawls sees the possibility of leaders to participate in the process through constitutional tradition and public policy by working towards developing the constitution in step with their faith-based analysis of social issues – in the case of this study, this will include issues of corruption and injustice. In

---

179. OSISA, *Constitutional Review and Reform*, 21.

180. The Constitutional Review Process was initiated by President Kikwete who appointed the Constitution Review Commission (CRC) to coordinate and supervise the constitution making process in Tanzania. The CRC was expected to complete its task by October 2013 with a goal of having a new constitution by April 2014, at the time when Tanzania would be celebrating its 50th anniversary of the Union. It was felt that a review of the Constitution is needed "to march with the demands and aspirations of a country that has attained half a century of nationhood" and to ensure that Tanzanians ended up with a "document that accommodates current dynamics and developments" (President Kikwete quoted in Felister, "Warioba Named Head"). After two drafts the new constitution was proposed, among others, limited the powers of the president, reduced the number of MPs, made new provisions for an independent electoral commission and judiciary, etc. The president proposed a date of 30 April 2015 for a referendum on the acceptance of the new Constitution. Interestingly enough, partly due to the pressure by church leaders, especially the Roman Catholic Bishop's Conference of Tanzania, the date was postponed indefinitely as it was felt that too little time was allowed for churches to educate their members as to the implications of the changes to the Constitution (cf. Kidanka, "Tanzanian Churches Reject," no page numbers).

this regard Stephen Macedo speaks of "transformative constitutionalism."[181] In this process ACT may also take into account Koopman's views of public and civic virtues (public wisdom, public justice, public temperance, public fortitude, public faith, public hope and public love) and his view of prophetic public theology as being engaged in policy discussions, and offering within it "broad visions" without "[d]etailed policy blueprints," but to show that "between these broad principles and detailed blueprints ethical parameters for policymaking should be developed"[182] (as in section 4.3.2.3).

In the same vein, Habermas reminds people of faith that they are, in this constitutional process "expected to appropriate the secular legitimation of constitutional principles under the premises of their own faith."[183] See also Habermas in *Between Naturalism and Religion*: "[t]he major religions must re-appropriate the normative foundations of the liberal state *on their own premises* . . ."[184] For Rawls, Christian "[c]itizens [should] affirm the ideal of public reason . . . from within their own reasonable doctrines."[185]

To conclude this subsection, it is important to again be reminded of Bentley's comment that the role being played by the church at the time of constitutional review may face many challenges due to the fact that changes in the wider culture are also highly significant. Equally important is also the fact that the church and ACT in particular will be working in an intensive competing environment with other (much more powerful) institutions such as those of the media, government, and economic life. However, all this said, as Tanzanians revise their constitution, law making and setting of policies, ACT's insights, conviction and commitment guided by Christian ethics and moral discourse contribute immensely towards a corruption-free and just Tanzania.

---

181. Macedo, "Transformative Constitutionalism."

182. Koopman, "Public Theology and the Public Role," 52; cf. "Some Contours for Public Theology," 48.

183. Habermas, "Notes on a Post-Secular Society," 27.

184. Habermas, *Between Naturalism and Religion*, 261 (emphasis in original).

185. Rawls, *Political Liberalism*, 147 and 218.

5.9 Conclusion

This chapter returned to the Tanzanian context. It had two main objectives: The first objective was to discuss the Anglican Church of Tanzania (also in its relationship with the wider Anglican Communion). The focal questions were:

- What has ACT done in the past, what is she doing in the present and what does she plan to do in the future with regard to the issue of corruption? Was it adequate and, if not, why?
- What are possible theological reasons behind the ACT's involvement (or not) in the public sphere? At the same time it was asked whether these reflect some of the theological-ethical considerations for doing so as identified in chapters 3 and 4 of this study – for example, considerations in light of theological perspectives on the nature of God and humanity, the nature and (holistic) mission of the church, kingdom values and norms and the church as locus for teaching these, speaking (prophetic) truth to power and the ways in which this may be done, biblical perspectives on good governance, the role of the church in the (moral) transformation of society, the importance of the integrity of the church, etc.

The following conclusions were drawn in meeting the above objectives: First, the chapter established that central to the church's mission of being a witnessing community, ACT has a role to play in the public square, a role which Pannenberg summarizes as "[b]y witnessing to the future fulfilment of humanity in God's kingdom, the church helps to stir the imagination for social action."[186]

To justify the role that the church has in public life, this chapter has been geared toward analyzing ACT's practice in public discourse on injustice and corruption. A critical descriptive assessment was conducted in which the study examined the historical and ongoing involvement of ACT in some spheres of public life as well as analyzing her potential to play a more extensive role in public life in addressing the problem of injustice, even if it has not done so explicitly with regard to corruption.

---

186. Pannenberg, *Theology and the Kingdom*, 84–85, 111.

The chapter also looked at the church's public responsibility and how the church has been fulfilling it. The overriding argument in the chapter was a strong belief that the church's involvement in combating corruption is not a matter of choice; it is an obligation that stems from the teaching of the Bible. This is God's call for ACT to be involved in the Tanzanian public sphere. In seeking to meet the requirements of this task, the study looked critically at what has been done, what is being done, and what it may do in in combating corruption in Tanzania by ACT.

In sum, therefore, the study of the Anglican Church of Tanzania as it seeks to bear faithful witness within the growing crisis of corruption in Tanzania reveals a considerable lack of focus on the issue. While history and the current trend indicate that the church has for a long time been doing well in areas such as health projects, schools, peace and reconciliation, poverty and environmental issues and even the issue of justice, unfortunately it seems as if the link between injustice and corruption has not been pronounced as corruption is not singled out as a specific and extremely urgent issue. It is not at the top of the agenda by the church. This fact, furthermore, reveals a limited awareness of the linkages between faith and spirituality, development work and in the case of this thesis, a theological-ethical discourse on corruption. Building from this argument, therefore, the study's tentative conclusion would be that despite some of the church leaders' noble intentions and activities, they have not had the desired impact. It is therefore imperative that ACT take action and address the problem of corruption in much more focused and unified manner. And behind this should be clear (public) theological and biblical-ethical considerations and foundations similar to the ones proposed in this study on which to base such action and efforts. After all, in the words of Koopman: ". . . Christian religion can be good news to societies if we develop constructive theologies. One of the acid tests for faithful public theology in the twenty-first century is to serve Christian communities with theological guidelines for participating in all walks of life."[187] This is also what this study hopes to do.

---

187. Koopman, "Public Theology as Prophetic Theology," 128.

CHAPTER 6

Summary, Conclusion and Recommendations

> Peace be with you! As the Father has sent me, I am sending you.
>
> John 20:21
>
> It's the servant attitude that gets faith communities to go . . . [t]heir footprint is where the pain is.
>
> Timothy Ewen Costello[1]

6.1 Introduction

This final chapter highlights the key arguments of this study and the contribution it wishes to make in this way to a theological discourse on corruption in Tanzania. The study, therefore, set out to offer biblical and theological-ethical reflections on the meaning and consequences of corruption and injustice and corruption *as* injustice in the country. The central aspect of the study was the theological link between corruption and/as injustice.

With regard to the context of the study, it sought to answer the following two questions:

1. What is the Anglican Church in Tanzania doing with regard to the issue of corruption?
2. What are possible theological-ethical principles or guidelines for ACT's combating corruption and promoting justice in this way in Tanzanian society?

---

1. Timothy Ewen Costello is an Australian Baptist minister and the current Chief Executive Officer of World Vision Australia. Quoted by Barney Zwartz, "Religion 'Denied Key Role' in Poverty Fight," in *The Sydney Morning Herald*, 5 December 2009.

This is the final chapter in which the study consists of two parts: In the first part, the study presents a summary of the arguments of the thesis, outlines the findings, and proposes answers to the thesis research questions. In the second part, some recommendations are offered to ACT for initiating effective action in combating corruption and injustice. The recommendations are in line with God's call to the church to live out its Christian witness both at local and national as well as personal and corporate levels.

6.2 Summary of Arguments and Research Findings

The study entitled *"Corruption Mocking at Justice": A Theological-Ethical Perspective on Public Life in Tanzania and Its Implications for the Anglican Church of Tanzania* is divided into six chapters with the following foci and some of their conclusions also listed below.

Chapter 1 served as an introduction to the study and discussed the primary and secondary research questions to be addressed. It argued that, in Tanzania, and indeed in the world, there is a growing awareness that humanity is threatened by continued forms of injustice perpetuated through corruption. Additionally, it was indicated that there is a need to explore how the church can present her unique ethical perspectives in order to effect change in societies beset with corruption.

Chapter 2 traced, assessed and located the problem of corruption in Tanzania itself. It reviewed the contextual and conceptual setting of the problem of corruption and injustice. Key components of the discussion included a general introduction to the issue of corruption, its historical-social background, as well as its extent, forms and trends within Tanzania. This paved the way for a substantive discussion of the theological-ethical aspects of corruption in subsequent chapters. The overview of Tanzanian society provided indicators of the magnitude of the problem in the country. It also offered necessary background to how the church may best become part of anti-corruption efforts.

In short, in chapter 2 the following was found to be the case:
- Corruption is not a new phenomenon in Tanzania. It was already there in pre-colonial times.
- Corruption in Tanzania is an indication of serious governance and developmental challenges.

- Corruption continues to be one of the major problems facing Tanzania.
- An evaluation of measures to prevent corruption by the government of Tanzania and in many civil organizations over the last decades have proved ineffective as can be seen in the continued increase in corruption.
- Many ethical values, which are fundamental to the eradication of corruption confirms and opens the door for the church to explore how it can play her role in addressing the problem.

Chapter 3 introduced the discussion of biblical-theological-ethical principles to the background of the moral reprehensibility, or in theological terms, the sinfulness of corruption. This was first done with reference to the nature and attributes of God. On this principle it was argued that the reasons for church rejection of corruption have to start with its beliefs regarding God, such as God as Creator and as a God of justice and God's plan for humanity and human society. Second, a Christian anthropological approach was used. Under the rubric of what in a biblical-theological sense constitutes humanity, issues were addressed of a biblical vision of humanity, human society, human dignity, relationality, human flourishing and the concept of living together, and norms and values for a just and peaceful human society.

It was thus concluded that:
- Theologically speaking, corruption amounts to sin and is a consequence of the fall of humankind.
- Corruption is not only a political, economic, legal, or developmental issue as it has for many decades been understood. Corruption is also a theological-ethical issue and as such of importance also to Christian churches.

Chapter 4 spelled out, with reference to biblical-theological and public-theological considerations, that the church does have a role to play in the struggle against corruption and injustice. It thus identified key foundations upon which the unique public role of the church in fighting corruption rests. The chapter also discussed what "the church" is and is not, also with regard to its involvement in fighting corruption. The conclusions of this chapter may be summarized as follows:

- Corruption is a result of moral failure and it is therefore a moral challenge. The task of the church is both theological and ethical as it to bears witness in the context of moral transformation.
- The Christian gospel must be central to the success of church's involvement in addressing the problem of corruption and injustice because it acts as a catalyst for change in the social order.

Chapter 5 presented a critical descriptive assessment of the Anglican Church of Tanzania's practice and participation in the public sphere on issues of corruption and justice. The chapter also reflected on the place, form and role of the Christian faith in relation to the problem of corruption in ACT. The biblical and theological-ethical guidelines and principles regarding the fight against corruption identified in previous chapters were also brought to bear on ACT. This chapter concluded that:

- The church's involvement in combating corruption is not a matter of choice; it is an obligation that stems from the teaching of the Bible.
- ACT has in some ways sought to provide effective leadership with regard to issues of justice in Tanzania.
- However, there exists a considerable lack of focus on the issue, both in terms of explicit theological discourse on as well as self-initiated programs of fighting corruption in ACT. While history and current trends indicate that the church has for a long time been doing well in areas such as health projects, schools, peace and reconciliation, poverty and climate change, unfortunately corruption has and is not singled out as a specific concern to be addressed by specific initiatives.
- A warning was given to ACT that avoiding political issues and describing them as "worldly concerns," will have dire consequences for the church and for society.
- Finally, the Anglican church was reminded that God's mission is about the realization of God's vision for the world; it implies a holistic mission of a new, peaceful, just and corruption-free society.

In the light of the above, a few succinct recommendations follow towards an appropriate response from the Anglican Church of Tanzania to the anti-corruption efforts in the country.

6.3 Recommendations

6.3.1 Theoretical Recommendations

At the heart of our theoretical recommendation rests the principles that calls for the church to know the character of God, humanity and society, both in theological terms as well as, in the case of the latter two, in secular terms.

The Anglican church is therefore confronted with a fundamental theological-ethical challenge of the dehumanizing effects of corruption and injustice which continues to cause severe suffering to Tanzanians. This reality places the cry of injustice squarely before the church's leaders and members, demanding an appropriate response from them. And this cry can only be responded to by applying clear biblical and theological-ethical principles and guidelines such as those proposed in this study, for example, humanity's sinfulness and need for redemption, but also more as the church's holistic mission implies; the guideline of a biblically informed concept of justice and good governance; and kingdom values and norms, etc.

6.3.2 Practical Recommendations

Building from the theoretical recommendations, ten areas are listed below where on a practical level ACT may increase or improve its engagement in the public sphere with regard to injustice and corruption.

- *Gospel clarity as a base for the war on corruption:* To ensure that the church does not lose focus, it is recommended that the Bible be brought to the center of every activity regarding the war on corruption. The Bible needs to be part of church decisions on every action, every programme, every effort to address corruption.
- *A holy church, accountable and transparent:* To maintain the church's integrity, which is key to fighting corruption and injustice, it is recommended that the church designs theological-ethical codes of conduct for church workers in

all its departments, projects and institutions so as to secure commitment from all stakeholders working towards ensuring the mission of God, through God's church, is being fulfilled.

- *Identifying and acting on the basis of the church's theological-ethical competence:* The church should identify and acknowledge its strengths, for example, its understanding of the dignity of human beings, the common good, the relational character of God's vision for society, solidarity with the poor, etc., and it should capitalize on these unique strengths as it addresses the issue of corruption.
- *Increases effectiveness of church governance, advocacy and partnership skills:* To strengthen the already present theological-ethical conviction within the church, that it and its leaders are critical social (often socio-political) players and that their engagement in governance and anti-corruption efforts can help ensure holistic approaches to address the underlying causes, it is recommended that church leaders seek to understand what is happening in other circles outside of the church, so that it can identify entry points and possibilities to forge partnership with other organizations in the struggle against corruption.
- *Give support to the faithful:* To strengthen peoples' commitment to fighting corruption, it is recommended that those who are already doing it, within and outside of the church, be supported by acknowledging their efforts and by offering them continued moral guidance and support.
- *Mainstream anti-corruption work with the existing programs:* To open up further opportunities to expand anti-corruption work, it is recommended that the future anti-corruption work should be mainstreamed with the already existing church relief and development programs, such as those which assist poor communities across Tanzania in areas of education, health, agriculture, environment, and economic development projects.
- *The church has to go public:* To affirm that the church is a public institution whose vision is to meet the needs of human beings personally and publically, it is recommended that the church

seeks to partner with other bodies without compromising its own mandate whose source is the Word of God. This means that in doing so the church should remember that although the focus is on human beings, engaging the state should continue to be high on its agenda. As Mugambi puts it, the church needs "to appreciate [peoples] aspirations, while restoring their hope and dignity by keeping the state and its representatives accountable to basic principles of good governance and democracy."[2]

- *The utilization of existing church structures and ministries:* One of the strengths that ACT has is its various structures and ministries – for example, the Mothers' Union, Fathers' Union, Youth and Children Fellowships and home groups. It is recommended that these be used to inculcate positive values within the community of believers as well outside.
- *Revisit current anti-corruption strategies:* In order to avoid the situation whereby the church is involved in anti-corruption work only by invitation from other organizations or government, important as these may be, it is recommended that the church also needs to come up with its *own* creative programs on anti-corruption if it is to have a lasting impact the state.
- *Spiritual formation, education of congregations and the empowerment of believers as a source of societal change:* In order to get church leaders and Christians involved in anti-corruption work more effectively, it is recommended that the church should understand and teach its own vision and ideals. This will empower people by challenging them and making them aware of the fact that they are called to live according to God's call to holiness, both as individuals and as institution. Words and deeds are crucial for the integrity and credibility of what believers do and how they integrated this in their day-to-day lives.

The final and key observation in this study regards issue of the internalization and implementation of practical and theoretical recommendations. Section 4.4 of this study highlighted the need for moral transformation,

---

2. Mugambi, *From Liberation to Reconstruction*, 176.

kingdom values/virtues and norms, and the church as a community of character, speaking the truth to power, prophetic witness, reconstruction and public policy advocacy and the integrity of the church. Similarly, in chapter 5, the fourth mark of Anglican mission was identified as "to seek to transform [the] unjust structures of society."

To do this one may refer to studies such as those of J. M. Vorster, Gustafson, and Theron and Lotter for guidance.[3] These scholars are all in clear agreement that for the people of God's kingdom, the church's main task regarding social problems lies within the domain of ethics. From this perspective it is proposed that individuals and groups in ACT may implement the practical proposals put forward in this chapter is by ensuring that the "church [lives] by its testimony and by its ministry" as it "[raises] ethical awareness."[4] The church is, after all, a community of moral discourse.[5] Vorster elaborates on the concept of testimony and ministry when he writes that "[p]ointing to Christ as the model of human conduct and attitude the churches should enhance the deeper meaning of honesty, fairness, responsibility, compassion, love and accountability."[6] This was also emphasized in this study with reference to the need for the church and its leaders to be morally upright before it goes out to face the public. Theron and Lotter call this "[f]ighting corruption with the proper attitude"[7] and by doing so then the church could fulfil other roles such as those of being "'watchdog' and a whistle blower in their monitoring role of public administration and the administration of justice."[8] To sum up the proposal for internalization and implementation we content with Vorster's three practical guidelines for the church that entail: *raising awareness of the problem, addressing the underlying attitude of self-interest,* and *calling for social justice.*[9]

---

3. Vorster, "Managing Corruption"; Gustafson, *Varieties of Moral Discourse*; Theron and Lotter, "Corruption."

4. Vorster, "Managing Corruption," 140.

5. Gustafson, *Varieties of Moral Discourse*, 53.

6. Vorster, "Managing Corruption," 145.

7. Theron and Lotter, "Corruption," 112.

8. Vorster, "Managing Corruption,' 140.

9. Ibid., 145.

6.4 Concluding Words

Corruption and injustice are an enormous global problem. They are destroying humanity by creating an environment where "[p]eople constantly are treated as less than human, prejudice does run rampant, the strong perpetually oppress the weak – and Christians must vigilantly champion the values we say we believe."[10] This presents a kairos moment for the global church and for ACT (see section 4.3.2.2).[11] In this moment, this study has identified deficiencies, but also possibilities and opportunities.

To this end, it is hoped that the study will contribute to the efforts in Tanzania to counter corruption. Perhaps most anti-corruption efforts have been conspicuously unsuccessful exactly because they have tended to focus on the issue solely from a political, social and economic perspectives and have ignored theological-ethical approaches to tackling corruption. The problem of corruption is complex – this has been said repeatedly in this study. It needs united efforts to stop it. The Anglican Church of Tanzania has a theological duty to perform, and to perform well, whereby corruption no longer "mocks at justice," but is indeed eradicated so that Tanzanians may testify that their country is a corruption-free state, one in which "peace and justice embrace."[12] May this eagerly awaited vision soon be fulfilled!

---

10. Stackhouse, *Making the Best of It*, 311.
11. Storrar, "*Kairos Moment for Public Theology*," 5.
12. Psalm 85:10.

Bibliography

Abbink, Jon. "Being Young in Africa: The Politics of Despair and Renewal." In *Vanguards and Vandals: Youth Politics and Youth in Africa*, edited by J. Abbink and I. Van Kessel, 1–36. Leiden: Brill Academic, 2005.

Achtemeier, Elizabeth. "Righteousness in the Old Testament." In *The Interpreter's Dictionary of the Bible*, edited by George Arthur Buttrik, 80–85. Philadelphia, PA: Westminster Press, 1962.

African Executive, The. "Corruption: Who Should Cast the First Stone?" 2015. https://africanexecutive.com/article.php?section_id=16&&article_id=522. Accessed 23 March 2015.

Agbasiere, Joseph.T., and Boniface K. Zabajungu, eds. *Church Contribution to Integral Development*. Eldoret, Kenya: AMECEA GABA, 1989.

Aidt, Toke S., and Jayasri Dutta. "Policy Compromises: Corruption and Regulation in a Democracy." *Economics and Politics* 20, no. 3 (2008): 335–360.

Akhter, Syed H. "Is Globalization What It's Cracked Up to Be? Economic Freedom, Corruption, and Human Development." *Journal of World Business* 39, no. 1 (2004): 283–295.

Akindele, S. T. "Corruption and Economic Retardation: A Retrospective Analysis of Nigeria's Experience since Independence." In *Readings in the Political Economy of Nigeria since Independence,* edited by O. A. Bamisaye. Lagos: Ventures Limited, Nigeria, 1990.

Alexander, Laura Grace. "Human Flourishing." 2011. http://www.genevaschool.org/wp-content/uploads/5-20-11_human_flourishing.pdf. Accessed 13 April 2014.

Alkire, Sabina. "Public Debate and Value Construction in Sen's Approach." In *Capabilities Equality: Basic Issues and Problems,* edited by Alexander Kaufman, 133–154. London: Routledge, 2006.

———. *Valuing Freedoms*. Oxford: Oxford University Press. 2002.

Allen, C. "Who Needs Civil Society?" *Review of African Political Economy* 24, no. 73 (1997): 329–337.

Alsop, R., ed. *Power, Rights and Poverty: Concepts and Connections*. Washington, DC: World Bank/DFID, 2004.

Alston, Phillip, and Mary Robinson, eds. *Human Rights and Development: Towards Mutual Reinforcement*. Oxford: Oxford University Press, 2005.

Amundsen, Inge. "Political Corruption: An Introduction to the Issues." CMI Working Paper 7. Bergen: Chr. Michelsen Institute,1999.

Anand, Vikas, Blake E. Ashforth, and Mahendra Joshi. "Business as Usual: The Acceptance and Perception of Corruption in Organizations." *Academy of Management Executive* 18, no. 2 (2004): 39–53.

Anderson, William B. *The Church in East Africa*. Dodoma: Central Tanganyika Press, 1981.

Anglican Church of Tanzania. *www.anglican.or.tz*. Accessed 14 October 2014.

Ansell, Nicholas. *The Annihilation of Hell: Universal Salvation and the Redemption of Time in the Eschatology of Jürgen Moltmann*. Milton Keynes: Paternoster, 2013.

Aquinas, Thomas. *Summa Theologica*. Translated by Fathers of the English Dominican Province. 5 vols. Westminster, MD: Christian Classics, 1948. Online edition by Kevin Knight, 2016.

Argandoña, A. "The 1996 ICC Report on Extortion and Bribery in International Business Transactions." *Business Ethics: A European Review*, 6 (1996): 134–146. http://www.iese.edu/research/pdfs/di-0326-e.pdf. Accessed 30 October 2011.

Aseka, Eric M. *Transformational Leadership in East Africa: Politics, Ideology and Community*. Kampala: Fountain Publishers, 2005.

Atkinson, Nigel. *Richard Hooker and the Authority of Scripture, Reason and Tradition*. Carlisle: Paternoster, 1997.

Augustine. *The City of God*. Edited by D. Knowles. Baltimore, MD: Penguin, 1972.

Avis, Paul. "Catholicity Outweighs Autonomy. Our Unity in Christ." 1 April 2011. http://livingchurch.org/catholicity-outweighs-autonomy. Accessed 18 May 2014.

———. *The Identity of Anglicanism: Essentials of Anglican Ecclesiology*. London: T&T Clark, 2007.

———. *Reshaping Ecumenical Theology: The Church Made Whole?* London: T&T Clark, 2010.

Ayittey, George B. N. *Africa Betrayed*. New York, NY: St. Martin's, 1992.

Babcock, Phillip, et al. *Webster's Third International Dictionary of the English Language*. Springfield, MA: Meriam Webster, 1986.

Bacio Terracino, J. "Corruption and Human Rights-Corruption as a Violation of Human Rights." Working Paper, International Council on Human

Rights Policy, 2008. http://www.ichrp.org/files/papers/150/131_terracino_en_2008.pdf. Accessed 11 October 2014.

Bain, C., Matthew Frost, and Paul Woolley. "Wholly Living: A New Perspective on International Development." London: Theos, 2010. http://www.theosthinktank.co.uk/publications/2010/10/10/wholly-living-a-new-perspective-on-international-development. Accessed 15 March 2013.

Baker, Deane-Peter. "Plantinga's Reformed Epistemology: What's the Question?" *International Journal for Philosophy of Religion* 57, no. 2 (2005): 84–95.

Banfield, Edward C. "Corruption as a Feature of Governmental Organization." *Journal of Law and Economics* 18 (1975): 587–609.

Barash, David P. *Introduction to Peace Studies.* Belmont, CA: Wadsworth, 1991.

Baregu, Mwesiga. "Tanzania's Hesitant and Disjointed Constitutional Reform Process." Unpublished paper Delivered at the Conference on Constitution-Making Processes in Southern Africa, Sheraton Hotel, Dar es Salaam, 26–28 July 2000.

Barkan, Joel D., ed. *Beyond Capitalism vs. Socialism in Kenya and Tanzania.* Boulder, CO: Lynne Rienner, 1994.

Barth, Karl. *Church Dogmatics, vol. 1, pt. 2: The Doctrine of the Word of God.* Edited by G. W. Bromiley and T. F. Torrance. Translated by H. Knight and G. T. Thomson. Edinburgh: T&T Clark, 1956.

———. *Community, State and Church: Three Essays.* Translated by A. M. Hall and G. R. Howe. Gloucester: Peter Smith, 1960.

———. *Evangelical Theology: An Introduction.* Grand Rapids, MI: Eerdmans, 1963.

———. *Ethics II.* Edited by D. Braun. Translated by G. W. Bromiley. Edinburgh: T&T Clark, 1981.

———. *The Humanity of God.* Westminster: John Knox, 1960.

Bauckham, Richard. *The Theology of Jürgen Moltmann.* Edinburgh: T&T Clark, 1995.

Baucum, T. J. Written essay in "Why Anglicanism? A Compilation of the Anglican Diocese of the Mid-Atlantic's Essay and Speaker Series Exploring the Topic of Anglicanism." Unpublished Essay. Edited by The Anglican Diocese of the Mid-Atlantic, The Anglican Church in North America. 2008. http://www.anglicandoma.org/uploads/ADV_booklet_Final_booklet.pdf. Accessed 14 March 2014.

Baucus, Melissa S., and Janet P. Near. "Can Illegal Corporate Behavior Be Predicted? An Event History Analysis." *Academy of Management Journal* 34, no. 1 (1991): 9–36.

Beasley-Murray, George R. *Jesus and the Kingdom of God.* Grand Rapids, MI: Exeter, 1986.

———. "The Kingdom of God in the Teaching of Jesus." *Journal of the Evangelical Theological Society* 35, no. 1 (1992): 19–30.

Beckhard, Richard, and Wendy Pritchard. *Changing the Essence: The Art of Creating and Leading Fundamental Change in Organizations.* San Francisco, CA: Jossey-Bass, 1992.

Bedford-Strohm, Heinrich. "Tilling and Caring for the Earth: Public Theology and Ecology." *International Journal of Public Theology* 1 (2007): 230–248.

Beilby, James K. *Epistemology as Theology: An Evaluation of Alvin Plantinga's Religious Epistemology.* Burlington, VT: Ashgate, 2005.

Beisner, E. Calvin. "Justice and Poverty: Two Views Contrasted." *Transformation* 10 (1993): 16–22.

Beker, Johan C. *Paul the Apostle: The Triumph of God in Life and Thought.* Philadelphia, PA: Fortress, 1980.

Bentley, Wessel. "Defining Christianity's 'Prophetic Witness' in the Post-Apartheid South African Democracy." *Studia Historiae Ecclesiasticae* 39, no. 1 (2013): 261–273.

———. *The Notion of Mission in Karl Barth's Ecclesiology.* Newcastle: Cambridge Scholars. 2010.

Berger, Peter. *The Social Reality of Religion.* London: Faber and Faber, 1969.

Berger, Peter, and Richard Neuhaus. *To Empower People: The Role of Mediating Structures in Public Policy.* Washington, DC: American Enterprise Institute for Public Policy Research, 1977.

Berger, Julia. "Religious Non-Governmental Organizations: An Exploratory Analysis." *Voluntas* 14, no. 1 (2003): 15–40.

Berkhof, Louis. *Systematic Theology.* Carlisle, PA: Banner of Truth, 1958.

Biéler, Andre. *Calvin's Economic and Social Thought.* Geneva: WCC, 2005.

Boesak, Allan. *The Tenderness of Conscience: African Renaissance and the Spirituality of Politics.* Glasgow: Wild Goose, 2005.

Boettner, Lorraine. *The Reformed Doctrine of Predestination.* Philipsburg, NJ: Presbyterian and Reformed, 1979.

Boff, Leonardo. *Church, Charisma and Power: Liberation Theology and the Institutional Church.* London: SCM, 1985.

Bolongaita, E. "Controlling Corruption in post-Conflict Countries." Kroc Institute Occasional Paper No. 26. *Third World Quarterly* 26, no. 4 (2005): 679–698.

Bosch, David. *Believing in the Future: Toward a Missiology of Western Culture.* Maryknoll, NY: Orbis, 1995.

———. *Transforming Mission: Paradigm Shifts in Theology of Mission.* Maryknoll, NY: Orbis, 1991.

Botman, H. Russel. "Good Governance: The Role of the Churches. A South African Perspective." Unpublished paper Delivered at the Joint Conference on Church and Development, Spier, Stellenbosch, South Africa: 2008. http://www3.gkke.org/fileadmin/files/publikationen/2008/spier_workshop-beitrag_botman.pdf. Accessed 12 May 2013.

———. "Towards a World-Formative Christianity in South Africa." In *Faith in Development: Partnership between the World Bank and the Churches in Africa*, edited by D. G. R. Belshaw, Robert Calderisi, and Chris Sugden, 72–79. Cape Town: Salty Print, 1997.

Boulton, Wayne G., Thomas D. Kennedy, and Allen Verhey, eds. *From Christ to the World: Introductory Readings in Christian Ethics*. Grand Rapids, MI: Eerdmans, 1994.

Bowers, Paul, ed. *Evangelical Theological Education Today*. Nairobi: Evangel, 1982.

———. "Theological Education in Africa: Why Does It Matter?" *African Journal of Evangelical Theology* 26, no. 2 (2007): 135–149.

Branch, Daniel, and Nic Cheeseman. "Democratization, Sequencing, and State Failure in East Africa: Lessons from Kenya." *African Affairs* 108, no. 430 (2008): 1–26.

Branch, Taylor. *At Canaan's Edge: America in the King Years 1965-68*. New York, NY: Simon & Schuster, 2006.

Bray, Gerald. *The Doctrine of God. Contours of Christian Theology*. Downers Grove, IL: InterVarsity, 1993.

Bretherton, Luke. *Christianity and Contemporary Politics: The Conditions and Possibilities of Faithful Witness*. Chichester: Wiley-Blackwell, 2010.

Breitenberg, E. Harold, Jr. "To Tell the Truth: Will the Real Public Theology Please Stand Up?" *Journal of the Society of Christian Ethics* 23, no. 2 (2003): 55–96.

Broughton, Geoff. "Restorative Justice: Opportunities for Christian Engagement." *International Journal of Public Theology* 3 (2009): 299–318.

Brueggemann, Walter. "Rethinking Church Models through Scripture." *Theology Today* 48, no. 2 (1991): 128–138.

———. *Theology of the Old Testament: Testimony, Dispute, Advocacy*. Minneapolis, MA: Fortress, 1997.

Brunkhorst, Hauke. *Solidarity: From Civic Friendship to a Global Legal Community*. Translated by Jeffrey Flynn. Cambridge: MIT Press, 2005.

Bulmer, Andrew, and Bob Hansford. *The Local Church and Its Engagement with Disasters*. Tearfund, June 2009. http://tilz.tearfund.org/~/media/files/tilz/topics/drr/publications/the_local_church__its_engagement_with_disasters.pdf.

Busch, Eberhard. *Karl Barth: His Life from Letters and Autobiographical Texts*. Grand Rapids, MI: Eerdmans, 1975.

Cady, Linell E. *Religion, Theology and American Public Life*. Albany, NY: SUNY, 1992.

Calderisi, Robert. *The Trouble with Africa: Why Foreign Aid Isn't Working*. New Haven, NJ: Yale University Press, 2006.

Calvin, John. *Institutes of the Christian Religion*. Vol. 2. Edited by John McNeill. Translated by F. L. Battles. Louisville, KY: Westminster John Knox, 1960.

———. *Institutes of the Christian Religion*. Vol. 4. Edited by John McNeill. Translated by F. L. Battles. Louisville, KY: Westminster John Knox, 1960.

CAPA. "Called to a Life of Faithfulness - Strategic Plan 2010-2014." Nairobi: CAPA, 2009.

Carr, David, and J. W. Steutel, eds., *Virtue Ethics and Moral Education*. London and New York, NY: Routledge, 1999.

Carson, D. A. *Right with God: Justification in the Bible and the World*. Grand Rapids, MI: Baker, 1992.

Casanova, José. *Public Religions in the Modern World*. Chicago, IL: University of Chicago Press, 1994.

Cerar, J. Written essay in "Why Anglicanism? A Compilation of the Anglican Diocese of the Mid-Atlantic's Essay and Speaker Series Exploring the Topic of Anglicanism." Unpublished essay. Edited by The Anglican Diocese of the Mid-Atlantic, The Anglican Church in North America. 2008. http://www.anglicandoma.org/uploads/ADV_booklet_Final_booklet.pdf. Accessed 14 March 2014.

Chachage, Chambi. *Corruption in Tanzania: Some Issues for Consideration*. Dar es Salaam: University of Dar es Salaam Economic Research Bureau, 1994.

———. "Globalization and Democratic Governance in Tanzania." Development Policy Management Forum, 2003. http://www.dpmf.org/Publications/OccassionalPapers/occasionalpaper10.pdf. Accessed 31 October 2013.

Chachage, Chambi, and Annar Cassam, eds. *Africa's Liberation: The Legacy of Nyerere*. Nairobi: Pambazuka, 2010.

Chaliga, Amon. "Uncritical Citizens or Patient Trustees? Tanzanians' Views of Political and Economic Reform." Afrobarometer Working Paper. No. 18. East Lansing, MI: Michigan State University, 2007.

Chambers, Robert. *Rural Development: Putting the Last First*. London: Longman, 1983.

Chapman, Mark. *Anglicanism: A Very Short Introduction*. Oxford: Oxford University Press, 2006.

———. *Anglican Theology*. London: T&T Clark, 2012.

Charry, E. T. "Sacramental Ecclesiology." In *The Community of the Word: Toward an Evangelical Ecclesiology*, edited by M. Husbands and D. J. Treier. Downers Grove, IL: InterVarsity, 2005.

Chêne, M. "Overview of Corruption in Tanzania." U4 Expert Answers. Estimate from Tanzania's Auditor General, 2009. http://www.u4.no/publications/overview-of-corruption-in-tanzania/. Accessed 24 April 2014.

Chitando, Ezra. "Religious Ethics, HIV and AIDS and Masculinities in South Africa." In *Persons in Community: African Ethics in a Global Culture*, edited by Ronald Nicolson, 45–64. Scottsville: University of KwaZulu-Natal Press, 2008.

Christie, Ian. "Human Flourishing and the Environment." Briefing Paper for the Theos/ CAFOD/ Tearfund *Wholly Living* Project, 9 October 2010, 1–31. http://www.theosthinktank.co.uk/files/files/05_Christie_Environment.pdf. Accessed 15 April 2013.

Clowney, Edmund P., and Gerald Lewis Bray. *The Church: Contours of Christian Theology*. Downers Grove, IL: InterVarsity, 1995.

Cole, Allan H. *Theology in Service to the Church: Global and Ecumenical Perspectives*. Eugene, OR: Wipf and Stock, 2014.

Collins, M. B. "Models of Training in Mission Institutions to Ensure the Planting of Theologically Balanced Churches in Training God's Servants." Association of Evangelicals in Africa (AEA). Nairobi: AEA, 1997: 92–119.

"Corruption Out of Control, Says Minister for Parliamentary Control, Philip Marmo." *The Citizen*, Tanzania, no. 1163. Friday 23 May 2008, 3.

Coulter, Paul. "What Does It Mean to Be Human?" 2008. http://www.bethinking.org/human-life/what-does-it-mean-to-be-human. Accessed 13 March 2012.

Couto, Richard. A., ed. *Political and Civic Leadership*. London: Sage. 2010.

CTS (Corruption Tracker System). Online Newsletter 013, June 2011.

Cunningham, David S. *These Three Are One. The Practice of Trinitarian Theology*. Oxford: Blackwell, 1998.

Curren, Randall R., *Aristotle on the Necessity of Public Education*. Lanham: Rowman & Littlefield, 2000.

Daboub, A. J., et. al. "Top Management Team Characteristics and Corporate Illegal Activity." *Academy of Management Review* 20, no. 1 (1995): 138–170.

Dackson, W. "Archbishop William Temple and Public Theology in Post-Christian Context." *Journal of Anglican Studies* 4 (2006): 239–251.

Dalziel, Murray, and Stephen C. Schoonover. *Changing Ways: A Practical Tool for Implementing Change within Organizations*. New York, NY: American Management Association, 1988.

Dames, Gordon E., ed. *Ethical Leadership and the Challenges of Moral Transformation*. Stellenbosch: Sun Press, 2009.

Dawkins, Richard. *The Selfish Gene*. Oxford: Oxford University Press, 1976.

Day, Katie. "The Construction of Public Theology: An Ethnographic Study of the Relationship between the Theological Academy and Local Clergy in South Africa." *International Journal of Public Theology* 2, no. 3 (2008): 354–378.

Deane-Drummond, Celia. "Why Human Flourishing? A Theological Commentary." 2010. http://www.theosthinktank.co.uk/files/files/01_Deane-Drummond_A_Theological_Commentary.pdf. Accessed 15 March 2013.

De Gruchy, Steve. "Christian Witnessing in a Secular State: Rethinking Church-State Relations in a New Democratic South Africa." In *An African Challenge to the Church in the 21st Century*, edited by Mongezi Guma and Leslie Milton. Cape Town: Salty Print, 1997.

———. "Engaging with the Biblical Guideline of the Oikos Journey." Unpublished paper delivered at Diakonia, Durban, South Africa, 12 September 2007.

———. "From Political to Public Theologies: The Role of Theology in Public Life in South Africa." In *Public Theology for the 21st Century: Essays in Honour of Duncan B. Forrester*, edited by William Storrar and Andrew R. Morton, 45–62. London and New York, NY: T&T Clark, 2004.

———. "Of Agency, Assets and Appreciation: Seeking Some Commonalities between Theology and Development." *Journal of Theology for Southern Africa* 117 (2003): 20–39.

De Sardan, Olivier J. P. "A Moral Economy of Corruption in Africa?" *Journal of Modern African Studies* 37, no. 1 (1999): 25–52.

Deheragora, K. "The Impact of Globalization on the Third World Cultures: Sri Lankan Experience." *Dialogue* (NS) XXIV (1997): 12.

Deji, Valentin. *Reconstruction and Renewal in Africa in Christian Theology*. Nairobi: Acton Publishers, 2003.

Dion, Michel. "What Is Corruption Corrupting? A Philosophical Viewpoint." *Journal of Money Laundering Control* 13, no. 1 (2010): 45–54.

Doak, Mary. *Reclaiming Narrative for Public Theology.* Albany, NY: State University of New York Press, 2004.

Dos Santos, J. F. "Planning Theological Education Inductively." *Theological Education Today* 11, no. 2 (1982): 1–14.

Downs, Perry. *Teaching for Spiritual Growth: An Introduction to Christian Education*. Grand Rapids, MI: Zondervan, 1994.

Dreyer, Yolanda A. "Pastoral Response to the Unhealed Wound of Gays Exacerbated by Indecision and Inarticulacy." *HTS Theological Studies* 64, no. 3 (2008): 1235–1254.

Dreze, Jean, and Amartya Sen *The Political Economy of Hunger*. Oxford: Clarendon, 1995.

Duby, Stephen J. "Classical Christian Theism and the Criterion of Particularity." *International Journal of Systematic Theology* 15, no. 2 (2013): 195–216.

Duchrow, Ulrich, and Dorothea Millwood. *Lutheran Churches: Salt or Mirror of Society?* Geneva: Lutheran World Federation, 1977.

Dukor, M. "Conceptions of Justice." *Indian Philosophical Quarterly* 24, no. 4 (1997): 457–476.

Dulles, Avery. *Models of the Church.* Expanded Edition. New York, NY: Images Books Doubleday, 1974.

Duty, Ronald W. "Congregations and Public Life." *Word & World* 26, no. 3 (2006): 277–288.

Ebeling, Gerhard. *Luther: An Introduction to His Thoughts.* Translated by R. A Wilson. Philadelphia, PA: Fortress, 1970.

Ekeh, Peter P. "Colonialism and the Two Publics in Africa: A Theoretical Statement." *Comparative Studies in Society and History* 17 (1975): 91–112.

Elliott, Kimberly Ann, ed. *Corruption and the Global Economy.* Washington, DC: Peterson Institute for International Economics, 1997.

Erickson, Millard J. *Christian Theology.* 2nd edition. Grand Rapids, MI: Baker, 1998.

———. *God the Father Almighty: A Contemporary Exploration of the Divine Attributes.* Grand Rapids, MI: Baker, 1998.

"Escrow Saga Dominates Sermons on Christmas." *The Citizen,* Tanzania. 26 December 2014. http://www.thecitizen.co.tz/News/Escrow-scandal-takes-centre-stage-on-Xmas/-/1840392/2569094/-/t52y9t/-/index.html. Accessed 12 March 2015.

Evans, Alex. *The Feeding of the Nine Billion: Global Food Security for the 21st Century.* London: Chatham House, 2009.

Evans, Bernard F. "Campaign for Human Development: Church Involvement in Social Change." *Review of Religious Research* 20 (1979): 264–278.

Evans, Bryan R. "The Cost of Corruption." A discussion paper on corruption, development and the poor. Tearfund. 2009. Available at http://auxbeacon.org/wp-content/uploads/2016/03/corruption23.pdf.

Evans, Mary. *Prophets of the Lord.* London: Paternoster, 1992.

Fashole-Luke, Edward, R. Gray, R. Hastings, and G. Tasie, eds. *Christianity in Independent Africa.* London: Rex Collings, 1978.

Feinberg, John S. *The Many Faces of Evil: Theological Systems and the Problem of Evil.* Grand Rapids, MI: Zondervan, 1994.

Felister, P. "Warioba Named Head of Constitution Commission." IPPMedia.com. 7 April 2012. http://www.ippmedia.com/frontend/index.php?l=40270/. Accessed 19 April 2014.

Ferguson, Sinclair B., and David F. Wright, eds. *New Dictionary of Theology.* Downer's Grove, IL: InterVarsity, 1988.

Fischer, Stanley, and Rudiger Dornbusch. *Economics.* New York, NY: McGraw-Hill, 1983.

Fjelstad, Odd-Helge. *Autonomy, Incentives and Patronage: A Study of Corruption in Tanzania and Uganda Authorities.* Bergen, Norway: Chr. Michelsen Institute, 2003.

Forrester, Duncan B. *Beliefs, Values and Policies: Conviction Politics in a Secular Age.* Oxford: Clarendon, 1989.

———. *Christian Justice and Public Policy.* Cambridge: Cambridge University Press, 1997.

———. "Leslie Newbigin as Public Theologian." In *A Scandalous Prophet: The Way of Mission after Newbigin*, edited by Thomas F. Foust, J. Andrew Kirk, Werner Ustorf, and George R. Hunsberger, 3–12. Grand Rapids, MI: Eerdmans, 2002.

———. *On Human Worth: A Christian Vindication of Equality.* London: SCM, 2001.

———. "The Scope of Public Theology." *Studies in Christian Ethics* 17, no. 2 (2004): 10–16.

———. *Theological Fragments: Essays in Unsystematic Theology.* New York, NY: T&T Clark, 2005.

———. *Theology and Politics.* Oxford: Basil Blackwell, 1988.

———. *The True Church and Morality: Reflections on Ecclesiology and Ethics.* Geneva: WCC Publications, 1997.

———. *Truthful Action: Explorations in Practical Theology.* Edinburgh: T&T Clark, 2001.

———. "Working in the Quarry: A Response to the Colloquium." In *Public Theology for the 21st Century: Essays in Honour of Duncan B. Forrester*, edited by W. Storrar and A. R. Morton. London. New York: T&T Clark, 2004.

Fortin, Ernest L. *Political Idealism and Christianity in the Thought of St. Augustine.* Villanova: Villanova University Press, 1971.

Fox, Michael V. *Proverbs 1–9.* AB 18a. New York, NY: Doubleday, 2000.

———. *Proverbs 10–31.* AB 18b. New Haven, NJ: Yale University Press, 2009.

Fraser, Nancy. "Rethinking the Public Sphere: A Contribution to the Critique of Actually Existing Democracy." In *The Phantom Public Sphere*, edited by Bruce Robbins, 1–32. Minneapolis, MI: University of Minnesota Press, 1993.

GAFCON. *Jerusalem Declaration: Being Faithful: The Shape of Historic Anglicanism Today.* London: Latimer Trust, 2008.

Gamble, A. J. "Justice." In *Encyclopedia of Biblical and Christian Ethics,* edited by R. K. Harrison, 217. Nashville, TN: Thomas Nelson, 1987.

Gaper, Des. "Sen's Capabilities Approach and Nussbaum's Capabilities Ethics." *Journal of International Development* 9, no. 2 (1997): 281–302.

George, S. K. *Called as Partners in Christ's Service. The Practice of God's Mission.* Louisville, KY: Geneva, 2004.

Gayer, Arthur D., eds. *Basic Economics: A Book of Readings*. Upper Saddle River, NJ: Prentice Hall, 1951.

Gibb, Richard. *Grace and Global Justice: The Socio-Political Mission of the Church in an Age of Globalization*. Bletchley: Paternoster, 2006.

Gibbs, Lee W. "Richard Hooker: Prophet of Anglicanism or English Magisterial Reformer?" *Anglican Theological Review* 84, no. 4 (2002): 943–960.

Gibbs, S., and D. Ajulu. *The Role of the Church in Advocacy: Case Studies from Southern and Eastern Africa*. Occasional Papers Series, no. 31. Oxford: INTRAC, 1999.

Giles, Kevin. *What on Earth Is the Church? An Exploration in New Testament Theology*. Downer's Grove, IL: InterVarsity, 1995.

Gitari, David. *In Season and Out of Season: Sermons to a Nation*. Carlisle: Regnum, 1996.

Global Integrity Report 2006. http://back.globalintegrity.org/reports/2006/tanzania/index.cfm. US State Department. Accessed 30 September 2014.

Goba, Bonganjalo. "Choosing Who We Are, a Christian Perspective on the Moral Crisis Confronting the South African Society." In *An African Challenge to the Church in the 21st Century*, edited by Mongezi Guman and Leslie Milton, 65–71. Cape Town: Salty Print, 1997.

———. "The Role of the Church in Moral Renewal." Unpublished Paper Presented at the Annual Meeting of the Diakonia Council of Churches, Durban on 23 June 2007.

Gordon, G. "Mission of Church and Role of Advocacy. Evangelical Advocacy: A Response to Global Poverty." Papers, PDF Files, and Presentations. Book 5, 2012. http://place.asburyseminary.edu/engaginggovernmentpapers/5. Accessed 22 July 2013.

Gordon, G, and B. Evans, "The Mission of the Church and the Role of Advocacy." Tearfund Discussion Paper, July 2002.

Gottfredson, Michael, and Travis Hirschi, T. *A General Theory of Crime*. Stanford, CA: Stanford University Press, 1990.

Government of Tanzania. "Commission Report on the State of Corruption in the Country." Dar es Salaam: Government of Tanzania, 1996.

———. *National Anti-Corruption Forum (NACF), Annexure 5: Forum Resolutions*. Dar es Salaam: Dar es Salaam University Press, 2009.

———. *National Anti-Corruption Strategy and Action Plan for Tanzania*. Dar es Salaam: President's Office, State House, 1990.

———. *The National Anti-Corruption Strategy and Action Plan for Tanzania. Report of the Presidential Commission of Inquiry against Corruption*. Two Volumes. Dar es Salaam: Government of Tanzania, 1999.

———. "The National Anti-Corruption Strategy and Action Plan - II (NACSAP II) Implementation Report." Dar es Salaam, 2009.

———. "National Strategy for Growth and Reduction of Poverty (NSGRP)." Poverty and Human Development Report 2011. Research and Analysis Working Group Monitoring System Ministry of Finance and Economic Affairs December 2011. Dar es Salaam.

———. "Prevention and Combating of Corruption: Causes of Corruption in Tanzania, 2011." http://www.tanzania.go.tz/pcb/corruption/causes.html. Accessed 7 November 2011.

GEPC (Government and Economic Policy Centre). "Is Corruption the Result of Moral Decay or Moral Willingness?" 2015. http://www.gepc.or.tz/?work=is-corruption-a-result-of-moral-decay-or-moral-willingness. Accessed 2 August 2015.

Geoconger. "Tanzania Church Rocked by Complaints over Election." *The Church of England Newspaper,* 17 March 2013. https://geoconger.wordpress.com/2013/03/24/tanzania-church-rocked-by-complaints-over-election-the-church-of-england-newspaper-march-17-2013-p-7/. Accessed 9 February 2014.

Graham, Elaine. "Power, Knowledge and Authority in Public Theology." *International Journal of Public Theology* 1 (2007): 42–62.

———. "Public Theology in an Age of Voter Apathy." In *Public Theology for the 21st Century: Essays in Honour of Duncan Forrester*, edited by William Storrar and Andrew Morton, 385–403. London and New York, NY: T&T Clark, 2004.

Graham, Elaine, and Esther Reed, eds. *The Future of Christian Social Ethics: Essays on the Work of Ronald H. Preston 1913 – 2001.* New York, NY/London: Continuum, 2004.

Graham, W. Fred. *The Constructive Revolutionary.* Richmond, VA: John Knox, 1971.

Green, Clifford, ed. *Karl Barth – Theologian of Freedom.* Minneapolis, MA: Augsburg Fortress, 1991.

Grenz, Stanley J. *Theology for the Community of God.* Grand Rapids, MI: Eerdmans, 2000.

Grenz, Stanley J., David Guretzki, and Cherith Fee Nordling. *Pocket Dictionary of Theological Terms.* Downer's Grove, IL: InterVarsity, 1999.

Grieb, A. K. "So That in Him We Might Become the Righteousness of God (2 Cor 5:21): Some Theological Reflections on the Church Becoming Justice." *Ex Auditu* 22 (2006): 58–80.

Grindle, Merilee, S. *Challenging the State: Crisis and Innovation in Latin America and Africa.* Cambridge: Cambridge University Press, 1996.

Groody, Daniel G. *Globalization, Spirituality, and Justice: Navigating the Path to Peace.* Theology in Global Perspective Series. Maryknoll, NY: Orbis, 2009.

Grudem, Wayne. *Politics according to the Bible*. Grand Rapids, MI: Zondervan, 2010.
Gruenberg, C. "Corruption and Human Rights: Integrating Human Rights into the Anti-Corruption Agenda." International Council on Human Rights Policy Working Paper. Versoix: ICHRP, 2009.
Guardini, Romano. *The End of the Modern World*. Wilmington, DE: ISI, 1998.
Guder, Darrell, ed. *Missional Church: A Vision for the Sending of the Church in North America*. Grand Rapids, MI: Eerdmans, 1998.
Gunton, C. *Act and Being: Towards a Theology of the Divine Attributes*. London: SCM Press, 2002.
———. "Being and Person: T. F. Torrance's Doctrine of God." In *The Promise of Trinitarian Theology: Theologians in Dialogue with T. F. Torrance*, edited by E. M. Colyer and M. D. Lanham, 115–137. Lanham, MD: Rowman & Littlefield, 2001.
———. *The Promise of Trinitarian Theology*. Edinburgh: T. & T. Clark, 1997.
Gupta, Akhil. "Blurred Boundaries: The Discourse of Corruption, the Culture of Politics, and the Imagined State." *American Ethnologist* 22, no. 2 (1995): 375–402.
Gupta, Sanjeev, Hamid Davoodi, and Rosa Alonso-Terme. "Does Corruption Affect Income Inequality and Poverty?" *IMF Working Paper No. 79*. Washington, DC: IMF, 1998.
Gupta, Sanjeev, Hamid Davoodi, and Erwin Tiongson. "Corruption and the Provision of Health Care and Education Services." IMF Working Paper No. 00/116. Washington, DC: IMF, 2000.
Gustafson, James M. *Theology and Ethics: Christian Ethics and the Community*. Philadelphia, PA: Pilgrim, 1977.
———. *Varieties of Moral Discourse. Prophetic, Narrative, Ethical, and Policy*. Grand Rapids, MI: Calvin College and Seminary, 1998.
Gutiérrez, Gustavo. *A Theology of Liberation: History, Politics and Salvation*. Translated by C. Inda and J. Eagleson. London: SCM, 1974.
Habermas, Jürgen. *Between Naturalism and Religion: Philosophical Essays*. Cambridge: Polity, 2008.
———. "Notes on a Post-Secular Society." *New Perspectives Quarterly* 25, no. 4 (2008): 17–29.
———. "The Public Sphere." In *Contemporary Political Philosophy*, edited by Robert E. Goodin and Philip Pettit, 103–106. Oxford: Blackwell, 1997.
———. *The Structural Transformation of the Public Sphere*. German Original 1962. Cambridge: Polity, 1989.
Haddad, Beverley. "Theologizing Development: A Gender Analysis of Poverty, Survival and Faith." *Journal of Theology for Southern Africa* 110 (2001): 5–19.

Haley, A. S. "Charges of TEC-Related Fraud and Bribery Filed R. E.: Election of Tanzanian Primate." *Standfrim,* 28 February 2013. http://www.standfirminfaith.com/?/sf/page/30153. Accessed 19 March 2014.

Haller, Dieter, and Cris Shore, eds. *Corruption: Anthropological Perspectives.* London: Pluto, 2005.

Hampden-Turner, Charles M., and Alfons Trompenaars. *Building Cross-Cultural Competence.* New York, NY: John Wiley & Sons, 2000.

Hanke, A. "Bribery." *The Zondervan Pictorial Encyclopedia of the Bible.* Vol. 1: 653. Nashville, TN: Thomas Nelson, 1975.

Hansen, Holger B., and Michael Twaddle, eds. *Religion and Politics in East Africa.* London: James Carrey, 1995.

Hansen, L., ed. *Christian in Public: Aims, Methodologies and Issues in Public Theology.* Stellenbosch: African Sun Media, 2007.

Hartley, J. E. *Leviticus.* Word Biblical Commentary 4. Dallas, TX: Word, 1992.

Hartropp, Andrew. *What Is Economic Justice? Biblical and Secular Perspectives Contrasted.* London: Paternoster, 2007.

Hassett, Miranda K. *Anglican Communion in Crisis: How Episcopal Dissidents and Their African Allies Are Reshaping Anglicanism.* Princeton, NJ: Princeton University Press, 2007.

Hauerwas, Stanley. *A Community of Character: Toward a Constructive Christian Social Ethics.* Notre Dame, IN: University of Notre Dame Press, 1981.

———. *In Good Company: The Church as Polis.* Notre Dame, IN: University of Notre Dame Press, 1997.

———. *Vision and Virtue: Essays in Christian Ethical Reflection.* Notre Dame, IN: University of Notre Dame Press, 1981.

Hauerwas, Stanley, and William H. Willimon. *Resident Aliens: Life in the Christian Colony.* Nashville, TN: Abingdon, 1989.

Havnevik, Kjell. *Tanzania: The Limits to Development from Above.* Stockholm: Nordiska Afrikainstitutet, 1993.

Havnevik, Kjell, and Aida C. Isinika, eds. *Tanzania in Transition: From Nyerere to Mkapa.* Dar es Salaam: Mkuki na Nyota, 2010.

Healey, Nick M. *Church, World and the Christian Life: Practical-Prophetic Ecclesiology.* Cambridge: Cambridge University Place, 2000.

Heath, Mark. "Church and Ministry: A Roman Catholic Perspective." *Review and Expositor* 79, no. 2 (1982): 315–328.

Heidenheimer, Arnold J. "Terms, Concepts, and Definitions: An Introduction." In *Political Corruption: A Handbook,* edited by Arnold J. Heidenheimer, Michael Johnston, and Victor T. Le Vine. New Brunswick, NJ: Transaction, 1989.

Heilman, Bruce E., and Paul J. Kaiser. "Religion, Identity and Politics in Tanzania." *Third World Quarterly* 23, no. 4 (2002): 691–709.

Henry, Sarojini A. "Fair and Just Economic Order in the World: Biblical Vision." *Theology for Our Times* 7 (2000): 108.

Henry, Carl F. H. "Reflections on the Kingdom of God." *Journal of the Evangelical Theological Society* 35, no. 1 (1992): 39–49.

Hermes, Niels, and Robert Lensink, eds. "Changing the Conditions for Development Aid: A New Paradigm?" *Journal of Development Studies Volume* 37, no. 6 (2001): 1–16.

Herstad, Britt. *The Role of Religious Communities in Addressing Gender-Based Violence and HIV*. Washington, DC: Futures Group, 2009.

Hodge, Charles. *Systematic Theology*. Grand Rapids, MI: Eerdmans, 1989.

Hofstede, G. *Culture's Consequences: Comparing Values, Behaviours, Institutions and Organisations across Nations*. London: Sage, 2001.

Hogue, Michael. "After the Secular: Toward a Pragmatic Public Theology." *Journal of the American Academy of Religion* 78, no. 2 (2010): 346–374.

Hollenbach, David. "Public Theology in America: Some Questions for Catholicism after John Courtney Murray." *Theological Studies* 37, no. 2 (1976): 290–303.

Holmquist, Frank, and Michael Ford. "Kenya: State and Civil Society the First Year after the Election." *Africa Today* 41, no. 4 (1994): 5–25.

Hope, Kempe Ronald. "Corruption and Development in Africa." In *Corruption and Development in Africa: Lessons from Country Case-Studies,* edited by Kempe Ronald Hope and Bornwell C. Chikulu, 17–39. New York: St Martin's Press, 2000.

———. *From Crisis to Renewal: Development Policy and Management in Africa*. Leiden: Brill, 2002.

Hope, Kempe Ronald, and Bornwell C. Chikulo, eds. *Corruption and Development in Africa: Lessons from Country Case Studies*. London: MacMillan, 1999.

Hordern, William. "Barth as Political Thinker." *The Christian Century* (26 March 1969): 412.

Horton, Michael. "The Law and the Gospel." 1996. http://www.whitehorseinn.org/free-articles/the-law-the-gospel-by-michael-horton.html. Accessed 15 June 2014.

House, H. W. "Creation and Redemption: A Study of Kingdom Interplay." *Journal of Evangelical Theological Society* 35, no. 1 (1992): 3–17.

House, Robert J., Paul J. Hanges, Mansour Javidan, Peter W. Dorfman, and Vipin Gupta. *Culture, Leadership and Organization: The Globe Study of 62 Societies*. Thousand Oaks, CA: SAGE, 2004.

Howard, Michael. *Problems of a Disarmed World*. Studies in War and Peace. New York, NY: Viking, 1977.

Hunsberger, George, and Craig Van Gelder, eds. *The Church between Gospel and Culture: The Emerging Mission in North America*. Grand Rapids, MI: Eerdmans, 1996.

Hunsinger, George. "Toward a Radical Barth." In *Karl Barth and Radical Politics*, edited by George Hunsinger. Philadelphia, PA: Westminster, 1976.

———, ed. *Karl Barth and Radical Politics*. Philadelphia, PA: Westminster, 1976.

Hyden, Goran. *No Shortcuts in Progress: African Development Management in Perspective*. London: Heinemann, 1983.

Hyden, Goran, and Maximillian Mmuya. *Power and Policy Slippage in Tanzania – Discussing National Ownership of Development*. Sida Studies No. 21. Stockholm: SIDA, 2008.

Ibhawoh, Bonny, and J. I. Dibua. "Deconstructing Ujamaa: The Legacy of Julius Nyerere in the Quest for Social and Economic Development in Africa." *Africa Journal of Political Science* 8, no. 1 (2003): 59–83.

Iliffe, John A. *A Modern History of Tanganyika*. Cambridge: Cambridge University Press, 1979.

Ilo, Stan Chu, Joseph Ogbonnaya, and Alex Ojacor. *The Church as Salt and Light: Path to an African Ecclesiology of Abundant Life*. Eugene, OR: Pickwick, 2011.

International Council on Human Rights Policy. "Corruption and Human Rights: Making the Connection." 2009. http://www.ichrp.org/files/reports/40/131_web.pdf. Accessed 11 November 2013.

The International Forum for Social Development. *Social Justice in an Open World. The Role of the United Nations*. New York, NY: United Nations, 2006.

Jackson, Michael, Elizabeth Kirby, Rodney Smith, and Lynn Thompson. "Sovereign Eyes: Legislators' Perception of Corruption." *Journal of Commonwealth and Comparative Politics* 32, no. 1 (1994): 54–67.

Jacob, W. M. *The Making of the Anglican Church Worldwide*. London: SPCK, 1997.

Jacobsen, Eneida. "Models of Public Theology." *International Journal of Public Theology* 6 (2012): 7–22.

Jain, Arvind K. "Corruption: A Review." *Journal of Economic Surveys* 15, no. 1 (2001): 71–121.

Jehl, Frank. *Ever Against the Stream. The Politics of Karl Barth, 1906-1968*. Grand Rapids, MI: Eerdmans, 2002.

Jeyaraj, J. B., *Christian Ministry-Models of Ministry and Training*. Bangalore: Theological Book Trust, 2002.

Johnson, Eleanor, and John Clark, eds. *Anglicans in Mission: A Transforming Journey*. London: SPCK, 2000.

Johnson, Kirsten D. "Theology, Political Theory and Pluralism: Beyond Tolerance and Difference." *International Journal of Public Theology* 1 (2007): 270–281.

Johnson, William. *The Mystery of God: Karl Barth and the Postmodern Foundations of Theology.* Louisville, KY: Westminster John Knox, 1997.

Johnston, M. "The Search for Definitions: The Vitality of Politics and the Issue of Corruption." *International Social Science Journal* 48, no. 3 (1996): 321–335.

Johnstone, Patrick. *Operation World: Pray for the World.* Carlisle: OM Publishing, 1993.

NORAD. "Joint Evaluation of Support to Anti-Corruption Efforts. Tanzania, Country Report 6/2011 – Study." http://www.oecd.org/countries/tanzania/48912823.pdf. Accessed 14 April 2014.

Kagashe, Beatus. "Tanzania: Over 30 Percent of Budget Eaten by Corrupt Officials, Says President." *The Citizen*, Tanzania, 10 July 2009. http://allafrica.com/stories/200907100964.html. Accessed 25 August 2012.

Kaiser, Paul J. "Structural Adjustment and the Fragile Nation: The Demise of Social Unity in Tanzania." *Journal of Modern African Studies* 34 (1996): 227–237.

Kalu, Ogbu. *African Christianity: An African Story.* Pretoria: University of Pretoria Press, 2005.

Kaniki, M. "TANU: The Party of Independence and National Consolidation." In *Toward Ujamaa: Twenty Years of TANU Leadership,* edited by Gabriel Ruhumbika, 1–31. Dar es Salaam: East African Literature Bureau, 1974.

Kaufmann, Daniel, Aart Kraay, and Pablo Zoido-Lobaton. "Governance Matters." The World Bank Development Research Group Macroeconomics and Growth and World Bank Institute Governance, Regulation and Finance - Policy Research Working Paper. Washington, DC: World Bank, 1999.

Keller, Tim. "The Gospel and the Poor." *Themelios* 33, no. 3 (2008): 8–22.

Kelsey, David H. *Eccentric Existence. A Theological Anthropology.* Louisville, KY: Westminster John Knox, 2009.

———. "On Human Flourishing: A Theocentric Perspective." A Paper Presented at the Yale Center for Faith and Culture Consultation on God's Power and Human Flourishing. Sponsored by the McDonald Agape Foundation (2008): 1–44. http://faith.yale.edu/sites/default/files/david_kelsey_-_gods_power_and_human_flourishing_0_0.pdf. Accessed 13 May 2014.

Kubiac, Anna. *Corruption in Everyday Experience.* Warsaw: Institute of Public Affairs, 2001.

Küng, Hans. *The Church.* London: Continuum, 1968.

Loyer, Kenneth M. "Dignity, Justice, and Flourishing within the Human Family: Methodist Theology and the Enrichment of Public Discourse and

Life." 2013. https://oimts.files.wordpress.com/2013/09/2013-3-loyer.pdf. Accessed 5 March 2014.

Kerr, Fergus. *Thomas Aquinas: A Very Short Introduction*. Oxford: Oxford University Press, 2009.

Kessler, Sanford. *Tocqueville's Civil Religion: American Religion and the Prospects of Freedom*. Albany, NY: State University of New York Press, 1994.

Khan, Mushtaq H. "A Typology of Corrupt Transactions in Developing Countries." *IDS Bulletin* 27, no. 2 (1996): 12–21.

Kidanka, Christopher. "Tanzanian Churches Reject Proposed Constitution Ahead of April Referendum." *The East African*, 13 March 2015. http://www.theeastafrican.co.ke/news/Tanzania-churches-reject-proposed-constitution/-/2558/2652494/-/9xd7m4z/-/index.html. Accessed 5 July 2015.

Kidner, Derek. *The Proverbs: An Introduction and Commentary*. Tyndale Old Testament Commentaries. Downer's Grove, IL: InterVarsity, 1984.

Kierkus, Christopher, and Douglas Baer. "Does the Relationship between Family Structure and Delinquency Vary According to Circumstances? An Investigation of Interaction Effects." *Canadian Journal of Criminology and Criminal Justice* 45, no. 4 (2003): 405–429.

Kikwete, J. M. "The Speech by His Excellency Dr Jakaya Mrisho Kikwete, President of the United Republic of Tanzania, at the Occasion of the 20th General Chapter of the Holy Ghost Congregation, 29th June, 2012." Bagamoyo, Tanzania, 2012.

Kim, Sebastian C. H. *Theology in the Public Sphere*. London: SCM, 2011.

Kim, Sebastian C. H., and Pauline Kollontai, eds. *Community Identity: Dynamics of Religion in Context*. London: T&T Clark, 2007.

Kirkpatrick, Martha. "'For God So Loved the World': An Incarnational Ecology." *Anglican Theological Review* 91, no. 2 (2009): 191–212.

———. "Incarnational Ecology." In *Modern Christian Thought. Vol. 2: Twentieth Century*, edited by James C. Livingstone and Francis Fiorenza. Second Edition. Upper Saddle River, NJ: Prentice Hall, 2010.

Klingebiel, Stephan, Bettina Eberle, Susanne Kühn, Jochen Möller, Stefan Nöthen, Katja Roehder, and Axel Ulmer. *Socio-Political Impact of Development Cooperation Measures in Tanzania: Analysing Impacts on Local Tensions and Conflicts*. Dar es Salaam/Berlin: German Development Institute, 2000.

Knack, Stephen, and Philip Keefer. "Institutions and Economic Performance: Institutional Measures Cross-Country Tests Using Alternative Institutional Measures." *Journal of Economics and Politics* 7, no. 3 (1995): 207–227.

Knight, Jonathan. *Luke's Gospel*. Routledge: London, 1998.

Koegelenberg, Renier, ed. *Transition and Transformation: A Challenge to the Church*. Cape Town: EFSA, 1994.

Kolstad, Ivar, Verena Fritz, and Tam O'Neil. "Corruption, Anti-Corruption Efforts and Aid: Do Donors Have the Right Approach?" Good Governance, Aid Modalities and Poverty Reduction Working Paper 3. January 2008. Westminster, UK: Overseas Development Institute, 2008.

Konrad-Adenauer-Stiftung. *The Role of Faith-Based Organizations in Good Governance: Interfaith Dialogue in Tanzania*. Dar es Salaam: KAS, 2010.

Koopman, Nico. "Churches and Public Policy Discourses in South Africa." 2008. http://www.csu.edu.au/data/assets/word_doc/0005/94784/Churches-and-public-policy-discourses-in-South-Africa.doc. Accessed 12 May 2014.

———. "Human Dignity and Human Rights as Guiding Principles for the Economy." In *The Humanisation of Globalisation: South African and German Perspectives*, edited by C. Le Bruyns and G. Ulshofer, 59–70. Frankfurt: Herchen Verlag, 2008.

———. "A Prophet for Dignity? A Theological Perspective." 2012. http://www.letterkunde.up.ac.za/argief/49_1/11%20Koopman%20WEB%2004.pdf. Accessed 12 October 2014.

———. "Public Theology and the Public Role of the Church in South Africa Today: Insights from the Confession of the Threefold Offices of Christ." In *Theology in Service to the Church: Global and Ecumenical Perspectives*, edited by Allan Hugh Cole, chapter 10. Eugene, OR: Wipf and Stock, 2008.

———. "Public Theology as Prophetic Theology. More Than Utopianism and Criticism." *Journal of Theology for Southern Africa* 133 (2009): 117–130.

———. "Some Comments on Public Theology." *Journal of Theology for Southern Africa* 117 (2003): 3–19.

———. "Some Contours for Public Theology." *International Journal of Practical Theology* 14, no. 1 (2010): 123–138.

Koopman, Nico N., and Dirk Jacobus Smit. "Public Witness in the Economic Sphere? On Human Dignity as a Theological Perspective." In *Christian in Public: Aims, Methodologies and Issues in Public Theology*, edited by Len Hansen, 271–282. Stellenbosch: African Sun Media, 2007.

Kretzschmar, Louise. "Christian Spirituality in Dialogue with Secular and African Spiritualities with Reference to Moral Formation and Agency." *Theologia Viatorum* 32, no. 1 (2008): 63–96.

———. "Cultural Pathways and Pitfalls in South Africa: a Reflection on Moral Agency and Leadership from a Christian Perspective." *Koers* 75, no. 3 (2010): 567–588.

Kumalo, R. S. "A Prophetic Church in the Democratization of the South African Society – A Myth or Reality?" Unpublished paper Delivered at Diakonia Council of Churches, Johannesburg, 7 November 2007.

Kunhiyop, Samuel W. *African Christian Ethics*. Grand Rapids, MI: Zondervan, 2008.

Kuyper, Lester J. "Righteousness and Salvation." *Scottish Journal of Theology* 30, no. 6 (1977): 233–252.

Laakso, Liisa, and Adebayo Olukoshi, eds. *Challenges to the Nation State in Africa*. Uppsala: Nordiska Afrikainstitutet, 1996.

Labelle, Huguette. Opening Speech during the 2012 Annual Membership Meeting of Transparency International, 2012. http://www.transparency.org/news/speech/fighting_corruption_in_2012. Accessed 5th March 2014.

Ladd, George E. *A Theology of the New Testament*. Grand Rapids, MI: Eerdmans, 1974.

Lange, Donald A. "Multidimensional Conceptualization of Organizational Corruption Control." *Academy of Management Review* 33, no. 3 (2008): 710–729.

Lausanne Theology Working Group. "The Whole Church Taking the Whole Gospel to the Whole World: Reflections of the Lausanne Theology Working Group." Cape Town, 2010. https://www.lausanne.org/content/twg-three-wholes.

Lambsdorff, Johann Graf. "Background Paper to the 2001 Corruption Perceptions Index. Framework Document." Transparency International and Gottingen University, 2001. http://www.transparency.org/files/content/tool/2001_CPI_Framework_EN.pdf

Laver, Roberto. "'Good News' in the Fight against Corruption." *The Review of Faith and International Affairs* 8, no. 4 (2010): 49–57. http://www.tandfonline.com/toc/rfia20/8/4. Accessed 30 October 2014.

Lawson, Andrew, and Lise Rakner. "Understanding Patterns of Accountability in Tanzania." Unpublished report by the Governance Working Group of the Development Partners to Tanzania in Collaboration with the Oxford Policy Management (OPM). Oxford, United Kingdom, 2005.

Le Bruyns, Clint. "Ethical Leadership in and through Religious Traditions." In *Ethical Leadership and the Challenges of Moral Transformation*, edited by Gordon E. Dames, 47–60. Stellenbosch: Sun Press, 2009.

———. "Religion and Economy? On Public Responsibility through Prophetic Intelligence, Theology and Solidarity." *Journal of Theology for Southern Africa*, 142 (2012): 80–97.

———. "Theological Perspectives on the World of Work: Problems and Prospects for Socio-Economic Transformation." Unpublished paper Presented at a Consultation on Theories for Social and Economic Justice, Stellenbosch Institute for Advanced Study, 30-31 July 2004, Stellenbosch University, 2009.

Lebacqz, Karen. *Justice in an Unjust World: Foundations for a Christian Approach to Justice*. Minneapolis, MN: Augsburg, 1987.

———. *Six Theories of Justice: Perspectives from Philosophical and Theological Ethics*. Minneapolis, MN: Augsburg, 1986.
Legal and Human Rights Center. "Public Engagement: Justice Watch Annual Report, 2007." Dar es Salaam: Legal and Human Rights Center, 2008.
Legum, Colin. *Africa since Independence*. Bloomington, IN: Indiana University Press, 1999.
Legum, Colin, and G. R. V. Mmari, eds. "*MWALIMU:* The Influence of Nyerere." Dar es Salaam: Mkuki na Nyota, 1995.
Leite, Carlos, and Jens Weidmann. "Does Mother Nature Corrupt? Natural Resources, Corruption, and Economic Growth." International Monetary Fund Working Paper 99/85. Washington, DC: IMF, 1999.
Lerisse, Fred, Donald Mmari, and Mgeni Baruani. "Vulnerability and Social Protection Programs in Tanzania." Research and Analysis Working Group. Dar es Salaam: URT, 2003.
Le Sage, A. "Africa's Irregular Security Threats: Challenges for US Engagement." *Strategic Forum-Institute for National Strategic University* (2010). https://www.ciaonet.org/attachments/16184/uploads. Accessed 7 November 2011.
Lewis, Robert, and Rob Wilkins. *The Church of the Irresistible Influence*. Grand Rapids, MI: Zondervan, 2001.
Lipsey, Richard. *An Introduction to Positive Economics*. London: Weidenfeld & Nicolson, 1963.
Livingstone, James C., and Francis Fiorenza. *Modern Christian Thought. Vol. 2: Twentieth Century.* Second Edition. Upper Saddle River, NJ: Prentice Hall, 2010.
Lonsdale, John. "Compromised Critics: Religion in Kenya's Politics." In *Religion and Politics in Kenya. Essays in Honor of Meddlesome Priest*, edited by Ben Knighton, 58–94. New York, NY: Palgrave, Macmillan, 2009.
Lonsdale, J., S. Booth-Clibborn, and A. Hake. "The Emerging Pattern of Church and State Cooperation in Kenya." In *Christianity in Independent Africa*, edited by Edward W. Fashiole-Luke, Richard Gray, Adrian Hastings, and Godwin Tasie, 267–284. London: Rex Collings, 1978.
Lorenzen, Thorwald. "Justice Anchored in Truth: A Theological Perspective on the Nature and Implementation of Justice." *International Journal of Public Theology* 3 (2009): 281–298.
Luanda, Nestor. "Christianity and Islam Contending for the Throne on Mainland Tanzania." In *Challenges to the Nation-State in Africa*, edited by Liisa Laakso and Adebayo Olukoshi. Uppsala: Nordiska Afrikainstitutet, 1996.
Lucas, George, and Rick W. Rubel. *The Moral Foundations of Leadership*. Boston, MA: Pearson Education, 2004.

Ludwig, Frieder. *Church and State in Tanzania: Aspects of Changing Relations, 1961–1994*. London: Routledge, 2001.
Lugongo, B., Venance George, Daniel Mjema, Rehema Matowo, and Awila Silla. "Let's Not Take TZ Peace for Granted, says Clergy." Website of the Archdiocese of Dar es Salaam, 2015. http://www.daressalaamarchdiocese.or.tz/lets-not-take-tz-peace-for-granted-says-clergy/. Accessed 19 July 2015.
Lupogo, Herman. "Tanzania: Civil-Military Relations and Political Stability." *African Security Review* 10, no. 1 (2001).
Luscombe, D. E. "The State of Nature and the Origin of the State." In *The Cambridge History of Later Medieval Philosophy*, edited by N. Kretzmann, A. Kenny, and J. Pinborg, 757–770. Cambridge: Cambridge University Press, 1982.
Luther, Martin. "On Secular Authority. To What Extent It Should Be Obeyed." In *Luther and Calvin on Secular Authority*, edited by Harro Hopfl, 1–45. Cambridge: Cambridge University Press, 1991.
Lyle, J. "Re-establishing Relationships in the Anglican Communion Will Be a 'Long Task,' says Archbishop." 2011. http://www.christiantoday.com/article/reestablishing.relationships.in.the.anglican.communion.will.be.a.long.task.says.archbishop/27442.htm. Accessed 19 August 2014.
Macedo, Stephen. "Transformative Constitutionalism and the Case of Religion: Defending the Moderate Hegemony of Liberalism." *Political Theory* 26, no. 1 (1998): 56–80.
Macquarrie, John. *Jesus Christ in Modern Thought*. London: SCM, 1990.
Mæstad, Ottar, and Aziza Mwisongo. "Informal Payments and the Quality of Health Care: Lessons from Tanzania." CMI Working Paper 5/2007. Bergen: Anti-Corruption Resource Centre – Chr. Michelsen Institute, 2007.
Makulilo, Alexander B. In *The Annual State of Constitutionalism in East Africa 2011*. Kampala: Fountain Publishers, 2013.
Malchow, Bruce. *Social Justice in the Hebrew Bible*. Minnesota, MN: Liturgical, 1996.
Maluleke, Tinyiko S. "Half a Century of African Christian Theologies: Elements of the Emerging Agenda for the Twenty First Century." In *African Christianity: An African Story*, edited by Ogbu Kalu, 480–492. Pretoria: Business Print Centre, 2005.
⸻ "The Rediscovery of the Agency of Africans: An Emerging Paradigm of post-Cold War and post-Apartheid Black and African Theology." *Journal of Theology for Southern Africa* 108 (2000): 19–37.
Mangalwadi, Vishal. *The Book That Made Your World: How the Bible Created the Soul of Western Civilization*. Nashville, TN: Thomas Nelson, 2011.
Markham, Ian S. "Theological Education in the 21st Century." *The Anglican Theological Review* 92, no. 1 (2010): 160–162.

Marshall, Christopher D. *Beyond Retribution: A New Testament Vision for Justice, Crime, and Punishment*. Grand Rapids: Eerdmans, 2001.

———. *The Little Book of Biblical Justice: A Fresh Approach to the Bible's Teaching on Justice*. Intercourse, PA: Good Books, 2005.

———. "The Meaning of Justice: Insights from the Biblical Tradition." In *Justice as the Basic Human Need*, edited by J. W. Taylor, 25–38. New York, NY: Nova Science, 2006.

Marshall, Katherine. "Sin, Corruption and What Religions Can Do About It." 22 July 2013. http://www.huffingtonpost.com/katherine-marshall/sin-corruption-and-what-religions-can-do-about-it_b_3316159.html. Accessed 26 July 2013.

Mathewes, Charles T. *A Theology of Public Life*. Cambridge: Cambridge University Press, 2007.

Mauro, Paolo. "Corruption and Composition of Government Expenditure." *Journal of Public Economics* 69 (1998): 263–279.

———. "Corruption and Growth." *Quarterly Journal of Economics* 110 (1995): 681–712.

———. "The Persistence of Corruption and Slow Economic Growth." *IMF Staff Papers* 51, no. 1 (2004): 1–18.

Mbaku, John Mukum. *Corruption and the Crisis of Institutional Reforms in Africa*. Lewiston; New York, NY: Edwin Mellen, 1998.

Mbiti, John S. *African Religions and Philosophy*. London: Heinemann, 1975.

———. "The Ethical Nature of God in African Religion as Expressed in African Proverbs." In *Embracing the Baobab Tree: The African Proverb in the 21st Century*, edited by Willem Saayman, 139–162. African Proverbs Series 5. Pretoria: Unisa, 1997.

———. *Introduction to African Religion*. London: Heinemann, 1977.

———. *New Testament Eschatology in an African Background*. London: London University Press, 1971.

Mbilinyi, Marjorie. "Equity, Justice and Transformation in Education: The Challenge of Mwalimu Julius Nyerere Today." In *Nyerere: Student, Teacher, Humanist and Statesman*, edited by Tom Molony and Kenneth King, 39–52. Occasional Papers no. 84. Edinburgh: Centre of African Studies, 2010.

Mbogo, R. "The Anglican Church of Kenya Mission Country Review Findings and Insights." Unpublished paper, 2012. http://www.anglicancommunion.org/ministry/mission/ecgi/documents/kenya_mission_country_review.pdf. Accessed 16 May 2014.

Mbonile, M. J. "Towards Breaking the Vicious Circle of Labor Migration in Tanzania: A Case of Makete District." *UTAFITI (New Series)* 3, no. 1 (1996): 91–109.

McBrien, Richard P. *Church: The Continuing Quest.* New York, NY: Newman, 1970.

McKenzie, Michael. "Christian Norms in the Ethical Square: An Impossible Dream?" *Journal of the Evangelical Theological Society* 38, no. 3 (1995): 413–427.

McCormack, Bruce L. *Engaging the Doctrine of God. Contemporary Protestant Perspectives.* Grand Rapids, MI: Baker, 2008.

McCormick, B. J. *Introducing Economics.* Harmondsworth: Penguin, 1974.

McGrade, Stephen A., ed. *Richard Hooker: Of the Laws of Ecclesiastical Polity, Vol. 1: Preface, Books I to IV.* Oxford: Oxford University Press, 2013.

McGrath, Alister. *Christian Theology: An Introduction.* Third Edition. Oxford: Blackwell, 2003.

———. *Justification by Faith.* Grand Rapids, MI: Zondervan, 2007.

McGrew, Timothy. "Has Plantinga Refuted the Historical Argument?" *Philosophia Christi* 6, no. 1 (2004): 7–26.

Meeks, M. Douglas. The Economy of Grace: Human Dignity in the Market System. In *God and Human Dignity*, edited by R. Kendall Soulen and Linda Woodhead, 197–214. Grand Rapids; MI: Eerdmans, 2006.

Mény, Yves. "'Fin de siècle' Corruption: Change, Crisis and Shifting Values." *International Social Science Journal* 48, no. 3 (1996): 309–320.

Mesaki, Simeon, and Mrisho Malipula. "Julius Nyerere's Influence and Legacy: From a Proponent of Familyhood to a Candidate for Sainthood." *International Journal of Sociology and Anthropology* 3, no. 3 (2011): 93–100.

———. "Religion and the State in Tanzania." *Cross-Cultural Communication* 7, no. 2 (2011): 249–259.

Mfumbusa, Bernardin. "The Church Is Growing. Corruption Is Growing." *The Media Project,* Wednesday, 11 August 2010. http://themediaproject.org/article/church-growing-corruption-growing?page=full. Accessed 17 September 2014.

Micah Challenge 2013. http://www.micahchallenge.org/beinformed/good-governance/theology-and-good-governance/338-goodness-and-good-governance. Accessed 2 June 2013.

Michael, Johnson. *Syndromes of Corruption: Wealth, Power and Democracy.* Cambridge: Cambridge University Press, 2005.

Miller, Seumas, and John Blacker. *Ethical Issues in Policing.* Aldershot: Ashgate, 2005.

Milovanovic, C. *Corruption and Human Rights: Making the Connection.* International Council on Human Rights Policy. Versoix: Switzerland, 2001.

Miner, Maureen, Martin Dowson, and Stuart Devenish. *Beyond Well-Being: Spirituality and Human Flourishing.* Charlotte, NC: Information Age, 2012.

Mkude, D. J. *Higher Education in Tanzania*, Oxford: James Currey; Dar es Salaam: Mkuki na Nyota, 2003.

———. "Morals for Good Governance." Unpublished paper presented at the Ethics as a Component of Quality Assurance Workshop for Senior Academic and Administrative/Management Staff of St. John's University of Tanzania, Dodoma, 26–27 November 2012.

Mo, Pak-Hung K. "Corruption and Economic Growth." *Journal of Comparative Economics* 29 (2001): 66–79.

Möller, Francois Petrus. *Kingdom of God, Church and Sacraments: Words of Light and Life*. Vol 4. Pretoria: J. L. van Schaik, 1998.

Moltmann, Jürgen. *The Church in the Power of the Spirit*. London: SCM Press, 1992 [1977].

———. *Experiences in Theology*. Philadelphia, PA: Fortress, 2000.

———. *Hope for the Church: Moltmann in Dialogue with Practical Theology*. Nashville, TN: Abingdon, 1979.

———. *Theology of Hope*. Translated by James W. Leitch. Minneapolis, MN: Fortress Press, 1967.

———. *The Way of Jesus Christ: Christology in Messianic Dimensions*, Minneapolis, MN: Fortress, 1993.

Mueller, William A. *Church and State in Luther and Calvin: A Comparative Study*. New York, NY: Anchor, Doubleday, 1965.

Mugambi, J. N. Kanyua. *The Biblical Basis for Evangelization*. Nairobi: Oxford University Press, 1989.

———. *Democracy and Development in Africa: The Role of the Churches*. Nairobi: AACC, 1997.

———. *From Liberation to Reconstruction: African Christian Theology after the Cold War*. Nairobi: East African Educational, 1995.

Mukandala, Rwekaza. "State Enterprise Control: The Case of Tanzania." In *State-Owned Enterprise in Africa*, edited by Barbara Grosh and Rwekaza Mukandala, chapter 5. Boulder, CO: Lynne Rienner, 1994.

Mulgan, Richard., Satish Chand, and Peter Larmour. "Corruption and Anti-Corruption." Policy Brief Paper 2. Acton: Crawford School of Economics and Government, 2006.

Murphy, Mark. "Consent, Custom and the Common Good in Aquinas' Account of Political Authority." *Review of Politics* 59 (1997): 323–350.

Mwakikagile, Godfrey. *Nyerere and Africa: End of an Era*. USA: Protea Publishing, 2002.

Mwaura, Philomena Njeri. "Reconstructing Mission: The Church in Africa in the Service of Justice, Peace and Reconciliation." Unpublished paper Presented at the Methodist World Mission Conference, Swanwick, UK, 2008.

National Probono Resource Centre. "What Is Social Justice?" Working Paper 1. Sydney: NPRC, 2011. http://probonocentre.org.au/wp-content/uploads/2015/09/Occ_1_What-is-Social-Justice_FINAL.pdf. Accessed 24 April 2014.

Nazir-Ali, Michael. "Breaking Faith with Britain." *Standpoint Issue* 1 (2008): 45–47.

Neville, David J. "Justice and Divine Judgment: Scriptural Perspectives for Public Theology." *International Journal of Public Theology* 3 (2009): 339–356.

Newbigin, Lesslie. *The Gospel in a Pluralist Society*. Grand Rapids, MI: Eerdmans, 1989.

Newman, John Henry. *Essays Critical and Historical: The Catholicity of the Anglican Church*. London: Basil Montagu Pickering, 1890.

Nielsen, Kai. "Conceptions of Justice." In *Encyclopedia of Government and Politics*, edited by Mary Hawkesworth. Vol 1. London: Routledge, 1996.

Ngara, Emmanuel. *Christian Leadership: A Challenge to the African Church*. Nairobi: Pauline, 2004.

Nicholls, Bruce. "The Witnessing Church in Dialogue." *Evangelical Review of Theology* 16, no. 1 (1992): 48–65.

Nichols, Shaun. "How Psychopaths Threaten Moral Rationalism, Or Is It Irrational to be Amoral?" *The Monist* 85, no. 2 (2002): 285–384.

Niebuhr, H. Richard. *Christ and Culture*. San Francisco, CA: Harper Collins, 2001.

———. *The Nature and Destiny of Man: A Christian Interpretation*. Louisville, KY: Westminster John Knox, [1941] 1996.

Njunwa, Mujwahuzi H. M. "Combating Corruption in Tanzania's Public Service: Successes and Challenges." Governance Initiatives to Fight Corruption in Tanzania. Unpublished paper. Mzumbe: Institute of Public Administration Mzumbe University, Tanzania, 2007.

———. "Cooperative Public Service Delivery in Tanzania: Is it Contributing to Social and Human Development?" *Journal of Administration and Governance* 2, no. 1 (2007): 32-39.

Noonan, John Thomas. *Bribes*. New York, NY: Macmillan, 1984.

Norwegian Church Aid. "NCA Country Plan 2011–2015." 2010. https://www.kirkensnodhjelp.no/contentassets/a11f250a5fc145dbb7bf932c8363c998/01384-4-norwegian-church-aid-strategy-for-tanzania-2011---2015.pdf.

Nthamburi, Z. "Morality in Public Life." In *Moral and Ethical Issues in African Christianity: Exploratory Essays in Moral Theology*, edited by J. N. Kanyua Mugambi and A. Nasimiyu-Wasike, 107–118. Nairobi: Acton, 1999.

Nürnberger, Klaus. *Prosperity, Poverty & Pollution: Managing the Approaching Crisis*. Pietermaritzburg: Cluster, 1999.

Nussbaum, Martha. *The Fragility of Goodness.* Cambridge: Cambridge University, 1986.
———. *Sex and Social Justice.* Oxford: Oxford University Press, 1999.
Nyirabu, Mohabe. "The Multiparty Reform Process in Tanzania: The Dominancy of the Ruling Party." *Africa Journal of Political Science* 7, no. 2 (2002): 99–112.
Nye, J. S. "Corruption and Political Development: A Cost-Benefit Analysis." *American Political Science Review* 61, no. 2 (1967): 417–427.
Nyerere, Julius K. *Freedom and Development.* Dar es Salaam: Oxford University Press, 1973.
———. *Freedom and Socialism.* Dar es Salaam: Oxford University Press, 1974.
———. *Freedom and Unity.* Dar es Salaam: Oxford University Press, 1966.
———. *Man and Development.* Dar es Salaam: Oxford University Press, 1974.
———. *Ujamaa: Essays on Socialism.* Dar es Salaam: Oxford University Press, 1977.
Nyiawung, Mbengu D. "The Prophetic Witness of the Church as an Appropriate Mode of Public Discourse in African Societies." *HTS Teologiese Studies/ Theological Studies* 66, no. 1 (2010), Art. #791, 8 pages.
Ochulor, Chinenye Leo, and Edet Patrick Bassey, "Analysis of Corruption from the Ethical and Moral Perspectives." *European Journal of Scientific Research* 44, no. 3 (2010): 466–476.
O'Collins, Gerald, and Edward G. Farrugia. *A Concise Dictionary of Theology.* New York, NY: Stimulus, 2000.
O'Donovan, Oliver. *Common Objects of Love: Moral Reflection and the Shaping of Community.* Grand Rapids, MI: Eerdmans, 2002.
———. *The Desire of the Nations: Rediscovering the Roots of Political Theology.* Cambridge: Cambridge University Press, 1999.
———. *Resurrection and Moral Order.* Grand Rapids, MI: Eerdmans, 1996.
———. *Resurrection and Moral Order: An Outline for Evangelical Ethics.* Grand Rapids, MI: Eerdmans, 1986.
———. *The Ways of Judgment.* Grand Rapids, MI: Eerdmans, 2005.
O'Donovan, Oliver, and Joan Lockwood O'Donovan. *Bonds of Imperfection: Christian Politics, Past and Present.* Grand Rapids, MI: Eerdmans, 2004.
———. *From Irenaeus to Grotius: A Sourcebook in Christian Political Thought 100-1625.* Grand Rapids, MI: Eerdmans, 1999.
Odhiambo, Eisha Stephen, T. I. Ouso, and J. F. M. Williams. *A History of East Africa.* London: Longman, 1977.
Okumu, Washington A. J. *The African Renaissance: History, Significance, and Strategy.* Trenton, NJ: African World, 2009.

Oliver, Anthony. "Righteousness of God and Man in the Prophets." *The Academic Journal of Caribbean Evangelical Theological Association Binah* 2 (1997): 29–44.

Olutayo, Akinpelu O., and Ayokunle O. Omobowale. "Capitalism, Globalisation and the Underdevelopment Process in Africa: History in Perpetuity." *Africa Development* 32, no. 2 (2007): 97–112.

OSISA, *Constitutional Review and Reform and the Adherence to Democratic Principles in Constitutions in Southern African Countries.* Johannesburg: Open Society Initiative for Southern Africa, 2007.

Osmer, Richard, and Friedrich Schweitzer. *Religious Education between Modernization and Globalization: New Perspectives on the United States and Germany.* Grand Rapids, MI: Eerdmans, 2003.

Overton, Roger N., ed. *God and Governing: Reflections on Ethics, Virtue, and Statesmanship.* Eugene, OR: Wipf and Stock, 2009.

Pace, Bradley. "Public Reason and Public Theology: How the Church Should Interfere." *Anglican Theological Review* 91, no. 2 (Spring 2009): 277. *Academic Search Complete*, EBSCO*host*. Accessed 12 October 2014.

Paeth, Scott R. *Exodus Church and Civil Society: Public Theology and Social Theory in the Work of Jürgen Moltmann.* Hampshire: Ashgate, 2008.

Pannenberg, Wolfhart. *Theology and the Kingdom of God.* Philadelphia, PA: Westminster Press, 1975.

Pavarala, Vinod, and Kanchan K. Malik. "Religion, Ethics and Attitudes towards Corruption: A Study of Perspectives in India." Religion and Development Research Programme, Working Paper 53. Birmingham, UK: International Development Department, University of Birmingham, 2010.

Payne, Stephen L. "Organization Ethics and Antecedents to Social Control Processes." *Academy of Management Review* 5, no. 3 (1980): 409–414.

Pazhayampallil, T. *Pastoral Guide. Vol. 1. Fundamental Moral Theology and Virtues.* Bangalore: Kristu Jyoti, 1995.

Pearson, Clive. "Alienated Neighbours: Interpreting the Cronulla Race Riots for Christ's Sake." *Forum on Public Policy: A Journal of the Oxford Round Table,* Summer 2008. http://www.forumonpublicpolicy.com/summer08papers/relsum08.html. Accessed 2 March 2014.

———. "What Is Public Theology?" 1993. http://www.csu.edu.au/__data/assets/pdf_file/0010/788590/What_is_Public_Theology.pdf. Accessed 13 May 2013.

Peels, Rik. "The Effects of Sin upon Human Moral Cognition." *Journal of Reformed Theology* 4 (2010): 42–69.

Pekenham, Thomas. *The Scramble for Africa: From 1876 to 1912.* New York, NY: Avon, 1991.

Peperzak, A. "Freedom." *International Philosophical Quarterly* 11, no. 3 (1971): 270–283.

Perkinson, J. W. "John S. Mbiti (1931–)." In *Empire: The Christian Tradition: New Readings of Classical Theologians,* edited by Pui-Lan Kwok, Don H. Compier and Joerg Rieger. Minneapolis, MN: Fortress. 2007.

Peterson, David. *Witness to the World.* Carlisle: Paternoster, 1999.

Peterson, L. M. "Extortion." In *Zondervan Pictorial Encyclopedia of the Bible*, Vol 2, edited by Merrill C. Tenney, 452. Grand Rapids: Zondervan, 1975.

Petty, Michael. "Introducing Anglicanism." Presentation IV: Dogmatic Theology. St. Peter's Anglican Church, Unpublished paper. Tallahassee, Florida USA, 2014.

Pfrimmer, David. "What Do Canadian Politicians Expect of the Churches?" In *Christian in Public: Aims, Methodologies and Issues in Public Theology,* edited by L. Hansen. Stellenbosch: African Sun Media, 2007.

Pink, Arthur. *The Attributes of God.* Swengel, PA: Reiner, 1968.

———. *The Sovereignty of God.* Grand Rapids, MI: Baker, 2008.

Pinsent, Andrew. *The Second-Person Perspective in Aquinas's Ethics.* London: Routledge, 2012.

Pityana, N. Barney, and Charles Villa-Vicencio, eds. *Being the Church in South Africa Today.* Johannesburg: SACC, 1995.

Plantinga, Jr. Cornelius. *Engaging God's World: A Christian Vision of Faith, Learning and Living.* Grand Rapids, MI: Eerdmans, 2002.

———. *Not the Way It's Supposed to Be: A Breviary of Sin.* Grand Rapids, MI: Eerdmans, 1995.

Pobee, John Samuel. "Lord, Creator-Spirit, Renew and Sustain the Whole Creation." *International Review of Mission* 29 (1990):151–158.

Pope, Jeremy. *Confronting Corruption: The Elements of a National Integrity System.* Berlin: TI, 2000. http://www.transparency.org/content/download/2439/14493/file/sourcebook.pdf.zip. Accessed 11 July 2012.

The Prevention and Combating of Corruption Bureau. *National Governance and Corruption Survey 2009 Report* Vol. 1: Analysis of Main Findings, Conclusions and Recommendations. Dar es Salaam: IFSD, 2009.

Procter, Paul, et al. *Cambridge International Dictionary of English.* Cambridge: Cambridge University Press, 1995.

Project Document on Democratic Empowerment Project (DEP) (January 2013–June 2016). https://info.undp.org/docs/pdc/Documents/TZA/DEP%20Prodoc.pdf. Accessed 12 July 2015.

Prozesky, Martin. "Corruption as a New Treason: Global Ethics, Africa's Moral Wisdom and the Corrupting of the Future." *Ubuntu: Journal of Conflict and Social Transformation* 2, no. 1&2 (2013): 7–19.

Ramphele, Mamphela. *Laying Ghosts to Rest: Dilemmas of the Transformation in South Africa.* Cape Town: Tafelberg, 2008

Ramsey, Michael. *The Gospel and the Catholic Church.* London: Longmans, 1990 [1956].

Rasheed, Sadig. "Promoting Ethics and Accountability in African Public Services." In *Development Management in Africa,* edited by Sadig Rasheed and David Fashole-Luke, 34–43. Boulder, CO: Westview, 1995.

Rawls, John. *Political Liberalism.* New York, NY: Colombia University Press, 1996.

———. *A Theory of Justice.* Cambridge, MA: Harvard University Press, 1971.

———. *A Theory of Justice.* Revised Edition. Cambridge, MA: Harvard University Press, 1999.

Reed, Esther D. *The Ethics on Human Rights: Contested Doctrinal and Moral Issues.* Waco, TX: Baylor University Press, 2007.

Reid, William Stanford. "The Ecumenicalism of John Calvin." *Westminster Theological Journal* 11, no. 1 (1948): 30–44.

Reiss, Albert, and Albert Biderman. *Data Sources on White Collar Lawbreaking.* Washington, DC: National Institute of Justice, 1980.

Reno, William. "The Politics of Insurgency in Collapsing States." *Development & Change* 33, no. 5 (2002): 837–358.

Reynolds, Douglas D. *Redeemed by God: Our Relationship with God through His Son, Jesus Christ.* Bloomington, IN: Trafford, 2006.

Ringer, Benjamin B., and Charles Y. Glock. "The Political Role of the Church as Defined by Its Parishioners." *Public Opinion Quarterly* 18 (1954): 337–347.

Robinson, Sandra L., and Rebecca J. Bennett. "A Typology of Deviant Workplace Behaviors: A Multidimensional Scaling Study." *Academy of Management Journal* 38, no. 2 (1995): 555–572.

Romzek, Barbara S. "Dynamics of Public Accountability in an Era of Reform." *International Review of Administrative Sciences* 66, no. 1 (2000): 21–44.

Rose-Ackerman, Susan. "Corruption and Development." Paper Prepared for the Annual World Bank Conference on Development Economics. Washington, DC, 30 April and 1 May 1997.

———. *Corruption and Government: Causes, Consequences and Reform.* Cambridge: Cambridge University Press, 1999.

———. "Corruption: Greed, Culture and the State." 2010 Yale Law and Economics Research Paper No. 409. *Yale Law Journal* 120 (2010): 125–140.

———. "The Political Economy of Corruption." In *Corruption and the Global Economy,* edited by Kimberly Ann Elliott, 31–60. Washington, DC: Institute for International Economics, 1997.

Rossouw, Gedeon J. "Defining and Understanding Fraud: A South African Case Study." *Business Ethics Quarterly* 10, no. 4 (2000): 885–896.

Rotberg, Robert I. *Corruption, Global Security, and World Order*. Washington, DC: Brookings Institution, 2009.

Rousseau, Jean-Jaques. *The Social Contract: Essays by Locke, Hume, and Rousseau*. Edited by Sir Ernest Barker. New York, NY: Oxford University Press, 1962.

Ruston, Roger. *Human Rights and the Image of God*. London: SCM, 2004.

Rwechungura, R. Z. "Ethics and Globalization: Managing Poverty and Corruption in Anglophone African Least Developed Nations, Tanzania as Case Study." Unpublished paper Presented at the Conference on Ethics and Integrity of Governance, Catholic University of Louvain, Belgium, 2–5 June 2005.

Sabar, Galia. *Church, State and Society in Kenya: From Mediation to Opposition 1963-1993*. London: Frank Cass, 2002.

Samuel, Vinay, and Chris Sugden. "Dialogue with Other Religions – An Evangelical View." In *Sharing Jesus in the Two-Thirds World*, edited by Vinay Samuel and Chris Sugden. Grand Rapids, MI: Eerdmans, 1984.

Sanneh, Lamin. *Abolitionists Abroad: American Blacks and the Making of Modern West Africa*. Cambridge, MA: Harvard University Press, 1999.

Schleifer, Andrei, and Robert W. Vishny. "Corruption." *The Quarterly Journal of Economics* 108, no. 3 (1993): 599–617. doi: 10.2307/2118402.

Schneiders, Sandra Marie. *The Revelatory Text: Interpreting the New Testament as Sacred Scripture*. Collegeville, MN: Liturgical, 1999.

Schreiner, Thomas R. *New Testament Theology*. Grand Rapids, MI: Baker, 2008.

Schubert, Ralph I. *A Christian-Ethical Comparison of Leadership Styles in the West and in Tanzania and Their Impact on Cross-Cultural Partnerships*. Nürnberg: VTR Publications, 2008.

Schwobel, Christoph. "Recovering Human Dignity." In *God and Human Dignity*, edited by R. Kendall Soulen and Linda Woodhead, 44–59. Grand Rapids; MI: Eerdmans, 2006.

Scott, M. "Political Corruption: An Introduction to the Issues." (In Inge Amundsen, 1972.) CMI Working Paper 7. Bergen: Chr. Michelsen Institute, 1999.

Sen, Amartya. "Capability and Well-Being." In *The Quality of Life*, edited by Amartya Sen and Martha Craven Nussbaum. Oxford: Oxford University Press, 1993.

———. "Capability and Well-being." WIDER Conference Paper, 1985.

———. *Commodities and Capabilities*. Oxford: Elsevier Science Publishers, 1985.

———. *Development as Freedom*. Oxford: Oxford University Press, 1999.

———. *The Idea of Justice*. London: Penguin, 2009.

———. *The Standard of Living*. Cambridge: Cambridge University Press, 1987.

———. "Well-being, Agency and Freedom: The Dewey Lectures 1984." *Journal of Philosophy* 82 (1985).

Sennett, James F. *Modality, Probability, and Rationality: A Critical Examination of Alvin Plantinga's Philosophy*. New York, NY: Peter Lang, 1992.

Setiloane, Gabriel. *Introduction to African Theology*. Johannesburg: Skotaville, 1986.

Sigmund, Paul E., ed. *St. Thomas Aquinas on Politics and Ethics*. New York, NY: Norton, 1988.

Sitta, Samuel. "Integrity Environment and Investment Promotion. The Case of Tanzania." Unpublished paper Presented at the OECD, Addis Ababa Conference 7–8 March 2005. http://www.oecd.org/daf/inv/investmentfordevelopment/34571058.pdf. Accessed 11 August 2011.

Skinner, Hannah. "Going Public with Public Theology: Developing Meaningful Discourse with the Wider World." In *Through the Eye of a Needle: Theological Conversations Over Political Economy*, edited by John Atherton and Hannah Skinner, 35–49. Peterborough: Epworth, 2007.

Sloane, Andrew. "Justifying Advocacy: A Biblical and Theological Rationale for Speaking the Truth to Power on Behalf of the Vulnerable." The John Saunders Annual Lecture, 19 October 2011. http://www.ethos.org.au/online-resources/Blog/Justifying-Advocacy---Speaking-Truth-to-Power. Accessed 18 August 2014.

Smit, Dirk J. "Challenges for Reformed Churches in Africa: A Contemporary Narrative." *International Journal for the Study of the Christian Church* 8, no. 4 (2008): 319–336.

———. *Essays on Being Reformed: Collected Essays 3*. Edited by Robert R. Vosloo. Stellenbosch: African Sun Media, 2009.

———. "Notions of the Public and Doing Theology." *International Journal of Public Theology* 1, no. 1 (2007): 431–454.

———. "On Learning to See? A Reformed Perspective on the Church and the Poor." In *Suffering, Poverty, and HIV-AIDS: International Practical Theological Perspectives*, edited by Pamela Couture and Bonnie J. Miller-McLemore, 55–77. Cardiff: Academic Press, 2003.

———. "Religion and Development: Crisis or New Opportunities?" Unpublished paper Delivered at the Free University, Amsterdam, the Netherlands, 14–15 June 2007.

Song, John Byung-Tek. "An Assessment of Robert Jenson's Hermeneutics on Divine Impassibility and the Emotions of God." *International Journal of Systematic Theology* 15, no. 1 (2013): 78–96.

Soulen, R. Kendall, and Linda Woodhead, eds. *God and Human Dignity*. Grand Rapids; MI: Eerdmans, 2006.

Spencer, Nick A. "Christian Vision of Human Flourishing." 2010. http://www.theosthinktank.co.uk/files/files/02_Spencer_A_Christian_Vision_of_Human_Flourishing.pdf. Accessed 5 March 2014.

Spillers, Hortense J. "Martin Luther King, Jr. and America's Civil Religion." *Nanzan Review of American Studies* 29 (2007): 39–49.

Stackhouse, John G. *Making the Best of It. Following Christ in the Real World.* Oxford: Oxford University Press, 2008.

Stackhouse, Max L. "God and Globalization." In *The Gospel and Globalization: Exploring the Religious Roots of a Globalized World*, edited by Michael W. Goheen and Erin Glanville. Vancouver, BC: Regent College, 2009.

———. *God and Globalization. Volume 4: Globalization and Grace.* New York, NY: Continuum, 2007.

———. "Public Theology." In *The Dictionary of the Ecumenical Movement*, edited by Nicolas Lossky, José Miguez Bonino, John Pobee, Tom F. Stransky, Geoffrey Wainwright and Pauline Webb, 1131–1133. Geneva: WCC, 2002.

———. "Public Theology and Ethical Judgment." *Theology Today* 54, no. 2 (2006): 165–191.

———. "Reflections on How and Why We Go Public." *International Journal of Public Theology* 1, no. 3/4 (2007): 421–430.

Stackhouse, Max L., and Don Browning, eds. *The Spirit and the Modern Authorities. Volume 2: God and Globalization.* Harrisburg, PA: Trinity, 2001.

Stackhouse, Max L., and Diane Obenchain, eds. *Christ and the Dominions of Civilization. Volume 3: God and Globalization.* Harrisburg, PA: Trinity, 2002.

Stackhouse, Max L., and Peter Paris, eds. *Religion and the Powers of the Common Life. Volume 1: God and Globalization.* Harrisburg, PA: Trinity, 2000.

Stackhouse, Max L., and L. M. Stratton. *Capitalism, Civil Society, Religion, and the Poor.* Wilmington: DE: Intercollegiate Studies Institute, 2002.

Stanford, R., and J. Stanford. "The Poverty and Inequality Report." Pathways: A Magazine on Poverty, Inequality and Social Policy, Special Issue 1997. http://inequality.stanford.edu/sites/default/files/. Accessed 12 December 2014.

Stassen, Glen Harold, and David P. Gushee. *Kingdom Ethics: Following Jesus in Contemporary Contexts.* Downers Grove, IL: InterVarsity, 2003.

Storrar, William. "A Kairos Moment for Public Theology." *International Journal of Public Theology* 1, no. 1 (2007): 5–25.

———. Symposium on "Responsible South African Public Theology in a Global Era: Perspectives and Proposals," Organized by the Beyers Naudé Centre for Public Theology, Stellenbosch University and the Faculty of Theology, University of Pretoria, 4–5 August 2008.

Storrar, William, and Andrew Morton, eds. *Public Theology for the 21st Century: Essays in Honour of Duncan B. Forrester*. London. New York: T&T Clark, 2004.

Stott, John R. W. *Christian Mission in the Modern World*. London: Falcon, 1975.

———. *The Lausanne Covenant: An Exposition and Commentary*. Minneapolis, MN: Worldwide, 1975.

Strauss, Richard. *The Joy of Knowing God*. Neptune, NJ: Loizeaux Brothers, 1984.

Strydom, J. G., and W. Wessels. *Prophetic Perspectives on Power and Social Justice*. Pretoria: Biblia, 2000.

Stückelberger, Christopher. *Corruption-Free Churches Are Possible. Experiences, Values, Solutions*. Geneva: Globethics.net, 2010.

Sweeney, Marvin A. *The Twelve Prophets*. Vol. 2. Collegeville, MN: Liturgical, 2000.

Sykes, Stephen. *Power and Christian Theology*. London: Continuum, 2006.

Szwajkowski, Eugene. "Organizational Illegality: Theoretical Integration and Illustrative Application." *Academy of Management Review* 10, no. 3 (1985): 558–567.

Tanner, N. "Islam and Christianity in Tanzania: The Relationship between the Religious Minorities of Muslims and Christians." (Paper) University of Berne, 2002.

Tanzania Corruption Tracker System. "Agenda Participation 2000." Online Newsletter 13, June 2011. http://www.corruptiontracker.or.tz/. Accessed 12 September 2013.

Tanzania Human Rights Report (THRR). Dar es Salaam: Legal and Human Rights Centre and Zanzibar Legal Aid Services, 2007.

Tanzi, Vito. "Corruption: Arm's-Length Relationships and Markets." In *The Economics of Organized Crime*, edited by Gianluca Fiorentini and Sam Pelzman, 161–180. Cambridge: Cambridge University Press, 1995.

———. "Corruption around the World: Causes, Consequences, Scope and Cures." *IMF Staff Papers* 45 (1998): 559–594.

Tarimo, Aquiline. *Applied Ethics and Africa's Social Reconstruction*. Nairobi: Acton, 2005.

Taylor, A. J. W. *Justice as a Basic Human Need*. New York, NY: Nova, 2006.

Temple, William. *Christianity and Social Order*. London: SPCK, [1942] 1976.

———. *Citizen and Churchman*. London: Eyre & Spottiswoode, 1941.

Temwende, O. K. "Tanzania: A Political and Historical Overview." Friedrich-Ebert-Stiftung (FES), 2004. http://tanzania.fes-international.de/doc/bot-historical-overview.pdf. Accessed 31 October 2013.

Thachuk, Kimberly. "Corruption and International Security." *SAIS Review* 25, no. 1 (2005): 143–152.

Theron, P. M., and G. A. Lotter. "Corruption: How Should Christians Respond?" *Acta Theologica* 32, no. 1 (2012): 96–117.
Thinking Anglicans. "News Items from around the Anglican Communion." 6 April 2013. http://www.thinkinganglicans.org.uk/archives/005990.html. Accessed 9 May 2013.
Thomson, H. "Satisfying Justice." *International Journal of Public Theology* 3 (2009): 339–356.
Tinder, Glenn. *The Political Meaning of Christianity: An Interpretation*. Baton Rouge, LA: Louisiana State University Press, 1989.
Tomberlin, James E., and P. Van Inwagen, eds. *An International Series of Contemporary Philosophers and Logicians, Vol. 5 of Profiles: Alvin Plantinga, Self-Profile*. Dordrecht: D. Reidel, 1985.
Torrance, Thomas F. *The Christian Doctrine of God: One Being Three Persons*. Edinburgh: T&T Clark, 1996.
———. *Karl Barth: Biblical and Evangelical Theologian*. Bloomsbury, IN: T&T Clark, 1991.
———. "Knowledge of God and Speech About Him According to John Calvin." In *Theology in Reconstruction*, edited by Thomas F Torrance, 76–98. London: SCM, 1965.
———. *The School of Faith: The Catechisms of the Reformed Church*. London: James Clarke, 1959.
Tozer, A. W. *The Knowledge of the Holy*. New York, NY: Harper and Row, 1961.
Tracy, David. *The Analogical Imagination: Christian Theology and the Culture of Pluralism*. New York, NY: Crossroad, 1981.
———. *Plurality and Ambiguity: Hermeneutics, Religion, Hope*. Chicago, IL: University of Chicago Press, 1994.
Tran, Ngoc Anh. "Corruption and Human Development." UNDP Working Paper Series No. 2008/07. Washington, DC: United Nations Development Fund, 2008.
Transparency International. "Integrating Human Rights in the Anti-Corruption Agenda: Challenges, Opportunities and Possibilities." Council on Human Rights Policy. 2010. http://r4d.dfid.gov.uk/PDF/Outputs/ICHRP/integrating-humrights%5D.pdf. Accessed 29 March 2014.
Tronvoll, Kjetil. "Citizens' Attitude to Good Governance and Corruption." Results from a 2011 Survey in Zanzibar. Oslo: International Law and Policy Institute, 2011.
Turiel, Elliot. *The Culture of Morality: Social Development, Context and Conflict*. Cambridge, UK: Cambridge University Press, 2002.
Turnbull, Richard. *Anglican and Evangelical?: Can They Agree?* London: Continuum, 2007.

United Nations. *Corruption: Threats and Trends in the Twenty-first Century*. New York: United Nations, 2005.

———. "Statement by the General Secretary at the UN Assembly on the Adoption of the United Nations Convention against Corruption (UNCAC), 2003." https://www.unodc.org/unodc/en/treaties/CAC/background/secretary-general-speech.html. Accessed 13 August 2013.

———. "United Nations Convention against Corruption" (UNCAC), 2003. www.unodc.org/unodc/en/treaties/CAC/.../secretary-general-speech. Accessed 13 August 2013.

United Nations Development Programme. *Human Development Report 2001*. New York/Oxford: Oxford University Press, 2001.

———. *Human Development Report 2010*. http://hdr.undp.org/. Accessed 8 November 2013.

———. *Human Development Report 2013*. http://hdr.undp.org/sites/default/files/reports/14/hdr2013_en_complete.pdf.

———. *Institutional Arrangement to Combat Corruption: A Comparative Study*. Bangkok: Keen, 2005.

———. UNDP Tanzania Success Stories Election Support 2010. http://www.tz.undp.org/content/dam/tanzania/UNDP%20Tanzania%20Success%20Stories%20-%20Election%20Support%202010.pdf. Accessed 12 March 2014.

———. UNDP 2000. Government of Tanzania, the National Anti-Corruption Strategy and Action Plan–II (NACSAP II) Implementation Report. Dar es Salaam, 2009.

URT (United Republic of Tanzania). *The Constitution of the United Republic of Tanzania of 1977*. (Incorporating and Consolidating All Amendments Made by the Constituent Assembly from 1977 to the 31 December 2008). Dar es Salaam: URT, 2008.

———. *National Land Policy. Ministry of Lands and Human Settlements Development*. Dar es Salaam: Government Printers, 2006.

———. *Population and Housing Census*. Dar es Salaam: URT, 2012.

———. President's Office, Planning Commission. *The Tanzania Five Year Development Plan 2011/12-2015/16: Unleashing Tanzania's Latent Growth Potentials May 2011*. Dar es Salaam: URT, 2011.

———. *Tanzania's Presidential Commission of Inquiry against Corruption*. Warioba Report. Dar es Salaam: URT, 1996.

USIPE (United States Institute of Peace). *Governance, Corruption, and Conflict*. Washington, DC: USIPE, 2010.

Uslaner, Eric M. *Corruption, Inequality and the Rule of Law*. Cambridge: Cambridge University Press, 2008.

Van Til, Henry. *The Calvinistic Concept of Culture*. Philadelphia, PA: Presbyterian and Reformed, 1959.
VanGemeren, Willem. *The Progress of Redemption*. Grand Rapids, MI: Zondervan, 1988.
Varughese. Alex, ed. *Discovering the New Testament Community and Faith*. Kansas City, MO: Beacon Hill, 2005.
Vellem, V. "Towards a Transformed Society: The Church and Social Transformation: Prophet, Priest and Political Voice." Unpublished Annual Lecture Presented at the Meeting of Diakonia, Durban, 13 August 2009.
Venter, Rian, ed. *Theology and the (Post)Aapartheid Condition: Genealogies and Future Directions*. Bloemfontein, South Africa: SUN Press, 2016.
Villa-Vicencio, Charles. "Towards a Transformed Society." In *The Church and Social Transformation: Prophet, Priest and Political Voice*. Diakonia Council of Churches Annual Lecture. Cape Town South Africa, 13 August, 2009.
Vine, W. E. *An Expository Dictionary of Bible Words*. Cambridge: Cambridge University Press, 1985.
Volf, M. "God, Justice, and Love: The Grounds for Human Flourishing." *Books and Culture: A Christian Review* (January/February 2009): 1–5. http://www.booksandculture.com/articles/2009/janfeb/16.26.html. Accessed 17 June 2014.
Vorster, J. M. "Managing Corruption in South Africa: The Ethical Responsibility of Churches." *Scriptura* 109 (2012): 133–147.
Vorster, Nico. "A Theological Evaluation of the South African Constitutional Value of Human Dignity." *Journal of Reformed Theology* 1 (2007): 320–339.
Walton, I. *The Works of That Learned and Judicious Divine Mr. Richard Hooker: With an Account of His Life and Death*. Oxford: Oxford University Press, 1845.
Ward, Kevin. *A History of Global Anglicanism*. Cambridge: Cambridge University Press, 2006.
Ward, Ted. "Evaluating Metaphors of Education." In *with an Eye on the Future: Development and Mission in the 21st Century. Essays in Honor of Ted W Ward*, edited by Duane Elmer and Lois McKinney, 43–52. Monrovia, CA: MARC, 1996.
Warfield, Benjamin B. *The Plan of Salvation*. Grand Rapids, MI: Eerdmans, 1970.
Watling, T. *Ecological Imaginations in the World Religions: An Ethnographic Analysis*. London; New York: Continuum, 2009.
WCC and UNESCO (The World Council of Churches and United Nations Educational, Scientific and Cultural Organization). "Final Report of the Seminar on the Role of Religion and Religious Institutions in the

Dismantling of Apartheid, 22–25 November." Geneva, Switzerland, 1991. http://unesdoc.unesco.org/images/0018/001888/188892eo.pdf.

Webber, Robert E. *The Secular Saint. A Case for Evangelical Social Responsibility.* Eugene, OR: Wipf and Stock, 1979.

Weithman, P. J. "Augustine's Political Philosophy." In *The Cambridge Companion to Augustine*, edited by Eleonore Stump and Norman Kretzmann, 234–252. Cambridge: Cambridge University Press, 2006. https://www3.nd.edu/~pweithma/professional_website/My%20Papers/Augustine's%20Political%20Thought.pdf. Accessed 14 May 2014.

———. "Complementarity and Equality in the Political Thought of Thomas Aquinas." *Theological Studies* 59, no. 2 (1998): 277–296.

———. "Nicholas Wolterstorff's 'Justice: Rights and Wrongs': An Introduction." *The Journal of Religious Ethics* 37, no. 2 (2009): 179–192.

"What Lessons Has Tanzania Drawn from Doctors' Strike?" *The Citizen*, Tanzania, 24 March 2012. http://thecitizen.co.tz/news/4-national-news/20904-what-lesson-has-tanzania-drawn-from-doctors-strike.html. Accessed 30 November 2011.

Williams, Rowan. "Archbishop's Message to the 4th Global South to South Encounter." http://rowanwilliams.archbishopofcanterbury.org/articles.php/984/archbishops-message-to-the-4th-global-south-to-south-encounter. Accessed 24 June 2015.

———. "The Challenge and Hope of Being an Anglican Today: A Reflection for the Bishops, Clergy and Faithful of the Anglican Communion." In *Community Identity: Dynamics of Religion in Context*, edited by C. H. Kim and P. Kollontai. London: T&T Clark, 2007.

———. *Faith in the Public Square.* London: Bloomsbury, 2012.

———. "Relations between the Church and State Today: What Is the Role of the Christian Citizen?" An address given by the Archbishop of Canterbury, Dr Rowan Williams, at Manchester University, 1 March 2011. http://rowanwilliams.archbishopofcanterbury.org/articles.php/2009/relations-between-the-church-and-state-today-what-is-the-role-of-the-christian. Accessed 5 March 2014.

———. "Theology and Economics: Two Different Worlds?" *Anglican Theological Review* 92, no. 4 (2010): 607–615.

———. "What Is the Church? In God's Company." *Christian Century* (2007): 23.

Wilson, Bryan. *Religion in Secular Society.* London: Penguin, 1966.

Windsor, D. "Corporate and Government Corruption: International Cooperation and Domestic regulation." In *Current Topics in Management, Vol. 9*, edited by M. Afzalur Rahim, Kenneth D. Mackenzie, and Robert T. Golembiewski. Greenwich, CT: JAI, 2004.

Witt, William. "General Convention 2003 and Its Aftermath: 'Non-Theological' Decisions and a Theological Alternative.'" *Trinity Journal for Theology & Ministry* 2, no. 2 (2008).

———. "What Is Anglican Theology?" 2013. http://willgwitt.org/wp-content/uploads/2013/01/What-is-Anglican-Theology.pdf. Accessed 14 April 2013.

Wogau, S. "Transitions to Good Governance: The Case of Tanzania." European Research Centre for Anti-Corruption and State-Building. Working Paper No. 19. Berlin: European Research Centre for Anti-Corruption and State-Building, 2010.

Wolff, Robert P. *About Philosophy*. Second Edition. Upper Saddle River, NJ: Prentice Hall, 1981.

Wolfson, Harry A. *Religious Philosophy*. Cambridge, MA: Harvard University Press, 1961.

Wolterstoff, Nicholas. *Justice: Rights and Wrongs*. Princeton, NJ: Princeton University Press, 2008.

———. *Until Justice and Peace Embrace*. Grand Rapids, MI: Eerdmans, 1983.

World Bank. *Bureaucrats in Business: The Economics and Politics of Government Ownership*. New York, NY: Oxford University Press, 1995.

———. *Governance. The World Bank's Experience*. Washington, DC: World Bank, 1994.

———. The New Anti-Corruption Home Page, 2002. www.WorldBank-homepage.htm.

———. *The Reform of Public Sector Management: Lessons from Experience*. Washington, DC: World Bank, 1991.

———. "Six Questions on the Cost of Corruption with World Bank Institute Global Governance Director Daniel Kaufmann." 2001. http://web.worldbank.org/WBSITE/EXTERNAL/NEWS/0,,contentMDK:20190295~menuPK:34457~pagePK:34370~piPK:34424~theSitePK:4607,00.html. Accessed 30 October 2011.

———. *Social Sector Review in Tanzania*. Washington, DC: World Bank, 1995.

———. *Sub-Saharan Africa: From Crisis to Sustainable Growth: A Long-Term Perspective Study*. Washington, DC: World Bank, 1989.

World Bank and the United States Agency for International Development. "Corruption in Slovakia: Results of Diagnostic Surveys." 2000. http://siteresources.worldbank.org/INTWBIGOVANTCOR/Resources/slovrep44.pdf.

World Council of Churches. "The Nature and Mission of the Church: A Stage in the Way to a Common Statement." Geneva: WCC, 2005.

World Vision. *About Us: Who We Are*. http://www.worldvision.org/worldvision/comms2.nsf/stable/whoweare?Open&lid=sitemap_whoweare&lpos=sitemap. Accessed 9 March 2013.

Wright, Christopher J. H. *Knowing Jesus through the Old Testament.* Downers Grove, IL: InterVarsity, 1992.
———. *The Mission of God.* Nottingham: IVP, 2006.
———. *The Mission of God: Unlocking the Bible's Grand Narrative.* Downers Grove, IL: InterVarsity, 2006.
———. *Old Testament Ethics for the People of God.* Leister, UK: IVP, 2004/2010.
———. *Salvation Belongs to Our God.* Downers Grove, IL: InterVarsity, 2007.
Wright, N. T. *On Becoming the Righteousness of God: 2 Corinthians 5:21.* In *Pauline Theology* Vol. 2, edited by D. M. Hay, 200–208. London: Fortress, 1993.
Wright, William J. *Martin Luther's Understanding of God's Two Kingdoms: A Response to the Challenge of Skepticism.* Grand Rapids, MI: Baker Academic Books, 2010.
Yansane, Aguibou Y., ed. *Prospects for Recovery and Sustainable Development in Africa.* Westport, CT: Greenwood, 1996.
Yoder, John H. *The Politics of Jesus.* Second Edition. Grand Rapids, MI: Eerdmans, 1994.
———. *The Priestly Kingdom: Social Ethics as Gospel.* Notre Dame: University of Notre Dame Press, 1984.
———. *The Royal Priesthood. Essays Ecclesiastical and Ecumenical.* Scottsdale, PA: Herald, 1998.
Young, Iris M. *Justice and the Politics of Difference.* Princeton, NJ: Princeton University Press, 1990.
Zaaiman, J. Power. "Towards a Third Generation Definition." *Koers* 72, no. 3 (2007): 357–375.
Zachariah, George. "Re-Imagining God of Life from the Margins." *Ecumenical Review* 65, no. 1 (2013): 35–50.
Zigarelli, Michael. "The Theology and Practice of Strategic Planning." *Regent Business Review* 13 (2004): 1–25.
Zigon, Jarett. *Morality: An Anthropological Perspective.* London: Berg, 2008.
Zizioulas, Jean D. *Being as Communion: Studies in Personhood and the Church.* New York, NY: St Vladimir's Seminary Press, 1985.

Corruption and injustice, like cancer, are both real and life threatening, both talked about more than actually understood. Efforts to combat corruption and injustice are incoherent and inadequate. Understanding the nature, the sources and the forms of corruption is critical to any viable war against it. Understanding the peculiar interplay between corruption and injustice is essential. What should the church, perhaps the most viable institution in the war against corruption and injustice, do in response to the scourge? Dr Sebahene's thesis deals with all these aspects and more. Quite likely, this work will generate needed discussion and subsequent action against corruption and injustice. I commend Dr Sebahene for an excellent piece on two interlinked critical contemporary social and spiritual issues and recommend his work to anyone desiring to contribute to the war against corruption and injustice.

Professor Emmanuel D. Mbennah, PhD
Vice-Chancellor, St John's University of Tanzania, Dodoma, Tanzania

Alfred Sebahene joins the discourse that follows the increased global consciousness of the negative effects of corruption on individuals and societies. He does so as an African, a Tanzanian and an Anglican theologian. Acutely aware of the prevalence of corruption in Africa in general, and in his country in particular, he takes up the urgent challenge to move beyond the notion of corruption as only a political, economic or cultural phenomenon and challenge, recognizing that corruption, at its core, also presents a theological challenge to Christian churches. As a public theologian and Christian ethicist, Sebahene highlights the theological "dynamic link between corruption and injustice," thus identifying corruption also as an issue of justice. He is both critical and appreciative of current and past efforts of the Tanzanian government and the Anglican Church of Tanzania in fighting corruption. However, acknowledging that not enough is being done, this research offers theological-ethical guidelines to the Anglican Church of Tanzania that could inform its role in the public sphere in general, but especially in addressing corruption. As such it is not only a necessary and timeous study, but a work that can serve the discourse on corruption and the role of churches across Africa well.

Len Hansen, DTh
Director of Research Development, Faculty of Theology,
Stellenbosch University, South Africa
Executive Director, NetACT Africa

In this important book, Alfred uw'lmana Sebahene discusses the role of the church in resisting corruption in Tanzania. He explains in some detail how corruption is manifested and outlines its devastating effects on the people of Tanzania. The value of this book on public theology lies in the fact that he explains the link between injustice and corruption from a theological-ethical perspective and draws on several other fields of study including philosophy, political science, sociology, economics, and historical studies.

Dr Sebahene argues that fighting corruption, also within its own ranks, is not an optional extra for the church, but inextricably part of its Christian witness. His theological analysis draws on Christian teaching, especially about God, humanity, society and the church, showing how a proper understanding can motivate Christian action in society. Rather than being marginalized, the church needs to be engaged in intellectual debates about political governance and the use of economic resources.

He contends that the influential Anglican Church of Tanzania needs to take action by promoting justice and curbing corruption more actively in society. It needs to ensure that its own house is in order, offering a courageous prophetic witness and acting in solidarity with the people of Tanzania. More specifically the Anglican Church can act through the Christian Social Services Commission, together with local and international Christian ecumenical groups, in interfaith collaborative initiatives, through strengthening the anti-corruption clubs in schools and at universities, facilitating the formation of moral character, fighting corruption from the pulpit, improving its theological education and meeting the challenge of developing moral and competent leaders for the church and society.

This book will also be of value to members of other countries, especially in Africa, who wish to understand why corruption has increased and what can be done to oppose this personal temptation and social scourge.

Louise Kretzschmar, PhD
Professor of Theological Ethics, University of South Africa

Langham Literature and its imprints are a ministry of Langham Partnership.

Langham Partnership is a global fellowship working in pursuit of the vision God entrusted to its founder John Stott –

> *to facilitate the growth of the church in maturity and Christ-likeness through raising the standards of biblical preaching and teaching.*

Our vision is to see churches in the majority world equipped for mission and growing to maturity in Christ through the ministry of pastors and leaders who believe, teach and live by the Word of God.

Our mission is to strengthen the ministry of the Word of God through:
- nurturing national movements for biblical preaching
- fostering the creation and distribution of evangelical literature
- enhancing evangelical theological education

especially in countries where churches are under-resourced.

Our ministry

Langham Preaching partners with national leaders to nurture indigenous biblical preaching movements for pastors and lay preachers all around the world. With the support of a team of trainers from many countries, a multi-level programme of seminars provides practical training, and is followed by a programme for training local facilitators. Local preachers' groups and national and regional networks ensure continuity and ongoing development, seeking to build vigorous movements committed to Bible exposition.

Langham Literature provides majority world preachers, scholars and seminary libraries with evangelical books and electronic resources through publishing and distribution, grants and discounts. The programme also fosters the creation of indigenous evangelical books in many languages, through writer's grants, strengthening local evangelical publishing houses, and investment in major regional literature projects, such as one volume Bible commentaries like *The Africa Bible Commentary* and *The South Asia Bible Commentary*.

Langham Scholars provides financial support for evangelical doctoral students from the majority world so that, when they return home, they may train pastors and other Christian leaders with sound, biblical and theological teaching. This programme equips those who equip others. Langham Scholars also works in partnership with majority world seminaries in strengthening evangelical theological education. A growing number of Langham Scholars study in high quality doctoral programmes in the majority world itself. As well as teaching the next generation of pastors, graduated Langham Scholars exercise significant influence through their writing and leadership.

To learn more about Langham Partnership and the work we do visit **langham.org**

www.ingramcontent.com/pod-product-compliance
Lightning Source LLC
Chambersburg PA
CBHW052012290426
44112CB00014B/2209